Building Large-Scale Web Applications with Angular

Your one-stop guide to building scalable and production-grade Angular web apps

Chandermani Arora
Kevin Hennessy
Christoffer Noring
Doguhan Uluca

BIRMINGHAM - MUMBAI

Building Large-Scale Web Applications with Angular

First Published: December 2018
Production Reference: 1191218

Published by Packt Publishing Ltd.
Livery Place, 35 Livery Street
Birmingham, B3 2PB, U.K.

ISBN 978-1-78995-956-7

www.packtpub.com

Contributors

About the authors

Chandermani Arora is a software craftsman, with love for technology and expertise on web stack. With years of experience, he has architected, designed, and developed various solutions for Microsoft platforms. He has been building apps on Angular 1 since its early days. Having a passion for the framework every project of his has an Angular footprint.

He tries to support the platform in every possible way by writing blogs on various Angular topics or helping fellow developers on StackOverflow, where he is an active member on the Angular channel. He also authored the first edition of this book.

Writing this book has just been a surreal experience and I would like to thank everyone on the Packt team including the reviewers who have helped me with this book.
I also want to express my gratitude towards my wife, my daughter and everyone else in my family. I am blessed to have you all in my life.

Kevin Hennessy is a Senior Software Engineer with Applied Information Sciences. He has 20 years' experience as a developer, team lead, and solutions architect, working on web-based projects, primarily using the Microsoft technology stack. Over the last several years, he has presented and written about single-page applications and JavaScript frameworks, including Knockout, Meteor, and Angular. He has spoken about Angular at the All Things Open conference.

I would like to thank my wife, Mary Gene Hennessy. Her unstinting love and support (and editorial suggestions) through the time that I spent writing this book, have made me ever more aware and appreciate how truly amazing it is to be married to her. I also want to thank my son, Aidan, who has informally tested the code in this book. He is a recent college graduate and his enthusiasm for technology has inspired me in writing this book.

Christoffer Noring, a software developer with over 10 years' experience, has successfully delivered software for industries ranging from telecom to aviation. He has worked on everything from databases to frontend. Frequently speaking on TDD, React, NativeScript, RxJS, and Angular, he writes books and blogs and holds the title of Google Developer Expert in Web Technologies and Angular.

Currently working for McKinsey as a full stack developer, he's the author and maintainer of *RxJS Ultimate*, and he has coauthored *Learning Angular - Second Edition*, a Packt title.

Thank you to my reviewers, Sachin, Andrew, Vince, Mashhood, and Ward, whose comments have been most helpful and have improved this book.
Sara, my wife, I wouldn't be in this place in my career without your valuable input and your saintly patience. Forever yours.
My brother, your suggestions and ongoing support have turned me into the writer I am today.
Mom and dad, thank you for your loving support and encouragement.

Doguhan Uluca is a software development expert for Excella Consulting in Washington, DC. He is the founder and director of the polyglot Tech Talk DC meetup and the creator of the DC Full Stack Web Summit conference. Doguhan has been published on DevPro and ACM. He is a speaker at international conferences, such as Ng-Conf, CodeStock, deliver:Agile and Agile XP. He is a full-stack JavaScript, Agile, and cloud engineering practitioner. Doguhan is an active contributor to the open source community, with libraries and tools published for JavaScript, Angular, Node, and MongoDB.

I would like to acknowledge my dear family, Chanda and Ada, for all their sacrifice and encouragement, allowing this book to happen. In addition, the amazing communities at NOVA Code Camp, NodeConf, ng-conf, Node DC, and Tech Talk DC for opening up my mind and embracing my ideas. Finally, my colleagues at Excella, who allowed an open, inquisitive, and daring environment to effect real change.

About the reviewer

Phodal Huang is a developer, creator, and author. He works in ThoughtWorks as a Senior Consultant, and focuses on IoT and frontend. He is the author of Design IoT System and Growth: Thinking in Full Stack in Chinese.

He is an open source enthusiast, and has created a series of projects in GitHub. After daily work, he likes to reinvent some wheels for fun. He created the micro-frontend framework Mooa for Angular. You can find out more wheels on his GitHub page, /phodal.

He loves designing, writing, hacking, traveling, you can also find out more about him on his personal website at phodal(dot)com.

Mashhood Rastgar is the founder and technical lead at Recurship, which is a JavaScript consultancy based in Karachi, Pakistan. He is also part of the Google Developer Experts for Web and Angular. Mashhood works startups working in EU and USA, to help them crawl through the technical maze and quickly build amazing products focused around the problems they are trying to solve. He specializes in using the latest technologies available to identify the best solutions. He is also a frequent international and local speaker at different web conferences.

Vinci Rufus is a Google Developer Expert and Senior Director with SapientRazorfish. He consults clients and teams on frontend architecture, mobile strategy, and user experience, primarily in the areas of content and commerce. His areas of interest involve progressive web apps, Angular, React, and web components. He is an author of *AngularJS Web Application Development Blueprints*.

> *A big shout out to my kids, Shannon and Jaden, and my nephew, Chris, who make it all worth it.*

Sachin Ohri is a technology architect with a keen interest in web-based technologies. He has been writing web applications for more than a decade, with technologies such as .NET, JavaScript, Durandal, Angular, and TypeScript. He works on providing technical solutions, including architectural design, technical support, and development expertise, to Fortune 500 companies. He holds various Microsoft certifications, such as Microsoft Azure Architect, Microsoft ASP.NET MVC web application, and Microsoft Programming with C#.

Andrew Leith Macrae first cut his programming teeth on an Apple IIe, poking bytes into the RAM. Over the years, he has developed interactive applications with Hypercard, Director, Flash, and more recently, Adobe AIR for mobile. He has also worked with HTML since there was HTML to work with and is currently working as a senior frontend developer at The Learning Channel, using Angular 4 with TypeScript.

Wyn B. Van Devanter is currently a managing consultant and senior developer with Excella, an Agile tech firm. He has experience in various industries and government with architecture, design, and implementation of software, largely with web-based applications. He also works heavily with DevOps, cloud, and container-based architectures and strives to be a good software craftsman using XP practices. He enjoys being involved in the community and regularly speaks and conducts workshops at events around the region. Wyn likes playing music, skiing, and conversations of intrigue.

Brendon Caulkins is a DC-based full stack developer at Excella. His focus is Java, but he still harbors a secret love for PHP. He holds a computer engineering degree from Purdue University (Boiler Up!) and refuses to give up playing with Legos. He has nearly a decade of hardware environmental testing and software product testing experience and is really, *really* good at breaking things. He is also an award-winning painter of tiny toy soldiers and goes by the name Plarzoid on the interwebs.

Packt is searching for authors like you

If you're interested in becoming an author for Packt, please visit `authors.packtpub.com` and apply today. We have worked with thousands of developers and tech professionals, just like you, to help them share their insight with the global tech community. You can make a general application, apply for a specific hot topic that we are recruiting an author for, or submit your own idea.

`mapt.io`

Mapt is an online digital library that gives you full access to over 5,000 books and videos, as well as industry leading tools to help you plan your personal development and advance your career. For more information, please visit our website.

Why subscribe?

- Spend less time learning and more time coding with practical eBooks and Videos from over 4,000 industry professionals

- Improve your learning with Skill Plans built especially for you

- Get a free eBook or video every month

- Mapt is fully searchable

- Copy and paste, print, and bookmark content

PacktPub.com

Did you know that Packt offers eBook versions of every book published, with PDF and ePub files available? You can upgrade to the eBook version at `www.PacktPub.com` and as a print book customer, you are entitled to a discount on the eBook copy. Get in touch with us at `service@packtpub.com` for more details.

At `www.PacktPub.com`, you can also read a collection of free technical articles, sign up for a range of free newsletters, and receive exclusive discounts and offers on Packt books and eBooks.

Table of Contents

Preface

If you have been burnt by unreliable JavaScript frameworks before, you will be amazed by the maturity of the Angular platform. Angular enables you to build fast, efficient, and real-world web apps. In this Learning Path, you'll learn Angular and to deliver high-quality and production-grade Angular apps from design to deployment.

You will begin by creating a simple fitness app, using the building blocks of Angular, and make your final app, Personal Trainer, by morphing the workout app into a full-fledged personal workout builder and runner with advanced directive building - the most fundamental and powerful feature of Angular.

You will learn the different ways of architecting Angular applications using RxJS, and some of the patterns that are involved in it. Later you'll be introduced to the router-first architecture, a seven-step approach to designing and developing mid-to-large line-of-business apps, along with popular recipes. By the end of this book, you will be familiar with the scope of web development using Angular, Swagger, and Docker, learning patterns and practices to be successful as an individual developer on the web or as a team in the Enterprise.

This Learning Path includes content from the following Packt products:

- Angular 6 by Example by Chandermani Arora, Kevin Hennessy
- Architecting Angular Applications with Redux, RxJS, and NgRx by Christoffer Noring
- Angular 6 for Enterprise-Ready Web Applications by Doguhan Uluca

Who this book is for

If you're a JavaScript or frontend developer looking to gain comprehensive experience of using Angular for end-to-end enterprise-ready applications, this Learning Path is for you.

What this book covers

Chapter 1, *Building Our First App – 7 Minute Workout*, teaches us how to build our first real Angular app. In the process, we will learn more about one of the primary building blocks of Angular, components. We will also be introduced to Angular's templating constructs, databinding capabilities, and services.

Chapter 2, *Personal Trainer*, introduces a new exercise where we morph the *7 Minute workout* into a generic Personal Trainer app. This app has the capability to create new workout plans other than the original 7 minute workout. This chapter covers Angular's form capabilities and how we can use them to build custom workouts.

Chapter 3, *Supporting Server Data Persistence*, deals with saving and retrieving workout data from the server. We augment Personal Trainer with persistence capabilities as we explore Angular's http client library and how it uses RxJS Observables.

Chapter 4, *Angular Directives in Depth*, goes deep into the inner workings of Angular directives and components. We build a number of directives to support Personal Trainer.

Chapter 5, *1.21 Gigawatt – Flux Pattern Explained*, teaches what the Flux pattern is and what concepts it consists of. It shows how to implement the Flux pattern using stores, a dispatcher, and several views.

Chapter 6, *Functional Reactive Programming*, drills down into certain properties of functional programming, such as higher-order functions, immutability, and recursion. Furthermore, we look at how to make code reactive and what reactive means.

Chapter 7, *Manipulating Stream and Their Values*, focuses a lot on educating the reader on operators, the thing that gives RxJS its power. The reader should leave this chapter with a lot more knowledge about how to manipulate data as well as Observables.

Chapter 8, *RxJS Advanced*, goes deeper and tries to explain more advanced concepts in RxJS, such as hot and cold Observables, subjects, error handling, and how to test your RxJS code with Marble testing.

Chapter 9, *Create a Local Weather Web Application*, introduces the Kanban method of software development with easy-to-use design tools used to communicate ideas. It also covers Angular fundamentals, unit testing, and leveraging CLI tools to maximize your impact.

Chapter 10, *Prepare Angular App for Production Release*, covers how to use containerization with Docker to enable cloud deployments.

Chapter 11, *Enhance Angular App with Angular Material*, introduces you to Angular material and explains how to use it to build great-looking apps.

Chapter 12, *Create a Router-First Line-of-Business App*, focuses on the Router-first architecture, a seven-step approach to the design and development of mid-to-large applications.

Chapter 13, *Continuous Integration and API Design,* goes over continuous integration using CircleCI and early integration with backend APIs using Swagger.

Chapter 14, *Design Authentication and Authorization,* dives into authentication- and authorization-related patterns in Angular and RESTful applications.

Chapter 15, *Angular App Design and Recipes,* contains recipes commonly needed for line-of-business applications.

Chapter 16, *Highly-Available Cloud Infrastructure on AWS,* moves beyond application features to go over provisioning a highly-available cloud infrastructure on AWS.

To get the most out of this book

We will be building our apps in the TypeScript language; therefore, it would be preferable if you have an IDE that makes development with TypeScript easy. IDEs such as Atom, Sublime, WebStorm, and Visual Studio (or VS Code) are great tools for this purpose.

Download the example code files

You can download the example code files for this book from your account at www.packtpub.com. If you purchased this book elsewhere, you can visit www.packtpub.com/support and register to have the files emailed directly to you.

You can download the code files by following these steps:

1. Log in or register at www.packtpub.com.
2. Select the **SUPPORT** tab.
3. Click on **Code Downloads & Errata**.
4. Enter the name of the book in the **Search** box and follow the onscreen instructions.

Once the file is downloaded, please make sure that you unzip or extract the folder using the latest version of:

- WinRAR/7-Zip for Windows
- Zipeg/iZip/UnRarX for Mac
- 7-Zip/PeaZip for Linux

The code bundle for the book is also hosted on GitHub at `https://github.com/chandermani/angular6byexample` and `https://github.com/PacktPublishing/Architecting-Angular-Applications-with-Redux-RxJs-and-NgRx`. The code bundle for the third module is hosted on author's GitHub repository at `https://github.com/duluca/local-weather-app` and `https://github.com/duluca/lemon-mart`. In case there's an update to the code, it will be updated on the existing GitHub repository.

We also have other code bundles from our rich catalog of books and videos available at `https://github.com/PacktPublishing/`. Check them out!

Conventions used

There are a number of text conventions used throughout this book.

`CodeInText`: Indicates code words in text, database table names, folder names, filenames, file extensions, pathnames, dummy URLs, user input, and Twitter handles. Here is an example: "We can see how the router combines the routes in `app.routes.ts` with the default route in `workout-builder.routes.ts`".

A block of code is set as follows:

```
"styles": [
    "node_modules/bootstrap/dist/css/bootstrap.min.css",
    "src/styles.css"
],
```

When we wish to draw your attention to a particular part of a code block, the relevant lines or items are set in bold:

```
const routes: Routes = [
    ...
    { path: 'builder', loadChildren: './workout-builder/workout-builder.module#WorkoutBuilderModule'},
    { path: '**', redirectTo: '/start' }
];
```

Any command-line input or output is written as follows:

```
ng new guessthenumber --inlineTemplate
```

Bold: Indicates a new term, an important word, or words that you see onscreen. For example, words in menus or dialog boxes appear in the text like this. Here is an example: "With the **Developer tools** open in the **Sources** tab"

Warnings or important notes appear like this.

Tips and tricks appear like this.

Get in touch

Feedback from our readers is always welcome.

General feedback: Email `feedback@packtpub.com` and mention the book title in the subject of your message. If you have questions about any aspect of this book, please email us at `questions@packtpub.com`.

Errata: Although we have taken every care to ensure the accuracy of our content, mistakes do happen. If you have found a mistake in this book, we would be grateful if you would report this to us. Please visit `www.packtpub.com/submit-errata`, selecting your book, clicking on the Errata Submission Form link, and entering the details.

Piracy: If you come across any illegal copies of our works in any form on the Internet, we would be grateful if you would provide us with the location address or website name. Please contact us at `copyright@packtpub.com` with a link to the material.

If you are interested in becoming an author: If there is a topic that you have expertise in and you are interested in either writing or contributing to a book, please visit `authors.packtpub.com`.

Reviews

Please leave a review. Once you have read and used this book, why not leave a review on the site that you purchased it from? Potential readers can then see and use your unbiased opinion to make purchase decisions, we at Packt can understand what you think about our products, and our authors can see your feedback on their book. Thank you!

For more information about Packt, please visit `packtpub.com`.

Building Our First App - 7 Minute Workout

We will be building a new app in Angular, and in the process, become more familiar with the framework. This app will also help us explore some new capabilities of Angular.

The topics that we will cover in this chapter include the following:

- **7 Minute Workout problem description**: We detail the functionality of the app that we build in this chapter.
- **Code organization**: For our first real app, we will try to explain how to organize code, specifically Angular code.
- **Designing the model**: One of the building blocks of our app is its model. We design the app model based on the app's requirements.
- **Understanding the data binding infrastructure**: While building the *7 Minute Workout* view, we will look at the data binding capabilities of the framework, which include *property*, *attribute*, *class*, *style*, and *event* bindings.
- **Exploring the Angular platform directives**: Some of the directives that we will cover are `ngFor`, `ngIf`, `ngClass`, `ngStyle`, and `ngSwitch`.

- **Cross-component communication with input properties**: As we build nested components, we learn how input properties can be used to pass data from the parent to its child components.
- **Cross-component communication with events**: Angular components can subscribe to and raise events. We get introduced to event binding support in Angular.
- **Angular pipes**: Angular pipes provide a mechanism to format view content. We explore some standard Angular pipes and build our own pipe to support conversions from seconds to hh:mm:ss.

Let's get started! The first thing we will do is to define our *7 Minute Workout* app.

What is 7 Minute Workout?

We want everyone reading this book to be physically fit. Therefore, this book should serve a dual purpose; it should not only stimulate your grey matter but also urge you to look after your physical fitness. What better way to do it than to build an app that targets physical fitness!

7 Minute Workout is an exercise/workout app that requires us to perform a set of 12 exercises in quick succession within the seven-minute time span. *7 Minute Workout* has become quite popular due to its bite-sized length and great benefits. We cannot confirm or refute the claims, but doing any form of strenuous physical activity is better than doing nothing at all. If you are interested to know more about the workout, then check out `http:/` `/well.blogs.nytimes.com/2013/05/09/the-scientific-7-minute-workout/`.

The technicalities of the app include performing a set of 12 exercises, dedicating 30 seconds for each of the exercises. This is followed by a brief rest period before starting the next exercise. For the app that we are building, we will be taking rest periods of 10 seconds each. So, the total duration comes out at a little more than seven minutes.

At the end of the chapter, we will have the *7 Minute Workout* app ready, which will look something like the following:

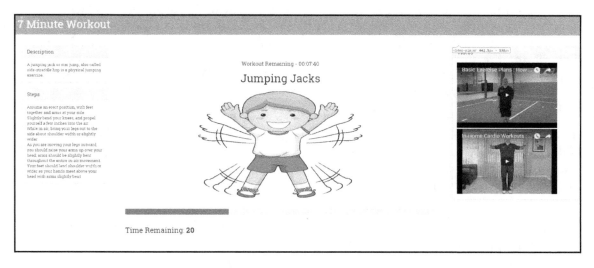

The 7 Minute Workout app

Downloading the code base

The code for this app can be downloaded from the GitHub site (`https://github.com/chandermani/angular6byexample`) dedicated to this book. Since we are building the app incrementally, we have created **multiple checkpoints** that map to **GitHub branches** such as `checkpoint2.1`, `checkpoint2.2`, and so on. During the narration, we will highlight the branch for reference. These branches will contain the work done on the app up until that point in time.

The *7 Minute Workout* code is available in the repository folder named `trainer`.

So, let's get started!

Setting up the build

Remember that we are building on a modern platform for which browsers still lack support. Therefore, directly referencing script files in HTML is out of the question (while common, it's a dated approach that we should avoid anyway). Browsers do not understand **TypeScript**; this implies that there has to be a process that converts code written in TypeScript into standard **JavaScript (ES5)**. Hence, having a build set up for any Angular app becomes imperative. And thanks to the growing popularity of Angular, we are never short of options.

If you are a frontend developer working on the web stack, you cannot avoid **Node.js**. This is the most widely used platform for web/JavaScript development. So, no prizes for guessing that most of the Angular build solutions out there are supported by Node. Packages such as **Grunt**, **Gulp**, **JSPM**, and **webpack** are the most common building blocks for any build system.

 Since we too are building on the Node.js platform, install Node.js before starting.

For this book and this sample app, we endorse **Angular CLI** (`http://bit.ly/ng6be-angular-cli`). A command line tool, it has a build system and a scaffolding tool that hugely simplifies Angular's development workflow. It is popular, easy to set up, easy to manage, and supports almost everything that a modern build system should have. More about it later.

As with any mature framework, Angular CLI is not the only option out there on the web. Some of the notable starter sites plus build setups created by the community are as follows:

Start site	Location
angular2-webpack-starter	http://bit.ly/ng2webpack
angular-seed	https://github.com/mgechev/angular-seed

Let's start with installing Angular CLI. On the command line, type the following:

```
npm i -g @angular/cli
```

Once installed, Angular CLI adds a new command `ng` to our execution environment. To create a new Angular project from the command line, run the following command:

```
ng new PROJECT-NAME
```

This generates a folder structure with a bunch of files, a boilerplate Angular application, and a preconfigured build system. To run the application from the command line, execute the following:

```
ng serve --open
```

And you can see a basic Angular application in action!

For our *7 Minute Workout* app, instead of starting from scratch, we are going to start from a version that is based on the project structure generated by ng new with minor modification. Start with the following steps:

 Curious about what the default project includes? Go ahead and run ng new PROJECT-NAME. Look at the generated content structure and the Angular CLI documentation to get an idea of what's part of a default setup.

1. Download the base version of this app from http://bit.ly/ngbe-base and unzip it to a location on your machine. If you are familiar with how Git works, you can just clone the repository and check out the base branch:

   ```
   git checkout base
   ```

   This code serves as the starting point for our app.

2. Navigate to the trainer folder from the command line and execute the command npm install from the command line to install the **package dependencies** for our application.

 Packages in the Node.js world are third-party libraries (such as Angular for our app) that are either used by the app or support the app's building process. **npm** is a command-line tool for pulling these packages from a remote repository.

3. Once npm pulls the app dependencies from the npm store, we are ready to build and run the application. From the command line, enter the following command:

```
ng serve --open
```

   This compiles and runs the app. If the build process goes fine, the default browser window/tab will open with a rudimentary app page (http://localhost:4200/). We are all set to begin developing our app in Angular!

But before we do that, it would be interesting to know a bit more about Angular CLI and the customization that we have done on the default project template that Angular CLI generates.

Angular CLI

Angular CLI was created with the aim of standardizing and simplifying the development and deployment workflow for Angular apps. As the documentation suggests:

> *"The Angular CLI makes it easy to create an application that already works, right out of the box. It already follows our best practices!"*

It incorporates:

- A build system based on **webpack**
- A **scaffolding tool** to generate all standard Angular artifacts including modules, directives, components, and pipes
- Adherence to **Angular style guide** (http://bit.ly/ngbe-styleguide), making sure we use community-driven standards for projects of every shape and size

You may have never heard the term style guide, or may not understand its significance. A style guide in any technology is a set of guidelines that help us organize and write code that is easy to develop, maintain, and extend. To understand and appreciate Angular's own style guide, some familiarity with the framework itself is desirable, and we have started that journey.

- A targeted **linter;** Angular CLI integrates with **codelyzer** (http://bit.ly/ngbe-codelyzer), a **static code analysis tool** that validates our Angular code against a set of rules to make sure that the code we write adheres to standards laid down in the Angular style guide
- Preconfigured **unit** and **end-to-end** (**e2e**) test framework

And much more!

Imagine if we had to do all this manually! The steep learning curve would quickly overwhelm us. Thankfully, we don't have to deal with it, Angular CLI does it for us.

The Angular CLI build setup is based on webpack, but it does not expose the underlying webpack configuration; this is intentional. The Angular team wanted to shield developers from the complexities and internal workings of webpack. The ultimate aim of Angular CLI is to eliminate any entry level barriers and make setting up and running Angular code simple.

It doesn't mean Angular CLI is not configurable. There is a *config file* (angular.json) that we can use to alter the build setup. We will not cover that here. Check the configuration file for 7 Minute Workout and read the documentation here: http://bit.ly/ng6be-angular-cli-config.

The tweaks that we have done to the default generated project template are:

- Referenced Bootstrap CSS in the style.css file.
- Upgraded some npm library versions.
- Changed the prefix configuration for generated code to use abe (short for Angular By Example) from app. With this change, all our components and directive selectors will be prefixed by abe instead of app. Check app.component.ts; the selector is abe-root instead of app-root.

While on the topic of Angular CLI and builds, there is something that we should understand before proceeding.

What happens to the TypeScript code we write?

Code transpiling

Browsers, as we all know, only work with JavaScript, they don't understand TypeScript. We hence need a mechanism to convert our TypeScript code into plain JavaScript (**ES5** is our safest bet). The **TypeScript compiler** does this job. The compiler takes the TypeScript code and converts it into JavaScript. This process is commonly referred to as **transpiling**, and since the TypeScript compiler does it, it's called a **transpiler**.

JavaScript as a language has evolved over the years with every new version adding new features/capabilities to the language. The latest avatar, ES2015, succeeds ES5 and is a major update to the language. While released in June 2015, some of the older browsers still lack support for the ES2015 flavor, of JavaScript making its adoption a challenge.

When transpiling code from TypeScript to JavaScript, we can specify the flavor of JavaScript to use. As mentioned earlier, ES5 is our safest bet, but if we plan to work with only the latest and greatest browsers, go for ES2015. For 7 Minute Workout, our code to transpile to is ES5 format. We set this TypeScript compiler configuration in `tsconfig.json` (see the `target` property).

Interestingly, transpilation can happen at both build/compile time and at runtime:

- **Build-time transpilation**: Transpilation as part of the build process takes the script files (in our case, TypeScript `.ts` files) and compiles them into plain JavaScript. Angular CLI does build-time transpilation.
- **Runtime transpilation**: This happens in the browser at runtime. We directly reference the TypeScript files (`.ts` in our case), and the TypeScript compiler, which is loaded in the browser beforehand, compiles these script files on the fly. This is a workable setup only for small examples/code snippets, as there is an additional performance overhead involved in loading the transpiler and transpiling the code on the fly.

The process of transpiling is not limited to TypeScript. Every language targeted towards the web, such as **CoffeeScript**, **ES2015**, (yes JavaScript itself!) or any other language that is not inherently understood by a browser needs transpilation. There are transpilers for most languages, and the prominent ones (other than TypeScript) are **tracuer** and **babel.**

The Angular CLI build system takes care of setting up the TypeScript compiler and sets up file watchers that recompile the code every time we make changes to our TypeScript file.

If you are new to TypeScript, remember that TypeScript does not depend on Angular; in fact, Angular has been built on TypeScript. I highly recommend that you look at the official documentation on TypeScript (https://www.typescriptlang.org/) and learn the language outside the realms of Angular.

Let's get back to the app we are building and start exploring the code setup.

Organizing code

The advantage of Angular CLI is that is dictates a code organization structure that works for applications of all sizes. Here is how the current code organization looks:

- `trainer` is the application root folder.
- The files inside `trainer` are configuration files and some standard files that are part of every standard node application.
- The `e2e` folder will contain end to end tests for the app.
- `src` is the primary folder where all the development happens. All the application artifacts go into `src`.
- The `assets` folder inside `src` hosts static content (such as images, CSS, audio files, and others).
- The `app` folder has the app's source code.
- The `environments` folder is useful to set configurations for different deployment environments (such as *dev, qa, production*).

To organize Angular code inside the `app` folder, we take a leaf from the Angular style guide (`http://bit.ly/ng6be-style-guide`) released by the Angular team.

Feature folders

The style guide recommends the use of **feature folders** to organize code. With feature folders, files linked to a single feature are placed together. If a feature grows, we break it down further into sub features and tuck the code into sub folders. Consider the app folder to be our first feature folder! As the application grows, app will add sub features for better code organization.

Let's get straight into building the application. Our first focus area, the app's model!

The 7 Minute Workout model

Designing the model for this app requires us to first detail the functional aspects of the *7 Minute Workout* app, and then derive a model that satisfies those requirements. Based on the problem statement defined earlier, some of the obvious requirements are as follows:

- Being able to start the workout.
- Providing a visual clue about the current exercise and its progress. This includes the following:
    - Providing a visual depiction of the current exercise
    - Providing step-by-step instructions on how to do a specific exercise
    - The time left for the current exercise
- Notifying the user when the workout ends.

Some other valuable features that we will add to this app are as follows:

- The ability to pause the current workout.
- Providing information about the next exercise to follow.
- Providing audio clues so that the user can perform the workout without constantly looking at the screen. This includes:
    - A timer click sound
    - Details about the next exercise
    - Signaling that the exercise is about to start
- Showing related videos for the exercise in progress and the ability to play them.

As we can see, the central themes for this app are **workout** and **exercise**. Here, a workout is a set of exercises performed in a specific order for a particular duration. So, let's go ahead and define the model for our workout and exercise.

Based on the requirements just mentioned, we will need the following details about an exercise:

- The name. This should be unique.
- The title. This is shown to the user.
- The description of the exercise.
- Instructions on how to perform the exercise.
- Images for the exercise.
- The name of the audio clip for the exercise.
- Related videos.

With TypeScript, we can define the classes for our model.

The Exercise class looks as follows:

```
export class Exercise {
  constructor(
    public name: string,
    public title: string,
    public description: string,
    public image: string,
    public nameSound?: string,
    public procedure?: string,
    public videos?: Array<string>) { }
}
```

TypeScript tips
Declaring constructor parameters with public or private is a shorthand for creating and initializing class members at one go. The ? suffix after nameSound, procedure, and videos implies that these are optional parameters.

For the workout, we need to track the following properties:

- The name. This should be unique.
- The title. This is shown to the user.
- The exercises that are part of the workout.
- The duration for each exercise.
- The rest duration between two exercises.

The model class to track workout progress (`WorkoutPlan`) looks as follows:

```
export class WorkoutPlan {
  constructor(
    public name: string,
    public title: string,
    public restBetweenExercise: number,
    public exercises: ExercisePlan[],
    public description?: string) { }

  totalWorkoutDuration(): number { ... }
}
```

The `totalWorkoutDuration` function returns the total duration of the workout in seconds.

`WorkoutPlan` has a reference to another class in the preceding definition, `ExercisePlan`. It tracks the exercise and the duration of the exercise in a workout, which is quite apparent once we look at the definition of `ExercisePlan`:

```
export class ExercisePlan {
  constructor(
    public exercise: Exercise,
    public duration: number) { }
}
```

Let me save you some typing and tell you where to get the model classes, but before that, we need to decide where to add them. We are ready for our first feature.

First feature module

The primary feature of *7 Minute Workout* is to execute a predefined set of exercises. Hence we are going to create a feature module now and later add the feature implementation to this module. We call this module `workout-runner`. Let's initialize the feature with Angular CLI's scaffolding capabilities.

From the command line, navigate to the `trainer/src/app` folder and run the following:

```
ng generate module workout-runner --module app.module.ts
```

Follow the console logs to know what files are generated. The command essentially:

- Creates a new Angular `WorkoutRunnerModule` module inside a new `workout-runner` folder
- Imports the newly created module into the main application module app (`app.module.ts`)

We now have a new **feature module**.

Give every feature its own module.

Make special note of the conventions Angular CLI follows when scaffolding Angular artifacts. From the preceding example, the module name provided with the command line was `workout-runner`. While the generated folder and filenames use the same name, the class name for the generated module is `WorkoutRunnerModule` (pascal case with the `Module` suffix).

Open the newly generated module definition (`workout-runner.module.ts`) and look at the generated content. `WorkoutRunnerModule` imports `CommonModule`, a module with common Angular directives such as `ngIf` and `ngFor`, allowing us to use these common directives across any component/directive defined in `WorkoutRunnerModule`.

Modules are Angular's way of organizing code. We will touch upon Angular modules shortly.

Copy the `model.ts` file from `http://bit.ly/ng6be-2-1-model-ts` into the `workout-runner` folder. Shortly, we will see how these model classes are utilized.

Since we have started with a preconfigured Angular app, we just need to understand how the app starts.

App bootstrapping

The app bootstrapping process for *7 Minute Workout* can be carried out from the `src` folder. There is a `main.ts` file that bootstraps the application by calling the following:

```
platformBrowserDynamic().bootstrapModule(AppModule)
    .catch(err => console.log(err));
```

The heavy lifting is done by the Angular CLI, which compiles the application, includes the script and CSS reference into `index.html`, and runs the application. We don't need to configure anything. These configurations are part of the default Angular CLI configuration (`.angular-cli.json`).

We have created a new module and added some model classes to the `module` folder. Before we go any further and start implementing the feature, let's talk a bit about **Angular modules**.

Exploring Angular modules

As the *7 Minute Workout* app grows and we add new components/directives/pipes/other artifacts to it, a need arises to organize these items. Each of these items needs to be part of an Angular module.

A naïve approach would be to declare everything in our app's root module (`AppModule`), as we did with `WorkoutRunnerComponent`, but this defeats the whole purpose of Angular modules.

To understand why a single-module approach is never a good idea, let's explore Angular modules.

Comprehending Angular modules

In Angular, **modules** are a way to organize code into chunks that belong together and work as a cohesive unit. Modules are Angular's way of grouping and organizing code.

An Angular module primarily defines:

- The components/directives/pipes it owns
- The components/directives/pipes it makes public for other modules to consume
- Other modules that it depends on
- Services that the module wants to make available application-wide

Any decent-sized Angular app will have modules interlinked with each other: some modules consuming artifacts from other, some providing artifacts to others, and some modules doing both.

As a standard practice, module segregation is feature-based. One divides the app into features or subfeatures (for large features) and modules are created for each of the features. Even the framework adheres to this guideline as all of the framework constructs are divided across modules:

- There is `CommonModule` that aggregates the standard framework constructs used in every browser-based Angular app
- There is `RouterModule` if we want to use the Angular routing framework
- There is `HtppModule` if our app needs to communicate with the server over HTTP

Angular modules are created by applying the `@NgModule` decorator to a TypeScript class. The decorator definition exposes enough metadata, allowing Angular to load everything the module refers to.

The decorator has multiple attributes that allow us to define:

- External dependencies (using `imports`).
- Module artifacts (using `declarations`).
- Module exports (using `exports`).
- The services defined inside the module that need to be registered globally (using `providers`).
- The main application view, called the **root component**, which hosts all other app views. Only the root module should set this using the `bootstrap` property.

This diagram highlights the internals of a module and how they link to each other:

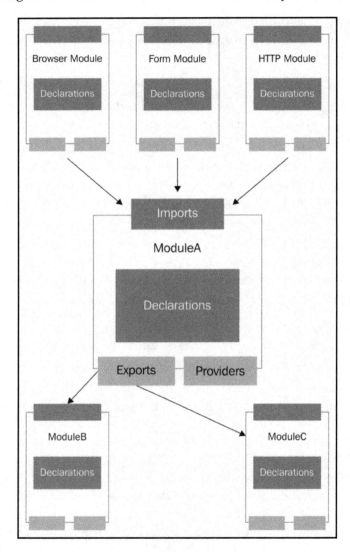

Modules defined in the context of Angular (using the @NgModule decorator) are different from modules we import using the import statement in our TypeScript file. Modules imported through the import statement are **JavaScript modules**, which can be in different formats adhering to *CommonJS, AMD,* or *ES2015* specifications, whereas Angular modules are constructs used by Angular to segregate and organize its artifacts. Unless the context of the discussion is specifically a JavaScript module, any reference to module implies an Angular module. We can learn more about this here: http://bit.ly/ng2be6-module-vs-ngmodule.

We hope one thing is clear from all this discussion: creating a single application-wide module is not the right use of Angular modules unless you are building something rudimentary.

It's time to get into the thick of the action; let's build our first component.

Our first component - WorkoutRunnerComponent

WorkoutRunnerComponent, is the central piece of our *7 Minute Workout* app and it will contain the logic to execute the workout.

What we are going to do in the WorkoutRunnerComponent implementation is as follows:

1. Start the workout
2. Show the workout in progress and show the progress indicator
3. After the time elapses for an exercise, show the next exercise
4. Repeat this process until all the exercises are over

We are ready to create (or scaffold) our component.

From the command line, navigate to the src/app folder and execute the following ng command:

```
ng generate component workout-runner -is
```

The generator generates a bunch of files (three) in the workout-runner folder and updates the module declaration in WorkoutRunnerModule to include the newly created WorkoutRunnerComponent.

The `-is` flag is used to stop generation of a separate CSS file for the component. Since we are using global styles, we do not need component-specific styles.

Remember to run this command from the `src/app` folder and not from the `src/app/workout-runner` folder. If we run the preceding command from `src/app/workout-runner`, Angular CLI will create a new subfolder with the `workout-runner` component definition.

The preceding `ng generate` command for component generates these three files:

- `<component-name>.component.html`: This is the component's view HTML.
- `<component-name>.component.spec.ts`: Test specification file used in unit testing.
- `<component-name>.component.ts`: Main component file containing component implementation.

Again, we will encourage you to have a look at the generated code to understand what gets generated. The Angular CLI component generator saves us some keystrokes and once generated, the boilerplate code can evolve as desired.

While we see only four decorator metadata properties (such as `templateUrl`), the component decorator supports some other useful properties too. Look at the Angular documentation for component to learn more about these properties and their application.

An observant reader might have noticed that the generated `selector` property value has a prefix `abe`; this is intentional. Since we are extending the HTML **domain-specific language (DSL)** to incorporate a new element, the prefix `abe` helps us demarcate HTML extensions that we have developed. So instead of using `<workout-runner></workout-runner>` in HTML we use `<abe-workout-runner></abe-workout-runner>`. The prefix value has been configured in `angular.json`, see the `prefix` property.

Always add a prefix to your component selector.

We now have the `WorkoutRunnerComponent` boilerplate; let's start adding the implementation, starting with adding the model reference.

In `workout-runner.component.ts`, import all the workout models:

```
import {WorkoutPlan, ExercisePlan, Exercise} from './model';
```

Next, we need to set up the workout data. Let's do that by adding some code in the generated `ngOnInit` function and related class properties to the `WorkoutRunnerComponent` class:

```
workoutPlan: WorkoutPlan;
restExercise: ExercisePlan;
ngOnInit() {
    this.workoutPlan = this.buildWorkout();
    this.restExercise = new ExercisePlan(
        new Exercise('rest', 'Relax!', 'Relax a bit', 'rest.png'),
        this.workoutPlan.restBetweenExercise);
}
```

`ngOnInit` is a special function that Angular calls when a component is initialized. We will talk about `ngOnInit` shortly.

The `buildWorkout` on `WorkoutRunnerComponent` sets up the complete workout, as we will define shortly. We also initialize a `restExercise` variable to track even the rest periods as exercise (note that `restExercise` is an object of type `ExercisePlan`).

The `buildWorkout` function is a lengthy function, so it's better to copy the implementation from the workout runner's implementation available in Git branch checkpoint2.1 (http://bit.ly/ng6be-2-1-workout-runner-component-ts). The `buildWorkout` code looks as follows:

```
buildWorkout(): WorkoutPlan {
let workout = new WorkoutPlan('7MinWorkout',
"7 Minute Workout", 10, []);
    workout.exercises.push(
        new ExercisePlan(
          new Exercise(
            'jumpingJacks',
            'Jumping Jacks',
            'A jumping jack or star jump, also called side-straddle hop
             is a physical jumping exercise.',
            'JumpingJacks.png',
            'jumpingjacks.wav',
            `Assume an erect position, with feet together and
             arms at your side. ...`,
            ['dmYwZH_BNd0', 'BABOdJ-2Z6o', 'c4DAnQ6DtF8']),
          30));
    // (TRUNCATED) Other 11 workout exercise data.
```

```
    return workout;
}
```

This code builds the `WorkoutPlan` object and pushes the exercise data into the `exercises` array (an array of `ExercisePlan` objects), returning the newly built workout.

The initialization is complete; now, it's time to actually implement the *start* workout. Add a `start` function to the `WorkoutRunnerComponent` implementation, as follows:

```
start() {
    this.workoutTimeRemaining =
    this.workoutPlan.totalWorkoutDuration();
    this.currentExerciseIndex = 0;
    this.startExercise(this.workoutPlan.exercises[this.currentExerciseIndex]);
}
```

Then declare the new variables used in the function at the top, with other variable declarations:

```
workoutTimeRemaining: number;
currentExerciseIndex: number;
```

The `workoutTimeRemaining` variable tracks the total time remaining for the workout, and `currentExerciseIndex` tracks the currently executing exercise index. The call to `startExercise` actually starts an exercise. This is how the code for `startExercise` looks:

```
startExercise(exercisePlan: ExercisePlan) {
    this.currentExercise = exercisePlan;
    this.exerciseRunningDuration = 0;
    const intervalId = setInterval(() => {
      if (this.exerciseRunningDuration >=  this.currentExercise.duration) {
        clearInterval(intervalId);
      }
      else { this.exerciseRunningDuration++; }
    }, 1000);
}
```

We start by initializing `currentExercise` and `exerciseRunningDuration`. The `currentExercise` variable tracks the exercise in progress and `exerciseRunningDuration` tracks its duration. These two variables also need to be declared at the top:

```
currentExercise: ExercisePlan;
exerciseRunningDuration: number;
```

We use the `setInterval` JavaScript function with a delay of one second (1,000 milliseconds) to make progress. Inside the `setInterval` callback, `exerciseRunningDuration` is incremented with each passing second. The nested `clearInterval` call stops the timer once the exercise duration lapses.

TypeScript arrow functions
The callback parameter passed to `setInterval (()=>{...})` is a lambda function (or an arrow function in ES 2015). Lambda functions are short-form representations of anonymous functions, with added benefits. You can learn more about them at `http://bit.ly/ng2be-ts-arrow-functions`.

The first cut of the component is almost complete, except it currently has a static view (UI) and hence we cannot verify the implementation. We can quickly rectify this situation by adding a rudimentary view definition. Open `workout-runner.component.ts`, comment out the `templateUrl` property, and add an inline template property (`template`) and set it to the following:

```
template: `<pre>Current Exercise: {{currentExercise | json}}</pre>
<pre>Time Left: {{currentExercise.duration -
exerciseRunningDuration}}</pre>`,
```

Strings enclosed in backticks (` ` `) are a new addition to ES2015. Also called template literals, such string literals can be multiline and allow expressions to be embedded inside (not to be confused with Angular expressions). Look at the MDN article at `http://bit.ly/template-literals` for more details.

Inline versus external view template

The preceding `template` property is an example of **inline component template**. This allows the component developer to specify the component template inline instead of using a separate HTML file. The inline template approach generally works for components with a trivial view. Inline templates have a disadvantage: formatting HTML becomes difficult and IDE support is very limited as the content is treated as a string literal. When we externalize HTML, we can develop a template as a normal HTML document. We recommend you use an **external template file** (specified using `templateUrl`) for elaborate views. Angular CLI by default generates an external template reference, but we can affect this behavior by passing the `--inline-template` flag to the `ng` component generation command, such as `--inline-template true`.

The preceding template HTML will render the raw `ExercisePlan` object and the exercise time remaining. It has an interesting expression inside the first interpolation: `currentExercise | json`. The `currentExercise` property is defined in `WorkoutRunnerComponent`, but what about the `|` symbol and what follows it (`json`)? In the Angular world, it is called a **pipe**. The sole purpose of a pipe is to transform/format template data.

The `json` pipe here does JSON data formatting. You will learn more about pipes later in this chapter, but to get a general sense of what the `json` pipe does, we can remove the `json` pipe plus the `|` symbol and render the template; we are going to do this next.

To render the new `WorkoutRunnerComponent` implementation, it has to be added to the root component's view. Modify `src/components/app/app.component.html` and replace the `h3` tag with the following code:

```
<div class="container body-content app-container">
    <abe-workout-runner></abe-workout-runner>
</div>
```

While the implementation may look complete, there is a crucial piece missing. Nowhere in the code do we actually start the workout. The workout should start as soon as we load the page.

Component lifecycle hooks are going to rescue us!

Component lifecycle hooks

The life of an Angular component is eventful. Components get created, change state during their lifetime, and finally, they are destroyed. Angular provides some **lifecycle hooks/functions** that the framework invokes (on the component) when such an event occurs. Consider these examples:

- When a component is initialized, Angular invokes `ngOnInit`
- When a component's data-bound properties change, Angular invokes `ngOnChanges`
- When a component is destroyed, Angular invokes `ngOnDestroy`

As developers, we can tap into these key moments and perform some custom logic inside the respective component.

The hook we are going to utilize here is `ngOnInit`. The `ngOnInit` function gets fired the first time the component's data-bound properties are initialized, but before the view initialization starts.

 While `ngOnInit` and the class constructor seem to look similar, they have a different purpose. *A constructor* is a language feature and it is used to initialize class members. `ngOnInit`, on the other hand, is used to do some initialization stuff once the component is ready. Avoid use of a constructor for anything other than member initialization.

Update the `ngOnInit` function to the `WorkoutRunnerComponent` class with a call to start the workout:

```
ngOnInit() {
    ...
    this.start();
}
```

Angular CLI as part of component scaffolding already generates the signature for `ngOnInit`. The `ngOnInit` function is declared on the `OnInit` interface, which is part of the core Angular framework. We can confirm this by looking at the import section of `WorkoutRunnerComponent`:

```
import {Component,OnInit} from '@angular/core';
...
export class WorkoutRunnerComponent implements OnInit {
```

There are a number of other lifecycle hooks, including `ngOnDestroy`, `ngOnChanges`, and `ngAfterViewInit`, that components support, but we are not going to dwell on any of them here. Look at the developer guide (`https://angular.io/guide/lifecycle-hooks`) on lifecycle hooks to learn more about other such hooks.

Implementing the interface (`OnInit` in the preceding example) is optional. These lifecycle hooks work as long as the function name matches. We still recommend you use interfaces to clearly communicate the intent.

Time to run our app! Open the command line, navigate to the `trainer` folder, and type this line:

```
ng serve --open
```

The code compiles, but no UI is rendered. What is failing us? Let's look at the browser console for errors.

Open the browser's dev tools (common keyboard shortcut `F12`) and look at the **console** tab for errors. There is a template parsing error. Angular is not able to locate the `abe-workout-runner` component. Let's do some sanity checks to verify our setup:

- `WorkoutRunnerComponent` implementation complete - *check*
- Component declared in `WorkoutRunnerModule`- *check*
- `WorkoutRunnerModule` imported into `AppModule` - *check*

Still, the `AppComponent` template cannot locate the `WorkoutRunnerComponent`. Is it because `WorkoutRunnerComponent` and `AppComponent` are in different modules? Indeed, that is the problem! While `WorkoutRunnerModule` has been imported into `AppModule`, `WorkoutRunnerModule` still does not export the new `WorkoutRunnerComponent` that will allow `AppComponent` to use it.

Remember, adding a component/directive/pipe to the `declaration` section of a module makes them available inside the module. It's only after we export the component/directive/pipe that it becomes available to be used across modules.

Let's export `WorkoutRunnerComponent` by updating the export array of the `WorkoutRunnerModule` declaration to the following:

```
declarations: [WorkoutRunnerComponent],
exports: [WorkoutRunnerComponent]
```

This time, we should see the following output:

```
Current Exercise: {
  "exercise": {
    "name": "jumpingJacks",
    "title": "Jumping Jacks",
    "description": "A jumping jack or star jump, also called side
    "image": "JumpingJacks.png",
    "nameSound": "jumpingjacks.wav",
    "procedure": "Assume an erect position, with feet together an
    "videos": [
      "dmYwZH_BNd0",
      "BABOdJ-2Z6o",
      "c4DAnQ6DtF8"
    ]
  },
  "duration": 30
}

Time Left: 28
```

Always export artifacts defined inside an Angular module if you want them to be used across other modules.

The model data updates with every passing second! Now you'll understand why interpolations ({{ }}) are a great debugging tool.

This will also be a good time to try rendering currentExercise without the json pipe and see what gets rendered.

We are not done yet! Wait long enough on the page and we realize that the timer stops after 30 seconds. The app does not load the next exercise data. Time to fix it!

Update the code inside the `setInterval` function:

```
if (this.exerciseRunningDuration >=  this.currentExercise.duration) {
  clearInterval(intervalId);
  const next: ExercisePlan = this.getNextExercise();
  if (next) {
    if (next !== this.restExercise) {
      this.currentExerciseIndex++;
      }
    this.startExercise(next);}
  else { console.log('Workout complete!'); }
}
```

The `if` condition `if (this.exerciseRunningDuration >= this.currentExercise.duration)` is used to transition to the next exercise once the time duration of the current exercise lapses. We use `getNextExercise` to get the next exercise and call `startExercise` again to repeat the process. If no exercise is returned by the `getNextExercise` call, the workout is considered complete.

During exercise transitioning, we increment `currentExerciseIndex` only if the next exercise is not a rest exercise. Remember that the original workout plan does not have a rest exercise. For the sake of consistency, we have created a rest exercise and are now swapping between rest and the standard exercises that are part of the workout plan. Therefore, `currentExerciseIndex` does not change when the next exercise is rest.

Let's quickly add the `getNextExercise` function too. Add the function to the `WorkoutRunnerComponent` class:

```
getNextExercise(): ExercisePlan {
    let nextExercise: ExercisePlan = null;
    if (this.currentExercise === this.restExercise) {
      nextExercise = this.workoutPlan.exercises[this.currentExerciseIndex +
1];
    }
    else if (this.currentExerciseIndex < this.workoutPlan.exercises.length
- 1) {
      nextExercise = this.restExercise;
    }
    return nextExercise;
}
```

The `getNextExercise` function returns the next exercise that needs to be performed.

Note that the returned object for `getNextExercise` is an `ExercisePlan` object that internally contains the exercise details and the duration for which the exercise runs.

The implementation is quite self-explanatory. If the current exercise is rest, take the next exercise from the `workoutPlan.exercises` array (based on `currentExerciseIndex`); otherwise, the next exercise is rest, given that we are not on the last exercise (the `else if` condition check).

With this, we are ready to test our implementation. The exercises should flip after every 10 or 30 seconds. Great!

 The current build setup automatically compiles any changes made to the script files when the files are saved; it also refreshes the browser after these changes. But just in case the UI does not update or things do not work as expected, refresh the browser window. If you are having a problem with running the code, look at the Git branch `checkpoint2.1` for a working version of what we have done thus far. Or if you are not using Git, download the snapshot of Checkpoint 2.1 (a ZIP file) from `http://bit.ly/ng6be-checkpoint2-1`. Refer to the `README.md` file in the `trainer` folder when setting up the snapshot for the first time.

We have done enough work on the component for now, let's build the view.

Building the 7 Minute Workout view

Most of the hard work has already been done while defining the model and implementing the component. Now, we just need to skin the HTML using the super-awesome data binding capabilities of Angular. It's going to be simple, sweet, and elegant!

For the *7 Minute Workout* view, we need to show the exercise name, the exercise image, a progress indicator, and the time remaining. Replace the local content of the `workout-runner.component.html` file with the content of the file from the Git branch `checkpoint2.2`, (or download it from `http://bit.ly/ng6be-2-2-workout-runner-component-html`). The view HTML looks as follows:

```
<div class="row">
  <div id="exercise-pane" class="col-sm">
    <h1 class="text-center">{{currentExercise.exercise.title}}</h1>
    <div class="image-container row">
      <img class="img-fluid col-sm" [src]="'/assets/images/' +
```

```
                                      currentExercise.exercise.image" />
    </div>
    <div class="progress time-progress row">
      <div class="progress-bar col-sm"
            role="progressbar"
            [attr.aria-valuenow]="exerciseRunningDuration"
            aria-valuemin="0"
            [attr.aria-valuemax]="currentExercise.duration"
  [ngStyle]="{'width':(exerciseRunningDuration/currentExercise.duration) *
                                                  100 +
'%'}">
      </div>
    </div>
    <h1>Time Remaining: {{currentExercise.duration-
exerciseRunningDuration}}</h1>
  </div>
</div>
```

WorkoutRunnerComponent currently uses an inline template; instead, we need to revert back to using an external template. Update the workout-runner.component.ts file and get rid of the template property, then uncomment templateUrl, which we commented out earlier.

Before we understand the Angular pieces in the view, let's just run the app again. Save the changes in workout-runner.component.html and if everything went fine, we will see the workout app in its full glory:

The basic app is now up and running. The exercise image and title show up, the progress indicator shows the progress, and exercise transitioning occurs when the exercise time lapses. This surely feels great!

If you are having a problem with running the code, look at the Git branch `checkpoint2.2` for a working version of what we have done thus far. You can also download the snapshot of `checkpoint2.2` (a ZIP file) from this GitHub location: `http://bit.ly/ng6be-checkpoint-2-2`. Refer to the `README.md` file in the `trainer` folder when setting up the snapshot for the first time.

Looking at the view HTML, other than some Bootstrap styles, there are some interesting Angular pieces that need our attention. Before we dwell on these view constructs in detail, let's break down these elements and provide a quick summary:

- `<h1 ...>{{currentExercise.exercise.title}}</h1>`: Uses **interpolation**
- `<img ... [src]="'/assets/images/' + currentExercise.exercise.image" .../>`: Uses **property binding** to bind the `src` property of the image to the component model property `currentExercise.exercise.image`
- `<div ... [attr.aria-valuenow]="exerciseRunningDuration" ... >`: Uses **attribute binding** to bind the aria attribute on *div* to `exerciseRunningDuration`
- `< div ... [ngStyle]="{'width':(exerciseRunningDuration/currentExercise.duration) * 100 + '%'}">`: Uses a **directive** `ngStyle` to bind the `style` property on the progress-bar `div` to an expression that evaluates the exercise progress

Phew! There is a lot of binding involved. Let's dig deeper into the binding infrastructure.

The Angular binding infrastructure

Most modern JavaScript frameworks today come with strong model-view binding support, and Angular is no different. The primary aim of any binding infrastructure is to reduce the boilerplate code that a developer needs to write to keep the model and view in sync. A robust binding infrastructure is always declarative and terse.

The Angular binding infrastructure allows us to transform template (raw) HTML into a live view that is bound to model data. Based on the binding constructs used, data can flow and be synced in both directions: from model to view and view to model.

The link between the component's model and its view is established using the `template` or `templateUrl` property of the `@Component` decorator. With the exception of the `script` tag, almost any piece of HTML can act as a template for the Angular binding infrastructure.

To make this binding magic work, Angular needs to take the view template, compile it, link it to the model data, and keep it in sync with model updates without the need for any custom boilerplate synchronization code.

Based on the data flow direction, these bindings can be of three types:

- **One-way binding from model to view**: In model-to-view binding, changes to the model are kept in sync with the view. Interpolations, property, attribute, class, and style bindings fall in this category.
- **One-way binding from view to model**: In this category, view changes flow towards the model. Event bindings fall in this category.
- **Two-way/bidirectional binding**: Two-way binding, as the name suggests, keeps the view and model in sync. There is a special binding construct used for two-way binding, `ngModel`, and some standard HTML data entry elements such as `input` and `select` support two-way binding.

Let's understand how to utilize the binding capabilities of Angular to support view templatization. Angular provides these binding constructs:

- Interpolations
- Property binding
- Attribute binding
- Class binding
- Style binding
- Event binding

This is a good time to learn about all these binding constructs. **Interpolation** is the first one.

Interpolations

Interpolations are quite simple. The expression (commonly known as a **template expression**) inside the interpolation symbols ({{ }}) is evaluated in the context of the model (or the component class members), and the outcome of the evaluation (string) is embedded in HTML. A handy framework construct to display a component's data/properties. We render the exercise title and the exercise time remaining using interpolation:

```
<h1>{{currentExercise.exercise.title}}</h1>
...
<h1>Time Remaining: {{currentExercise.duration?-
exerciseRunningDuration}}</h1>
```

Remember that interpolations synchronize model changes with the view. Interpolation is one way of binding from a model to a view.

 View bindings in Angular are always evaluated in the context of the component's scope.

Interpolations, in fact, are a special case of property binding, which allows us to bind any HTML element/component properties to a model. We will shortly discuss how an interpolation can be written using property binding syntax. Consider interpolation as syntactical sugar over property binding.

Property binding

Property bindings allow us to bind native HTML/component properties to the component's model and keep them in sync (from model->view). Let's look at property binding from a different context.

Look at this view excerpt from the 7 Minute Workout's component view (`workout-runner.component.html`):

```
<img class="img-responsive" [src]="'/static/images/' +
currentExercise.exercise.image" />
```

It seems that we are setting the `src` attribute of `img` to an expression that gets evaluated at runtime. But are we really binding to an attribute? Or is this a property? Are properties and attributes different?

In Angular realms, while the preceding syntax looks like it is setting an HTML element's attribute, it is, in fact, doing **property binding**. Moreover, since many of us are not aware of the difference between an HTML element's properties and its attributes, this statement is very confusing. Therefore, before we look at how property bindings work, let's try to grasp the difference between an element's property and its attribute.

Property versus attribute

Take any DOM element API and you will find attributes, properties, functions, and events. While events and functions are self-explanatory, it is difficult to understand the difference between properties and attributes. In daily use, we use these words interchangeably, which does not help much either. Take, for example, this line of code:

```
<input type="text" value="Awesome Angular">
```

When the browser creates a DOM element (`HTMLInputElement` to be precise) for this input textbox, it uses the `value` attribute on `input` to set the initial state of the `value` property of `input` to `Awesome Angular`.

After this initialization, any changes to the `value` property of `input` do not reflect on the `value` attribute; the attribute always has `Awesome Angular` (unless set explicitly again). This can be confirmed by querying the `input` state.

Suppose we change the `input` data to `Angular rocks!` and query the `input` element state:

```
input.value // value property
```

The `value` property always returns the current input content, which is `Angular rocks!`. Whereas this DOM API function:

```
input.getAttribute('value')  // value attribute
```

Returns the `value` attribute, and is always the `Awesome Angular` that was set initially.

The primary role of an element attribute is to initialize the state of the element when the corresponding DOM object is created.

There are a number of other nuances that add to this confusion. These include the following:

- Attribute and property synchronization is not consistent across properties. As we saw in the preceding example, changes to the `value` property on `input` do not affect the `value` attribute, but this is not true for all property-value pairs. The `src` property of an image element is a prime example of this; changes to property or attribute values are always kept in sync.

- It's surprising to learn that the mapping between attributes and properties is also not one-to-one. There are a number of properties that do not have any backing attribute (such as `innerHTML`), and there are also attributes that do not have a corresponding property defined on the DOM (such as `colspan`).

- Attribute and property mapping adds to this confusion too, as they do not follow a consistent pattern. An excellent example of this is available in the Angular developer's guide, which we are going to reproduce here verbatim:

The `disabled` attribute is another peculiar example. A button's `disabled` property is `false` by default so the button is enabled. When we add the disabled attribute, its presence alone initializes the button's `disabled` property to `true` so the button is disabled. Adding and removing the disabled attribute disables and enables the button. The value of the attribute is irrelevant, which is why we cannot enable a button by writing `<button disabled="false">Still Disabled</button>`.

The aim of this discussion is to make sure that we understand the difference between the properties and attributes of a DOM element. This new mental model will help us as we continue to explore the framework's property and attribute binding capabilities. Let's get back to our discussion on property binding.

Property binding continued...

Now that we understand the difference between a property and an attribute, let's look at the binding example again:

```
<img class="img-responsive" [src]="'/static/images/' +
currentExercise.exercise.image" />
```

The `[propertName]` square bracket syntax is used to bind the `img.src` property to an Angular expression.

The general syntax for property binding looks as follows:

```
[target]="sourceExpression";
```

In the case of property binding, the `target` is a property on the DOM element or component. With property binding, we can literally bind to any property on the element's DOM. The `src` property on the `img` element is what we use; this binding works for any HTML element and every property on it.

Expression target can also be an event, as we will see shortly when we explore event binding.

Binding source and target

It is important to understand the difference between source and target in an Angular binding. The property appearing inside `[]` is a target, sometimes called **binding target**. The target is the consumer of the data and always refers to a property on the component/element. The **source** expression constitutes the data source that provides data to the target.

At runtime, the expression is evaluated in the context of the component's/element's property (the `WorkoutRunnerComponent.currentExercise.exercise.image` property in the preceding case).

Always remember to add square brackets `[]` around the target. If we don't, Angular treats the expression as a string constant and the target is simply assigned the string value.
Property binding, event binding, and attribute binding do not use the interpolation symbol. The following is invalid:
`[src]="{{'/static/images/' + currentExercise.exercise.image}}"`.

If you have worked on AngularJS, property binding together with event binding allows Angular to get rid of a number of directives, such as `ng-disable`, `ng-src`, `ng-key*`, `ng-mouse*`, and a few others.

From a data binding perspective, Angular treats components in the same way as it treats native elements. Hence, property binding works on component properties too! Components can define **input** and **output properties** that can be bound to the view, such as this:

```
<workout-runner [exerciseRestDuration]="restDuration"></workout-runner>
```

This hypothetical snippet binds the `exerciseRestDuration` property on the `WorkoutRunnerComponent` class to the `restDuration` property defined on the container component (parent), allowing us to pass the rest duration as a parameter to the `WorkoutRunnerComponent`. As we enhance our app and develop new components, you will learn how to define custom properties and events on a component.

 We can enable property binding using the `bind-` syntax, which is a canonical form of property binding. This implies that `[src]="'/assets/images/' + currentExercise.exercise.image"` is equivalent to the following: `bind-src="'/static/images/' + currentExercise.exercise.image"`.

 Property binding, like interpolation, is unidirectional, from the component/element source to the view. Changes to the model data are kept in sync with the view.

The template view that we just created has only one property binding (on `[src]`). The other bindings with square brackets aren't property bindings. We will cover them shortly.

Interpolation syntactic sugar over property binding

We concluded the section on interpolations by describing interpolation as syntactical sugar over property binding. The intent was to highlight how both can be used interchangeably. The interpolation syntax is terser than property binding and hence is very useful. This is how Angular interprets an interpolation:

```
<h3>Main heading - {{heading}}</h3>
<h3 [text-content]="' Main heading - '+ heading"></h3>
```

Angular translates the interpolation in the first statement into the `textContent` property binding (second statement).

Interpolation can be used in more places than you can imagine. The following example contrasts the same binding using interpolation and property binding:

```
<img [src]="'/assets/images/' + currentExercise.exercise.image" />
<img src="/assets/images/{{currentExercise.exercise.image}}" />        //
interpolation on attribute

<span [text-content]="helpText"></span>
<span>{{helpText}}</span>
```

While property binding (and interpolations) makes it easy for us to bind any expression to the target property, we should be careful with the expression we use. Angular's change detection system will evaluate your expression binding multiple times during the life cycle of the application, as long as our component is alive. Therefore, while binding an expression to a property target, keep these two guidelines in mind.

Quick expression evaluation

A property binding expression should evaluate quickly. Slow expression evaluation can kill your app's performance. This happens when a function performing CPU intensive work is part of an expression. Consider this binding:

```
<div>{{doLotsOfWork()}}</div>
```

Angular will evaluate the preceding `doLotsOfWork()` expression every time it performs a change detection run. These change detection runs happen more often than we imagine and are based on some internal heuristics, so it becomes imperative that the expressions we use evaluate quickly.

Side effect-free binding expressions

If a function is used in a binding expression, it should be side effect-free. Consider yet another binding:

```
<div [innerHTML]="getContent()"></div>
```

And the underlying function, `getContent`:

```
getContent() {
  var content=buildContent();
  this.timesContentRequested +=1;
  return content;
}
```

The `getContent` call changes the state of the component by updating the `timesContentRequested` property every time it is called. If this property is used in views such as:

```
<div>{{timesContentRequested}}</div>
```

Angular throws errors such as:

```
Expression '{{getContent()}}' in AppComponent@0:4' has changed after it was
checked. Previous value: '1'. Current value: '2'
```

 The Angular framework works in two modes, dev and production. If we enable production mode in the application, the preceding error does not show up. Look at the framework documentation at `http://bit.ly/enableProdMode` for more details.

The bottom line is that your expression used inside property binding should be side effect-free.

Let's now look at something interesting, `[ngStyle]`, which looks like a property binding, but it's not. The target specified in `[]` is not a component/element property (`div` does not have an `ngStyle` property), it's a directive.

Two new concepts need to be introduced, **target selection** and **directives**.

Angular directives

As a framework, Angular tries to enhance the HTML **DSL** (short for **Domain-Specific Language**):

- Components are referenced in HTML using custom tags such as `<abe-workout-runner></abe-workout-runner>` (not part of standard HTML constructs). This highlights the first extension point.
- The use of `[]` and `()` for property and event binding defines the second.
- And then there are **directives**, the third extension point which are further classified into **attribute** and **structural directives**, and **components** (components are directive too!).

While components come with their own view, attribute directives are there to enhance the appearance and/or behavior of existing elements/components.

Structural directives do not have their own view too; they change the DOM layout of the elements on which they are applied. We will dedicate a complete section later in the chapter to understanding these structural directives.

The `ngStyle` directive used in the `workout-runner` view is, in fact, an attribute directive:

```
<div class="progress-bar" role="progressbar"
  [ngStyle] = "{'width':(exerciseRunningDuration/currentExercise.duration) *
100 + '%'}"></div>
```

The `ngStyle` directive does not have its own view; instead, it allows us to set multiple styles (`width` in this case) on an HTML element using binding expressions. We will be covering a number of framework attribute directives later in this book.

Directive nomenclature

Directives is an umbrella term used for component directives (also known as components), attribute directives, and structural directives. Throughout the book, when we use the term directive, we will be referring to either an attribute directive or a structural directive depending on the context. Component directives are always referred to as components.

With a basic understanding of the directive types that Angular has, we can comprehend the process of target selection for binding.

Target selection for binding

The target specified in `[]` is not limited to a component/element property. While the property name is a common target, the Angular templating engine actually does heuristics to decide the target type. Angular first searches the registered known directives (attribute or structural) that have matching selectors before looking for a property that matches the target expression. Consider this view fragment:

```
<div [ngStyle]='expression'></div>
```

The search for a target starts with a framework looking at all internal and custom directives with a matching selector (`ngStyle`). Since Angular already has an `NgStyle` directive, it becomes the target (the directive class name is `NgStyle`, whereas the selector is `ngStyle`). If Angular did not have a built-in `NgStyle` directive, the binding engine would have looked for a property called `ngStyle` on the underlying component.

If nothing matches the target expression, an unknown directive error is thrown.

That completes our discussion on target selection. The next section is about attribute binding.

Attribute binding

The only reason attribute binding exists in Angular is that there are HTML attributes that do not have a backing DOM property. The `colspan` and `aria` attributes are some good examples of attributes without backing properties. The progress bar div in our view uses attribute binding.

 If attribute directives are still playing your head, I cannot blame you, it can become a bit confusing. Fundamentally, they are different. Attribute directives (such as `[ngStyle]`) change the appearance or behavior of DOM elements and as the name suggests are directives. There is no attribute or property named `ngStyle` on any HTML element. Attribute binding, on the other hand, is all about binding to HTML attributes that do not have backing for a DOM property.

The *7 Minute Workout* uses attribute binding at two places, `[attr.aria-valuenow]` and `[attr.aria-valuemax]`. We may ask a question: can we use standard interpolation syntax to set an attribute? No, that does not work! Let's try it: open `workout-runner.component.html` and replace the two aria attributes `attr.aria-valuenow` and `attr.aria-valuemax` enclosed in `[]` with this highlighted code:

```
<div class="progress-bar" role="progressbar"
    aria-valuenow = "{{exerciseRunningDuration}}"
    aria-valuemin="0"
    aria-valuemax= "{{currentExercise.duration}}"  ...> </div>
```

Save the view and if the app is not running, run it. This error will pop up in the browser console:

```
Can't bind to 'ariaValuenow' since it isn't a known native property in
WorkoutRunnerComponent ...
```

Angular is trying to search for a property called `ariaValuenow` in the `div` that does not exist! Remember, interpolations are actually property bindings.

We hope that this gets the point across: to bind to an HTML attribute, use attribute binding.

Angular binds to properties by default and not to attributes.

To support attribute binding, Angular uses a prefix notation, `attr`, within `[]`. An attribute binding looks as follows:

```
[attr.attribute-name]="expression"
```

Revert to the original aria setup to make attribute binding work:

```
<div ... [attr.aria-valuenow]="exerciseRunningDuration"
    [attr.aria-valuemax]="currentExercise.duration" ...>
```

Remember that unless an explicit `attr.` prefix is attached, attribute binding does not work.

While we have not used style and class-based binding in our workout view, these are some binding capabilities that can come in handy. Hence, they are worth exploring.

Style and class binding

We use **class binding** to set and remove a specific class based on the component state, as follows:

```
[class.class-name]="expression"
```

This adds `class-name` when `expression` is `true` and removes it when it is `false`. A simple example can look as follows:

```
<div [class.highlight]="isPreferred">Jim</div> // Toggles the highlight
class
```

Use style bindings to set inline styles based on the component state:

```
[style.style-name]="expression";
```

While we have used the `ngStyle` directive for the workout view, we could have easily used style binding as well, as we are dealing with a single style. With style binding, the same `ngStyle` expression would become the following:

```
[style.width.%]="(exerciseRunningDuration/currentExercise.duration) * 100"
```

`width` is a style, and since it takes units too, we extend our target expression to include the `%` symbol.

 Remember that `style.` and `class.` are convenient bindings for setting a single class or style. For more flexibility, there are corresponding attribute directives: `ngClass` and `ngStyle`.

Earlier in the chapter, we formally introduced directives and their classifications. One of the directives types, attribute directives (again, don't confuse them with attribute binding, which we introduced in the preceding section) are the focus of our attention in the next section.

Attribute directives

Attribute directives are HTML extensions that change the look, feel or behavior of a component/element. As described in the section on Angular directives, these directives do not define their own view.

Other than `ngStyle` and `ngClass` directives, there are a few more attribute directives that are part of the core framework. `ngValue`, `ngModel`, `ngSelectOptions`, `ngControl`, and `ngFormControl` are some of the attribute directives that Angular provides.

Since *7 Minute Workout* uses the `ngStyle` directive, it would be wise to dwell more on this directive and its close associate `ngClass`.

 While the next section is dedicated to learning how to use the `ngClass` and `ngStyle` attribute directives, it is not until Chapter 4, *Angular Directives in Depth*, that we learn how to create our own attribute directives.

Styling HTML with ngClass and ngStyle

Angular has two excellent directives that allow us to dynamically set styles on any element and toggle CSS classes. For the bootstrap progress bar, we use the `ngStyle` directive to dynamically set the element's style, `width`, as the exercise progresses:

```
<div class="progress-bar" role="progressbar" ...
    [ngStyle]="{'width':(exerciseRunningDuration/currentExercise.duration)
* 100 + '%'}"> </div>
```

`ngStyle` allows us to bind one or more styles to a component's properties at once. It takes an object as a parameter. Each property name on the object is the style name, and the value is the Angular expression bound to that property, such as the following example:

```
<div [ngStyle]= "{
'width':componentWidth,
'height':componentHeight,
'font-size': 'larger',
'font-weight': ifRequired ? 'bold': 'normal' }"></div>
```

The styles can not only bind to component properties (`componentWidth` and `componentHeight`), but also be set to a constant value (`'larger'`). The expression parser also allows the use of the ternary operator (`?:`); check out `isRequired`.

If styles become too unwieldy in HTML, we also have the option of writing in our component a function that returns the object hash, and setting that as an expression:

```
<div [ngStyle]= "getStyles()"></div>
```

Moreover, `getStyles` on the component looks as follows:

```
getStyles () {
    return {
      'width':componentWidth,
      ...
    }
}
```

`ngClass` works on the same lines too, except that it is used to toggle one or multiple classes. For example, check out the following code:

```
<div [ngClass]= "{'required':inputRequired, 'email':whenEmail}"></div>
```

The `required` class is applied when `inputRequired` is `true` and is removed when it evaluates to `false`.

 Directives (custom or platform) like any other Angular artifact, always belong to a module. To use them across modules, the module needs to be imported. Wondering where `ngStyle` is defined? `ngStyle` is part of the core framework module, `CommonModule,`, and has been imported in the workout runner module definition (`workout-runner.module.ts`). `CommonModule` defines a number of handy directives that are used across Angular.

Well! That covers everything we had to learn about our newly developed view.

 And as described earlier, if you are having a problem with running the code, look at the Git branch `checkpoint2.2`. If not using Git, download the snapshot of `checkpoint2.2` (a ZIP file) from `http://bit.ly/ng2be-checkpoint2-2`. Refer to the `README.md` file in the `trainer` folder when setting up the snapshot for the first time.

Time to add some enhancements and learn a bit more about the framework!

Learning more about an exercise

For people who are doing this workout for the first time, it will be good to detail the steps involved in each exercise. We can also add references to some YouTube videos for each exercise to help the user understand the exercise better.

We are going to add the exercise description and instructions in the left panel and call it the **description panel**. We will also add references to YouTube videos in the right panel, which is the video player panel. To make things more modular and learn some new concepts, we are going to create independent components for each description panel and video panel.

The model data for this is already available. The `description` and `procedure` properties in the `Exercise` class (see `model.ts`) provide the necessary details about the exercise. The `videos` array contains some related YouTube video IDs, which will be used to fetch these videos.

Adding descriptions and video panels

An Angular app is nothing but a hierarchy of components, similar to a tree structure. As of now, *7 Minute Workout* has two components, the root component, `AppComponent`, and its child, `WorkoutRunnerComponent`, in line with the HTML component layout, which now looks as follows:

```
<abe-root>
    ...
    <abe-workout-runner>...</abe-workout-runner>
</abe-root>
```

Run the app and do a view source to verify this hierarchy. As we all more components to implement new features in the application this component tree grows and branches out.

We are going to add two subcomponents to `WorkoutRunnerComponent`, one each to support the exercise description and exercise videos. While we could have added some HTML directly to the `WorkoutRunnerComponent` view, what we are hoping here is to learn a bit more about cross-component communication. Let's start with adding the description panel on the left and understand how a component can accept inputs.

Component with inputs

Navigate to the `workour-runner` folder and generate a boilerplate exercise description component:

```
ng generate component exercise-description -is
```

To the generated `exercise-description.component.ts` file, add the highlighted code:

```
import { Component, OnInit, Input } from '@angular/core';
...
export class ExerciseDescriptionComponent {
  @Input() description: string;
  @Input() steps: string;
}
```

The `@Input` decorator signifies that the component property is available for data binding. Before we dig into the `@Input` decorator, let's complete the view and integrate it with `WorkoutRunnerComponent`.

Copy the view definition for exercise description, `exercise-description.component.html`, from the Git branch `checkpoint2.3`, in the `workout-runner/exercise-description` folder. Look at the highlighted HTML for the exercise description:

```
<div class="card-body">
    <div class="card-text">{{description}}</div>
</div>
...
<div class="card-text">
    {{steps}}
</div>
```

The preceding interpolation references the input properties of `ExerciseDescriptionComponent`: `description` and `steps`.

The component definition is complete. Now, we just need to reference `ExerciseDescriptionComponent` in `WorkoutRunnerComponent` and provide values for `description` and `steps` for the `ExerciseDescriptionComponent` view to render correctly.

Open `workout-runner.component.html` and update the HTML fragments as highlighted in the following code. Add a new div called `description-panel` before the `exercise-pane` div and adjust some styles on the `exercise-pane` div, as follows:

```
<div class="row">
    <div id="description-panel" class="col-sm-3">
        <abe-exercise-description
            [description]="currentExercise.exercise.description"
            [steps]="currentExercise.exercise.procedure"></abe-exercise-
description>
    </div>
    <div id="exercise-pane" class="col-sm-6">
    ...
```

If the app is running, the description panel should show up on the left with the relevant exercise details.

`WorkoutRunnerComponent` **was able to use**
`ExerciseDescriptionComponent` **because it has been declared on**
`WorkoutRunnerModule` **(see the** `workout-`
`runner.module.ts` declaration property). The Angular CLI component generator does this work for us.

Look back at the `abe-exercise-description` declaration in the preceding view. We are referring to the `description` and `steps` properties in the same manner as we did with the HTML element properties earlier in the chapter (`<img [src]='expression' ...`). Simple, intuitive, and very elegant!

The Angular data binding infrastructure makes sure that whenever the `currentExercise.exercise.description` and `currentExercise.exercise.procedure` properties on `WorkoutRunnerComponent` change, the bound properties on `ExerciseDescriptionComponent`, `description`, and `steps` are also updated.

The `@Input` decoration can take a property alias as a parameter, which means the following: consider a property declaration such as: `@Input("myAwesomeProperty") myProperty:string`. It can be referenced in the view as follows: `<my-component [myAwesomeProperty]="expression"....`

The power of the Angular binding infrastructure allows us to use any component property as a bindable property by attaching the `@Input` decorator (and `@Output` too) to it. We are not limited to basic data types such as `string`, `number`, and `boolean`; there can be complex objects too, which we will see next as we add the video player:

The `@Input` decorator can be applied to complex objects too.

Generate a new component in the `workout-runner` directory for the video player:

```
ng generate component video-player -is
```

Update the generated boilerplate code by copying implementation from `video-player.component.ts` and `video-player.component.html` available in the Git branch `checkpoint2.3` in the `trainer/src/components/workout-runner/video-player` folder (GitHub location: `http://bit.ly/ng6be-2-3-video-player`).

Let's look at the implementation for the video player. Open `video-player.component.ts` and check out the `VideoPlayerComponent` class:

```
export class VideoPlayerComponent implements OnInit, OnChanges {
  private youtubeUrlPrefix = '//www.youtube.com/embed/';

  @Input() videos: Array<string>;
  safeVideoUrls: Array<SafeResourceUrl>;

  constructor(private sanitizer: DomSanitizationService) { }

  ngOnChanges() {
    this.safeVideoUrls = this.videos ?
      this.videos
        .map(v =>
this.sanitizer.bypassSecurityTrustResourceUrl(this.youtubeUrlPrefix + v))
      : this.videos;
  }
}
```

The `videos` input property here takes an array of strings (YouTube video codes). While we take the `videos` array as input, we do not use this array directly in video player view; instead, we transform the input array into a new array of `safeVideoUrls` and bind it. This can be confirmed by looking at the view implementation:

```
<div *ngFor="let video of safeVideoUrls">
  <iframe width="198" height="132" [src]="video" frameborder="0"
allowfullscreen></iframe>
</div>
```

The view also uses a new Angular directive called `ngFor` to bind to the `safeVideoUrls` array. The ngFor directive belongs to a class of directives called **structural directives**. The directive's job is to take an HTML fragment and regenerate it based on the number of elements in the bound collection.

If you are confused about how the `ngFor` directive works with `safeVideoUrls`, and why we need to generate `safeVideoUrls` instead of using the `videos` input array, wait for a while as we are shortly going to address these queries. But, let's first complete the integration of `VideoPlayerComponent` with `WorkoutRunnerComponent` to see the final outcome.

Update the `WorkoutRunnerComponent` view by adding the component declaration after the `exercise-pane` div:

```
<div id="video-panel" class="col-sm-3">
    <abe-video-player [videos]="currentExercise.exercise.videos"></abe-
video-player>
</div>
```

The `VideoPlayerComponent`'s `videos` property binds to the exercise's videos collection.

Start/refresh the app and the video thumbnails should show up on the right.

 If you are having a problem with running the code, look at the Git branch `checkpoint2.3` for a working version of what we have done thus far. You can also download the snapshot of `checkpoint2.3` (a ZIP file) from `http://bit.ly/ng6be-checkpoint-2-3`. Refer to the `README.md` file in the `trainer` folder when setting up the snapshot for the first time.

Now, it's time to go back and look at the parts of the `VideoPlayerComponent` implementation. We specifically need to understand:

- How the `ngFor` directive works
- Why there is a need to transform the input `videos` array into `safeVideoUrls`
- The significance of the Angular component life cycle event `OnChanges` (used in the video player)

To start with, it's time to formally introduce `ngFor` and the class of directives it belongs to: structural directives.

Structural directives

The third categorization of directives, structural directives, work on the components/elements to manipulate their layout.

The Angular documentation describes structural directives in a succinct manner:

> *"Instead of defining and controlling a view like a Component Directive, or modifying the appearance and behavior of an element like an Attribute Directive, the Structural Directive manipulates the layout by adding and removing entire element sub-trees."*

Since we have already touched upon component directives (such as `workout-runner` and `exercise-description`) and attribute directives (such as `ngClass` and `ngStyle`), we can very well contrast their behaviors with structural directives.

The `ngFor` directive belongs to this class. We can easily identify such directives by the `*` prefix. Other than `ngFor`, Angular comes with some other structural directives such as `ngIf` and `ngSwitch`.

The ever-so-useful NgForOf

Every templating language has constructs that allow the templating engine to generate HTML (by repetition). Angular has `NgForOf`. The `NgForOf` directive is a super useful directive used to duplicate a piece of an HTML fragment n number of times. Let's again look at how we have used `NgForOf` in the video player:

```
<div *ngFor="let video of safeVideoUrls">
    <iframe width="198" height="132" [src]="video" frameborder="0"
allowfullscreen></iframe>
</div>
```

The directive selector for `NgForOf` is `{selector: '[ngFor][ngForOf]'}`, so we can use either `ngFor` or `ngForOf` in the view template. We also at times refer to this directive as `ngFor`.

The preceding code repeats the `div` fragment for each exercise video (using the `safeVideoUrls` array). The `let video of safeVideoUrls` string expression is interpreted as follows: take each video in the `safeVideoUrls` array and assign it to a template input variable, `video`.

This input variable can now be referenced inside the `ngFor` template HTML, as we do when we set the `src` property binding.

Interestingly, the string assigned to the `ngFor` directive is not a typical Angular expression. Instead, it's a **microsyntax**—a micro language, which the Angular engine can parse.

You can learn more about microsyntax in Angular's developer guide: `http://bit.ly/ng6be-micro-syntax`.

This microsyntax exposes a number of iteration context properties that we can assign to template input variables and use them inside the ngFor HTML block.

One such example is index. index increases from 0 to the length of the array for each iteration, something similar to a for loop, in any programming language. The following example shows how to capture it:

```
<div *ngFor="let video of videos; let i=index">
    <div>This is video - {{i}}</div>
</div>
```

Other than index, there are some more iteration context variables; these include first, last, even, and odd. This context data allows us to do some nifty stuff. Consider this example:

```
<div *ngFor="let video of videos; let i=index; let f=first">
    <div [class.special]="f">This is video - {{i}}</div>
</div>
```

It applies a special class to the first video div.

The NgForOf directive can be applied to HTML elements as well as our custom components. This is a valid use of NgForOf:

```
<user-profile *ngFor="let userDetail of users" [user]= "userDetail"></user-
profile>
```

Always remember to add an asterisk (*) before ngFor (and other structural directives). * has a significance.

Asterisk (*) in structural directives

The * prefix is a terser format to represent a structural directive. Take, for example, the usage of ngFor by the video player. The ngFor template:

```
<div *ngFor="let video of safeVideoUrls">
    <iframe width="198" height="132" [src]="video" frameborder="0"
allowfullscreen></iframe>
</div>
```

Actually expands to the following:

```
<ng-template ngFor let-video [ngForOf]="safeVideoUrls">
    <div>
        <iframe width="198" height="132"  [src]="video" ...></iframe>
    </div>
</ng-template>
```

The `ng-template` tag is an Angular element that has a declaration for `ngFor`, a template input variable (`video`), and a property (`ngForOf`) that points to the `safeVideoUrls` array. Both the preceding declarations are a valid usage of `ngFor`.

Not sure about you, but I prefer the terser first format for `ngFor`!

NgForOf performance

Since `NgForOf` generates HTML based on collection elements, it is notorious for causing performance issues. But we cannot blame the directive. It does what it is supposed to do: iterate and generate elements! If the underlying collection is huge, UI rendering can take a performance hit, especially if the collection changes too often. The cost of continuously destroying and creating elements in response to a changing collection can quickly become prohibitive.

One of the performance tweaks for `NgForOf` allows us to alter the behavior of `ngForOf` when it comes to creating and destroying DOM elements (when the underlying collection elements are added or removed).

Imagine a scenario where we frequently get an array of objects from the server and bind it to the view using `NgForOf`. The default behavior of `NgForOf` is to regenerate the DOM every time we refresh the list (since Angular does a standard object equality check). However, as developers, we may very well know not much has changed. Some new objects may have been added, some removed, and maybe some modified. But Angular just regenerates the complete DOM.

To alleviate this situation, Angular allows us to specify a custom **tracking function**, which lets Angular know when two objects being compared are equal. Have a look at the following function:

```
trackByUserId(index: number, hero: User) { return user.id; }
```

A function such as this can be used in the `NgForOf` template to tell Angular to compare the *user* object based on its `id` property instead of doing a reference equality check.

This is how we then use the preceding function in the `NgForOf` template:

```
<div *ngFor="let user of users; trackBy: trackByUserId">{{user.name}}</div>
```

`NgForOf` will now avoid recreating DOM for users with IDs already rendered.

Remember, Angular may still update the existing DOM elements if the bound properties of a user have changed.

That's enough on the `ngFor` directive; let's move ahead.

We still need to understand the role of the `safeVideoUrls` and the `OnChange` life cycle events in the `VideoPlayerComponent` implementation. Let's tackle the former first and understand the need for `safeVideoUrls`.

Angular security

The easiest way to understand why we need to bind to `safeVideoUrls` instead of the `videos` input property is by trying the `videos` array out. Replace the existing `ngFor` fragment HTML with the following:

```
<div *ngFor="let video of videos">
    <iframe width="198" height="132"
        [src]="'//www.youtube.com/embed/' + video"  frameborder="0"
allowfullscreen></iframe>
</div>
```

And look at the browser's console log (a page refresh may be required). There are a bunch of errors thrown by the framework, such as:

```
Error: unsafe value used in a resource URL context (see
http://g.co/ng/security#xss)
```

No prize for guessing what is happening! Angular is trying to safeguard our application against a **Cross-Site Scripting** (**XSS**) attack.

Such an attack enables the attacker to inject malicious code into our web pages. Once injected, the malicious code can read data from the current site context. This allows it to steal confidential data and also impersonate the logged-in user, hence gaining access to privileged resources.

Angular has been designed to block these attacks by sanitizing any external code/script that is injected into an Angular view. Remember, content can be injected into a view through a number of mechanisms, including property/attribute/style bindings or interpolation.

Consider an example of binding HTML markup through a component model to the `innerHTML` property of an HTML element (property binding):

```
this.htmlContent = '<span>HTML content.</span>'    // Component

<div [innerHTML]="htmlContent"> <!-- View -->
```

While the HTML content is emitted, any unsafe content (such as a *script*) if present is stripped.

But what about Iframes? In our preceding example, Angular is blocking property binding to Iframe's `src` property too. This is a warning against third-party content being embedded in our own site using Iframe. Angular prevents this too.

All in all, the framework defines four security contexts around content sanitization. These include:

1. **HTML content sanitization**, when HTML content is bound using the `innerHTML` property
2. **Style sanitization**, when binding CSS into the `style` property
3. **URL sanitization**, when URLs are used with tags such as `anchor` and `img`
4. **Resource sanitization**, when using `Iframes` or `script` tags; in this case, content cannot be sanitized and hence it is blocked by default

Angular is trying its best to keep us out of danger. But at times, we know that the content is safe to render and hence want to circumvent the default sanitization behavior.

Trusting safe content

To let Angular know that the content being bound is safe, we use `DomSanitizer` and call the appropriate method based on the security contexts just described. The available functions are as follows:

- `bypassSecurityTrustHtml`
- `bypassSecurityTrustScript`
- `bypassSecurityTrustStyle`
- `bypassSecurityTrustUrl`
- `bypassSecurityTrustResourceUrl`

In our video player implementation, we use `bypassSecurityTrustResourceUrl`; it converts the video URL into a trusted `SafeResourceUrl` object:

```
this.videos.map(v =>
this.sanitizer.bypassSecurityTrustResourceUrl(this.youtubeUrlPrefix + v))
```

The `map` method transforms the videos array into a collection of `SafeResourceUrl` objects and assigns it to `safeVideoUrls`.

Each of the methods listed previously takes a string parameter. This is the content we want Angular to know is safe. The return object, which could be any of `SafeStyle`, `SafeHtml`, `SafeScript`, `SafeUrl`, or `SafeResourceUrl`, can then be bound to the view.

 A comprehensive treatment of this topic is available in the framework security guide available at `http://bit.ly/ng6be-security`. A highly recommended read!

The last question to answer is why do this in the `OnChanges` Angular life cycle event?

OnChange life cycle event

The `OnChanges` life cycle event is triggered whenever the component's input(s) change. In the case of `VideoPlayerComponent`, it is the `videos` array input property that changes whenever a new exercise is loaded. We use this life cycle event to recreate the `safeVideoUrls` array and re-bind it to the view. Simple!

Video panel implementation is now complete. Let's add a few more minor enhancements and explore it a bit more in Angular.

Formatting exercise steps with innerHTML binding

One of the sore points in the current app is the formatting of the exercise steps. It's a bit difficult to read these steps.

The steps should either have a line break (`<br>`) or be formatted as an HTML `list` for easy readability. This seems to be a straightforward task, and we can just go ahead and change the data that is bound to the step interpolation, or write a pipe that can add some HTML formatting using the line delimiting convention (`.`). For a quick verification, let's update the first exercise steps in `workout-runner.component.ts` by adding a break (`<br>`) after each line:

```
`Assume an erect position, with feet together and arms at your side. <br>
  Slightly bend your knees, and propel yourself a few inches into the air.
<br>
  While in air, bring your legs out to the side about shoulder width or
slightly wider. <br>
  ...
```

As the workout restarts, look at the first exercise steps. The output does not match our expectations, as shown here:

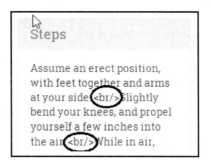

The break tags were literally rendered in the browser. Angular did not render the interpolation as HTML; instead, it escaped the HTML characters, and we know why, security!

How to fix it? Easy! Replace the interpolation with the property binding to bind step data to the element's `innerHTML` property (in `exercise-description.html`), and you are done!

```
<div class="card-text" [innerHTML]="steps">
```

Refresh the workout page to confirm.

Preventing Cross-Site Scripting Security (XSS) issues
By using `innerHTML`, we instruct Angular to not escape HTML, but
Angular still sanitizes the input HTML as described in the security section
earlier. It removes things such as `<script>` tags and other JavaScript to
safeguard against XSS attacks. If you want to dynamically inject
styles/scripts into HTML, use the `DomSanitizer` to bypass this
sanitization check.

Time for another enhancement! It's time to learn about Angular pipes.

Displaying the remaining workout duration using pipes

It will be nice if we can tell the user the time left to complete the workout and not just the
duration of the exercise in progress. We can add a countdown timer somewhere in the
exercise pane to show the overall time remaining.

The approach that we are going to take here is to define a component property called
`workoutTimeRemaining`. This property will be initialized with the total time at the start of
the workout and will reduce with every passing second until it reaches zero. Since
`workoutTimeRemaining` is a numeric value, but we want to display a timer in the
`hh:mm:ss` format, we need to make a conversion between the seconds data and the time
format. **Angular pipes** are a great option for implementing such a feature.

Angular pipes

The primary aim of a pipe is to format the data displayed in the view. **Pipes** allow us to
package this content transformation logic (formatting) as a reusable element. The
framework itself comes with multiple predefined pipes, such as `date`, `currency`,
`lowercase`, `uppercase`, `slice`, and others.

This is how we use a pipe with a view:

```
{{expression | pipeName:inputParam1}}
```

An expression is followed by the pipe symbol (|), which is followed by the pipe name and then an optional parameter (`inputParam1`) separated by a colon (:). If the pipe takes multiple inputs, they can be placed one after another separated by a colon, such as the inbuilt `slice` pipe, which can slice an array or string:

```
{{fullName | slice:0:20}} //renders first 20 characters
```

The parameter passed to the pipe can be a constant or a component property, which implies we can use template expressions with pipe parameter. See the following example:

```
{{fullName | slice:0:truncateAt}} //renders based on value truncateAt
```

Here are some examples of the use of the `date` pipe, as described in the Angular `date` documentation. Assume that `dateObj` is initialized to *June 15, 2015 21:43:11* and locale is *en-US*:

```
{{ dateObj | date }}              // output is 'Jun 15, 2015          '
{{ dateObj | date:'medium' }}     // output is 'Jun 15, 2015, 9:43:11 PM'
{{ dateObj | date:'shortTime' }}  // output is '9:43 PM              '
{{ dateObj | date:'mmss' }}       // output is '43:11'
```

Some of the most commonly used pipes are the following:

- **date**: As we just saw, the date filter is used to format the date in a specific manner. This filter supports quite a number of formats and is locale-aware too. To know about the other formats supported by the date pipe, check out the framework documentation at `http://bit.ly/ng2-date`.

- **uppercase** and **lowercase**: These two pipes, as the name suggests, change the case of the string input.

- **decimal** and **percent**: `decimal` and `percent` pipes are there to format decimal and percentage values based on the current browser locale.

- **currency**: This is used to format numeric values as a currency based on the current browser locale:

```
{{14.22|currency:"USD" }} <!-Renders USD 14.22 -->
{{14.22|currency:"USD":'symbol'}}  <!-Renders $14.22 -->
```

- **json**: This is a handy pipe for debugging that can transform any input into a string using `JSON.stringify`. We made good use of it at the start of this chapter to render the `WorkoutPlan` object (see the Checkpoint 2.1 code).

- **slice**: This pipe allows us to split a list or a string value to create a smaller trimmed down list/string. We saw an example in the preceding code.

We are not going to cover the preceding pipes in detail. From a development perspective, as long as we know what pipes are there and what they are useful for, we can always refer to the platform documentation for exact usage instructions.

Pipe chaining

A really powerful feature of pipes is that they can be chained, where the output from one pipe can serve as the input to another pipe. Consider this example:

```
{{fullName | slice:0:20 | uppercase}}
```

The first pipe slices the first 20 characters of `fullName` and the second pipe transforms them to uppercase.

Now that we have seen what pipes are and how to use them, why not implement one for the *7 Minute Workout* app: a **seconds to time** pipe?

Implementing a custom pipe - SecondsToTimePipe

`SecondsToTimePipe`, as the name suggests, should convert a numeric value into the `hh:mm:ss` format.

Create a folder `shared` in the `workout-runner` folder and from the shared folder invoke this CLI command to generate the pipe boilerplate:

```
ng generate pipe seconds-to-time
```

The `shared` folder has been created to add common components/directives/pipes that can be used in the `workout-runner` module. It is a convention we follow to organize shared code at different levels. In the future, we can create a shared folder at the app module level, which has artifacts shared globally. In fact, if the second to time pipe needs to be used across other application modules, it can also be moved into the app module.

Copy the following `transform` function implementation into `seconds-to-time.pipe.ts`(the definition can also be downloaded from the Git branch `checkpoint.2.4` on the GitHub site at `http://bit.ly/nng6be-2-4-seconds-to-time-pipe-ts`):

```
export class SecondsToTimePipe implements PipeTransform {
  transform(value: number): any {
    if (!isNaN(value)) {
      const hours = Math.floor(value / 3600);
      const minutes = Math.floor((value - (hours * 3600)) / 60);
      const seconds = value - (hours * 3600) - (minutes * 60);

      return ('0' + hours).substr(-2) + ':'
        + ('0' + minutes).substr(-2) + ':'
        + ('0' + seconds).substr(-2);
    }
    return;
  }
}
```

In an Angular pipe, the implementation logic goes into the `transform` function. Defined as part of the `PipeTransform` interface, the preceding `transform` function transforms the input seconds value into an *hh:mm:ss* string. The first parameter to the `transform` function is the pipe input. The subsequent parameters, if provided, are the arguments to the pipe, passed using a colon separator (`pipe:argument1:arugment2..`) from the view.

For `SecondsToTimePipe`, while Angular CLI generates a boilerplate argument (`args?:any`), we do not make use of any pipe argument as the implementation does not require it.

The pipe implementation is quite straightforward, as we convert seconds into hours, minutes, and seconds. Then, we concatenate the result into a string value and return the value. The addition of 0 on the left for each of the `hours`, `minutes`, and `seconds` variables is done to format the value with a leading 0 in case the calculated value for hours, minutes, or seconds is less than 10.

The pipe that we just created is just a standard TypeScript class. It's the Pipe decorator (`@Pipe`) that instructs Angular to treat this class as a pipe:

```
@Pipe({
  name: 'secondsToTime'
})
```

The pipe definition is complete, but to use the pipe in `WorkoutRunnerComponent` the pipe has to be declared on `WorkoutRunnerModule`. Angular CLI has already done this for us as part of the boilerplate generation (see the `declaration` section in `workout-runner.module.ts`).

Now we just need to add the pipe in the view. Update `workout-runner.component.html` by adding the highlighted fragment:

```
<div class="exercise-pane" class="col-sm-6">
    <h4 class="text-center">Workout Remaining - {{workoutTimeRemaining |
secondsToTime}}</h4>
    <h1 class="text-center">{{currentExercise.exercise.title}}</h1>
```

Surprisingly, the implementation is still not complete! There is one more step left. We have a pipe definition, and we have referenced it in the view, but `workoutTimeRemaining` needs to update with each passing second for `SecondsToTimePipe` to be effective.

We have already initialized `WorkoutRunnerComponent`'s `workoutTimeRemaining` property in the `start` function with the total workout time:

```
start() {
    this.workoutTimeRemaining = this.workoutPlan.totalWorkoutDuration();
    ...
}
```

Now the question is: how to update the `workoutTimeRemaining` variable with each passing second? Remember that we already have a `setInterval` set up that updates `exerciseRunningDuration`. While we can write another `setInterval` implementation for `workoutTimeRemaining`, it will be better if a single `setInterval` setup can take care of both the requirements.

Add a function called `startExerciseTimeTracking` to `WorkoutRunnerComponent`; it looks as follows:

```
startExerciseTimeTracking() {
    this.exerciseTrackingInterval = window.setInterval(() => {
      if (this.exerciseRunningDuration >= this.currentExercise.duration) {
        clearInterval(this.exerciseTrackingInterval);
        const next: ExercisePlan = this.getNextExercise();
        if (next) {
          if (next !== this.restExercise) {
            this.currentExerciseIndex++;
          }
          this.startExercise(next);
        }
```

```
    else {
      console.log('Workout complete!');
    }
    return;
  }
  ++this.exerciseRunningDuration;
  --this.workoutTimeRemaining;
}, 1000);
}
```

As you can see, the primary purpose of the function is to track the exercise progress and flip the exercise once it is complete. However, it also tracks `workoutTimeRemaining` (it decrements this counter). The first `if` condition setup just makes sure that we clear the timer once all the exercises are done. The inner `if` conditions are used to keep `currentExerciseIndex` in sync with the running exercise.

This function uses a numeric instance variable called `exerciseTrackingInterval`. Add it to the class declaration section. We are going to use this variable later to implement an exercise pausing behavior.

Remove the complete `setInterval` setup from `startExercise` and replace it with a call to `this.startExerciseTimeTracking();`. We are all set to test our implementation. If required, refresh the browser and verify the implementation:

The next section is about another inbuilt Angular directive, `ngIf`, and another small enhancement.

Adding the next exercise indicator using ngIf

It will be nice for the user to be told what the next exercise is during the short rest period between exercises. This will help them prepare for the next exercise. So let's add it.

To implement this feature, we can simply output the title of the next exercise from the `workoutPlan.exercises` array. We show the title next to the `Time Remaining` countdown section.

Change the workout div (`class="exercise-pane"`) to include the highlighted content, and remove existing `Time Remaining` h1:

```
<div class="exercise-pane">
<!-- Exiting html -->
    <div class="progress time-progress">
        <!-- Exiting html -->
    </div>
     <div class="row">
       <h4 class="col-sm-6 text-left">Time Remaining:
         <strong>{{currentExercise.duration-
exerciseRunningDuration}}</strong>
       </h4>
       <h4 class="col-sm-6 text-right"
*ngIf="currentExercise.exercise.name=='rest'">Next up:
         <strong>{{workoutPlan.exercises[currentExerciseIndex +
1].exercise.title}}</strong>
       </h4>
     </div>
</div>
```

We wrap the existing `Time Remaining` h1 and add another h3 tag to show the next exercise inside a new `div` with some style updates. Also, there is a new directive, `ngIf`, in the second h3. The `*` prefix implies that it belongs to the same set of directives that `ngFor` belongs: **structural directives**. Let's talk a bit about `ngIf`.

The `ngIf` directive is used to add or remove a specific section of the DOM based on whether the expression provided to it returns `true` or `false`. The DOM element is added when the expression evaluates to `true` and is destroyed otherwise. Isolate the `ngIf` declaration from the preceding view:

```
ngIf="currentExercise.details.name=='rest'"
```

The directive expression checks whether we are currently in the rest phase and accordingly shows or hides the linked h3.

Also in the same h3, we have an interpolation that shows the name of the exercise from the `workoutPlan.exercises` array.

A word of caution here: `ngIf` adds and destroys the DOM element, and hence it is not similar to the visibility constructs that we employed to show and hide elements. While the end result of `style`, `display:none` is the same as that of `ngIf`, the mechanism is entirely different:

```
<div [style.display]="isAdmin" ? 'block' : 'none'">Welcome Admin</div>
```

Versus this line:

```
<div *ngIf="isAdmin" ? 'block' : 'none'">Welcome Admin</div>
```

With `ngIf`, whenever the expression changes from `false` to `true`, a complete re-initialization of the content occurs. Recursively, new elements/components are created and data binding is set up, starting from the parent down to the children. The reverse happens when the expression changes from `true` to `false`: all of this is destroyed. Therefore, using `ngIf` can sometimes become an expensive operation if it wraps a large chunk of content and the expression attached to it changes very often. But otherwise, wrapping a view in `ngIf` is more performant than using CSS/style-based show or hide, as neither the DOM is created nor the data binding expressions are set up when the `ngIf` expression evaluates to `false`.

New version of Angular support branching constructs too. This allows us to implement the **if then else** flow in the view HTML. The following sample has been lifted directly from the platform documentation of `ngIf`:

```
<div *ngIf="show; else elseBlock">Text to show</div>
<ng-template #elseBlock>Alternate text while primary text is hidden</ng-template>
```

The `else` binding points to a `ng-template` with template variable `#elseBlock`.

There is another directive that belongs in this league: `ngSwitch`. When defined on the parent HTML, it can swap the child HTML elements based on the `ngSwitch` expression. Consider this example:

```
<div id="parent" [ngSwitch] ="userType">
<div *ngSwitchCase="'admin'">I am the Admin!</div>
<div *ngSwitchCase="'powerUser'">I am the Power User!</div>
<div *ngSwitchDefault>I am a normal user!</div>
</div>
```

We bind the `userType` expression to `ngSwitch`. Based on the value of `userType` (`admin`, `powerUser`, or any other `userType`), one of the inner div elements will be rendered. The `ngSwitchDefault` directive is a wildcard match/fallback match, and it gets rendered when `userType` is neither `admin` nor `powerUser`.

If you have not realized it yet, note that there are three directives working together here to achieve switch-case-like behavior:

- `ngSwitch`
- `ngSwitchCase`
- `ngSwitchDefault`

Coming back to our next exercise implementation, we are ready to verify the implementation, start the app, and wait for the rest period. There should be a mention of the next exercise during the rest phase, as shown here:

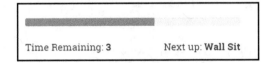

The app is shaping up well. If you have used the app and done some physical workouts along with it, you will be missing the exercise pause functionality badly. The workout just does not stop until it reaches the end. We need to fix this behavior.

Pausing an exercise

To pause an exercise, we need to stop the timer. We also need to add a button somewhere in the view that allows us to pause and resume the workout. We plan to do this by drawing a button overlay over the exercise area in the center of the page. When clicked on, it will toggle the exercise state between paused and running. We will also add keyboard support to pause and resume the workout using the key binding p or P. Let's update the component.

Update the `WorkoutRunnerComponent` class, add these three functions, and add a declaration for the `workoutPaused` variable:

```
workoutPaused: boolean;
...
pause() {
    clearInterval(this.exerciseTrackingInterval);
    this.workoutPaused = true;
}

resume() {
    this.startExerciseTimeTracking();
    this.workoutPaused = false;
}
```

```
pauseResumeToggle() {
    if (this.workoutPaused) { this.resume();      }
    else {         this.pause();      }
}
```

The implementation for pausing is simple. The first thing we do is cancel the existing `setInterval` setup by calling `clearInterval(this.exerciseTrackingInterval);`. While resuming, we again call `startExerciseTimeTracking`, which again starts tracking the time from where we left off.

Now we just need to invoke the `pauseResumeToggle` function for the view. Add the following content to `workout-runner.html`:

```
<div id="exercise-pane" class="col-sm-6">
    <div id="pause-overlay" (click)="pauseResumeToggle()">
        <span class="pause absolute-center"
            [ngClass]="{'ion-md-pause' : !workoutPaused, 'ion-md-play' :
workoutPaused}">
        </span>
    </div>
    <div class="row workout-content">
```

The `click` event handler on the div toggles the workout running state, and the `ngClass` directive is used to toggle the class between `ion-md-pause` and `ion-md-play`- standard Angular stuff. What is missing now is the ability to pause and resume on a *P* key press.

One approach could be to apply a `keyup` event handler on the div:

```
<div id="pause-overlay" (keyup)= "onKeyPressed($event)">
```

But there are some shortcomings to this approach:

- The `div` element does not have a concept of focus, so we also need to add the `tabIndex` attribute on the div to make it work
- Even then, it works only when we have clicked on the div at least once

There is a better way to implement this; attach the event handler to the global `window` event `keyup`. This is how the event binding should be applied on the `div`:

```
<div id="pause-overlay" (window:keyup)= "onKeyPressed($event)">
```

Make note of the special `window:` prefix before the `keyup` event. We can use this syntax to attach events to any global object, such as the `document`. A handy and very powerful feature of Angular binding infrastructure! The `onKeyPressed` event handler needs to be added to `WorkoutRunnerComponent`. Add this function to the class:

```
onKeyPressed(event: KeyboardEvent) {
    if (event.which === 80 || event.which === 112) {
      this.pauseResumeToggle();
    }
  }
```

The `$event` object is the standard **DOM event object** that Angular makes available for manipulation. Since this is a keyboard event, the specialized class is `KeyboardEvent`. The `which` property is matched to ASCII values of `p` or `P`. Refresh the page and you should see the play/pause icon when your mouse hovers over the exercise image, as follows:

While we are on the topic of **event binding**, it would be a good opportunity to explore Angular's event binding infrastructure

The Angular event binding infrastructure

Angular event binding allows a component to communicate with its parent through events.

If we look back at the app implementation, what we have encountered thus far are the property/attribute bindings. Such bindings allow a component/element to take inputs from the outside world. The data flows into the component.

Event bindings are the reverse of property bindings. They allow a component/element to inform the outside world about any state change.

As we saw in the pause/resume implementation, event binding employs round brackets (`()`) to specify the target event:

```
<div id="pause-overlay" (click)="pauseResumeToggle()">
```

This attaches a `click` event handler to the `div` that invokes the expression `pauseResumeToggle()` when the `div` is clicked.

 Like properties, there is a canonical form for events too. Instead of using round brackets, the `on-` prefix can be used: `on-click="pauseResumeToggle()"`

Angular supports all types of events. Events related to keyboard inputs, mouse movements, button clicks, and touches. The framework even allows us to define our own event for the components we create, such as:

```
<workout-runner (paused)= "stopAudio()"></workout-runner>
```

It is expected that events have side effects; in other words, an event handler may change the state of the component, which in turn may trigger a chain reaction in which multiple components react to the state change and change their own state. This is unlike a property binding expression, which should be side-effect-free. Even in our implementation, clicking on the `div` element toggles the exercise run state.

Event bubbling

When Angular attaches event handlers to standard HTML element events, the event propagation works in the same way as standard DOM event propagation works. This is also called **event bubbling**. Events on child elements are propagated upwards, and hence event binding is also possible on a parent element, as follows:

```
<div id="parent " (click)="doWork($event)"> Try
  <div id="child ">me!</div>
</div>
```

Clicking on either of the divs results in the invocation of the doWork function on the parent div. Moreover, $event.target contains the reference to the div that dispatched the event.

 Custom events created on Angular components do not support event bubbling.

Event bubbling stops if the expression assigned to the target evaluates to a falsey value (such as void, false). Therefore, to continue propagation, the expression should evaluate to true:

```
<div id="parent" (click)="doWork($event) || true">
```

Here too, the $event object deserves some special attention.

Event binding an $event object

Angular makes an $event object available whenever the target event is triggered. This $event contains the details of the event that occurred.

The important thing to note here is that the shape of the $event object is decided based on the event type. For HTML elements, it is a DOM event object (https://developer. mozilla.org/en-US/docs/Web/Events), which may vary based on the actual event.

But if it is a custom component event, what is passed in the $event object is decided by the component implementation.

We have now covered most of the data binding capabilities of Angular, with the exception of two-way binding. A quick introduction to the two-way binding constructs is warranted before we conclude the chapter.

Two-way binding with ngModel

Two-way binding helps us keep the model and view in sync. Changes to the model update the view and changes to the view update the model. The obvious area where two-way binding is applicable is form input. Let's look at a simple example:

```
<input [(ngModel)]="workout.name">
```

The `ngModel` directive here sets a two-way binding between the `input`'s `value` property and the `workout.name` property on the underlying component. Anything that the user enters in the preceding `input` is synced with `workout.name`, and any changes to `workout.name` are reflected back on the preceding `input`.

Interestingly, we can achieve the same result without using the `ngModel` directive too, by combining both property and event binding syntax. Consider the next example; it works in the same way as `input` before:

```
<input [value]="workout.name"
    (input)="workout.name=$event.target.value" >
```

There is a property binding set up on the `value` property and an event binding set up on the `input` event that make the bidirectional sync work.

We will get into more details on two-way binding in `Chapter 2`, *Personal Trainer*, where we build our own custom workouts.

We have created a diagram that summarizes the data flow patterns for all the bindings that we have discussed thus far. Here is a handy diagram to help you memorize each of the binding constructs and how data flows:

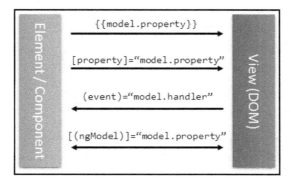

We now have a fully functional *7 Minute Workout*, with some bells and whistles too, and hopefully you had fun creating the app. It's time to conclude the chapter and summarize the lessons.

 If you are having a problem with running the code, look at the Git branch `checkpoint2.4` for a working version of what we have done thus far. You can also download a snapshot of `checkpoint2.4` (a ZIP file) from this GitHub location: `http://bit.ly/ng6be-checkpoint-2-4`. Refer to the `README.md` file in the `trainer` folder when setting up the snapshot for the first time.

Cross-component communication using Angular events

It's time now to look at eventing in more depth. Let's add audio support to *7-Minute Workout*.

Tracking exercise progress with audio

For the *7-Minute Workout* app, adding sound support is vital. One cannot exercise while constantly staring at the screen. Audio clues help the user perform the workout effectively as they can just follow the audio instructions.

Here is how we are going to support exercise tracking using audio clues:

- A ticking clock soundtrack progress during the exercise
- A half-way indicator sounds, indicating that the exercise is halfway through
- An exercise-completion audio clip plays when the exercise is about to end
- An audio clip plays during the rest phase and informs users about the next exercise

There will be an audio clip for each of these scenarios.

Modern browsers have good support for audio. The HTML5 `<audio>` tag provides a mechanism to embed audio clips into HTML content. We too will use the `<audio>` tag to play back our clips.

Since the plan is to use the HTML <audio> element, we need to create a wrapper directive that allows us to control audio elements from Angular. Remember that directives are HTML extensions without a view.

 The checkpoint3.4 Git and the trainer/static/audio folder contain all the audio files used for playback; copy them first. If you are not using Git, a snapshot of the chapter code is available at http://bit.ly/ng6be-checkpoint-3-4. Download and unzip the contents and copy the audio files.

Building Angular directives to wrap HTML audio

If you have worked a lot with JavaScript and jQuery, you may have realized we have purposefully shied away from directly accessing the DOM for any of our component implementations. There has not been a need to do it. The Angular data-binding infrastructure, including property, attribute, and event binding, has helped us manipulate HTML without touching the DOM.

For the audio element too, the access pattern should be Angularish. In Angular, the only place where direct DOM manipulation is acceptable and practiced is inside directives. Let's create a directive that wraps access to audio elements.

Navigate to trainer/src/app/shared and run this command to generate a template directive:

```
ng generate directive my-audio
```

 Since it is the first time we are creating a directive, we encourage you to look at the generated code.

Since the directive is added to the shared module, it needs to be exported too. Add the MyAudioDirective reference in the exports array too (shared.module.ts). Then update the directive definition with the following code:

```
import {Directive, ElementRef} from '@angular/core';

@Directive({
  selector: 'audio',
  exportAs: 'MyAudio'
})
export class MyAudioDirective {
```

```
        private audioPlayer: HTMLAudioElement;
        constructor(element: ElementRef) {
          this.audioPlayer = element.nativeElement;
        }
      }
```

The MyAudioDirective class is decorated with @Directive. The @Directive decorator is similar to the @Component decorator except we cannot have an attached view. Therefore, no template or templateUrl is allowed!

The preceding selector property allows the framework to identify where to apply the directive. We have replaced the generated [abeMyAudioDirective] attribute selector with just audio. Using audio as the selector makes our directive load for every <audio> tag used in HTML. The new selector works as an element selector.

 In a standard scenario, directive selectors are attribute-based (such as [abeMyAudioDirective] for the generated code), which helps us identify where the directive has been applied. We deviate from this norm and use an element selector for the MyAudioDirective directive. We want this directive to be loaded for every audio element, and it becomes cumbersome to go to each audio declaration and add a directive-specific attribute. Hence an element selector.

The use of exportAs becomes clear when we use this directive in view templates.

The ElementRef object injected in the constructor is the Angular element (audio in this case) for which the directive is loaded. Angular creates the ElementRef instance for every component and directive when it compiles and executes the HTML template. When requested in the constructor, the DI framework locates the corresponding ElementRef and injects it. We use ElementRef to get hold of the underlying audio element in the code (the instance of HTMLAudioElement). The audioPlayer property holds this reference.

The directive now needs to expose an API to manipulate the audio player. Add these functions to the MyAudioDirective directive:

```
stop() {
  this.audioPlayer.pause();
}

start() {
  this.audioPlayer.play();
}
get currentTime(): number {
  return this.audioPlayer.currentTime;
```

```
  }

  get duration(): number {
    return this.audioPlayer.duration;
  }

  get playbackComplete() {
    return this.duration == this.currentTime;
  }
```

The `MyAudioDirective` API has two functions (`start` and `stop`) and three getters (`currentTime`, `duration`, and a Boolean property called `playbackComplete`). The implementations for these functions and properties just wrap the audio element functions.

 Learn about these audio functions from the MDN documentation here: `http://bit.ly/html-media-element`.

To understand how we use the audio directive, let's create a new component that manages audio playback.

Creating WorkoutAudioComponent for audio support

If we go back and look at the audio cues that are required, there are four distinct audio cues, and hence we are going to create a component with five embedded `<audio>` tags (two audio tags work together for next-up audio).

From the command line go to the `trainer/src/app/workout-runner` folder and add a new `WorkoutAudioComponent` component using Angular CLI.

Open `workout-audio.component.html` and replace the existing view template with this HTML snippet:

```html
<audio #ticks="MyAudio" loop src="/assets/audio/tick10s.mp3"></audio>
<audio #nextUp="MyAudio" src="/assets/audio/nextup.mp3"></audio>
<audio #nextUpExercise="MyAudio" [src]="'/assets/audio/' +
nextupSound"></audio>
<audio #halfway="MyAudio" src="/assets/audio/15seconds.wav"></audio>
<audio #aboutToComplete="MyAudio" src="/assets/audio/321.wav"></audio>
```

There are five `<audio>` tags, one for each of the following:

- **Ticking audio**: The first audio tag produces the ticking sound and is started as soon as the workout starts.
- **Next up audio and exercise audio**: There next two audio tags work together. The first tag produces the "Next up" sound. And the actual exercise audio is handled by the third tag (in the preceding code snippet).
- **Halfway audio**: The fourth audio tag plays halfway through the exercise.
- **About to complete audio**: The final audio tag plays a piece to denote the completion of an exercise.

Did you notice the usage of the # symbol in each of the `audio` tags? There are some variable assignments prefixed with #. In the Angular world, these variables are known as **template reference variables** or at times **template variables**.

As the platform guide defines:

A template reference variable is often a reference to a DOM element or directive within a template.

 Don't confuse them with the template input variables that we have used with the `ngFor` directive earlier, `*ngFor="let video of videos"`. The **template input variable's** (`video` in this case) scope is within the HTML fragment it is declared, whereas the template reference variable can be accessed across the entire template.

Look at the last section where `MyAudioDirective` was defined. The `exportAs` metadata is set to `MyAudio`. We repeat that same `MyAudio` string while assigning the `template reference variable` for each audio tag:

```
#ticks="MyAudio"
```

The role of `exportAs` is to define the name that can be used in the view to assign this directive to a variable. Remember, a single element/component can have multiple directives applied to it. `exportAs` allows us to select which directive should be assigned to a template-reference variable based on what is on the right side of equals.

Typically, template variables, once declared, give access to the view element/component they are attached to, to other parts of the view, something we will discuss shortly. But in our case, we will use template variables to refer to the multiple `MyAudioDirective` from the parent component's code. Let's understand how to use them.

Update the generated `workout-audio.compnent.ts` with the following outline:

```
import { Component, OnInit, ViewChild } from '@angular/core';
import { MyAudioDirective } from '../../shared/my-audio.directive';

@Component({
  ...
})
export class WorkoutAudioComponent implements OnInit {
  @ViewChild('ticks') private ticks: MyAudioDirective;
  @ViewChild('nextUp') private nextUp: MyAudioDirective;
  @ViewChild('nextUpExercise') private nextUpExercise: MyAudioDirective;
  @ViewChild('halfway') private halfway: MyAudioDirective;
  @ViewChild('aboutToComplete') private aboutToComplete: MyAudioDirective;
  private nextupSound: string;

  constructor() { }
  ...
}
```

The interesting bit in this outline is the `@ViewChild` decorator against the five properties. The `@ViewChild` decorator allows us to inject a child component/directive/element reference into its parent. The parameter passed to the decorator is the template variable name, which helps DI match the element/directive to inject. When Angular instantiates the main `WorkoutAudioComponent`, it injects the corresponding audio directives based on the `@ViewChild` decorator and the template reference variable name passed. Let's complete the basic class implementation before we look at `@ViewChild` in detail.

 Without `exportAs` set on the `MyAudioDirective` directive, the `@ViewChild` injection injects the related `ElementRef` instance instead of the `MyAudioDirective` instance. We can confirm this by removing the `exportAs` attribute from `myAudioDirective` and then looking at the injected dependencies in `WorkoutAudioComponent`.

The remaining task is to just play the correct audio component at the right time. Add these functions to `WorkoutAudioComponent`:

```
stop() {
    this.ticks.stop();
    this.nextUp.stop();
    this.halfway.stop();
    this.aboutToComplete.stop();
    this.nextUpExercise.stop();
  }
  resume() {
    this.ticks.start();
```

```
    if (this.nextUp.currentTime > 0 && !this.nextUp.playbackComplete)
        { this.nextUp.start(); }
    else if (this.nextUpExercise.currentTime > 0 &&
!this.nextUpExercise.playbackComplete)
        { this.nextUpExercise.start(); }
    else if (this.halfway.currentTime > 0 &&
!this.halfway.playbackComplete)
        { this.halfway.start(); }
    else if (this.aboutToComplete.currentTime > 0 &&
!this.aboutToComplete.playbackComplete)
        { this.aboutToComplete.start(); }
  }

  onExerciseProgress(progress: ExerciseProgressEvent) {
    if (progress.runningFor === Math.floor(progress.exercise.duration / 2)
      && progress.exercise.exercise.name != 'rest') {
      this.halfway.start();
    }
    else if (progress.timeRemaining === 3) {
      this.aboutToComplete.start();
    }
  }

  onExerciseChanged(state: ExerciseChangedEvent) {
    if (state.current.exercise.name === 'rest') {
      this.nextupSound = state.next.exercise.nameSound;
      setTimeout(() => this.nextUp.start(), 2000);
      setTimeout(() => this.nextUpExercise.start(), 3000);
    }
  }
```

Having trouble writing these functions? They are available in the `checkpoint3.3` Git branch.

There are two new model classes used in the preceding code. Add their declarations to `model.ts`, as follows (again available in `checkpoint3.3`):

```
export class ExerciseProgressEvent {
    constructor(
        public exercise: ExercisePlan,
        public runningFor: number,
        public timeRemaining: number,
        public workoutTimeRemaining: number) { }
}

export class ExerciseChangedEvent {
    constructor(
        public current: ExercisePlan,
```

```
        public next: ExercisePlan) { }
}
```

These are model classes to track progress events.

The `WorkoutAudioComponent` implementation consumes this data. Remember to import the reference for `ExerciseProgressEvent` and `ExerciseProgressEvent` in `workout-audio.component.ts`.

To reiterate, the audio component consumes the events by defining two event handlers: `onExerciseProgress` and `onExerciseChanged`. How the events are generated becomes clear as we move along.

The `start` and `resume` functions stop and resume audio whenever a workout starts, pauses, or completes. The extra complexity in the resume function it to tackle cases when the workout was paused during next up, about to complete, or half-way audio playback. We just want to continue from where we left off.

The `onExerciseProgress` function should be called to report the workout progress. It's used to play the halfway audio and about-to-complete audio based on the state of the workout. The parameter passed to it is an object that contains exercise progress data.

The `onExerciseChanged` function should be called when the exercise changes. The input parameter contains the current and next exercise in line and helps `WorkoutAudioComponent` to decide when to play the next up exercise audio.

We touched upon two new concepts in this section: template reference variables and injecting child elements/directives into the parent. It's worth exploring these two concepts in more detail before we continue with the implementation. We'll start with learning more about template reference variables.

Understanding template reference variables

Template reference variables are created on the view template and are mostly consumed from the view. As you have already learned, these variables can be identified by the # prefix used to declare them.

One of the greatest benefits of template variables is that they facilitate cross-component communication at the view template level. Once declared, such variables can be referenced by sibling elements/components and their children. Check out the following snippet:

```
<input #emailId type="email">Email to {{emailId.value}}
<button (click)= "MailUser(emaild.value)">Send</button>
```

This snippet declares a template variable, `emailId`, and then references it in the interpolation and the button `click` expression.

The Angular templating engine assigns the DOM object for `input` (an instance of `HTMLInputElement`) to the `emailId` variable. Since the variable is available across siblings, we use it in a button's `click` expression.

Template variables work with components too. We can easily do this:

```
<trainer-app>
  <workout-runner #runner></workout-runner>
  <button (click)= "runner.start()">Start Workout</button>
</trainer-app>
```

In this case, `runner` has a reference to the `WorkoutRunnerComponent` object, and the button is used to start the workout.

> The `ref-` prefix is the canonical alternative to `#`. The `#runner` variable can also be declared as `ref-runner`.

Template variable assignment

You may not have noticed but there is something interesting about the template variable assignments described in the last few sections. To recap, the three examples that we have used are:

```
<audio #ticks="MyAudio" loop src="/static/audio/tick10s.mp3"></audio>
<input #emailId type="email">Email to {{emailId.value}}

<workout-runner #runner></workout-runner>
```

What got assigned to the variable depends on where the variable was declared. This is governed by rules in Angular:

- If a directive is present on the element, such as `MyAudioDirective` in the first example shown previously, the directive sets the value.
  The `MyAudioDirective` directive sets the `ticks` variable to an instance of `MyAudioDirective`.
- If there is no directive present, either the underlying HTML DOM element is assigned or a component object is assigned (as shown in the `input` and `workout-runner` examples).

We will be employing this technique to implement the workout audio component integration with the workout runner component. This introduction gives us the head start that we need.

The other new concept that we promised to cover is child element/directive injection using the `ViewChild` and `ViewChildren` decorators.

Using the @ViewChild decorator

The `@ViewChild` decorator instructs the Angular DI framework to search for some specific child component/directive/element in the component tree and inject it into the parent. This allows the parent component to interact with child components/element using the reference to the child, a new communication pattern!

In the preceding code, the audio element directive (the `MyAudioDirective` class) is injected into the `WorkoutAudioComponent` code.

To establish the context, let's recheck a view fragment from `WorkoutAudioComponent`:

```
<audio #ticks="MyAudio" loop src="/static/audio/tick10s.mp3"></audio>
```

Angular injects the directive (`MyAudioDirective`) into the `WorkoutAudioComponent` property: `ticks`. The search is done based on the selector passed to the `@ViewChild` decorator. Let's see the audio example again:

```
@ViewChild('ticks') private ticks: MyAudioDirective;
```

The selector parameter on `ViewChild` can be a string value, in which case Angular searches for a matching template variable, as before.

Or it can be a *type*. This is valid and should inject an instance of `MyAudioDirective`:

```
@ViewChild(MyAudioDirective) private ticks: MyAudioDirective;
```

However, it does not work in our case. Why? Because there are multiple `MyAudioDirective` directives declared in the `WorkoutAudioComponent` view, one for each of the `<audio>` tags. In such a scenario, the first match is injected. Not very useful. Passing the type selector would have worked if there was only one `<audio>` tag in the view!

Properties decorated with @ViewChild are sure to be set before the ngAfterViewInit event hook on the component is called. This implies such properties are null if accessed inside the constructor.

Angular also has a decorator to locate and inject multiple child components/directives: @ViewChildren.

The @ViewChildren decorator

@ViewChildren works similarly to @ViewChild, except it can be used to inject multiple child types into the parent. Again taking the previous audio component above as an example, using @ViewChildren, we can get all the MyAudioDirective directive instances in WorkoutAudioComponent, as shown here:

```
@ViewChildren(MyAudioDirective) allAudios: QueryList<MyAudioDirective>;
```

Look carefully; allAudios is not a standard JavaScript array, but a custom class, QueryList<Type>. The QueryList class is an immutable collection that contains the reference to the components/directives that Angular was able to locate based on the filter criteria passed to the @ViewChildren decorator. The best thing about this list is that Angular will keep this list in sync with the state of the view. When directives/components get added/removed from the view dynamically, this list is updated too. Components/directives generated using ng-for are a prime example of this dynamic behavior. Consider the preceding @ViewChildren usage and this view template:

```
<audio *ngFor="let clip of clips" src="/static/audio/ "+{{clip}}></audio>
```

The number of MyAudioDirective directives created by Angular depends upon the number of clips. When @ViewChildren is used, Angular injects the correct number of MyAudioDirective instances into the allAudio property and keeps it in sync when items are added or removed from the clips array.

While the usage of @ViewChildren allows us to get hold of all MyAudioDirective directives, it cannot be used to control the playback. You see, we need to get hold of individual MyAudioDirective instances as the audio playback timing varies. Hence the distinct @ViewChild implementation.

Once we get hold of the MyAudioDirective directive attached to each audio element, it is just a matter of playing the audio tracks at the right time.

Integrating WorkoutAudioComponent

While we have componentized the audio playback functionality into WorkoutAudioComponent, it is and always will be tightly coupled to the WorkoutRunnerComponent implementation. WorkoutAudioComponent derives its operational intelligence from WorkoutRunnerComponent. Hence the two components need to interact. WorkoutRunnerComponent needs to provide the WorkoutAudioComponent state change data, including when the workout started, exercise progress, workout stopped, paused, and resumed.

One way to achieve this integration would be to use the currently exposed WorkoutAudioComponent API (stop, resume, and other functions) from WorkoutRunnerComponent.

Something can be done by injecting WorkoutAudioComponent into WorkoutRunnerComponent, as we did earlier when we injected MyAudioDirective into WorkoutAudioComponent.

Declare the WorkoutAudioComponent in the WorkoutRunnerComponent's view, such as:

```
<div class="row pt-4">...</div>
<abe-workout-audio></abe-workout-audio>
```

Doing so gives us a reference to the WorkoutAudioComponent inside the WorkoutRunnerComponent implementation:

```
@ViewChild(WorkoutAudioComponent) workoutAudioPlayer:
WorkoutAudioComponent;
```

The WorkoutAudioComponent functions can then be invoked from WorkoutRunnerComponent from different places in the code. For example, this is how pause would change:

```
pause() {
    clearInterval(this.exerciseTrackingInterval);
    this.workoutPaused = true;
    this.workoutAudioPlayer.stop();
}
```

And to play the next-up audio, we would need to change parts of the startExerciseTimeTracking function:

```
this.startExercise(next);
this.workoutAudioPlayer.onExerciseChanged(new ExerciseChangedEvent(next,
this.getNextExercise()));
```

This is a perfectly viable option where WorkoutAudioComponent becomes a dumb component controlled by WorkoutRunnerComponent. The only problem with this solution is that it adds some noise to the WorkoutRunnerComponent implementation. WorkoutRunnerComponent now needs to manage audio playback too.

There is an alternative, however.

WorkoutRunnerComponent can expose events that are triggered during different times of workout execution, such as workout started, exercise started, and workout paused. The advantage of having WorkoutRunnerComponent expose events is that it allows us to integrate other components/directives with WorkoutRunnerComponent using the same events. Be it the WorkoutAudioComponent or components we create in future.

Exposing WorkoutRunnerComponent events

Till now we have only explored how to consume events. Angular allows us to raise events too. Angular components and directives can expose custom events using the EventEmitter class and the @Output decorator.

Add these event declarations to WorkoutRunnerComponent at the end of the variable declaration section:

```
workoutPaused: boolean;
@Output() exercisePaused: EventEmitter<number> =
    new EventEmitter<number>();
@Output() exerciseResumed: EventEmitter<number> =
    new EventEmitter<number>()
@Output() exerciseProgress:EventEmitter<ExerciseProgressEvent> =
    new EventEmitter<ExerciseProgressEvent>();
@Output() exerciseChanged: EventEmitter<ExerciseChangedEvent> =
    new EventEmitter<ExerciseChangedEvent>();
@Output() workoutStarted: EventEmitter<WorkoutPlan> =
    new EventEmitter<WorkoutPlan>();
@Output() workoutComplete: EventEmitter<WorkoutPlan> =
    new EventEmitter<WorkoutPlan>();
```

The names of the events are self-explanatory, and within our `WorkoutRunnerComponent` implementation, we need to raise them at the appropriate times.

Remember to add the `ExerciseProgressEvent` and `ExerciseChangeEvent` imports to the `model` already declared on top. And add the `Output` and `EventEmitter` imports to `@angular/core`.

Let's try to understand the role of the `@Output` decorator and the `EventEmitter` class.

The @Output decorator

We covered a decent amount of Angular eventing capabilities in this chapter. Specifically, we learned how we can consume any event on a component, directive, or DOM element using the `bracketed ()` syntax. How about raising our own events?

In Angular, we can create and raise our own events, events that signify something noteworthy has happened in our component/directive. Using the `@Output` decorator and the `EventEmitter` class, we can define and raise custom events.

 It's also a good time to refresh what we learned about events.

Remember this: it is through events that components can communicate with the outside world. When we declare:

```
@Output() exercisePaused: EventEmitter<number> = new
EventEmitter<number>();
```

It signifies that `WorkoutRunnerComponent` exposes an event, `exercisePaused` (raised when the workout is paused).

To subscribe to this event, we can do the following:

```
<abe-workout-runner (exercisePaused)="onExercisePaused($event)"></abe-
workout-runner>
```

This looks absolutely similar to how we did the DOM event subscription in the workout runner template. See this sample stipped from the workout-runner's view:

```
<div id="pause-overlay" (click)="pauseResumeToggle()"
(window:keyup)="onKeyPressed($event)">
```

The `@Output` decorator instructs Angular to make this event available for template binding. Events created without the `@Output` decorator cannot be referenced in HTML.

 The `@Output` decorator can also take a parameter, signifying the name of the event. If not provided, the decorator uses the property name: `@Output("workoutPaused") exercisePaused: EventEmitter<number>` .... This declares a `workoutPaused` event instead of `exercisePaused`.

Like any decorator, the `@Output` decorator is there just to provide metadata for the Angular framework to work with. The real heavy lifting is done by the `EventEmitter` class.

Eventing with EventEmitter

Angular embraces **reactive programming** (also dubbed **Rx**-style programming) to support asynchronous operations with events. If you are hearing this term for the first time or don't have much idea about what reactive programming is, you're not alone.

Reactive programming is all about programming against **asynchronous data streams**. Such a stream is nothing but a sequence of ongoing events ordered based on the time they occur. We can imagine a stream as a pipe generating data (in some manner) and pushing it to one or more subscribers. Since these events are captured asynchronously by subscribers, they are called asynchronous data streams.

The data can be anything, ranging from browser/DOM element events to user input to loading remote data using AJAX. With *Rx* style, we consume this data uniformly.

In the Rx world, there are Observers and Observables, a concept derived from the very popular **Observer design pattern**. **Observables** are streams that emit data. **Observers**, on the other hand, subscribe to these events.

The `EventEmitter` class in Angular is primarily responsible for providing eventing support. It acts both as an *observer* and *observable*. We can fire events on it and it can also listen to events.

There are two functions available on `EventEmitter` that are of interest to us:

- `emit`: As the name suggests, use this function to raise events. It takes a single argument that is the event data. `emit` *is the observable side.*
- `subscribe`: Use this function to subscribe to the events raised by `EventEmitter`. `subscribe` is the observer side.

Let's do some event publishing and subscriptions to understand how the preceding functions work.

Raising events from WorkoutRunnerComponent

Look at the `EventEmitter` declaration. These have been declared with the `type` parameter. The `type` parameter on `EventEmitter` signifies the type of data emitted.

Let's add the event implementation to `workout-runner.component.ts`, starting from the top of the file and moving down.

Add this statement to the end of the `start` function:

```
this.workoutStarted.emit(this.workoutPlan);
```

We use the `emit` function of `EventEmitter` to raise a `workoutStarted` event with the current workout plan as an argument.

To `pause`, add this line to raise the `exercisePaused` event:

```
this.exercisePaused.emit(this.currentExerciseIndex);
```

To `resume`, add the following line:

```
this.exerciseResumed.emit(this.currentExerciseIndex);
```

Each time, we pass the current exercise index as an argument to `emit` when raising the `exercisePaused` and `exerciseResumed` events.

Inside the `startExerciseTimeTracking` function, add the highlighted code after the call to `startExercise`:

```
this.startExercise(next);
this.exerciseChanged.emit(new ExerciseChangedEvent(next,
this.getNextExercise()));
```

The argument passed contains the exercise that is going to start (`next`) and the next exercise in line (`this.getNextExercise()`).

To the same function, add the highlighted code:

```
this.tracker.endTracking(true);
this.workoutComplete.emit(this.workoutPlan);
this.router.navigate(['finish']);
```

The event is raised when the workout is completed.

In the same function, we raise an event that communicates the workout progress. Add this statement:

```
--this.workoutTimeRemaining;
this.exerciseProgress.emit(new ExerciseProgressEvent(
    this.currentExercise,
    this.exerciseRunningDuration,
    this.currentExercise.duration -this.exerciseRunningDuration,
    this.workoutTimeRemaining));
```

That completes our eventing implementation.

As you may have guessed, `WorkoutAudioComponent` now needs to consume these events. The challenge here is how to organize these components so that they can communicate with each other with the minimum dependency on each other.

Component communication patterns

As the implementation stands now, we have:

- A basic `WorkoutAudioComponent` implementation
- Augmented `WorkoutRunnerComponent` by exposing workout life cycle events

These two components just need to talk to each other now.

If the parent needs to communicate with its children, it can do this by:

- **Property binding**: The parent component can set up a property binding on the child component to push data to the child component. For example, this property binding can stop the audio player when the workout is paused:

```
<workout-audio [stopped]="workoutPaused"></workout-audio>
```

Property binding, in this case, works fine. When the workout is paused, the audio is stopped too. But not all scenarios can be handled using property bindings. Playing the next exercise audio or halfway audio requires a bit more control.

- **Calling functions on child components**: The parent component can also call functions on the child component if it can get hold of the child component. We have already seen how to achieve this using the @ViewChild and @ViewChildren decorators in the WorkoutAudioComponent implementation. This approach and its shortcomings have also been discussed briefly in the *Integrating WorkoutAudioComponent* section.

There is one more not-so-good option. Instead of the parent referencing the child component, the child references the parent component. This allows the child component to call the parent component's public functions or subscribe to parent component events.

We are going to try this approach and then scrap the implementation for a better one! A lot of learning can be derived from the not-so-optimal solution we plan to implement.

Injecting a parent component into a child component

Add the WorkoutAudioComponent to the WorkoutRunnerComponent view just before the last closing div:

```
<abe-workout-audio></abe-workout-audio>
```

Next, inject WorkoutRunnerComponent into WorkoutAudioComponent. Open workout-audio.component.ts and add the following declaration and update the constructor:

```
private subscriptions: Array<any>;

constructor( @Inject(forwardRef(() => WorkoutRunnerComponent))
    private runner: WorkoutRunnerComponent) {
    this.subscriptions = [
      this.runner.exercisePaused.subscribe((exercise: ExercisePlan) =>
          this.stop()),
      this.runner.workoutComplete.subscribe((exercise: ExercisePlan) =>
          this.stop()),
      this.runner.exerciseResumed.subscribe((exercise: ExercisePlan) =>
          this.resume()),
      this.runner.exerciseProgress.subscribe((progress:
ExerciseProgressEvent) =>
          this.onExerciseProgress(progress)),
```

```
        this.runner.exerciseChanged.subscribe((state: ExerciseChangedEvent)
=>
        this.onExerciseChanged(state))];
    }
```

And remember to add these imports:

```
import {Component, ViewChild, Inject, forwardRef} from '@angular/core';
import {WorkoutRunnerComponent} from '../workout-runner.component'
```

Let's try to understand what we have done before running the app. There is some amount of trickery involved in the construction injection. If we directly try to inject `WorkoutRunnerComponent` into `WorkoutAudioComponent`, it fails with Angular complaining of not being able to find all the dependencies. Read the code and think carefully; there is a subtle dependency cycle issue lurking. `WorkoutRunnerComponent` is already dependent on `WorkoutAudioComponent`, as we have referenced `WorkoutAudioComponent` in the `WorkoutRunnerComponent` view. Now by injecting `WorkoutRunnerComponent` in `WorkoutAudioComponent`, we have created a dependency cycle.

Cyclic dependencies are challenging for any DI framework. When creating a component with a cyclic dependency, the framework has to somehow resolve the cycle. In the preceding example, we resolve the circular dependency issue by using an `@Inject` decorator and passing in the token created using the `forwardRef()` global framework function.

Once the injection is done correctly, inside the constructor, we attach a handler to the `WorkoutRunnerComponent` events, using the `subscribe` function of `EventEmitter`. The arrow function passed to `subscribe` is called whenever the event occurs with a specific event argument. We collect all the subscriptions into a `subscription` array. This array comes in handy when we unsubscribe, which we need to, to avoid memory leaks.

A bit about `EventEmitter`: the `EventEmmiter` subscription (`subscribe` function) takes three arguments:

```
subscribe(generatorOrNext?: any, error?: any, complete?: any) : any
```

- The first argument is a callback, which is invoked whenever an event is emitted
- The second argument is an error callback function, invoked when the observable (the part that is generating events) errors out
- The final argument takes a callback function that is called when the observable is done publishing events

We have done enough to make audio integration work. Run the app and start the workout. Except for the ticking audio, all the \ audio clips play at the right time. You may have to wait some time to hear the other audio clips. What is the problem?

As it turns out, we never started the ticking audio clip at the start of the workout. We can fix it by either setting the `autoplay` attribute on the `ticks` audio element or using the component life cycle events to trigger the ticking sound. Let's take the second approach.

Using component life cycle events

The injected `MyAudioDirective` in `WorkoutAudioComponent`, shown as follows, is not available till the view is initialized:

```
<audio #ticks="MyAudio" loop src="/assets/audio/tick10s.mp3"></audio>
<audio #nextUp="MyAudio" src="/assets/audio/nextup.mp3"></audio>
. . .
```

We can verify it by accessing the `ticks` variable inside the constructor; it will be null. Angular has still not done its magic and we need to wait for the children of `WorkoutAudioComponent` to be initialized.

The component's life cycle hooks can help us here. The `AfterViewInit` event hook is called once the component's view has been initialized and hence is a safe place from which to access the component's child directives/elements. Let's do it quickly.

Update `WorkoutAudioComponent` by adding the interface implementation, and the necessary imports, as highlighted:

```
import {..., AfterViewInit} from '@angular/core';
. . .
export class WorkoutAudioComponent implements OnInit, AfterViewInit {
    ngAfterViewInit() {
        this.ticks.start();
    }
}
```

Go ahead and test the app. The app has come to life with full-fledged audio feedback. Nice!

While everything looks fine and dandy on the surface, there is a memory leak in the application now. If, in the middle of the workout, we navigate away from the workout page (to the start or finish page) and again return to the workout page, multiple audio clips play at random times.

It seems that `WorkoutRunnerComponent` is not getting destroyed on route navigation, and due to this, none of the child components are destroyed, including `WorkoutAudioComponent`. The net result? A new `WorkoutRunnerComponent` is being created every time we navigate to the workout page but is never removed from the memory on navigating away.

The primary reason for this memory leak is the event handlers we have added in `WorkoutAudioComponent`. We need to unsubscribe from these events when the audio component unloads, or else the `WorkoutRunnerComponent` reference will never be dereferenced.

Another component lifecycle event comes to our rescue here: `OnDestroy` Add this implementation to the `WorkoutAudioComponent` class:

```
ngOnDestroy() {
  this.subscriptions.forEach((s) => s.unsubscribe());
}
```

Also, remember to add references to the `OnDestroy` event interface as we did for `AfterViewInit`.

Hope the `subscription` array that we created during event subscription makes sense now. One-shot unsubscribe!

This audio integration is now complete. While this approach is not an awfully bad way of integrating the two components, we can do better. Child components referring to the parent component seems to be undesirable.

 Before proceeding, delete the code that we have added to `workout-audio.component.ts` from the *Injecting a parent component into a child component* section onward.

Sibling component interaction using events and template variables

What if `WorkoutRunnerComponent` and `WorkoutAudioComponent` were organized as sibling components?

If WorkoutAudioComponent and WorkoutRunnerComponent become siblings, we can make good use of Angular's *eventing* and *template reference variables*. Confused? Well, to start with, this is how the components should be laid out:

```
<workout-runner></workout-runner>
<workout-audio></workout-audio>
```

Does it ring any bells? Starting from this template, can you guess how the final HTML template would look? Think about it before you proceed further.

Still struggling? As soon as we make them sibling components, the power of the Angular templating engine comes to the fore. The following template code is enough to integrate WorkoutRunnerComponent and WorkoutAudioComponent:

```
<abe-workout-runner (exercisePaused)="wa.stop()"
    (exerciseResumed)="wa.resume()"
    (exerciseProgress)= "wa.onExerciseProgress($event)"
    (exerciseChanged)= "wa.onExerciseChanged($event)"
    (workoutComplete)="wa.stop()"
    (workoutStarted)="wa.resume()">
</abe-workout-runner>
<abe-workout-audio #wa></abe-workout-audio>
```

The WorkoutAudioComponent template variable, wa, is being manipulated by referencing the variable in the event handler expressions on WorkoutRunnerComponent. Quite elegant! We still need to solve the biggest puzzle in this approach: Where does the preceding code go? Remember, WorkoutRunnerComponent is loaded as part of route loading. Nowhere in the code have we had a statement like this:

```
<workout-runner></workout-runner>
```

We need to reorganize the component tree and bring in a container component that can host WorkoutRunnerComponent and WorkoutAudioComponent. The router then loads this container component instead of WorkoutRunnerComponent. Let's do it.

Generate a new component code from command line by navigating to trainer/src/app/workout-runner and executing:

```
ng generate component workout-container -is
```

Copy the HTML code with the events described to the template file. The workout container component is ready.

We just need to rewire the routing setup. Open `app-routing.module.ts`. Change the route for the workout runner and add the necessary import:

```
import {WorkoutContainerComponent}
        from './workout-runner/workout-container/workout-
container.component';
..
{ path: '/workout', component: WorkoutContainerComponent },
```

And we have a working audio integration that is clear, concise, and pleasing to the eye!

It's time now to wrap up the chapter, but not before addressing the video player dialog glitch introduced in the earlier sections. The workout does not stop/pause when the video player dialog is open.

We are not going to detail the fix here, and urge the readers to give it a try without consulting the `checkpoint3.4` code.

Here is an obvious hint. Use the eventing infrastructure!

And another one: raise events from `VideoPlayerComponent`, one for each playback started and ended.

And one last hint: the `open` function on the dialog service (`Modal`) returns a promise, which is resolved when the dialog is closed.

If you are having a problem with running the code, look at the `checkpoint3.4` Git branch for a working version of what we have done thus far. Or if you are not using Git, download the snapshot of `checkpoint3.4` (a ZIP file) from `http://bit.ly/ng6be-checkpoint-3-4`. Refer to the `README.md` file in the `trainer` folder when setting up the snapshot for the first time.

Summary

We started this chapter with the aim of creating a complex Angular app. The *7 Minute Workout* app fitted the bill, and you learned a lot about the Angular framework while building this app.

To build the app, we started off by defining the model of the app. Once the model was in place, we started the actual implementation by building an **Angular component**. Angular components are nothing but classes that are decorated with a framework-specific decorator, @Component.

We also learned about **Angular modules** and how Angular uses them to organize code artifacts.

Once we had a fully functional component, we created a supporting view for the app. We also explored the data binding capabilities of the framework, including **property, attribute, class, style,** and **event binding**. Plus, we highlighted how **interpolations** are a special case of property binding.

Components are a special class of directives that have an attached view. We touched upon what directives are and the special classes of directives, including **attribute** and **structural directives**.

We learned how to perform cross-component communication using **input properties**. The two child components that we put together (ExerciseDescriptionComponent and VideoPlayerComponent) derived their inputs from the parent WorkoutRunnerComponent using input properties.

We then covered another core construct in Angular, **pipes**. We saw how to use pipes such as the date pipe and how to create one of our own.

Throughout the chapter, we touched upon a number of Angular directives, including the following:

- `ngClass`/`ngStyle`: For applying multiple styles and classes using Angular binding capabilities
- `ngFor`: For generating dynamic HTML content using a looping construct
- `ngIf`: For conditionally creating/destroying DOM elements
- `ngSwitch`: For creating/destroying DOM elements using the switch-case construct

We now have a basic *7 Minute Workout* app. For a better user experience, we have added a number of small enhancements to it too, but we are still missing some good-to-have features that would make our app more usable. From the framework perspective, we have purposefully ignored some core/advanced concepts such as **change detection**, **dependency injection**, **component routing**, and data flow patterns.

Lastly, we touched upon an important topic: cross-component communication, primarily using Angular eventing. We detailed how to create custom events using the `@Output` decorator and `EventEmitter`.

The `@ViewChild` and `@ViewChildren` decorators that we touched upon in this chapter helped us understand how a parent can get hold of a child component for use. Angular DI also allows injecting a parent component into a child.

We concluded this chapter by building a `WorkoutAudioComponent` and highlighted how sibling-component communication can happen using Angular events and template variables.

What's next? We are going to build a new app, *Personal Trainer*. This app will allow us to build our own custom workouts. Once we can create our own workout, we are going to morph the *7-Minute Workout* app into a generic *Workout Runner* app that can run workouts that we build using *Personal Trainer*.

For the next chapter, we'll showcase Angular's form capabilities while we build a UI that allows us to create, update, and view our own custom workouts/exercises.

2
Personal Trainer

The *7 Minute Workout* app has been an excellent opportunity for us to learn about Angular. Working through the app, we have covered a number of Angular constructs. Still, there are areas such as Angular form support and client-server communication that remain unexplored. This is partially due to the fact that 7 Minute Workout, from a functional standpoint, has limited touch points with the end user. Interactions are limited to starting, stopping, and pausing the workout. Also, the app neither consumes nor produces any data (except workout history).

In this chapter, we plan to delve deeper into one of the two aforementioned areas, Angular form support. Keeping up with the health and fitness theme (no pun intended), we plan to build a *Personal Trainer* app. The new app will be an extension to *7 Minute Workout*, allowing us to build our own customized workout plans that are not limited to the *7 Minute Workout* plans we already have.

This chapter is dedicated to understanding Angular forms and how to put them to use as we build out our *Personal Trainer* app.

The topics that we will cover in this chapter are as follows:

- **Defining Personal Trainer requirements**: Since we are building a new app in this chapter, we start with defining the app requirements.
- **Defining the Personal Trainer model**: Any app design starts with defining its model. We define the model for *Personal Trainer*, which is similar to the *7 Minute Workout* app built earlier.
- **Defining the Personal Trainer layout and navigation**: We define the layout, navigation patterns, and views for the new app. We also set up a navigation system that is integrated with Angular routes and the main view.
- **Adding support pages**: Before we focus on the form capability and build a Workout component, we build some supporting components for workout and exercise listing.

- **Defining the Workout Builder component structure**: We lay out the Workout Builder components that we will use to manage workouts.
- **Building forms**: We make extensive use of HTML forms and input elements to create custom workouts. In the process, we will learn more about Angular Forms. The concepts that we cover include:
    - **Form types**: The two types of form that can be built with Angular are template-driven and reactive. We're working with both template-driven and reactive forms in this chapter.
    - **ngModel**: This provides two-way data binding for template driven forms and allows us to track changes and validate form input.
    - **Reactive Form Controls**: These include the form builder, form control, form group, and form array. These are used to construct forms programmatically.
    - **Data formatting**: These are the CSS classes that permit us to style our feedback to the user.
    - **Input validation**: We will learn about the validation capabilities of Angular forms.

Personal Trainer requirements

Based on the notion of managing workouts and exercises, these are some of the requirements that our *Personal Trainer* app should fulfill:

- The ability to list all available workouts.
- The ability to create and edit a workout. While creating and editing a workout, it should have:
    - The ability to add workout attributes including name, title, description, and rest duration
    - The ability to add/remove multiple exercises for workouts
    - The ability to order exercises in the workout
    - The ability to save workout data
- The ability to list all available exercises.

- The ability to create and edit an exercise. While creating and editing an exercise, it should have:
  - The ability to add exercise attributes such as name, title, description, and procedure
  - The ability to add pictures for the exercise
  - The ability to add related videos for the exercise
  - The ability to add audio clues for the exercise

All the requirements seem to be self-explanatory, so let's start with the design of the application. As customary, we first need to think about the model that can support these requirements.

Getting started with the code for Personal Trainer

First, download the base version of the new *Personal Trainer* app from `checkpoint4.1` in the GitHub repository for the book.

 The code is available on GitHub `https://github.com/chandermani/` `angular6byexample` for everyone to download. Checkpoints are implemented as branches in GitHub. The branch to download is as follows: `GitHub Branch: checkpoint4.1`. If you are not using Git, download the snapshot of Checkpoint 4.1 (a ZIP file) from the following GitHub location: `https://github.com/chandermani/angular6byexample/` `archive/checkpoint4.1.zip`. Refer to the `README.md` file in the `trainer` folder when setting up the snapshot for the first time.

This code has the complete *7 Minute Workout (Workout Runner)* app. We have added some more content to support the new *Personal Trainer* app. Some of the relevant updates are:

- Adding the new `WorkoutBuilder` feature. This feature contains implementations pertaining to *Personal Trainer*.
- Updating the layout and styles of the app.

- Adding some components and HTML templates with placeholder content for *Personal Trainer* in the `workout-builder` folder under `trainer/src/app`.
- Defining a new route to the `WorkoutBuilder` feature. We will cover setting up this route within the app in the coming section.
- As we just mentioned, moving the existing `model.ts` file into the `core` folder.

Let's discuss how we will be using the model.

Using the Personal Trainer model in Workout Builder services

Services are useful for sharing data across controllers and other Angular constructs. Open the `model.ts` file present in the `core` folder under `app`. In this class, we essentially do not have any data, but a blueprint that describes the shape of the data. The plan is to use services to expose this model structure. We have already done that in Workout Runner. Now, we will do the same in Workout Builder.

 The `model.ts` file has been moved into the `core` folder as it is shared across the *Workout Builder* and *Workout Runner* apps. Note: in `checkpoint4.1` we have updated the import statements in `workout-runner.component.ts`, `workout-audio.component.ts`, and `workout-history-tracker-service.ts` to reflect this change.

In `Chapter 1`, *Building Our First App - 7 Minute Workout*, we reviewed the class definitions in the model file: `Exercise`, `ExercisePlan`, and `WorkoutPlan`. As we then mentioned, these three classes constitute our base model. We will now start using this base model in our new app.

That's all on the model design front. The next thing we are going to do is define the structure for the new app.

The Personal Trainer layout

The skeleton structure of *Personal Trainer* looks like this:

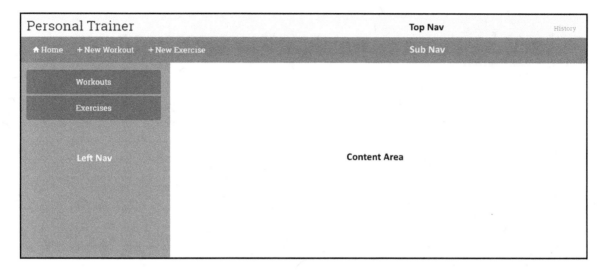

This has the following components:

- **Top Nav**: This contains the app branding title and history link.
- **Sub Nav**: This has navigation elements that change based on the active component.
- **Left Nav**: This contains elements that are dependent upon the active component.
- **Content Area**: This is where the main view for our component will display. This is where most of the action happens. We will create/edit exercises and workouts and show a list of exercises and workouts here.

Look at the source code files; there is a new folder `workout-builder` under `trainer/src/app`. It has files for each component that we described previously, with some placeholder content. We will be building these components as we go along in this chapter.

However, we first need to link up these components within the app. This requires us to define the navigation patterns for the Workout Builder app and accordingly define the app routes.

Personal Trainer navigation with routes

The navigation pattern that we plan to use for the app is the list-detail pattern. We will create list pages for the exercises and workouts available in the app. Clicking on any list item takes us to the detailed view for the item where we can perform all CRUD operations (create/read/update/delete). The following routes adhere to this pattern:

Route	Description
/builder	This just redirects to **builder/workouts**
/builder/workouts	This lists all the available workouts. It is the landing page for *Workout Builder*
/builder/workout/new	This creates a new workout
/builder/workout/:id	This edits an existing workout with the specific ID
/builder/exercises	This lists all the available exercises
/builder/exercise/new	This creates a new exercise
/builder/exercise/:id	This edits an existing exercise with the specific ID

Getting started with Personal Trainer navigation

At this point, if you look at the route configuration in `app-routing.module.ts` in the `src/app` folder, you will find one new route definition, `builder`:

```
const routes: Routes = [
    ...
    { path: 'builder', component: WorkoutBuilderComponent },
    ...
];
```

And if you run the application, you will see that the start screen shows another link, **Create a Workout**:

Behind the scenes, we have added another router link for this link into `start.component.html`:

```
<a routerLink="/builder" class="btn btn-primary btn-lg btn-block"
role="button" aria-pressed="true">
    <span>Create a Workout</span>
    <span class="ion-md-add"></span>
</a>
```

And if you click on this link, you will be taken to the following view:

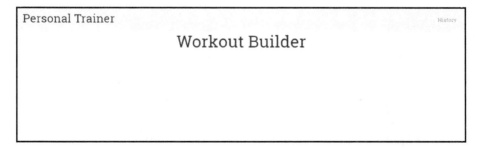

Again, behind the scenes we have added `workout-builder.component.ts` to the `trainer/src/app/workout-builder` folder with the following inline template:

```
template: `
  <div class="row">
    <div class="col-sm-3"></div>
    <div class="col-sm-6">
        <h1 class="text-center">Workout Builder</h1>
    </div>
    <div class="col-sm-3"></div>
  </div>
```

And this view is displayed on the screen under the header using the router outlet in our `app.component.html` template:

```
<div class="container body-content app-container">
    <router-outlet></router-outlet>
</div>`
```

We have wrapped this component (along with the other files we have stubbed out for this feature) in a new module named `workout-builder.module.ts`:

```
import { NgModule } from '@angular/core';
import { CommonModule } from '@angular/common';

import { WorkoutBuilderComponent } from './workout-builder.component';
import { ExerciseComponent } from './exercise/exercise.component';
import { ExercisesComponent } from './exercises/exercises.component';
import { WorkoutComponent } from './workout/workout.component';
import { WorkoutsComponent } from './workouts/workouts.component';

@NgModule({
  imports: [
    CommonModule
  ],
  declarations: [WorkoutBuilderComponent, ExerciseComponent,
ExercisesComponent, WorkoutComponent, WorkoutsComponent]
})
export class WorkoutBuilderModule { }
```

The only thing that might look different here from the other modules that we have created is that we are importing `CommonModule` instead of `BrowserModule`. This avoids importing the whole of `BrowserModule` a second time, which would generate an error when we get to implementing lazy loading for this module.

Finally, we have added an import for this module to `app.module.ts`:

```
...
@NgModule({
  imports: [
    ...
    WorkoutBuilderModule],
...
```

So, nothing surprising here. Following these patterns, we should now begin to think about adding the additional navigation outlined previously for our new feature. However, before we jump into doing that, there are a couple of things we need to consider.

First, if we start adding our routes to the `app.routing-module.ts` file, then the number of routes stored there will grow. These new routes for *Workout Builder* will also be intermixed with the routes for *Workout Runner*. While the number of routes we are now adding might seem insignificant, over time this could get to be a maintenance problem.

Second, we need to take into consideration that our application now consists of two features—*Workout Runner* and *Workout Builder*. We should be thinking about ways to separate these features within our application so that they can be developed independently of each other.

Put differently, we want **loose coupling** between the features that we build. Using this pattern allows us to swap out a feature within our application without affecting the other features. For example, somewhere down the line, we may want to convert the *Workout Runner* into a mobile app but leave the *Workout Builder* intact as a web-based application.

This ability to separate our components from each other is one of the key advantages of using the **component design pattern** that Angular implements. Fortunately, Angular's router gives us the ability to separate out our routing into logically organized **routing configurations** that closely match the features in our application.

In order to accomplish this separation, Angular allows us to use **child routing**, where we can isolate the routing for each of our features. In this chapter, we will use **child routing** to separate out the routing for *Workout Builder*.

Introducing child routes to Workout Builder

Angular supports our goal of isolating the routing for our new *Workout Builder* by providing us with the ability to create a hierarchy of router components within our application. We currently have just one router component, which is in the root component of our application. But Angular allows us to add what are called **child router components** under our root component. This means that one feature can be ignorant of the routes the other is using and each is free to adapt its routes in response to changes within that feature.

Getting back to our application, we can use **child routing** in Angular to match the routing for the two features of our application with the code that will be using them. So in our application, we can structure the routing into the following routing hierarchy for our *Workout Builder* (at this point, we are leaving the *Workout Runner* as is to show the before and after comparison):

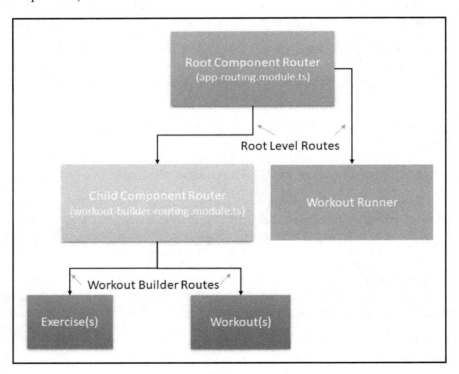

With this approach, we can create a logical separation of our routes by feature and make them easier to manage and maintain.

So, let's get started by adding child routing to our application.

From this point on in this section, we'll be adding to the code that we downloaded earlier for this chapter. If you want to see the complete code for this next section, you can download it from `checkpoint 4.2` in the GitHub repository. If you want to work along with us as we build out the code for this section, still be sure to add the changes in `styles.css` in the `trainer/src` folder that are part of this checkpoint, since we won't be discussing them here. Also be sure and add the files for exercise(s) ,workout(s), and navigation from the `trainer/src/app/workout-builder` folder in the repository. At this stage, these are just stub files, which we will implement later in this chapter. However, you will need these stub files here in order to implement navigation for the *Workout Builder* module. The code is available to download on GitHub at `https://github.com/chandermani/angular6byexample`. Checkpoints are implemented as branches in GitHub. The branch to download is as follows: `GitHub Branch: checkpoint4.2`. If you are not using Git, download the snapshot of `Checkpoint 4.2` (a ZIP file) from the following GitHub location: `https://github.com/chandermani/angular6byexample/archive/checkpoint4.2.zip`. Refer to the `README.md` file in the `trainer` folder when setting up the snapshot for the first time.

Adding the child routing component

In the `workout-builder` directory, add a new TypeScript file named `workout-builder.routing.module.ts` with the following imports:

```
import { NgModule } from '@angular/core';
import { Routes, RouterModule } from '@angular/router';
import { WorkoutBuilderComponent } from './workout-builder.component';
import { WorkoutsComponent } from './workouts/workouts.component';
import { WorkoutComponent } from './workout/workout.component';
import { ExercisesComponent } from './exercises/exercises.component';
import { ExerciseComponent } from './exercise/exercise.component';
```

As you can see, we are importing the components we just mentioned; they will be part of our *Workout Builder* (exercise, exercises, workout, and workouts). Along with those imports, we are also importing `NgModule` from the Angular core module and `Routes` and `RouterModule` from the Angular router module. These imports will give us the ability to add and export child routes.

 We are not using the Angular CLI here because it does not have a standalone blueprint for creating a routing module. However, you can have the CLI create a routing module at the time that you create a module using the `--routing` option. In this case, we already had an existing module created so we couldn't use that flag. See `https://github.com/angular/angular-cli/blob/master/docs/documentation/stories/routing.md` for more details about how to do this.

Then, add the following route configuration to the file:

```
const routes: Routes = [
  {
    path: 'builder',
    component: WorkoutBuilderComponent,
    children: [
        {path: '', pathMatch: 'full', redirectTo: 'workouts'},
        {path: 'workouts', component: WorkoutsComponent },
        {path: 'workout/new', component: WorkoutComponent },
        {path: 'workout/:id', component: WorkoutComponent },
        {path: 'exercises', component: ExercisesComponent},
        {path: 'exercise/new', component: ExerciseComponent },
        {path: 'exercise/:id', component: ExerciseComponent }
    ]
  },
];
```

The first configuration, `path: 'builder'`, sets the base URL for the child routes so that each of the child routes prepends it. The next configuration identifies the `WorkoutBuilder` component as the feature area root component for the child components in this file. This means it will be the component in which each of the child components is displayed using `router-outlet`. The final configuration is a list of one or more children that defines the routing for the child components.

One thing to note here is that we have set up `Workouts` as the default for the child routes with the following configuration:

```
{path:'', pathMatch: 'full', redirectTo: 'workouts'},
```

This configuration indicates that if someone navigates to `builder`, they will be redirected to the `builder/workouts` route. The `pathMatch: 'full'` setting means that the match will only be made if the path after workout/builder is an empty string. This prevents the redirection from happening if the routes are something else, such as `workout/builder/exercises` or any of the other routes we have configured within this file.

Finally, add the following class declaration preceded by an `@NgModule` decorator that defines imports and exports for our module:

```
@NgModule({
  imports: [RouterModule.forChild(routes)],
  exports: [RouterModule]
})
export class WorkoutBuilderRoutingModule { }
```

This import is very similar to the one in `app.routing-module.ts`, with one difference - instead of `RouterModule.forRoot`, we are using `RouterModule.forChild`. The reason for the difference may seem self-explanatory: we are creating child routes, not the routes in the root of the application, and this is how we signify that. Under the hood, however, there is a significant difference. This is because we cannot have more than one router service active in our application. `forRoot` creates the router service but `forChild` does not.

Updating the WorkoutBuilder component

We next need to update the `WorkoutBuilder` component to support our new child routes. To do so, change the `@Component` decorator for Workout Builder to:

1. Remove the `selector`
2. Add a `<abe-sub-nav-main>` custom element to the template
3. Add a `<router-outlet>` tag to the template

The decorator should now look like the following:

```
@Component({
  template: `<div class="container-fluid fixed-top mt-5">
                <div class="row mt-5">
                  <abe-sub-nav-main></abe-sub-nav-main>
                </div>
                <div class="row mt-2">
                  <div class="col-sm-12">
                    <router-outlet></router-outlet>
                  </div>
```

```
            </div>
        <div>`
    })
```

We are removing the selector because `WorkoutBuilderComponent` will not be embedded in the application root, `app.component.ts`. Instead, it will be reached from `app.routing-module.ts` through routing. And while it will handle incoming routing requests from `app.routes.ts`, it will, in turn, be routing them to the other components contained in the Workout Builder feature.

And those components will display their views using the `<router-outlet>` tag that we have just added to the `WorkoutBuilder` template. Given that the template for `Workout BuilderComponent` will be simple, we are using an inline `template` instead of a `templateUrl`.

 Typically, for a component's view we recommend using a `templateUrl` that points to a separate HTML template file. This is especially true when you anticipate that the view will involve more than a few lines of HTML. In that situation, it is much easier to work with a view inside its own HTML file.

We are also adding an `<abe-sub-nav-main>` element that will be used to create a secondary top-level menu for navigating within the *Workout Builder* feature. We'll discuss that a little later in this chapter.

Updating the Workout Builder module

Now, let's update `WorkoutBuilderModule`. First, add the following import to the file:

```
import { WorkoutBuilderRoutingModule } from './workout-builder-
routing.module';
```

It imports the child routing that we just set up. Next, update the `@NgModule` decorator to add `workoutBuilderRoutingModule`:

```
...
@NgModule({
  imports: [
    CommonModule,
    WorkoutBuilderRoutingModule
  ],
  ...
})
```

Finally, add the imports and declarations for the new navigation components that can be found in `checkpoint4.2`:

```
import { LeftNavExercisesComponent } from './navigation/left-nav-
exercises.component';
import { LeftNavMainComponent } from './navigation/left-nav-
main.component';
import { SubNavMainComponent } from './navigation/sub-nav-main.component';
...
  declarations: [
    ...
    LeftNavExercisesComponent,
    LeftNavMainComponent,
    SubNavMainComponent]
```

Updating App Routing module

One last step: return to `app.routing-module.ts` and remove the import of the `WorkoutBuilderComponent` and the route definition that points to the builder:`{ path: 'builder', component: WorkoutBuilderComponent },`.

 Be sure to leave the import of the `WorkoutBuilderModule` in `app.module.ts` unchanged. We'll discuss removing that in the next section when we cover lazy loading.

Putting it all together

We now have area or feature routing that contains child routes, and all the routes related to the *Workout Builder* are now separately contained in their own routing configuration. This means that we can manage all the routing for *Workout Builder* in the `WorkoutBuilderRoutes` component without affecting other parts of the application.

We can see how the router combines the routes in `app.routes.ts` with the default route in `workout-builder.routes.ts`, if we now navigate from the start page to the Workout Builder:

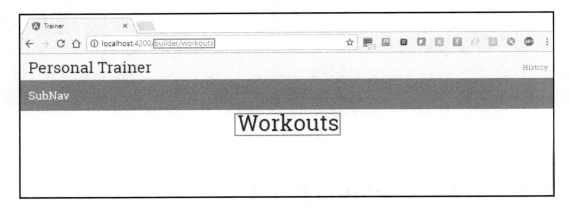

If we look at the URL in the browser, it is `/builder/workouts`. You'll recall that the router link on the start page is `['/builder']`. So how did the router take us to this location?

It does it this way: when the link is clicked, the Angular router first looks to `app-routing.module.ts` for the `builder` path because that file contains the configuration for the root routes in our application. The router does not find that path because we have removed it from the routes in that file.

However, `WorkoutBuilderModule` has been imported into our `AppModule` and that module in turn imports `workoutBuilderRoutingModule`. The latter file contains the child routes that we just configured. The router finds that `builder` is the parent route in that file and so it uses that route. It also finds the default setting that redirects to the child path `workouts` in the event that the `builder` path ends with an empty string, which it does in this case.

If you look at the screen, you will see it is displaying the view for `Workouts` (and not as previously *Workout Builder*). This means that the router has successfully routed the request to `WorkoutsComponent`, which is the component for the default route in the child route configuration that we set up in `workoutBuilderRoutingModule`.

This process of route resolution is illustrated here:

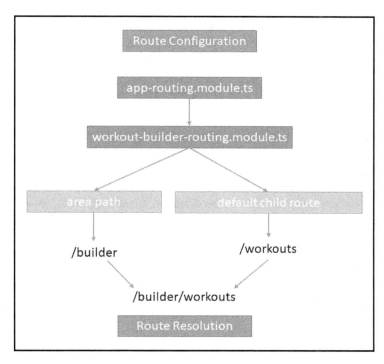

One final thought on child routing. When you look at our child routing component, workout-builder.component.ts, you will see that it has no references to its parent component, app.component.ts (the <selector> tag has been removed, so WorkoutBuilderComponent is not being embedded in the root component). This means that we have successfully encapsulated WorkoutBuilderComponent (and all of its related components that are imported in the WorkoutBuilderModule) in a way that will allow us to move all of it elsewhere in the application, or even into a new application.

Now, it's time for us to move on to converting our routing for the Workout Builder to use lazy loading and building out its navigation menus. If you want to see the completed code for this next section, you can download it from the companion codebase in checkpoint 4.3. Again, if you are working along with us as we build the application, be sure and update the styles.css file, which we are not discussing here.

The code is also available on GitHub: `https://github.com/chandermani/` `angular6byexample`. Checkpoints are implemented as branches in GitHub. The branch to download is as follows: `GitHub Branch:` `checkpoint4.3 (folder - trainer)`. If you are not using Git, download the snapshot of `Checkpoint 4.3` (a ZIP file) from the following GitHub location: `https://github.com/chandermani/angular6byexample/` `archive/checkpoint4.3.zip`. Refer to the `README.md` file in the `trainer` folder when setting up the snapshot for the first time.

Lazy loading of routes

When we roll out our application, we expect that our users will be accessing the Workout Runner every day (and we know that this will be the case for you!). But, we anticipate that they will only occasionally be using the Workout Builder to construct their exercises and workout plans. It would, therefore, be nice if we could avoid the overhead of loading the Workout Builder when our users are just doing their exercises in the Workout Runner. Instead, we would prefer to load Workout Builder only on demand when a user wants to add to or update their exercises and workout plans. This approach is called **lazy loading**. Lazy loading allows us to employ an asynchronous approach when loading our modules. This means that we can load just what is required to get the application started and then load other modules as we need them.

Under the hood, when we use the Angular CLI to build and serve our application, it uses WebPack's bundling and chunking capabilities to accomplish lazy loading. We'll be discussing these capabilities as we work through how to implement lazy loading in our application.

So in our *Personal Trainer*, we want to change the application so that it only loads the **Workout Builder** on demand. And the Angular router allows us to do just that using lazy loading.

But before we get started implementing lazy loading, let's take a look at our current application and how it is loading our modules. With the developer tools open in the **Sources** tab, start up the application; when the start page appears in your browser, if you look under the webpack node in the source tree, you will see that all the files in the application have loaded, including both the *Workout Runner* and *Workout Builder* files:

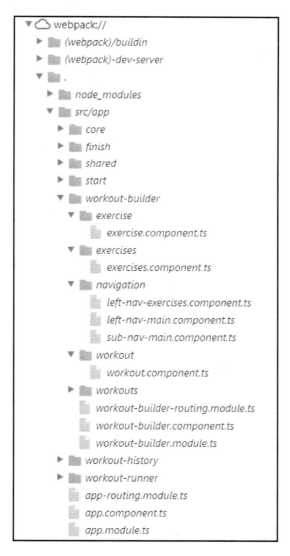

So, even though we may just want to use the *Workout Runner,* we have to load the *Workout Builder* as well. In a way, this makes sense if you think of our application as a **Single Page Application (SPA)**. In order to avoid round trips to the server, an SPA will typically load all the resources that will be needed to use the application when it is first started up by a user. But in our case, the important point is that we do not need the *Workout Builder* when the application is first loaded. Instead, we would like to load those resources only when the user decides that they want to add or change a workout or exercise.

So, let's get started with making that happen.

First, modify `app.routing-module.ts` to add the following route configuration for `WorkoutBuilderModule`:

```
const routes: Routes = [
    ...
    { path: 'builder', loadChildren: './workout-builder/workout-
builder.module#WorkoutBuilderModule'},
    { path: '**', redirectTo: '/start' }
];
```

Notice that the `loadChildren` property is:

```
module file path + # + module name
```

This configuration provides the information that will be needed to load and instantiate `WorkoutBuilderModule`.

Next go back to `workout-builder-routing.module.ts` and change the `path` property to an empty string:

```
export const Routes: Routes = [
    {
        path: '',
    . . .
    }
];
```

We are making this change because we are now setting the path (`builder`) to the `WorkoutBuilderRoutes` in the new configuration for them that we added in `app.routing-module.ts`.

Finally go back to `app-module.ts` and remove the `WorkoutBuilderModule` import in the `@NgModule` configuration in that file. What this means is that instead of loading the **Workout Builder** feature when the application first starts, we only load it when a user accesses the route to *Workout Builder.*

```
PS C:\Users\Kevin.Hennessy\Github\angular6byexample\trainer> ng serve
** NG Live Development Server is listening on localhost:4200, open your browser on http://localhost:4200/ **
 40% building modules 256/260 modules 4 active ...dules\cDate: 2018-02-27T20:11:56.286Z
Hash: a40fda64678f63423b5e
Time: 11933ms
chunk {inline} inline.bundle.js (inline) 5.79 kB [entry] [rendered]
chunk {main} main.bundle.js (main) 205 kB [initial] [rendered]
chunk {polyfills} polyfills.bundle.js (polyfills) 545 kB [initial] [rendered]
chunk {styles} styles.bundle.js (styles) 691 kB [initial] [rendered]
chunk {vendor} vendor.bundle.js (vendor) 8.3 MB [initial] [rendered]
chunk {workout-builder.module} workout-builder.module.chunk.js () 45.9 kB  [rendered]

webpack: Compiled successfully.
```

What's interesting here is the last line that shows a separate file for the `workout.builder.module` called `workout-builder.module.chunk.js.`. **WebPack** has used what is called code splitting to carve out our workout builder module into a separate chunk. This chunk will not be loaded in our application until it is needed (that is when the router navigates to `WorkoutBuilderModule`).

Now, keeping the **Sources** tab open in the Chrome developer tools bring up the application in the browser again. When the start page loads, only the files related to the *Workout Runner* appear and not those related to the *Workout Builder*, as shown here:

Then, if we clear the **Network** tab and click on the **Create a Workout link**, we'll see the `workout-builder.module` chunk load:

Name	Status	Type	Initiator	Size	Time
workout-builder.module.chunk.js	200	script	inline.bundle.js:109	45.1 KB	318 ms

This means that we have achieved encapsulation of our new feature and with asynchronous routing we are able to use lazy loading to load all its components only when needed.

Child and asynchronous routing make it straightforward to implement applications that allow us to have our cake and eat it too. On one hand, we can build SPAs with powerful client-side navigation, while on the other hand we can also encapsulate features in separate child routing components and load them only on demand.

This power and flexibility of the Angular router give us the ability to meet user expectations by closely mapping our application's behavior and responsiveness to the ways they will use the application. In this case, we have leveraged these capabilities to achieve what we set out to do: immediately load *Workout Runner* so that our users can get to work on their exercises right away, but avoid the overhead of loading *Workout Builder* and instead only serve it when a user wants to build a workout.

Now that we have the routing configuration in place in the *Workout Builder*, we will turn our attention to building out the sub-level and left navigation; this will enable us to use this routing. The next sections cover implementing this navigation.

Integrating sub- and side-level navigation

The basic idea around integrating sub- and side-level navigation into the app is to provide context-aware sub-views that change based on the active view. For example, when we are on a list page as opposed to editing an item, we may want to show different elements in the navigation. An e-commerce site is a great example of this. Imagine Amazon's search result page and product detail page. As the context changes from a list of products to a specific product, the navigation elements that are loaded also change.

Sub-level navigation

We'll start by adding sub-level navigation to the *Workout Builder*. We have already imported our `SubNavMainComponent` into the *Workout Builder*. But, currently it is just displaying placeholder content:

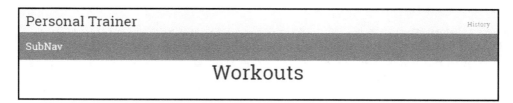

We'll now replace that content with three router links: **Home**, **New Workout**, and **New Exercise**.

Open the `sub-nav-main.component.html` file and change the HTML in it to the following:

```
<nav class="navbar fixed-top navbar-dark bg-primary mt-5">
    <div>
        <a [routerLink]="['/builder/workouts']" class="btn btn-primary">
        <span class="ion-md-home"></span> Home
        </a>
        <a [routerLink]="['/builder/workout/new']" class="btn btn-primary">
        <span class="ion-md-add"></span> New Workout
        </a>
        <a [routerLink]="['/builder/exercise/new']" class="btn btn-
primary">
        <span class="ion-md-add"></span> New Exercise
        </a>
    </div>
</nav>
```

Now, rerun the application and you will see the three navigation links. If we click on the **New Exercise** link button, we will be routed to `ExerciseComponent` and its view will appear in the **Router Outlet** in the *Workout Builder* view:

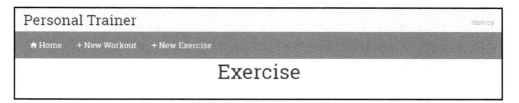

The **New Workout** link button will work in a similar fashion; when clicked on, it will take the user to the `WorkoutComponent` and display its view in the router outlet. Clicking on the **Home** link button will return the user to the `WorkoutsComponent` and view.

Side navigation

Side-level navigation within the *Workout Builder* will vary depending on the child component that we navigate to. For instance, when we first navigate to the *Workout Builder*, we are taken to the **Workouts** screen because the `WorkoutsComponent` route is the default route for the *Workout Builder*. That component will need side navigation; it will allow us to select to view a list of workouts or a list of exercises.

The component-based nature of Angular gives us an easy way to implement these context-sensitive menus. We can define new components for each of the menus and then import them into the components that need them. In this case, we have three components that will need side menus: **Workouts**, **Exercises**, and **Workout**. The first two of these components can actually use the same menu so we really only need two side menu components: `LeftNavMainComponent`, which will be like the preceding menu and will be used by the `Exercises` and `Workouts` components, and `LeftNavExercisesComponent`, which will contain a list of existing exercises and will be used by the `Workouts` component.

We already have files for the two menu components, including template files, and have imported them into `WorkoutBuilderModule`. We will now integrate these into the components that need them.

First, modify the `workouts.component.html` template to add the selector for the menu:

```
<div class="row">
    <div>
        <abe-left-nav-main></abe-left-nav-main>
    </div>
    <div class="col-sm-10 builder-content">
        <h1 class="text-center">Workouts</h1>
    </div>
</div>
```

Then, replace the placeholder text in the `left-nav-main.component.html` with the navigation links to `WorkoutsComponent` and `ExercisesComponent`:

```
<div class="left-nav-bar">
    <div class="list-group">
        <a [routerLink]="['/builder/workouts']" class="list-group-item
list-group-item-action">Workouts</a>
        <a [routerLink]="['/builder/exercises']" class="list-group-item
```

```
list-group-item-action">Exercises</a>
    </div>
</div>
```

Run the application and you should see the following:

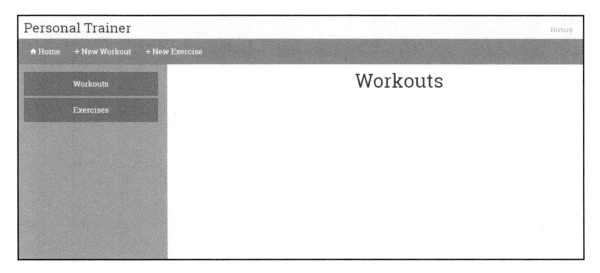

Follow the exact same steps to complete the side menu for the Exercises component.

 We won't show the code for this menu here, but you can find it in the
workout-builder/exercises folder under trainer/src/app in
checkpoint 4.3 of the GitHub repository.

For the menu for the **Workout** screen, the steps are the same except that you should change
left-nav-exercises.component.html to the following:

```
<div class="left-nav-bar">
  <h3>Exercises</h3>
</div>
```

We will use this template as the starting point for building out a list of exercises that will
appear on the left-hand side of the screen and can be selected for inclusion in a workout.

Implementing workout and exercise lists

Even before we start implementing the **Workout** and **Exercise** list pages, we need a data store for exercise and workout data. The current plan is to have an in-memory data store and expose it using an Angular service. In Chapter 3, *Supporting Server Data Persistence*, where we talk about server interaction, we will move this data to a server store for long-term persistence. For now, the in-memory store will suffice. Let's add the store implementation.

WorkoutService as a workout and exercise repository

The plan here is to create a WorkoutService instance that is responsible for exposing the exercise and workout data across the two applications. The main responsibilities of the service include:

- **Exercise-related CRUD operations**: Get all exercises, get a specific exercise based on its name, create an exercise, update an exercise, and delete it
- **Workout-related CRUD operations**: These are similar to the exercise-related operations, but targeted toward the workout entity

The code is available to download on GitHub at https://github.com/chandermani/angular6byexample. The branch to download is as follows: **GitHub Branch: checkpoint4.4** (folder trainer). If you are not using Git, download the snapshot of Checkpoint 4.4 (a ZIP file) from the following GitHub location: https://github.com/chandermani/angular6byexample/archive/checkpoint4.4.zip. Refer to the README.md file in the trainer folder when setting up the snapshot for the first time. Again, if you are working along with us as we build the application, be sure to update the styles.css file, which we are not discussing here. Because some of the files in this section are rather long, rather than showing the code here, we are also going to suggest at times that you simply copy the files into your solution.

Locate `workout-service.ts` in the `trainer/src/core` folder. The code in that file should look like the following, except for the implementation of the two methods `setupInitialExercises` and `setupInitialWorkouts`, which we have left out because of their length:

```
import {Injectable} from '@angular/core';
import {ExercisePlan} from './model';
import {WorkoutPlan} from './model';
import {Exercise} from "./model";
import { CoreModule } from './core.module';

@Injectable({
  providedIn: CoreModule
})
export class WorkoutService {
    workouts: Array<WorkoutPlan> = [];
    exercises: Array<Exercise> = [];

    constructor() {
        this.setupInitialExercises();
        this.setupInitialWorkouts();
    }

    getExercises(){
        return this.exercises;
    }

    getWorkouts(){
        return this.workouts;
    }
    setupInitialExercises(){
     // implementation of in-memory store.
    }

    setupInitialWorkouts(){
     // implementation of in-memory store.
    }
}}
```

As we have mentioned before, the implementation of an Angular service is straightforward. Here, we are declaring a class with the name `WorkoutService` and decorating it with `@Injectable`. Within the `@Injectable` decorator, we have set the `provided-in` property to `CoreModule`. This registers `WorkoutService` as a provider with Angular's **Dependency Injection** framework and makes it available throughout our application.

In the class definition, we first create two arrays: one for `Workouts` and one for `Exercises`. These arrays are of types `WorkoutPlan` and `Exercise` respectively, and we, therefore, need to import `WorkoutPlan` and `Exericse` from `model.ts` to get the type definitions for them.

The constructor calls two methods to set up the **Workouts** and **Services List**. At the moment, we are just using an in-memory store that populates these lists with data.

The two methods, `getExercises` and `getWorkouts`, as the names suggest, return a list of exercises and workouts respectively. Since we plan to use the in-memory store to store workout and exercise data, the `Workouts` and `Exercises` arrays store this data. As we go along, we will be adding more functions to the service.

Time to build out the components for the workout and exercise lists!

Workout and exercise list components

First, open the `workouts.component.ts` file in the `trainer/src/app/workout-builder/workouts` folder and update the imports as follows:

```
import { Component, OnInit } from '@angular/core';
import { Router } from '@angular/router';

import { WorkoutPlan } from '../../core/model';
import { WorkoutService } from '../../core/workout.service';;
```

This new code imports the Angular `Router` as well as `WorkoutService` and the `WorkoutPlan` type.

Next, replace the class definition with the following code:

```
export class WorkoutsComponent implements OnInit {
    workoutList:Array<WorkoutPlan> = [];

    constructor(
        public router:Router,
```

```
        public workoutService:WorkoutService) {}

    ngOnInit() {
        this.workoutList = this.workoutService.getWorkouts();
    }

    onSelect(workout: WorkoutPlan) {
        this.router.navigate( ['./builder/workout', workout.name] );
    }
}
```

This code adds a constructor into which we are injecting the `Router` and the `WorkoutService`. The `ngOnInit` method then calls the `getWorkouts` method on the `WorkoutService` and populates a `workoutList` array with a list of `WorkoutPlans` returned from that method call. We'll use that `workoutList` array to populate the list of workout plans that will display in the `Workouts` component's view.

You'll notice that we are putting the code for calling `WorkoutService` into the `ngOnInit` method. We want to avoid placing this code in the constructor. Eventually, we will be replacing the in-memory store that this service uses with a call to an external data store and we do not want the instantiation of our component to be affected by this call. Adding these method calls to the constructor would also complicate testing the component.

To avoid such unintended side effects, we instead place the code in the `ngOnInit` method. This method implements one of Angular's lifecycle hooks, `OnInit`, which Angular calls after creating an instance of the service. This way, we rely on Angular to call this method in a predictable way that does not affect the instantiation of the component.

Next, we'll make almost identical changes to the `Exercises` component. As with the `Workouts` component, this code injects the workout service into our component. This time, we then use the workout service to retrieve the exercises.

 As it is similar to the `Workouts` component, we won't show that code here. Just add it from the `workout-builder/exercises` folder in `checkpoint 4.4`.

Workout and exercise list views

Now, we need to implement the list views that have so far been empty!

In this section, we will be updating the code from `checkpoint 4.3` with `checkpoint 4.4`. So if you are coding along with us, simply follow the steps laid out in this section. If you want to see the finished code, then just copy the files from `checkpoint 4.4` into your solution.

Workouts list views

To get the view working, open `workouts.component.html` and add the following markup:

```
<div class="row">
    <div>
        <abe-left-nav-main></abe-left-nav-main>
    </div>
    <div class="col-sm-10 builder-content">
        <h1 class="text-center">Workouts</h1>
        <div *ngFor="let workout of workoutList|orderBy:'title'"
class="workout tile" (click)="onSelect(workout)">
            <div class="title">{{workout.title}}</div>
            <div class="stats">
                <span class="duration" title="Duration"><span class="ion-md-
time"></span> - {{(workout.totalWorkoutDuration?
workout.totalWorkoutDuration(): 0)|secondsToTime}}</span>
                <span class="float-right" title="Exercise Count"><span
class="ion-md-list"></span> - {{workout.exercises.length}}</span>
            </div>
        </div>
    </div>
</div>
```

We are using one of the Angular core directives, `ngFor`, to loop through the list of workouts and display them in a list on the page. We add the `*` sign in front of `ngFor` to identify it as an Angular directive. Using a `let` statement, we assign `workout` as a local variable that we use to iterate through the workout list and identify the values to be displayed for each workout (for example, `workout.title`). We then use one of our custom pipes, `orderBy`, to display a list of workouts in alphabetical order by title. We are also using another custom pipe, `secondsToTime`, to format the time displayed for the total workout duration.

If you are coding along with us, you will need to move the
secondsToTime pipe into the shared folder and include it in the
SharedModule. Then, add SharedModule to WorkoutBuilderModule as
an additional import. That change has already been made in checkpoint
4.4 in the GitHub repository.

Finally, we bind the click event to the following onSelect method that we add to our
component:

```
onSelect(workout: WorkoutPlan) {
    this.router.navigate( ['/builder/workout', workout.name] );
}
```

This sets up navigation to the workout details page. This navigation happens when we click
on an item in the workout list. The selected workout name is passed as part of the
route/URL to the workout detail page.

Go ahead and refresh the builder page (/builder/workouts); one workout is listed, the 7
Minute Workout. Click on the tile for that workout. You'll be taken to the **Workout** screen
and the workout name, 7MinWorkout, will appear at the end of the URL:

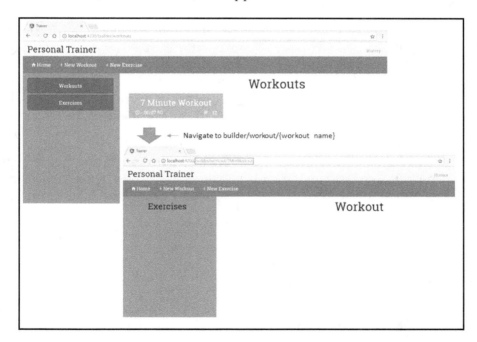

The Workout screen

Exercises list views

We are going to follow the same approach for the `Exercises` list view as we did for the `Workouts` list view, except that in this case, we will actually be implementing two views: one for the `Exercises` component (which will display in the main content area when a user navigates to that component) and one for the `LeftNavExercisesComponent` exercises context menu (which will display when the user navigates to the `Workouts` component to create or edit a workout).

For the `Exercises` component, we will follow an approach that is almost identical to what we did to display a list of workouts in the `Workouts` component. So, we won't show that code here. Just add the files for `exercises.component.ts` and `exercises.component.html` from `checkpoint 4.4`.

When you are done copying the files, click on the **Exercises** link in the left navigation to load the 12 exercises that you have already configured in `WorkoutService`.

As with the `Workouts` list, this sets up the navigation to the exercise detail page. Clicking on an item in the exercises list takes us to the exercise detail page. The selected exercise name is passed as part of the route/URL to the exercise detail page.

In the final list view, we will add a list of exercises that will display in the left context menu for the *Workout Builder* screen. This view is loaded in the left navigation when we create or edit a workout. Using Angular's component-based approach, we will update the `leftNavExercisesComponent` and its related view to provide this functionality. Just add the files for `left-nav-exercises.component.ts` and `left-nav-exercises.component.html` from the `trainer/src/app/navigation` folder in `checkpoint 4.4`.

Once you are done copying those files, click on the **New Workout** button on the sub-navigation menu in the *Workout Builder* and you will now see a list of exercises displayed in the left navigation menu—exercises that we have already configured in `WorkoutService`.

Time to add the ability to load, save, and update exercise/workout data!

Building a workout

The core functionality *Personal Trainer* provides centers around workout and exercise building. Everything is there to support these two functions. In this section, we focus on building and editing workouts using Angular.

The `WorkoutPlan` model has already been defined, so we are aware of the elements that constitute a workout. The *Workout Builder* page facilitates user input and lets us build/persist workout data.

Once complete, the *Workout Builder* page will look like this:

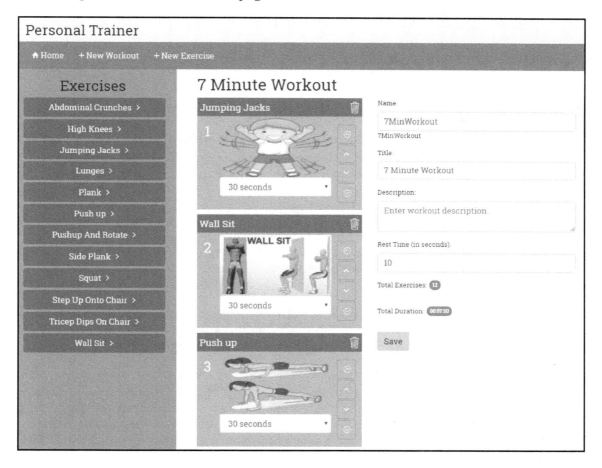

The page has a left navigation that lists all the exercises that can be added to the workout. Clicking on the arrow icon on the right adds the exercise to the end of the workout.

The center area is designated for workout building. It consists of exercise tiles laid out in order from top to bottom and a form that allows the user to provide other details about the workout such as name, title, description, and rest duration.

This page operates in two modes:

- **Create/New**: This mode is used for creating a new workout. The URL is `#/builder/workout/new`.
- **Edit**: This mode is used for editing the existing workout. The URL is `#/builder/workout/:id`, where `:id` maps to the name of the workout.

With this understanding of the page elements and layout, it's time to build each of these elements. We will start with left nav (navigation).

Finishing left nav

At the end of the previous section, we updated the left navigation view for the `Workout` component to show a list of exercises. Our intention was to let the user click on an arrow next to an exercise to add it to the workout. At the time, we deferred implementing the `addExercise` method in the `LeftNavExercisesComponent` that was bound to that click event. Now, we will go ahead and do that.

We have a couple of options here. The `LeftNavExercisesComponent` is a child component of the `WorkoutComponent`, so we can implement child/parent inter-component communication to accomplish that. We covered this technique in the previous chapter while working on *7 Minute Workout*.

However, adding an exercise to the workout is part of a larger process of building the workout and using child/parent inter-component communication would make the implementation of the `AddExercise` method differ from the other functionality that we will be adding going forward.

For this reason, it makes more sense to follow another approach for sharing data, one that we can use consistently throughout the process of building a workout. That approach involves using a service. As we get into adding the other functionality for creating an actual workout, such as save/update logic and implementing the other relevant components, the benefits of going down the service route will become increasingly clear.

So, we introduce a new service into the picture: `WorkoutBuilderService`. The ultimate aim of `WorkoutBuilderService` service is to coordinate between `WorkoutService` (which retrieves and persists the workout) and the components (such as `LeftNavExercisesComponent` and others we will add later), while the workout is being built, hence reducing the amount of code in `WorkoutComponent` to the bare minimum.

Adding WorkoutBuilderService

WorkoutBuilderService monitors the state of the workout that a user of the application is building. It:

- Tracks the current workout
- Creates a new workout
- Loads the existing workout
- Saves the workout

Copy workout-builder-service.ts from the workout-builder/builder-services folder under trainer/src/app in checkpoint 4.5.

> The code is also available for everyone to download on GitHub at https://github.com/chandermani/angular6byexample. Checkpoints are implemented as branches in GitHub. The branch to download is as follows: GitHub Branch: checkpoint4.5 (folder—trainer). If you are not using Git, download the snapshot of Checkpoint 4.5 (a ZIP file) from the following GitHub location: https://github.com/chandermani/angular6byexample/archive/checkpoint4.5.zip. Refer to the README.md file in the trainer folder when setting up the snapshot for the first time. Again, if you are working along with us as we build the application, be sure to update the styles.css file, which we are not discussing here.

While we normally make services available application-wide, WorkoutBuilderService will only be used in the *Workout Builder* feature. Therefore, instead of registering it with the providers in AppModule, we have registered it in the provider array of WorkoutBuilderModule as follows (after adding it as an import at the top of the file):

```
@NgModule({
....
  providers: [WorkoutBuilderService]
})
```

Adding it as a provider here means that it will only be loaded when the *Workout Builder* feature is being accessed and it cannot be reached outside this module. This means that it can be evolved independently of other modules in the application and can be modified without affecting other parts of the application.

Let's look at some of the relevant parts of the service.

`WorkoutBuilderService` needs the type definitions for `WorkoutPlan`, `ExercisePlan`, and `WorkoutService`, so we import these into the component:

```
import { WorkoutPlan, ExercisePlan } from '../../core/model';
import { WorkoutService } from '../../core/workout.service';
```

`WorkoutBuilderService` has a dependency on `WorkoutService` to provide persistence and querying capabilities. We resolve this dependency by injecting `WorkoutService` into the constructor for `WorkoutBuilderService`:

```
constructor(public workoutService: WorkoutService) {}
```

`WorkoutBuilderService` also needs to track the workout being built. We use the `buildingWorkout` property for this. The tracking starts when we call the `startBuilding` method on the service:

```
startBuilding(name: string){
    if(name){
        this.buildingWorkout = this.workoutService.getWorkout(name)
        this.newWorkout = false;
    }else{
        this.buildingWorkout = new WorkoutPlan("", "", 30, []);
        this.newWorkout = true;
    }
    return this.buildingWorkout;
}
```

The basic idea behind this tracking function is to set up a `WorkoutPlan` object (`buildingWorkout`) that will be made available to components to manipulate the workout details. The `startBuilding` method takes the workout name as a parameter. If the name is not provided, it implies we are creating a new workout, and hence a new `WorkoutPlan` object is created and assigned; if not, we load the workout details by calling `WorkoutService.getWorkout(name)`. In any case, the `buildingWorkout` object has the workout being worked on.

The `newWorkout` object signifies whether the workout is new or an existing one. It is used to differentiate between save and update situations when the `save` method on this service is called.

The rest of the methods, removeExercise, addExercise, and moveExerciseTo, are self-explanatory and affect the exercise list that is part of the workout (buildingWorkout).

WorkoutBuilderService is calling a new method, getWorkout, on WorkoutService, which we have not added yet. Go ahead and copy the getWorkout implementation from the workout-service.ts file in the services folder under trainer/src in checkpoint 4.5. We will not dwell on the new service code as the implementation is quite simple.

Let's get back to left nav and implement the remaining functionality.

Adding exercises using ExerciseNav

To add exercises to the workout we are building, we just need to import WorkoutBuilderService and ExercisePlan, inject WorkoutBuilderService into the LeftNavExercisesComponent, and call its addExercise method, passing the selected exercise as a parameter:

```
constructor(
    public workoutService:WorkoutService,
    public workoutBuilderService:WorkoutBuilderService) {}
. . .
addExercise(exercise:Exercise) {
    this.workoutBuilderService.addExercise(new ExercisePlan(exercise, 30));
}
```

Internally, WorkoutBuilderService.addExercise updates the buildingWorkout model data with the new exercise.

The preceding implementation is a classic case of sharing data between independent components. The shared service exposes the data in a controlled manner to any component that requests it. While sharing data, it is always a good practice to expose the state/data using methods instead of directly exposing the data object. We can see that in our component and service implementations too. LeftNavExercisesComponent does not update the workout data directly; in fact, it does not have direct access to the workout being built. Instead, it relies upon the service method, addExercise, to change the current workout's exercise list.

Since the service is shared, there are pitfalls to be aware of. As services are injectable through the system, we cannot stop any component from taking dependency on any service and calling its functions in an inconsistent manner, leading to undesired results or bugs. For example, `WorkoutBuilderService` needs to be initialized by calling `startBuilding` before `addExercise` is called. What happens if a component calls `addExercise` before the initialization takes place?

Implementing the Workout component

The `WorkoutComponent` is responsible for managing a workout. This includes creating, editing, and viewing the workout. Due to the introduction of `WorkoutBuilderService`, the overall complexity of this component will be reduced. Other than the primary responsibility of integrating with, exposing, and interacting with its template view, we will delegate most of the other work to `WorkoutBuilderService`.

The `WorkoutComponent` is associated with two `routes/views`, namely `/builder/workout/new` and `/builder/workout/:id`. These routes handle both creating and editing workout scenarios. The first job of the component is to load or create the workout that it needs to manipulate.

Route parameters

But before we get to building out the `WorkoutComponent` and its associated view, we need to touch briefly on the navigation that brings a user to the screen for that component. This component handles both creating and editing workout scenarios. The first job of the component is to load or create the workout that it needs to manipulate. We plan to use Angular's routing framework to pass the necessary data to the component, so that it will know whether it is editing an existing workout or creating a new one, and in the case of an existing workout, which component it should be editing.

How is this done? The `WorkoutComponent` is associated with two routes, namely `/builder/workout/new` and `/builder/workout/:id`. The difference in these two routes lies in what is at the end of these routes; in one case, it is `/new`, and in the other, `/:id`. These are called **route parameters.** The `:id` in the second route is a token for a route parameter. The router will convert the token to the ID for the workout component. As we saw earlier, this means that the URL that will be passed to the component in the case of *7 Minute Workout* will be `/builder/workout/7MinuteWorkout`.

How do we know that this workout name is the right parameter for the ID? As you recall, when we set up the event for handling a click on the **Workout** tiles on the **Workouts** screen that takes us to the **Workout** screen, we designated the workout name as the parameter for the ID, like so:

```
onSelect(workout: WorkoutPlan) {
    this.router.navigate( ['./builder/workout', workout.name] );
}
```

Here, we are constructing the route using the programmatic interface for the router. The `router.navigate` method accepts an array. This is called the **link parameters array**. The first item in the array is the path of the route, and the second is a route parameter that specifies the ID of the workout. In this case, we set the `id` parameter to the workout name. We can also construct the same type of URL as part of a router link or simply enter it in the browser to get to the **Workouts** screen and edit a particular workout.

The other of the two routes ends with `/new`. Since this route does not have a `token` parameter, the router will simply pass the URL unmodified to the `WorkoutComponent`. The `WorkoutComponent` will then need to parse the incoming URL to identify that it should be creating a new component.

Route guards

But before the link takes the user to the `WorkoutComponent`, there is another step along the way that we need to consider. The possibility always exists that the ID that is passed in the URL for editing a workout could be incorrect or missing. In those cases, we do not want the component to load, but instead, we want to have the user redirected to another page or back to where they came from.

Angular offers a way to accomplish this result with **route guards**. As the name implies, route guards **provide a way to prevent navigation to a route**. A route guard can be used to inject custom logic that can do things such as check authorization, load data, and make other verifications to determine whether the navigation to the component needs to be canceled or not. And all of this is done before the component loads so it is never seen if the routing is canceled.

Angular offers several route guards, including `CanActivate`, `CanActivateChild`, `CanDeActivate`, `Resolve`, and `CanLoad`. At this point, we are interested in the `Resolve` route guard. The `Resolve` guard will allow us not only to check for the existence of a workout, but also to load the data associated with a workout before loading the `WorkoutComponent`. The advantage of doing the latter is that we avoid the necessity of checking to make sure the data is loaded in the `WorkoutComponent` and it eliminates adding conditional logic throughout its component template to make sure that the data is there when it is rendered. This will be especially useful when in the next chapter when we start using `observables` where we must wait for the observable to complete before we are guaranteed of having the data that it will provide. The `Resolve` guard will handle waiting for the observable to complete, which means that the `WorkoutComponent` will be guaranteed to have the data that it needs before it loads.

Implementing the resolve route guard

The `Resolve` guard allows us to prefetch the data for a workout. In our case, what we want to do is use `Resolve` to check the validity of any ID that is passed for an existing workout. Specifically, we will run a check on that ID by making a call to the `WorkoutBuilderService` to retrieve the Workout Plan and see if it exists. If it exists, we will load the data associated with the Workout Plan so that it is available to the `WorkoutComponent`; if not we will redirect back to the Workouts screen.

Copy `workout.resolver.ts` from the `workout-builder/workout` folder under `trainer/src/app/workout` in `checkpoint 4.5` and you will see the following code:

```
import 'rxjs/add/operator/map';
import 'rxjs/add/operator/take';
import { Injectable } from '@angular/core';
import { Observable } from 'rxjs/Observable';
import { Router, Resolve, RouterStateSnapshot,
        ActivatedRouteSnapshot } from '@angular/router';
import { WorkoutPlan } from '../../core/model';
import { WorkoutBuilderService } from '../builder-services/workout-builder.service';


@Injectable()
export class WorkoutResolver implements Resolve<WorkoutPlan> {
  public workout: WorkoutPlan;

  constructor(
    public workoutBuilderService: WorkoutBuilderService,
    public router: Router) {}
```

```
resolve(
  route: ActivatedRouteSnapshot,
  state: RouterStateSnapshot): WorkoutPlan {
  let workoutName = route.paramMap.get('id');

  if (!workoutName) {
      workoutName = '';
  }

  this.workout = this.workoutBuilderService.startBuilding(workoutName);

  if (this.workout) {
      return this.workout;
  } else { // workoutName not found
      this.router.navigate(['/builder/workouts']);
      return null;
  }
  }
}
```

As you can see, the WorkoutResolver is an injectable class that implements the Resolve interface. The code injects the WorkoutBuilderService and Router into the class and implements the interface with the resolve method. The resolve method accepts two parameters; ActivatedRouteSnapshot and RouterStateSnapshot. In this case, we are only interested in the first of these two parameters, ActivatedRouteSnapshot. It contains a paramMap from which we extract the ID parameter for the route.

The resolve method then calls the startBuilding method of WorkoutBuildingService using the parameter supplied in the route. If the workout exists, then resolve returns the data and the navigation proceeds; if not, it re-routes the user to the workouts page and returns false. If new is passed as an ID, WorkoutBuilderService will load a new workout and the Resolve guard will allow navigation to proceed to the WorkoutComponent.

The resolve method can return a Promise , an Observable, or a synchronous value. If we return an Observable, we will need to make sure that the Observable completes before proceeding with navigation. In this case, however, we are making a synchronous call to a local in-memory data store, so we are just returning a value.

To complete the implementation of the `WorkoutResolver`, first make sure to import and add it to `WorkoutBuilderModule` as a provider:

```
....
import { WorkoutResolver } from './workout/workout.resolver';

@NgModule({
....
  providers: [WorkoutBuilderService, WorkoutResolver]
})
....
```

Then, add it to the route configuration for `WorkoutComponent` by updating `workout-builder-routing.module.ts` as follows:

```
....
import { WorkoutResolver } from './workout/workout.resolver';
....
const routes: Routes = [
  {
    path: '',
    component: WorkoutBuilderComponent,
    children: [
        {path: '', pathMatch: 'full', redirectTo: 'workouts'},
        {path: 'workouts', component: WorkoutsComponent },
        {path: 'workout/new', component: WorkoutComponent, resolve: {
workout: WorkoutResolver} },
        {path: 'workout/:id', component: WorkoutComponent, resolve: {
workout: WorkoutResolver} },
        {path: 'exercises', component: ExercisesComponent},
        {path: 'exercise/new', component: ExerciseComponent },
        {path: 'exercise/:id', component: ExerciseComponent }
    ]
  },
];
```

As you can see, we add `WorkoutResolver` to the routing module's imports. Then, we add `resolve { workout: WorkoutResolver }` to the end of the route configuration for `workout/new` and `workout/:id`. This instructs the router to use the `WorkoutResolver` resolve method and assign its return value to `workout` in the route's data. This configuration means that `WorkoutResolver` will be called prior to the router navigating to `WorkoutComponent` and that the workout data will be available to the `WorkoutComponent` when it loads. We'll see how to extract this data in the `WorkoutComponent` in the next section.

Implementing the Workout component continued...

Now that we have established the routing that takes us to the `Workout` component, let's turn to completing its implementation. So, copy the `workout.component.ts` file from the `workout-builder/workout` folder under `trainer/src/app` in checkpoint `4.5`. (Also, copy `workout-builder.module.ts` from the `workout-builder` folder. We'll discuss the changes in this file a little later when we get to Angular forms.)

Open `workout.component.ts` and you'll see that we have added a constructor that injects `ActivatedRoute` and `WorkoutBuilderService`:

```
constructor(
public route: ActivatedRoute,
public workoutBuilderService:WorkoutBuilderService){ }
```

In addition, we have added the following `ngOnInit` method:

```
ngOnInit() {
    this.sub = this.route.data
        .subscribe(
          (data: { workout: WorkoutPlan }) => {
            this.workout = data.workout;
          }
        );
}
```

The method subscribes to the `route` and extracts the `workout` from the `route.data`. There is no need to check the workout exists because we have already done that in the `WorkoutResolver`.

 We are subscribing to the `route.data` because as an `ActivatedRoute`, the `route` exposes its `data` as an `Observable`, which can change during the lifetime of the component. This gives us the ability to reuse the same component instance with different parameters, even though the `OnInit` life cycle event for that component is called only once. We'll cover `Observables` in detail in the next chapter.

In addition to this code, we have also added a series of methods to the `Workout Component` for adding, removing, and moving a workout. These methods all call corresponding methods on the `WorkoutBuilderService` and we will not review them in detail here. We've also added an array of `durations` for populating the duration drop-down list.

For now, this is enough for the **component** class implementation. Let's update the associated `Workout` template.

Implementing the Workout template

Now, copy the `workout.component.html` files from the `workout-builder/workout` folder under `trainer/src/app` in `checkpoint 4.5`. Run the app, navigate to `/builder/workouts`, and double-click on the *7 Minute Workout* tile. This should load the *7 Minute Workout* details with a view similar to the one shown at the start of the *Building a workout* section.

 In the event of any problem, you can refer to the `checkpoint 4.5` code in the `GitHub repository: Branch: checkpoint 4.5` (folder - `trainer`).

We will be dedicating a lot of time to this view, so let's understand some specifics here.

The exercise list div (`id="exercise-list"`) lists the exercises that are part of the workout in order. We display them as top-to-bottom tiles in the left part of the content area. Functionally, this template has:

- The **Delete** button to delete the exercise
- Reorder buttons to move the exercise up and down the list, as well as to the top and bottom

We use `ngFor` to iterate over the list of exercises and display them:

```
<div *ngFor="let exercisePlan of workout.exercises; let i=index"
class="exercise-item">
```

You will notice that we are using the * asterisk in front of `ngFor`, which is shorthand for the `<template>` tag. We are also using `let` to set two local variables: `exerisePlan` to identify an item in the list of exercises and `i` to set up an index value that we will use to show a number for the exercises as they are displayed on the screen. We will also use the index value to manage reordering and deleting exercises from the list.

The second div element for workout data (`id="workout-data"`) contains the HTML input element for details such as name, title, and rest duration, and a button to save workout changes.

The complete list has been wrapped inside the HTML form element so that we can make use of the form-related capabilities that Angular provides. So, what are these capabilities?

Angular forms

Forms are such an integral part of HTML development that any framework that targets client-side development just cannot ignore them. Angular provides a small but well-defined set of constructs that make standard form-based operations easier.

If we think carefully, any form of interaction boils down to:

- Allowing user inputs
- Validating those inputs against business rules
- Submitting the data to the backend server

Angular has something to offer for all the preceding use cases.

For user input, it allows us to create two-way bindings between the form input elements and the underlying model, hence avoiding any boilerplate code that we may have to write for model input synchronization.

It also provides constructs to validate the input before it can be submitted.

Lastly, Angular provides HTTP services for client-server interaction and persisting data to the server. We'll cover those services in `Chapter 3`, *Supporting Server Data Persistence*.

Since the first two use cases are our main focus in this chapter, let's learn more about Angular user input and data validation support.

Template-driven and reactive forms

Angular offers two types of forms: **template-driven** and **reactive**. We'll be discussing both types of form in this chapter. Because the Angular team indicates that many of us will primarily use **template-driven forms**, that is what we will start in this chapter.

Template-driven forms

As the name suggests, **template-driven forms** place the emphasis on developing a form within an HTML template and handling most of the logic for the form inputs, data validation, saving, and updating in-form directives placed within that template. The result is that very little form-related code is required in the component class that is associated with the form's template.

Template-driven forms make heavy use of the ngModel form directive. We will be discussing it in the next sections. It provides two-way data binding for form controls, which is a nice feature indeed. It allows us to write much less boilerplate code to implement a form. It also helps us to manage the state of the form (such as whether the form controls have changed and whether these changes have been saved). And, it also gives us the ability to easily construct messages that display if the validation requirements for a form control have not been met (for example, a required field not provided, email not in the right format, and so on).

Getting started

In order to use Angular forms in our Workout component, we must first add some additional configuration. Open workout-buider.module.ts from the workout-builder folder under trainer/src/app in checkpoint 4.5. You will see that it imports FormsModule:

```
....
import { FormsModule } from '@angular/forms';
....
@NgModule({
    imports: [
        CommonModule,
        FormsModule,
        SharedModule,
        workoutBuilderRouting
    ],
```

This brings in all that we will need to implement our form, including:

- NgForm
- ngModel

Let's start using these to build our form.

Using NgForm

In our template (`workout.component.html`), we have added the following `form` tag:

```
<form #f="ngForm" class="row" name="formWorkout"
(ngSubmit)="save(f.form)">. . .
</form>
```

Let's take a look at what we have here. One interesting thing is that we are still using a standard `<form>` tag and not a special Angular tag. We've also used # to define a local variable `f` to which we have assigned `ngForm`. Creating this local variable provides us with the convenience of being able to use it for form-related activity in other places within the form. For example, you can see that we are using it at the end of the opening `form` tag in a parameter, `f.form`, which is being passed to the `onSubmit` event bound to `(ngSubmit)`.

That last binding to `(ngSubmit)` should tell us that something different is going on here. Even though we did not explicitly add the `NgForm` directive, our `<form>` now has additional events such as `ngSubmit` to which we can bind actions. How did this happen? Well, this was not triggered by our assigning `ngForm` to a local variable. Instead, it happened *automagically* because we imported the forms module into `workout-builder.module.ts`.

With that import in place, Angular scanned our template for a `<form>` tag and wrapped that `<form>` tag within an `NgForm` directive. The Angular documentation indicates that `<form>` elements in the component will be upgraded to use the Angular form system. This is important because it means that various capabilities of `NgForm` are now available to use with the form. These include the `ngSubmit` event, which signals when a user has triggered a form submission and provides the ability to validate the entire form before submitting it.

ngModel

One of the fundamental building blocks for template-driven forms is ngModel, and you will find it being used throughout our form. One of the primary roles of ngModel is to support two-way binding between user input and an underlying model. With such a setup, changes in the model are reflected in the view, and updates to the view too are reflected back on the model. Most of the other directives that we have covered so far only support one-way binding from models to views. ngModel goes both ways. But, be aware that it is only available within NgForm for use with elements that allow user input.

As you know, we already have a model that we are using for the **Workout** page, WorkoutPlan. Here is the WorkoutPlan model from model.ts:

```
export class WorkoutPlan {
  constructor(
    public name: string,
    public title: string,
    public restBetweenExercise: number,
    public exercises: ExercisePlan[],
    public description?: string) {
  }
totalWorkoutDuration(): number{
  . . . [code calculating the total duration of the workout]. . .
}
```

Note the use of the ? after description. This means that it is an optional property in our model and is not required to create a WorkoutPlan. In our form, this will mean that we will not require that a description be entered and everything will work fine without it.

Within the WorkoutPlan model, we also have a reference to an array made up of instances of another type of model: ExercisePlan. ExercisePlan in turn is made up of a number (duration) and another model (Exercise), which looks like this:

```
export class Exercise {
    constructor(
        public name: string,
        public title: string,
        public description: string,
        public image: string,
        public nameSound?: string,
        public procedure?: string,
        public videos?: Array<string>) { }
}
```

The use of these nested classes shows that we can create complex hierarchies of models that can all be data-bound within our form using NgModel. So throughout the form, whenever we need to update one of the values in a WorkoutPlan or an ExercisePlan, we can use NgModel to do that (the WorkoutPlan model will be represented by a local variable named workout in the following examples).

Using ngModel with input and textarea

Open workout-component.html and look for ngModel. It has been applied to form elements that allow user data input. These include input, textarea, and select. The workout name input setup looks like this:

```
<input type="text" name="workoutName" class="form-control" id="workout-
name" placeholder="Enter workout name. Must be unique."
[(ngModel)]="workout.name">
```

The preceding [(ngModel)] directive sets up a two-way binding between the input control and the workout.name model property. The brackets and parentheses should each look familiar. Previously, we used them separately from each other: the [] brackets for property binding and the () parentheses for event binding. In the latter case, we usually bound the event to a call to a method in the component associated with the template. You can see an example of this in the form with the button that a user clicks on to remove an exercise:

```
<span class="btn float-right trashcan"
(click)="removeExercise(exercisePlan)"><span class="ion-ios-trash-
outline"></span></span>
```

Here, the click event is explicitly bound to a method called removeExercise in our Workout component class. But for the workout.name input, we do not have an explicit binding to a method on the component. So what's going on here and how does the update happen without us calling a method on the component? The answer to that question is that the combination [( )] is shorthand for both binding a model property to the input element and wiring up an event that updates the model.

Put differently, if we reference a model element in our form, ngModel is smart enough to know that what we want to do is update that element (workout.name here) when a user enters or changes the data in the input field to which it is bound. Under the hood, Angular creates an update method similar to what we would otherwise have to write ourselves. Nice! This approach keeps us from having to write repetitive code to update our model.

Angular supports most of the HTML5 input types, including text, number, select, radio, and checkbox. This means binding between a model and any of these input types just works out of the box.

The `textarea` element works the same as the input:

```
<textarea name="description" . . .
[(ngModel)]="workout.description"></textarea>
```

Here, we bind `textarea` to `workout.description`. Under the hood, `ngModel` updates the workout description in our model with every change we type into the text area.

To test out how this works, why don't we verify this binding? Add a model interpolation expression at the end of any of the linked inputs, such as this one:

```
<input type="text". . . [(ngModel)]="workout.name">{{workout.name}}
```

Open the **Workout** page, type something in the input, and see how the interpolation is updated instantaneously. The magic of two-way binding!

Using ngModel with select

Let's look at how `select` has been set up:

```
<select . . . name="duration" [(ngModel)]="exercisePlan.duration">
    <option *ngFor="let duration of durations"
[value]="duration.value">{{duration.title}}</option>
</select>
```

We are using `ngFor` here to bind to an array, `durations`, which is in the `Workout` component class. The array looks like this:

```
[{ title: "15 seconds", value: 15 },
 { title: "30 seconds", value: 30 }, ...]
```

The `ngFor` component will loop over the array and populate the drop-down values with the corresponding values in the array with the title for each item being displayed using interpolation, `{{duration.title}}`. And `[(ngModel)]` then binds the drop-down selection to the `exercisePlan.duration` in the model.

Notice here that we are binding to the nested model: `ExercisePlan`. And, we may have multiple exercises to which we will be applying this binding. With that being the case, we have to make use of another Angular form directive—`ngModelGroup`—to handle these bindings. `ngModelGroup` will allow us to create a nested group within our model that will contain the list of exercises included in the workout and then in turn loop over each exercise to bind its duration to the model.

To start with, we will add `ngModelGroup` to the div tag that we have created within the form to hold our list of exercises:

```
<div id="exercises-list" class="col-sm-2 exercise-list"
ngModelGroup="exercises">
```

That takes care of creating the nested list of exercises. Now, we have to handle the individual exercises within that list, and we can do that by adding another `ngModelGroup` to the individual divs that contain each exercise:

```
<div class="exercise tile" [ngModelGroup]="i">
```

Here, we are using the index in our for loop to dynamically create an individual model group for each of our exercises. These model groups will be nested inside the first model group that we created. Temporarily, add the tag `<pre>{{ f.value | json }}</pre>` to the bottom of the form and you will be able to see the structure of this nested model:

```
{
  "exercises": {
    "0": {
      "duration": 15
    },
    "1": {
      "duration": 60
    },
    "2": {
      "duration": 45
```

```
  },
  "exerciseCount": 3
},
"workoutName": "1minworkout",
"title": "1 Minute Workout",
"description": "desc",
"restBetweenExercise": 30
}
```

This is powerful stuff that enables us to create complicated forms with nested models, all of which can use ngModel for databinding.

 You may have noticed a subtle difference in the two ngModelGroup directive tags we just introduced. The second of the two is wrapped in angle brackets, [], while the first is not. This is because with the first tag we are just naming our model group, whereas with the second we are binding it dynamically to each exercise's div tag using the index of our for loop.

Like input, select too supports two-way binding. We saw how changing select updates a model, but the model-to-template binding may not be apparent. To verify that a model to a template binding works, open the *7 Minute Workout* app and verify the duration dropdowns. Each one has a value that is consistent with the model value (30 seconds).

Angular does an awesome job of keeping the model and view in sync using ngModel. Change the model and see the view updated; change the view and watch as the model is updated instantaneously.

Now, let's add validation to our form.

 The code for the next section is also available for everyone to download on GitHub at https://github.com/chandermani/angular6byexample. Checkpoints are implemented as branches in GitHub. The branch to download is as follows: GitHub Branch: checkpoint4.6 (folder—trainer). Or if you are not using Git, download the snapshot of Checkpoint 4.6 (a ZIP file) from the following GitHub location: https://github.com/chandermani/angular6byexample/archive/checkpoint4.6.zip. Refer to the README.md file in the trainer folder when setting up the snapshot for the first time. Again, if you are working along with us as we build the application, be sure and update the styles.css file, which we are not discussing here.

Angular validation

As the saying goes, *never trust user input*. Angular has support for validation, including the standard required, min, max, and pattern, as well as custom validators.

ngModel

ngModel is the building block that we will use to implement validation. It does two things for us: it maintains the model state and provides a mechanism for identifying validation errors and displaying validation messages.

To get started, we need to assign ngModel to a local variable in all of our form controls that we will be validating. In each case, we need to use a unique name for this local variable. For example, for workout name we add #name="ngModel" within the input tag for that control along with the HTML 5 required attribute. The workout name input tag should now look like this:

```
<input type="text" name="workoutName" #name="ngModel" class="form-control"
id="workout-name" placeholder="Enter workout name. Must be unique."
[(ngModel)]="workout.name" required>
```

Continue through the form, assigning ngModel to local variables for each of the inputs. Also, add the required attribute for all the required fields.

The Angular model state

Whenever we use NgForm, every element within our form, including input, text area, and select, has some states defined on the associated model. ngModel tracks these states for us. The states tracked are:

- pristine: The value of this is true as long as the user does not interact with the input. Any update to the input field and ng-pristine is set to false.

- dirty: This is the reverse of ng-pristine. This is true when the input data has been updated.

- touched: This is true if the control ever had focus.

- untouched: This is true if the control has never lost focus. This is just the reverse of ng-touched.

- `valid`: This is `true` if there are validations defined on the `input` element and none of them are failing.
- `invalid`: This is `true` if any of the validations defined on the element are failing.

`pristinedirty` or `toucheduntouched` are useful properties that can help us decide when error labels are shown.

Angular CSS classes

Based on the model state, Angular adds some CSS classes to an input element. These include the following:

- `ng-valid`: This is used if the model is valid
- `ng-invalid`: This is used if the model is invalid
- `ng-pristine`: This is used if the model is pristine
- `ng-dirty`: This is used if the model is dirty
- `ng-untouched`: This is used when the input is never visited
- `ng-touched`: This is used when the input has focus

To verify it, go back to the `workoutName` input tag and add a template reference variable named `spy` inside the `input` tag:

```
<input type="text" name="workoutName" #name="ngModel" class="form-control"
id="workout-name" placeholder="Enter workout name. Must be unique."
[(ngModel)]="workout.name" required #spy>
```

Then, below the tag, add the following label:

```
<label>{{spy.className}}</label>
```

Reload the application and click on the **New Workout** link in the *Workout Builder*. Before touching anything on the screen, you will see the following displayed:

> **Name:**
>
> Enter workout name. Must be unique.
>
> **form-control ng-untouched ng-pristine ng-invalid**

Add some content into the **Name** input box and tab away from it. The label changes to this:

What we are seeing here is Angular changing the CSS classes that apply to this control as the user interacts with it. You can also see these changes by inspecting the `input` element in the developer console.

These CSS class transitions are tremendously useful if we want to apply visual clues to the element depending on its state. For example, look at this snippet:

```
input.ng-invalid {  border:2px solid red; }
```

This draws a red border around any input control that has invalid data.

As you add more validations to the Workout page, you can observe (in the developer console) how these classes are added and removed as the user interacts with the `input` element.

Now that we have an understanding of model states and how to use them, let's get back to our discussion of validations (before moving on, remove the variable name and label that you just added).

Workout validation

The workout data needs to be validated for a number of conditions.

After taking the step of adding the local variable references for `ngModel` and the required attribute to our `input` fields, we have been able to see how `ngModel` tracks changes in the state of these controls and how it toggles the CSS styles.

Displaying appropriate validation messages

Now, the input needs to have a value; otherwise, the validation fails. But, how can we know if the validation has failed? `ngModel` comes to our rescue here. It can provide the validation state of the particular input. And that gives us what we need to display an appropriate validation message.

Let's go back to the input control for the Workout name. In order to get a validation message to display, we have to first modify the input tag to the following:

```
<input type="text" name="workoutName" #name="ngModel" class="form-control"
id="workout-name" placeholder="Enter workout name. Must be unique."
[(ngModel)]="workout.name" required>
```

We have added a local variable called `#name` and assigned `ngModel` to it. This is called a template reference variable and we can use it with the following label to display a validation message for the input:

```
<label *ngIf="name.control.hasError('required') && (name.touched)"
class="alert alert-danger validation-message">Name is required</label>
```

We are showing the validation message in the event that the name is not provided and the control has been touched. To check the first condition, we retrieve the `hasError` property of the control and see if the error type is `required`. We check to see if the name input has been `touched` because we do not want the message to display when the form first loads for a new workout.

 You will notice that we are using a somewhat more verbose style to identify validation errors than is required in this situation. Instead of `name.control.hasError('required')`, we could have used `!name.valid` and it would have worked perfectly fine. However, using the more verbose approach allows us to identify validation errors with greater specificity, which will be essential when we start adding multiple validators to our form controls. We'll look at using multiple validators a little later in this chapter. For consistency, we'll stick with the more verbose approach.

Load the new Workout page (`/builder/workouts/new`) now. Enter a value in the name input box and then delete it. The error label appears as shown in the following screenshot:

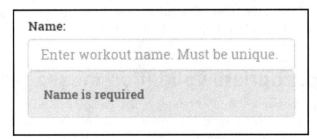

Adding more validation

Angular provides several out-of-the-box validators, including:

- `required`
- `minLength`
- `maxLength`
- `email`
- `pattern`

For the complete list of out-of-the box validators, see the documentation for the `Validators` class at `https://angular.io/api/forms/Validators`.

We've seen how the `required` validator works. Now, let's look at two of the other out-of-the-box validators: `minLength` and `maxLength`. In addition to making it required, we want the title of the workout to be between 5 and 20 characters (we'll look at the `pattern` validator a little later in this chapter).

So, in addition to the `required` attribute we added previously to the title input box, we will add the `minLength` attribute and set it to `5`, and add the `maxLength` attribute and set it to `20`, like so:

```
<input type="text" . . . minlength="5" maxlength="20" required>
```

Then, we add another label with a message that will display when this validation is not met:

```
<label *ngIf="(title.control.hasError('minlength') ||
title.control.hasError('maxlength')) && workout.title.length > 0"
class="alert alert-danger validation-message">Title should be between 5 and
20 characters long.</label>
```

Managing multiple validation messages

You'll see that the conditions for displaying the message now test for the length not being zero. This prevents the message from displaying in the event that the control is touched but left empty. In that case, the title required message should display. This message only displays if nothing is entered in the field and we accomplish this by checking explicitly to see if the control's `hasError` type is `required`:

```
<label *ngIf="title.control.hasError('required')" class="alert alert-danger
validation-message">Title is required.</label>
```

Since we are attaching two validators to this input field, we can consolidate the check for the input being touched by wrapping both validators in a div tag that checks for that condition being met:

```
<div *ngIf="title.touched">
   . . . [the two validators] . . .
</div>
```

What we just did shows how we can attach multiple validations to a single input control and also display the appropriate message in the event that one of the validation conditions is not met. However, it's pretty clear that this approach will not scale for more complicated scenarios. Some inputs contain a lot of validations and controlling when a validation message shows up can become complex. As the expressions for handling the various displays get more complicated, we may want to refactor and move them into a custom directive. Creating a custom directive will be covered in detail in Chapter 4, *Angular Directives in Depth*.

Custom validation messages for an exercise

A workout without any exercise is of no use. There should at least be one exercise in the workout and we should validate this restriction.

The problem with exercise count validation is that it is not something that the user inputs directly and the framework validates. Nonetheless, we still want a mechanism to validate the exercise count in a manner similar to other validations on this form.

What we will do is add a hidden input box to the form that contains the count of the exercises. We will then bind this to ngModel and add a pattern validator that will check to make sure that there is more than one exercise. We will set the value of the input box to the count of the exercises:

```
<input type="hidden" name="exerciseCount" #exerciseCount="ngModel"
ngControl="exerciseCount" class="form-control" id="exercise-count"
[(ngModel)]="workout.exercises.length" pattern="[1-9][0-9]*">
```

Then, we will attach a validation message to it similar to what we just did with our other validators:

```
<label *ngIf="exerciseCount.control.hasError('pattern')" class="alert
alert-danger extended-validation-message">The workout should have at least
one exercise!</label>
```

We are not using `ngModel` in its true sense here. There is no two-way binding involved. We are only interested in using it to do custom validation.

Open the new Workout page, add an exercise, and remove it; we should see this error:

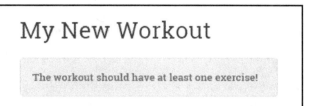

What we did here could have been easily done without involving any model validation infrastructure. But, by hooking our validation into that infrastructure, we do derive some benefits. We can now determine errors with a specific model and errors with the overall form in a consistent and familiar manner. Most importantly, if our validation fails here, the entire form will be invalidated.

 Implementing custom validation the way we just did is not what you would want to do very often. Instead, it will usually make more sense to implement this kind of complicated logic inside a custom directive. We'll cover creating custom directives in detail in `Chapter 4`, *Angular Directives in Depth*.

One nuisance with our newly implemented `Exercise Count` validation is that it shows when the screen for a new `Workout` first appears. With this message, we are not able to use `ng-touched` to hide the display. This is because the exercises are being added programmatically and the hidden input we are using to track their count never changes from untouched as exercises are added or removed.

To fix this problem, we need an additional value to check when the state of the exercise list has been reduced to zero, except when the form is first loaded. The only way that situation can happen is if the user adds and then removes exercises from a workout to the point that there are no more exercises. So, we'll add another property to our component that we can use to track whether the remove method has been called. We call that value `removeTouched` and set its initial value to `false`:

```
removeTouched: boolean = false;
```

Then, in the remove method we will set that value to `true`:

```
removeExercise(exercisePlan: ExercisePlan) {
    this.removeTouched = true;
    this.workoutBuilderService.removeExercise(exercisePlan);
}
```

Next, we will add `removeTouched` to our validation message conditions, like so:

```
<label *ngIf="exerciseCount.control.hasError('pattern') && (removeTouched)"
```

Now, when we open a new workout screen, the validation message will not display. But if the user adds and then removes all the exercises, then it will display.

To understand how model validation rolls up into form validation, we need to understand what form-level validation has to offer. However, even before that, we need to implement saving the workout and calling it from the workout form.

Saving the workout

The workout that we are building needs to be persisted (in-memory only). The first thing that we need to do is extend `WorkoutService` and `WorkoutBuilderService`.

`WorkoutService` needs two new methods, `addWorkout` and `updateWorkout`:

```
addWorkout(workout: WorkoutPlan){
    if (workout.name){
        this.workouts.push(workout);
        return workout;
    }
}

updateWorkout(workout: WorkoutPlan){
    for (var i = 0; i < this.workouts.length; i++) {
        if (this.workouts[i].name === workout.name) {
            this.workouts[i] = workout;
            break;
        }
    }
}
```

The `addWorkout` method does a basic check on the workout name and then pushes the workout into the workout array. Since there is no backing store involved, if we refresh the page, the data is lost. We will fix this in the next chapter where we persist the data to a server.

The `updateWorkout` method looks for a workout with the same name in the existing workouts array and if found, updates and replaces it.

We only add one save method to `WorkoutBuilderService` as we are already tracking the context in which workout construction is going on:

```
save(){
    let workout = this.newWorkout ?
        this._workoutService.addWorkout(this.buildingWorkout) :
        this._workoutService.updateWorkout(this.buildingWorkout);
    this.newWorkout = false;
    return workout;
}
```

The `save` method calls either `addWorkout` or `updateWorkout` in the `Workout` service based on whether a new workout is being created or an existing one is being edited.

From a service perspective, that should be enough. Time to integrate the ability to save workouts into the `Workout` component and learn more about the form directive!

Before we look at `NgForm` in more detail, let's add the save method to `Workout` to save the workout when the `Save` button is clicked on. Add this code to the `Workout` component:

```
save(formWorkout:any){
    if (!formWorkout.valid) return;
    this.workoutBuilderService.save();
    this.router.navigate(['/builder/workouts']);
}
```

We check the validation state of the form using its invalid property and then call the `WorkoutBuilderService.save` method if the form state is valid.

More on NgForm

Forms in Angular have a different role to play as compared to traditional forms that post data to the server. If we go back and look again at the form tag, we will see that it is missing the standard action attribute. The standard form behavior of posting data to the server using full-page post-back does not make sense with an SPA framework such as Angular. In Angular, all server requests are made through asynchronous invocations originating from directives or services.

Under the hood, Angular is also turning off the browser's inbuilt validation. As you have seen in this chapter, we are still using validation attributes such as `required` that look the same as native HTML validation attributes. However, as the Angular documentation explains, inside an Angular form "Angular uses directives to match these attributes with validator functions in the framework." See `https://angular.io/guide/form-validation#template-driven-validation`.

The form here plays a different role. When the form encapsulates a set of input elements (such as input, textarea, and select) it provides an API for:

- Determining the state of the form, such as whether the form is dirty or pristine based on the input controls on it
- Checking validation errors at the form or control level

 If you still want the standard form behavior, you can add an `ngNoForm` attribute to the `form` element, but this will definitely cause a full-page refresh. You can also turn on the browser's inbuilt validation by adding the `ngNativeValidate` attribute. We'll explore the specifics of the `NgForm` API a little later in this chapter when we look at saving the form and implementing validation.

The state of the `FormControl` objects within the form is being monitored by `NgForm`. If any of them are invalid, then `NgForm` sets the entire form to invalid. In this case, we have been able to use `NgForm` to determine that one or more of the `FormControl` objects is invalid and therefore the state of the form as a whole is invalid too.

Let's look at one more issue before we finish this chapter.

Fixing the saving of forms and validation messages

Open a new Workout page and directly click on the **Save** button. Nothing is saved as the form is invalid, but validations on individual form input do not show up at all. It now becomes difficult to know what elements have caused validation failure. The reason behind this behavior is pretty obvious. If we look at the error message binding for the name input element, it looks like this:

```
*ngIf="name.control?.hasError('required') && name.touched"
```

Remember that, earlier in the chapter, we explicitly disabled showing validation messages until the user has touched the input control. The same issue has come back to bite us and we need to fix it now.

We do not have a way to explicitly change the touched state of our controls to untouched. Instead, we will resort to a little trickery to get the job done. We'll introduce a new property called `submitted`. Add it at the top of the `Workout` class definition and set its initial value to `false`, like so:

```
submitted: boolean = false;
```

The variable will be set to `true` on the **Save** button click. Update the save implementation by adding the highlighted code:

```
save(formWorkout){
    this.submitted = true;
    if (!formWorkout.valid) return;
    this._workoutBuilderService.save();
    this.router.navigate(['/builder/workouts']);
}
```

However, how does this help? Well, there is another part to this fix that requires us to change the error message for each of the controls we are validating. The expression now changes to:

```
*ngIf="name.control.hasError('required') && (name.touched || submitted)"
```

With this fix, the error message is shown when the control is touched or the form submit button is pressed (`submitted` is `true`). This expression fix now has to be applied to every validation message where a check appears.

If we now open the new **Workout** page and click on the **Save** button, we should see all validation messages on the input controls:

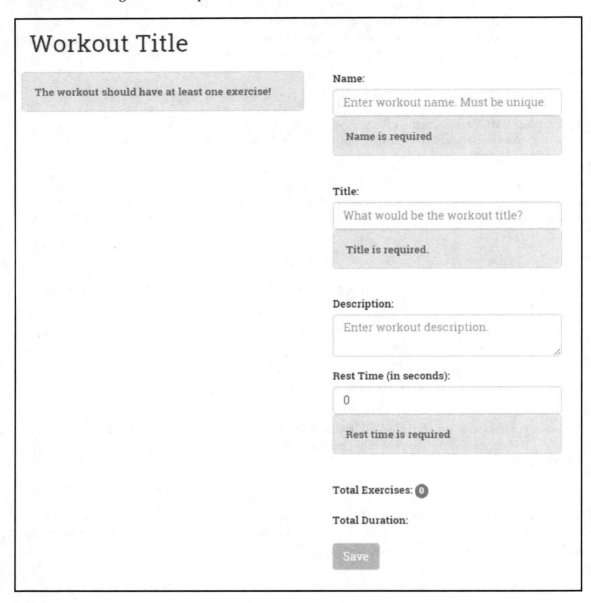

Reactive forms

The other type of form that Angular supports is called **reactive** forms. **Reactive forms** start with a model that is constructed in a component class. With this approach, we use the **form builder API** to create a form in code and associate it with a model.

Given the minimal code we have to write to get template-driven forms working, why and when should we consider using reactive forms? There are several situations in which we might want to use them. These include cases where we want to take programmatic control of creating the form. This is especially beneficial, as we will see, when we are trying to create form controls dynamically based on data we are retrieving from the server.

If our validation gets complicated, it is often easier to handle it in code. Using reactive forms, we can keep this complicated logic out of the HTML template, making the template syntax simpler.

Another significant advantage of reactive forms is that they make unit-testing the form possible, which is not the case with **template-driven forms.** We can simply instantiate our form controls in our tests and then test them outside the markup on our page.

Reactive forms use three new form directives that we haven't discussed before: `FormGroup`, `FormControl`, and `FormArray`. These directives allow the form object that is constructed in code to be tied directly to the HTML markup in the template. The form controls that are created in the component class are then directly available in the form itself. Technically speaking, this means that we don't need to use `ngModel` (which is integral to template-driven forms) with reactive forms (although it can be used). The overall approach is a cleaner and less cluttered template with more focus on the code that drives the form. Let's get started with building a reactive form.

Getting started with reactive forms

We'll make use of reactive forms to build the form to add and edit **Exercises**. Among other things, this form will allow the user to add links to exercise videos on YouTube. And since they can add any number of video links, we will need to be able to add controls for these video links dynamically. This challenge will present a good test of how effective reactive forms can be in developing more complex forms.

Here is how the form will look:

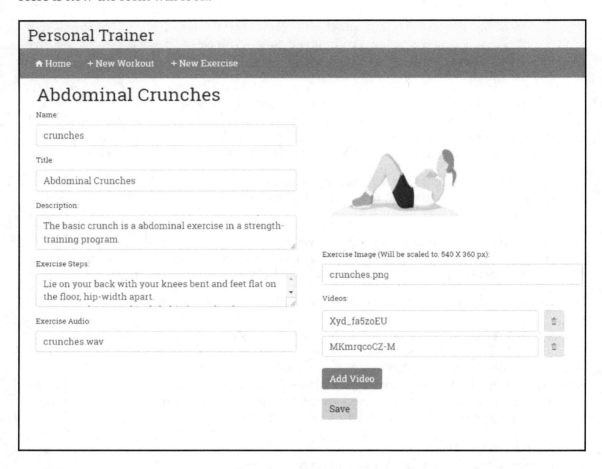

To get started, open `workout-builder.module.ts` and add the following `import`:

```
import { FormsModule, ReactiveFormsModule }   from '@angular/forms';
  ...
@NgModule({
    imports: [
        CommonModule,
        FormsModule,
        ReactiveFormsModule,
        SharedModule,
        workoutBuilderRouting
    ],
```

`ReactiveFormsModule` contains what we will need to build reactive forms.

Next, copy `exercise-builder-service.ts` from the `workout-builder/builder-services` folder under `trainer/src/app` in `checkpoint 4.6` and import it into `workout-builder.module.ts`:

```
import { ExerciseBuilderService } from "./builder-services/exercise-
builder-service";
```

Then, add it as an additional provider to the providers array in that same file:

```
@NgModule({
   . . .
  providers: [
    WorkoutBuilderService,
    WorkoutResolver,
    ExerciseBuilderService,
    ExerciseResolver
    ]
})
```

You will notice here that we also have added `ExerciseResolver` as a provider. We won't be covering that here, but you should copy it from the `exercise` folder as well and also copy the updated `workout-builder-routing.module.ts`, which adds it as a route guard for the navigation to `ExerciseComponent`.

Now, open `exercise.component.ts` and add the following import statement:

```
import { Validators, FormArray, FormGroup, FormControl, FormBuilder } from
'@angular/forms';
```

This brings in the following, which we will use to construct our form:

- FormBuilder
- FormGroup
- FormControl
- FormArray

Finally, we inject `FormBuilder` (as well as `Router`, `ActivatedRoute`, and `ExerciseBuilderService`) into the constructor of our class:

```
constructor(
    public route: ActivatedRoute,
    public router: Router,
```

```
        public exerciseBuilderService: ExerciseBuilderService,
        public formBuilder: FormBuilder
    ) {}
```

With these preliminary steps out of the way, we can now go ahead and start building out our form.

Using the FormBuilder API

The `FormBuilder` API is the foundation for reactive forms. You can think of it as a factory for turning out the forms we are constructing in our code. Go ahead and add the `ngOnInit` lifecycle hook to your class, as follows:

```
ngOnInit() {
  this.sub = this.route.data
      .subscribe(
        (data: { exercise: Exercise }) => {
          this.exercise = data.exercise;
        }
      );

    this.buildExerciseForm();
}
```

When `ngOnInit` fires, it will extract the data for an existing or new `exercise` from the route data that has been retrieved and returned by `ExerciseResolver`. This is the same pattern we followed with initializing the `Workout` component.

Now, let's implement the `buildExerciseForm` method by adding the following code:

```
buildExerciseForm(){
    this.exerciseForm = this.formBuilder.group({
        'name': [this.exercise.name, [Validators.required,
AlphaNumericValidator.invalidAlphaNumeric]],
        'title': [this.exercise.title, Validators.required],
        'description': [this.exercise.description, Validators.required],
        'image': [this.exercise.image, Validators.required],
        'nameSound': [this.exercise.nameSound],
        'procedure': [this.exercise.procedure],
        'videos': this.addVideoArray()
    })
}
```

Let's examine this code. To start with, we are using the injected instance of `FormBuilder` to construct the form and assign it to a local variable, `exerciseForm`. Using `formBuilder.group`, we add several form controls to our form. We add each of them by a simple key/value mapping:

```
'name': [this.exercise.name, Validators.required],
```

The left side of the mapping is the name of the `FormControl`, and the right is an array containing as its first element the value of the control (in our case, the corresponding element on our exercise model) and the second a validator (in this case, the out-of-the-box required validator). Nice and neat! It's definitely easier to see and reason about our form controls by setting them up outside the template.

We can not only build up `FormControls` in our form this way but also add `FormControlGroups` and `FormControlArray`, which contain `FormControls` within them. This means we can create complex forms that contain nested input controls. In our case, as we have mentioned, we are going to need to accommodate the possibility of our users adding multiple videos to an exercise. We can do this by adding the following code:

```
'videos': this.addVideoArray()
```

What we are doing here is assigning a `FormArray` to videos, which means we can assign multiple controls in this mapping. To construct this new `FormArray`, we add the following `addVideoArray` method to our class:

```
addVideoArray(){
    if(this.exercise.videos){
        this.exercise.videos.forEach((video : any) => {
            this.videoArray.push(new FormControl(video,
Validators.required));
        });
    }
    return this.videoArray;
}
```

This method constructs a `FormControl` for each video; each is then added each to a `FormArray` that is assigned to the videos control in our form.

Adding the form model to our HTML view

So far, we have been working behind the scenes in our class to construct our form. The next step is to wire up our form to the view. To do this, we use the same controls that we used to build the form in our code: `formGroup`, `formControl`, and `formArray`.

Open `exercise.component.html` and add a `form` tag as follows:

```
<form class="row" [formGroup]="exerciseForm"
(ngSubmit)="onSubmit(exerciseForm)">
```

Within the tag, we are first assigning the `exerciseForm` that we just built in code to `formGroup`. This establishes the connection between our coded model and the form in the view. We also wire up the `ngSubmit` event to an `onSubmit` method in our code (we'll discuss this method a little later).

Adding form controls to our form inputs

Next, we start constructing the inputs for our form. We'll start with the input for the name of our exercise:

```
<input name="name" formControlName="name" class="form-control" id="name"
placeholder="Enter exercise name. Must be unique.">
```

We assign the name of our coded form control to `formControlName`. This establishes the link between the control in our code and the `input` field in the markup. Another item of interest here is that we do not use the `required` attribute.

Adding validation

The next thing that we do is add a validation message to the control that will display in the event of a validation error:

```
<label *ngIf="exerciseForm.controls['name'].hasError('required') &&
(exerciseForm.controls['name'].touched || submitted)" class="alert alert-
danger validation-message">Name is required</label>
```

Notice that this markup is very similar to what we used in template-driven forms for validation, except that the syntax for identifying the control is somewhat more verbose Again, it checks the state of the `hasError` property of the control to make sure it is valid.

But wait a minute! How can we validate this input? Haven't we removed the required attribute from our tag? This is where the control mappings that we added in our code come into play. If you look back at the code for the form model, you can see the following mapping for the `name` control:

```
'name': [this.exercise.name, Validators.required],
```

The second element in the mapping array assigns the required validator to the name form control. This means that we don't have to add anything to our template; instead, the form control itself is attached to the template with a required validator. The ability to add a validator in our code enables us to conveniently add validators outside our template. This is especially useful when it comes to writing custom validators with complex logic behind them.

Adding dynamic form controls

The **Exercise** form that we are building requires that we allow the user to add one or more videos to the exercise. Since we don't know how many videos the user may want to add, we will have to build the `input` fields for these videos dynamically as the user clicks on the **Add Video** button. Here's how it will look:

We have already seen the code in our component class that we use to do this. Now, let's take a look at how it is implemented in our template.

We first use `ngFor` to loop through our list of videos. Then, we assign the index in our videos to a local variable, `i`. No surprises so far:

```
<div *ngFor="let video of videoArray.controls; let i=index" class="form-row
align-items-center">
```

Inside the loop, we do three things. First, we dynamically add a video `input` field for each of the videos currently in our exercise:

```
<div class="col-sm-10">
    <input type="text" class="form-control" [formControlName]="i"
placeholder="Add a related youtube video identified."/>
</div>
```

Next, we add a button to allow the user to delete a video:

```
<span class="btn alert-danger" title="Delete this video."
(click)="deleteVideo(i)">
    <span class="ion-ios-trash-outline"></span>
</span>
```

We bind a `deleteVideo` method in our component class to the button's `click` event and pass to it the index of the video being deleted.

We then add a validation message for each of the video `input` fields:

```
<label
*ngIf="exerciseForm.controls['videos'].controls[i].hasError('required') &&
(exerciseForm.controls['videos'].controls[i].touched || submitted)"
class="alert alert-danger validation-message">Video identifier is
required</label>
```

The validation message follows the same pattern for displaying the message that we have used elsewhere in this chapter. We drill into the `exerciseFormControls` group to find the particular control by its index. Again, the syntax is verbose but easy enough to understand.

Saving the form

The final step in building out our reactive form is to handle saving the form. When we constructed the form tag earlier, we bound the `ngSubmit` event to the following `onSubmit` method in our code:

```
onSubmit(formExercise: FormGroup) {
    this.submitted = true;
    if (!formExercise.valid) { return; }
    this.mapFormValues(formExercise);
    this.exerciseBuilderService.save();
    this.router.navigate(['/builder/exercises']);
}
```

This method sets `submitted` to `true`, which will trigger the display of any validation messages that might have been previously hidden because the form had not been touched. It also returns without saving in the event that there are any validation errors on the form. If there are none, then it calls the following `mapFormValues` method, which assigns the values from our form to the `exercise` that will be saved:

```
mapFormValues(form: FormGroup) {
    this.exercise.name = form.controls['name'].value;
    this.exercise.title = form.controls['title'].value;
    this.exercise.description = form.controls['description'].value;
    this.exercise.image = form.controls['image'].value;
    this.exercise.nameSound = form.controls['nameSound'].value;
    this.exercise.procedure = form.controls['procedure'].value;
    this.exercise.videos = form.controls['videos'].value;
}
```

It then calls the save method in `ExerciseBuilderService` and routes the user back to the exercise list screen (remember that any new exercise will not display in that list because we have not yet implemented data persistence in our application).

We hope this makes it clear; reactive forms offer many advantages when we are trying to build more complicated forms. They allow programming logic to be removed from the template. They permit validators to be added to the form programmatically. And, they support building forms dynamically at runtime.

Custom validators

Now, we'll take a look at one more thing before we conclude this chapter. As anyone who has worked on building web forms (either in Angular or any other web technology) knows, we are often called on to create validations that are unique to the application we are building. Angular provides us with the flexibility to enhance our reactive form validation by building custom validators.

In building our exercise form, we need to be sure about what is entered, as a name contains only alphanumeric characters and no spaces. This is because when we get to storing the exercises in a remote data store, we are going to use the name of the exercise as its key. So, in addition to the standard required field validator, let's build another validator that checks to make sure that the name entered is in alphanumeric form only.

Creating a custom control is quite straightforward. In its simplest form, an Angular custom validator is a function that takes a control as an input parameter, runs the validation check, and returns true or false. So, let's start by adding a TypeScript file with the name `alphanumeric-validator.ts`. In that file, first import `FormControl` from `@angular/forms`, then add the following class to that file:

```
export class AlphaNumericValidator {
    static invalidAlphaNumeric(control: FormControl): { [key: string]:
boolean } {
        if ( control.value.length && !control.value.match(/^[a-z0-9]+$/i) )
{
            return {invalidAlphaNumeric: true };
        }
        return null;
    }
}
```

The code follows the pattern for creating a validator that we just mentioned. The only thing that may be a little surprising is that it returns true when the validation fails! As long as you are clear on this one quirk, you should have no problem writing your own custom validator.

Integrating a custom validator into our forms

So how do we plug our custom validator into our form? If we are using reactive forms, the answer is pretty simple. We add it just like a built-in validator when we build our form in code. Let's do that. Open `exercise.component.ts` and first add an import for our custom validator:

```
import { AlphaNumericValidator } from '../alphanumeric-validator';
```

Then, modify the form builder code to add the validator to the `name` control:

```
buildExerciseForm(){
    this.exerciseForm = this._formBuilder.group({
    'name': [this.exercise.name, [Validators.required,
AlphaNumericValidator.invalidAlphaNumeric]],
    . . . [other form controls] . . .
    });
}
```

Since the name control already has a required validator, we add `AlphaNumericValidator` as a second validator using an array that contains both validators. The array can be used to add any number of validators to a control.

The final step is to incorporate the appropriate validation message for the control into our template. Open `workout.component.html` and add the following label just below the label that displays the message for the required validator:

```
<label *ngIf="exerciseForm.controls['name'].hasError('invalidAlphaNumeric')
&& (exerciseForm.controls['name'].touched || submitted)" class="alert
alert-danger validation-message">Name must be alphanumeric</label>
```

The exercise screen will now display a validation message if a non-alphanumeric value is entered in the name input box:

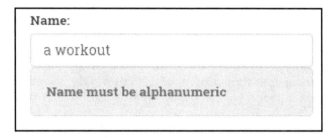

As we hope you can see, reactive forms give us the ability to add custom validators to our forms in a straightforward manner that allows us to maintain the validation logic in our code and easily integrate it into our templates.

You may have noticed that in this chapter, we have not covered how to use custom validators in template-driven forms. That is because implementing them requires the additional step of building a custom directive. We'll cover that in `Chapter 4`, *Angular Directives in Depth*.

Configuration options for running validation

Before we move on from validation, there is one more topic to cover and that is configuration options for running the validations. So far, we have been using the default option, which runs validation checks on every input event. However, you have the choice of configuring them to run either on "blur"(that is when the user leaves an input control) or when the form is submitted. You can set this configuration at the form level or on a control-by-control basis.

For example, we might decide that to avoid the complexity of handling missing exercises in the workout form, we will set that form to validate only upon submit. We can set this by adding the following highlighted assignment of NgFormOptions to the form tag:

```
<form #f="ngForm" name="formWorkout" (ngSubmit)="save(f.form)"
[ngFormOptions]="{updateOn: 'submit'}" class="row">
```

This instructs Angular to run our validations only upon submit. Try it and you'll see that no validations appear when you make entries into the form. Leave the form blank and press the **Save** button, and you will see the validation messages appear. Taking this approach, of course, means that there are no visual cues to the user regarding validation until they press the Save button.

There are also a couple of other unintended side effects to using this approach in our form. The first is that the title no longer updates at the top of the screen as we type into the title input box. That value will only be updated when we press **Save**. Second, you will also see a validation message appear if you add one or more workouts and then remove all of them. This is because of the special conditions we set up for this control, which cause it to fire outside the normal validation flow.

So, maybe we should take a different approach. Angular provides the option of implementing more fine-grained control of the validation flow by allowing us to make such configurations at the control level using ngModelOptions. For example, let's remove the ngFormOptions assignment from the form tag and modify the title input control to add ngModelOptions as follows:

```
<input type="text" name="title" class="form-control" #title="ngModel"
id="workout-title" placeholder="What would be the workout title?"
[(ngModel)]="workout.title" [ngModelOptions]="{updateOn: 'blur'}"
minlength="5" maxlength="20" required>
```

You'll then notice that as you type the title into the input box, it does not update the title on the screen until you move off it (which triggers the `updateOn` event):

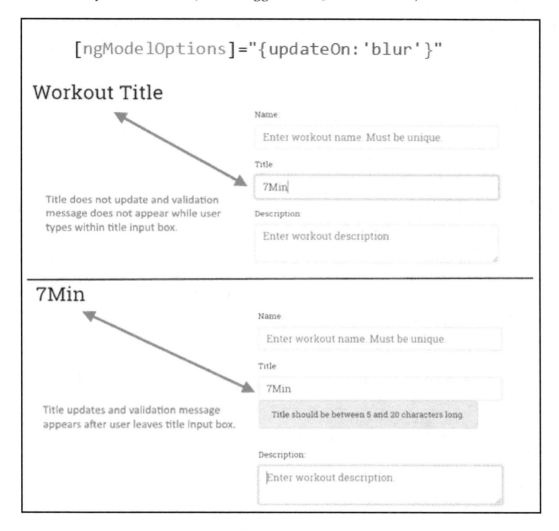

As you will remember, the default option caused the title to update with every keystroke. This is a contrived example but it illustrates how the differences in these configurations work.

You probably don't see the need to use the on blur setting here. But, in case where you may be doing validation by calling an external data store, this approach could be helpful in limiting the number of calls that are being made. And making such remote calls is exactly what we will be doing in Chapter 4, *Angular Directives in Depth*, when we implement a custom directive. The directive will be checking for duplicate names that already exist in our remote data store. So, let's remove this configuration from the title input control and place it instead on the name input control, like so:

```
<input type="text" name="workoutName" #name="ngModel" class="form-control"
id="workout-name" placeholder="Enter workout name. Must be unique."
[(ngModel)]="workout.name" [ngModelOptions]="{updateOn: 'blur'}" required>
```

We also can set the validation timing options within a reactive form. From what we have already learned about reactive forms, you will not be surprised to learn that we will be applying these settings in our code rather than the template. For example, to set them for a form group you use the following syntax:

```
new FormGroup(value, {updateOn: 'blur'}));
```

We can also apply them to individual form controls and that is what we will do in the case of our exercise form. Like the workout form, we will want to be able to validate the uniqueness of the name by making a remote call. So, we will want to limit the validation checking in a similar manner. We'll do that by adding the following to the code that creates the name form control:

```
buildExerciseForm() {
    this.exerciseForm = this.formBuilder.group({
        'name': [
          this.exercise.name,
        {
          updateOn: 'blur',
          validators: [Validators.required,
AlphaNumericValidator.invalidAlphaNumeric]
        }
      ],
      ....
    });
}
```

Note that we are putting the setting, along with the validators array, in the options object inside a pair of curly braces.

Summary

We now have a *Personal Trainer* app. The process of converting a specific *7 Minute Workout* app to a generic *Personal Trainer* app helped us learn a number of new concepts. We started the chapter by defining the new app requirements. Then, we designed the model as a shared service.

We defined some new views and corresponding routes for the *Personal Trainer* app. We also used both child and asynchronous routing to separate out *Workout Builder* from the rest of the app.

We then turned our focus to workout building. One of the primary technological focuses in this chapter was on Angular forms. The *Workout Builder* employed a number of form input elements and we implemented a number of common form scenarios using both template-driven and reactive forms. We also explored Angular validation in depth, and implemented a custom validator. We also covered configuring the timing options for running validation.

The next chapter is all about client-server interaction. The workouts and exercises that we create need to be persisted. In the next chapter, we build a persistence layer, which will allow us to save workout and exercise data on the server.

Before we conclude this chapter, here is a friendly reminder. If you have not completed the exercise building routine for *Personal Trainer*, go ahead and do it. You can always compare your implementation with what has been provided in the companion code base. There are also things you can add to the original implementation, such as file uploads for the exercise image, and once you are more familiar with client-server interaction, a remote check to determine whether the YouTube videos actually exist.

3
Supporting Server Data Persistence

It's now time to talk to the server! There is no fun in creating a workout, adding exercises, and saving it to later realize that all our efforts are lost because the data did not persist anywhere. We need to fix this.

Seldom are applications self-contained. Any consumer app, irrespective of its size, has parts that interact with elements outside its boundary. With web-based applications, the interaction is mostly with a server. Apps interact with the server to authenticate, authorize, store/retrieve data, validate data, and perform other such operations.

This chapter explores the constructs that Angular provides for client-server interaction. In the process, we add a persistence layer to *Personal Trainer* that loads and saves data to a backend server.

The topics we cover in this chapter include the following:

- **Provisioning a backend to persist workout data**: We set up a MongoLab account and use its Data API to access and store workout data.
- **Understanding the Angular HttpClient**: The `HttpClient` allows us to interact with a server over HTTP. You'll learn how to make all types of `GET`, `POST`, `PUT`, and `DELETE` requests with the `HttpClient`.
- **Implementing the loading and saving of workout data**: We use the `HTTPClient` to load and store workout data in the MongoLab databases.
- **Two ways in which we can use the HttpClient's XMLHttpRequest**: Either Observables or with promises.
- **Using RxJS and Observables**: To subscribe to and query streams of data.

- **Using promises**: In this chapter, we will see how to use promises as part of HTTP invocation and response.
- **Working with cross-domain access**: As we are interacting with a MongoLab server in a different domain, you will learn about browser restrictions on cross-domain access. You will also learn how JSONP and CORS help us make cross-domain access easy and about Angular JSONP support.

Let's set the ball rolling.

Angular and server interactions

Any client-server interaction typically boils down to sending HTTP requests to a server and receiving responses from a server. For heavy JavaScript apps, we depend on the AJAX request/response mechanism to communicate with the server. To support AJAX-based communication, Angular provides the Angular `HttpClient` module. Before we delve into the `HttpClient` module, we need to set up our server platform that stores the data and allows us to manage it.

Setting up the persistence store

For data persistence, we use a document database called MongoDB (`https://www.mongodb.com/`), hosted over MongoLab (`https://www.mlab.com/`), as our data store. The reason we zeroed in on MongoLab is that it provides an interface to interact with the database directly. This saves us the effort of setting up server middleware to support MongoDB interaction.

It is never a good idea to expose the data store/database directly to the client. But in this case, since our primary aim is to learn about Angular and client-server interaction, we take this liberty and directly access the MongoDB instance hosted in MongoLab. There is also a new breed of apps that are built over **noBackend** solutions. In such a setup, frontend developers build apps without the knowledge of the exact backend involved. Server interaction is limited to making API calls to the backend. If you are interested in knowing more about these noBackend solutions, do check out `http://nobackend.org/`.

Our first task is to provision an account on MongoLab and create a database:

1. Go to `https://mlab.com` and sign up for an mLab account by following the instructions on the website
2. Once the account is provisioned, log in and create a new Mongo database by clicking on the **Create New** button on the home page
3. On the database creation screen, you need to make some selections to provision the database. See the following screenshot to select the free database tier and other options:

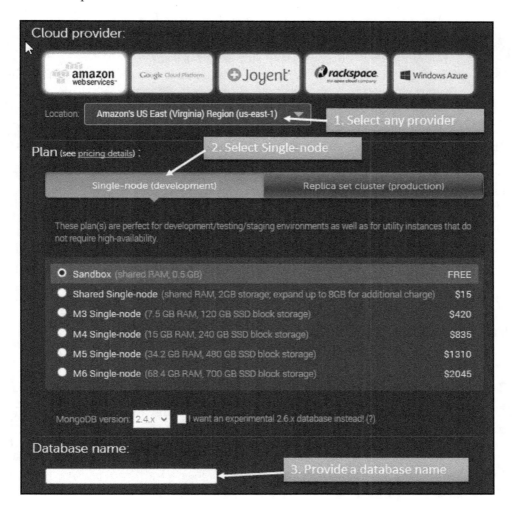

4. Create the database and make a note of the database name that you create
5. Once the database is provisioned, open the database and add two collections to it from the **Collection** tab:
   - `exercises`: This stores all *Personal Trainer* exercises
   - `workouts`: This stores all *Personal Trainer* workouts

Collections in the MongoDB world equate to a database table.

 MongoDB belongs to a breed of databases called **document databases**. The central concepts here are documents, attributes, and their linkages. And unlike traditional databases, the schema is not rigid. We will not be covering what document databases are and how to perform data modeling for document-based stores in this book. *Personal Trainer* has a limited storage requirement and we manage it using the two previously mentioned document collections. We may not even be using the document database in its true sense.

Once the collections are added, add yourself as a user to the database from the **Users** tab.

The next step is to determine the API key for the MongoLab account. The provisioned API key has to be appended to every request made to MongoLab. To get the API key, perform the following steps:

1. Click on the username (not the account name) in the top-right corner to open the user profile.
2. In the section titled **API Key**, the current API key is displayed; copy it. At the same time, click on the button below the API key to **Enable Data API access**. This is disabled by default.

The data store schema is complete. We now need to seed these collections.

Seeding the database

The *Personal Trainer* app already has a predefined workout and a list of 12 exercises. We need to seed the collections with this data.

Open `seed.js` in the `trainer/db` folder for checkpoint 5.1 from the companion code base. It contains the seed JSON script and detailed instructions on how to seed data into the MongoLab database instance.

Once seeded, the database will have one workout in the workouts collection and 12 exercises in the exercises collection. Verify this on the MongoLab site; the collections should show the following:

NAME	DOCUMENTS	CAPPED?	SIZE
exercises	12	false	19.30 KB
workouts	1	false	8.97 KB

Everything has been set up now, so let's start our discussion of the `HttpClient` module and implement workout/exercise persistence for the *Personal Trainer* app.

The basics of the HTTPClient module

At the core of the `HTTPClient` module is the `HttpClient`. It performs HTTP requests using `XMLHttpRequest` as the default backend (JSONP is also available, as we will see later in this chapter). It supports requests such as `GET`, `POST`, `PUT`, and `DELETE`. In this chapter, we will use the `HttpClient` to make all of these types of requests. As we will see, the `HttpClient` makes it easy to make these calls with a minimal amount of setup and complexity. None of this terminology will come as a surprise to anyone who has previously worked with Angular or built JavaScript applications that communicate with a backend data store.

However, there is a substantial change in the way Angular handles HTTP requests. Calling a request now returns an Observable of HTTP responses. It does so by using the RxJS library, which is a well-known open source implementation of the asynchronous Observable pattern.

You can find the RxJS project on GitHub at `https://github.com/ Reactive-Extensions/RxJS`. The site indicates that the project is being actively developed by Microsoft in collaboration with a community of open source developers. We will not be covering the asynchronous Observable pattern in great detail here, and we encourage you to visit that site to learn more about the pattern and how RxJS implements it. The version of RxJS that Angular is using is beta 5.

In the simplest of terms, using Observables allows a developer to think about the data that flows through an application as streams of information that the application can dip into and use whenever it wants. These streams change over time, which allows the application to react to these changes. This quality of Observables provides a foundation for **functional reactive programming** (**FRP**), which fundamentally shifts the paradigm for building web applications from imperative to reactive.

The RxJS library provides operators that allow you to subscribe to and query these data streams. Moreover, you can easily mix and combine them, as we will see in this chapter. Another advantage of Observables is that it is easy to cancel or unsubscribe from them, making it possible to seamlessly handle errors inline.

While it is still possible to use promises, the default method in Angular uses Observables. We will also cover promises in this chapter.

Personal Trainer and server integration

As described in the previous section, client-server interaction is all about asynchronicity. As we alter our *Personal Trainer* app to load data from the server, this pattern becomes self-evident.

In the previous chapter, the initial set of workouts and exercises was hardcoded in the WorkoutService implementation. Let's see how to load this data from the server first.

Loading exercise and workout data

Earlier in this chapter, we seeded our database with a data form, the seed.js file. We now need to render this data in our views. The MongoLab Data API is going to help us here.

 The MongoLab Data API uses an API key to authenticate access requests. Every request made to the MongoLab endpoints needs to have a query string parameter, apikey=<key>, where key is the API key that we provisioned earlier in the chapter. Remember that the key is always provided to a user and associated with their account. Avoid sharing your API keys with others.

The API follows a predictable pattern to query and update data. For any MongoDB collection, the typical endpoint access pattern is one of the following (given here is the base URL: `https://api.mongolab.com/api/1/databases`):

- `/<dbname>/collections/<name>?apiKey=<key>`: This has the following requests:
    - `GET`: This action gets all objects in the given collection name.
    - `POST`: This action adds a new object to the collection name. MongoLab has an `_id` property that uniquely identifies the document (object). If not provided in the posted data, it is auto-generated.
- `/<dbname>/collections/<name>/<id>?apiKey=<key>`: This has the following requests:
    - `GET`: This gets a specific document/collection item with a specific ID (a match done on the `_id` property) from the collection name.
    - `PUT`: This updates the specific item (`id`) in the collection name.
    - `DELETE`: This deletes the item with a specific ID from the collection name.

 For more details on the Data API interface, visit the MongoLab Data API documentation at `http://docs.mlab.com/data-api`.

Now we are in a position to start implementing exercise/workout list pages.

 The code that we are starting with in this chapter is `checkpoint 4.6` (folder: `trainer`) in the GitHub repository for this book. It is available on GitHub (`https://github.com/chandermani/angular6byexample`). Checkpoints are implemented as branches in GitHub. If you are not using Git, download the snapshot of checkpoint 4.6 (a ZIP file) from the following GitHub location: `https://github.com/chandermani/angular6byexample/tree/checkpoint4.6`. Refer to the `README.md` file in the `trainer` folder when setting up the snapshot for the first time.

Loading exercise and workout lists from a server

To pull exercise and workout lists from the MongoLab database, we have to rewrite our `WorkoutService` service methods: `getExercises` and `getWorkouts`. But before we can do that, we have to set up our service to work with Angular's HTTPClient module.

Adding the HTTPClient module and RxJS to our project

The Angular HTTPClient module is included in the Angular bundles that you have already installed. To use it, we need to import it into `app.module.ts`, like so (make sure that the import follows `BrowserModule`):

```
import { HttpClientModule } from '@angular/common/http';
. . .
@NgModule({
  imports: [
    BrowserModule,
    HttpClientModule,
. . .
})
```

We also need an external third-party library: **Reactive Extensions for JavaScript** (RxJS). RxJS implements the Observable pattern and it is used by Angular with the HTTPClient module. It is included in the Angular bundles that are already part of our project.

Updating workout-service to use the HTTPClient module and RxJS

Open `workout.service.ts` from `trainer/src/app/core`. In order to use the HTTPClient and RxJS within the `WorkoutService`, we need to add the following imports to that file:

```
import { HttpClient } from '@angular/common/http';
import { Observable } from 'rxjs/Observable';
import { catchError } from 'rxjs/operators';
```

We are importing the `HTTPClient` module along with `Observable` from RxJS and one additional RxJS operator: `catchError`. We'll see how this operator is used as we work through the code in this section.

In the class definition, add the following properties, which include a workout property and ones that set the URL for the collections in our Mongo database and the key to that database as well as another property: params, which sets up the API key as a query string for API access:

```
workout: WorkoutPlan;
collectionsUrl = "https://api.mongolab.com/api/1/
databases/<dbname>/collections";
apiKey = <key>
params = '?apiKey=' + this._apiKey;
```

Replace the <dbname> and <key> tokens with the database name and API key of the database that we provisioned earlier in the chapter.

Next, inject the HTTPClient module into the WorkoutServiceconstructor using the following line of code:

```
constructor(public http: HttpClient) {
}
```

Then change the getExercises() method to the following:

```
getExercises() {
    return this.http.get<ExercisePlan>(this.collectionsUrl + '/exercises' +
this.params)
        .pipe(catchError(WorkoutService.handleError));
}
```

If you are used to working with promises for asynchronous data operations, what you see here will look different. Instead of a promise that has a call to then() chained to it, what happens here is that the http.get method returns an Observable from the RxJS library. Notice that we are also setting the response to be of type <ExercisePlan> to make explicit to our upstream callers what type of Observable is being returned from our HTTP GET call.

 Returning an Observable is the default response when using the HTTPClient module's get method. The Observable can, however, be converted to a promise. And, as we will see later in this chapter, the option to return JSONP also exists.

Before we move on, there is one more thing to touch upon in this code. Notice that we are using a pipe method to add a catchError operator. This operator accepts a method, handleError, for handling a failed response. The handleError method takes the failed response as a parameter. We log the error to the console and use Observable.throw to return the error to the consumer:

```
static handleError (error: Response) {
    console.error(error);
    return Observable.throw(error || 'Server error');
}
```

To be clear, this is not production code, but it will give us the opportunity to show how to write code upstream to handle errors that are generated as part of data access.

 It is important to understand that at this stage no data is flowing through the Observable until there is a subscription to it. This can bring about a gotcha moment for things such as adds and updates if you are not careful to add subscriptions to your Observables.

Modifying getWorkouts() to use the HTTPClient module

The change in the code for retrieving workouts is almost identical to that for the exercises:

```
getWorkouts() {
    return this.http.get<WorkoutPlan[]>(this.collectionsUrl + '/workouts' +
this.params)
        .pipe(catchError(WorkoutService.handleError));
}
```

Again we are specifying the type of Observable—in this case <WorkoutPlan[]>—that will be returned by our HTTP GET call and using pipe to add a catchError operator.

Now that the getExercises and getWorkouts methods are updated, we need to make sure that they work with the upstream callers.

Updating the workout/exercise list pages

The exercise and workout list pages (as well as `LeftNavExercises`) call either the `getExercises` or `getWorkouts` method in `model.ts`. In order to get these working with the remote calls that are now being made using the `HTTPClient` module, we need to modify those calls to subscribe to the Observable that is being returned by the `HTTPClient` module. So, update the code in the `ngOnInit` method in `exercises.component.ts` to the following:

```
ngOnInit() {
  this.workoutService.getExercises()
  .subscribe(
      exercises => this.exerciseList = exercises,
      (err: any) => console.error
  );
```

Our method now subscribes to the Observable that is being returned by the `getExercises` method; at the point when the response arrives, it assigns the results to `exerciseList`. If there is an error, it assigns it to a `console.error` call that displays the error in the console. All of this is now being handled asynchronously using the `HTTPClient` module with RxJS.

Go ahead and make similar changes to the `ngOnInit` methods in `workouts.component.ts` and `left-nav-exercises.component.ts`.

Refresh the workout/exercise list page and the workout and exercise data will be loaded from the database server.

Look at the complete implementation in checkpoint 5.1 in the GitHub repository if you are having difficulty in retrieving/showing data. Note that in this checkpoint, we have disabled navigation links to the workout and exercise screens because we still have to add the Observable implementation to them. We'll do that in the next section. Also remember to replace the database name and API key before you run the code from `Checkpoint 5.1`. If you are not using Git, download the snapshot of `Checkpoint 5.1` (a ZIP file) from the following GitHub location: `https://github.com/chandermani/angular6byexample/tree/checkpoint5.1`. Refer to the `README.md` file in the `trainer` folder when setting up the snapshot for the first time.

This looks good and the lists are loading fine. Well, almost! There is a small glitch in the workout list page. We can easily spot it if we look carefully at any list item (in fact, there is only one item):

The workout duration calculations are not working anymore! What could be the reason? We need to look back at how these calculations were implemented. The `WorkoutPlan` service (in `model.ts`) defines a `totalWorkoutDuration` method that does the math for this.

The difference is in the workout array that is bound to the view. In the previous chapter, we created the array with model objects that were created using the `WorkoutPlan` service. But now, since we are retrieving data from the server, we bind a simple array of JavaScript objects to the view, which for obvious reasons has no calculation logic.

We can fix this problem by mapping a server response to our model class objects and returning them to any upstream caller.

Mapping server data to application models

Mapping server data to our model and vice versa may be unnecessary if the model and server storage definition match. If we look at the `Exercise` model class and the seed data that we have added for the exercise in MongoLab, we will see that they do match and hence mapping becomes unnecessary.

Mapping a server response to the model data becomes imperative if:

- Our model defines any methods
- A stored model is different from its representation in code
- The same model class is used to represent data from different sources (this can happen for mashups, where we pull data from disparate sources)

The `WorkoutPlan` service is a prime example of an impedance mismatch between a model representation and its storage. Look at the following screenshot to understand these differences:

The two major differences between the model and server data are as follows:

- The model defines the totalWorkoutDuration method.
- The exercises array representation also differs. The exercises array of the model contains the full Exercise object, while the server data stores just the exercise identifier or name.

This clearly means that loading and saving a workout requires model mapping.

The way we will do this is by adding another operator to transform the Observable response object. So far, we have only returned a plain JavaScript object as the response. The nice thing is that the pipe method that we used to add error handling also allows us to add additional operators that we can use to transform the JavaScript object into the WorkoutPlan type in our model.

Let's rewrite the getWorkouts method in the workout-service.ts file to the following:

```
getWorkouts(): Observable<WorkoutPlan[]> {
    return this.http.get<WorkoutPlan[]>(this.collectionsUrl +
'/workouts' + this.params)
        .pipe(
            map((workouts: Array<any>) => {
                const result: Array<WorkoutPlan> = [];
                if (workouts) {
                    workouts.forEach((workout) => {
                        result.push(
                            new WorkoutPlan(
```

```
                                   workout.name,
                                   workout.title,
                                   workout.restBetweenExercise,
                                   workout.exercises,
                                   workout.description
                              ));
                });
          }
          return result;
        }),
        catchError(this.handleError<WorkoutPlan[]>('getWorkouts',
  []))
             );
      }
```

We have added a `map` operator that transforms this Observable into one made up of `WorkoutPlan` objects. Each `WorkoutPlan` object (we have only one at the moment) will then have the `totalWorkoutDuration` method that we need.

Looking at the code you can see that we operate on the JSON results HTTPClient response, which is why we are using the `<any>` type. And then we create a typed array of `WorkoutPlans` and iterate through the first array using a fat arrow `forEach` function, assigning each JavaScript object to a `WorkoutPlan` object.

We return the results of these mappings to the callers that subscribe to them, `workouts.component.ts` in this case. We have also updated the `catchError` operator with a new `handleError` method which you can find in `Checkpoint 5.2`. The callers do not need to make any changes to the code they use to subscribe to our workouts Observable. Instead, the model mapping can take place at one spot in the application and then be used throughout it.

If you rerun the application, you will see that the total number of seconds now displays properly:

Checkpoint 5.2 in the GitHub repository contains the working implementation for what we have covered so far. The GitHub branch is `checkpoint5.2` (folder: `trainer`).

Loading exercise and workout data from the server

Just as we fixed the `getWorkouts` implementation in `WorkoutService` earlier, we can implement other get operations for exercise- and workout-related stuff. Copy the service implementation for the `getExercise` and `getWorkout` methods of `WorkoutService` from `workout.service.ts` in the `trainer/src/app/core` folder in checkpoint 5.2.

 The `getWorkout` and `getExercise` methods use the name of the workout/exercise to retrieve results. Every MongoLab collection item has an `_id` property that uniquely identifies the item/entity. In the case of our `Exercise` and `WorkoutPlan` objects, we use the name of the exercise for unique identification. Hence, the `name` and `_id` property of each object always match.

At this point, we will need to add one more import to `workout.service.ts`:

```
import { forkJoin } from 'rxjs/observable/forkJoin';
```

This import brings in the `forkJoin` operator, which we will be discussing shortly.

Pay special attention to the implementation of the `getWorkout` method because there is a decent amount of data transformation happening due to the model and data storage format mismatch. This is how the `getWorkout` method now looks:

```
getWorkout(workoutName: string): Observable<WorkoutPlan> {
    return forkJoin (
        this.http.get(this.collectionsUrl + '/exercises' + this.params),
        this.http.get(this.collectionsUrl + '/workouts/' + workoutName +
this.params))
        .pipe(
            map(
                (data: any) => {
                    const allExercises = data[0];
                    const workout = new WorkoutPlan(
                        data[1].name,
                        data[1].title,
                        data[1].restBetweenExercise,
                        data[1].exercises,
                        data[1].description
                    );
                    workout.exercises.forEach(
                        (exercisePlan: any) => exercisePlan.exercise =
allExercises.find(
```

```
                              (x: any) => x.name === exercisePlan.name
                    )
                );
                return workout;
            }
        ),
        catchError(this.handleError<WorkoutPlan>(`getWorkout
    id=${workoutName}`))
        );
    }
```

There is a lot happening inside `getWorkout` that we need to understand.

The `getWorkout` method uses Observable and its `forkJoin` operator to return two Observable objects: one that retrieves the `Workout` and another that retrieves a list of all the `Exercises`. What is interesting about the `forkJoin` operator is that not only does it allow us to return multiple Observable streams, but it also waits until both Observable streams have retrieved their data before further processing the results. In other words, it enables us to stream the responses from multiple concurrent HTTP requests and then operate on the combined results.

Once we have the `Workout` details and the complete list of exercises, we then `pipe` the results to the `map` operator (which we saw previously with the code for the `Workouts` list), which we use to change the `exercises` array of the workout to the correct `Exercise` class object. We do this by searching the `allExercises` Observable for the name of the exercise in the `workout.exercises` array returned from the server, and then assigning the matching exercise to the workout services array. The end result is that we have a complete `WorkoutPlan` object with the `exercises` array set up correctly.

These `WorkoutService` changes warrant fixes in upstream callers too. We have already fixed the lists of exercises in the `LeftNavExercises` and `Exercises` components and the workouts in the `Workouts` component. Now let's fix the `Workout` and `Exercise` components along similar lines. The `getWorkout` and `getExercise` methods in the workout services are not directly called by these components, but by builder services. So we'll have to fix the builder services together with the `Workout` and `Exercise` components and the two resolvers—`WorkoutResolver` and `ExerciseResolver`—that we have added to the routes for these components.

Fixing the builder services

Now that we have `WorkoutService` set up to retrieve a workout from our remote data store, we have to modify `WorkoutBuilderService` to be able to retrieve that workout as an Observable. The method that pulls the `Workout` details is `startBuilding`. In order to do that, we will break the current `startBuilding` method into two methods, one for new workouts and one for existing workouts that we have retrieved from the server. Here is the code for new workouts:

```
startBuildingNew() {
  const exerciseArray: ExercisePlan[] = [];
  this.buildingWorkout = new WorkoutPlan('', '', 30, exerciseArray);
  this.newWorkout = true;
  return this.buildingWorkout;
}
```

For existing workouts, we add the following code:

```
startBuildingExisting(name: string) {
  this.newWorkout = false;
  return this.workoutService.getWorkout(name);
}
```

We'll let you make the same fixes in `ExerciseBuilderService`.

Updating the resolvers

As we move on to using Observable types with our data access, we are going to have to make some adjustments to the resolvers that we have created for the routes leading to workout and exercise screens. We start with the `WorkoutResolver` in `workout-resolver.ts` that can be found in the `workout` folder.

First, add the following imports from RxJs:

```
import { Observable } from 'rxjs/Observable';
import { of } from 'rxjs/observable/of';
import { map, catchError } from 'rxjs/operators';
```

Next update the `resolve` method as follows:

```
resolve(
  route: ActivatedRouteSnapshot,
  state: RouterStateSnapshot): Observable<WorkoutPlan> {
  const workoutName = route.paramMap.get('id');

  if (!workoutName) {
      return this.workoutBuilderService.startBuildingNew();
  } else {
      return
this.workoutBuilderService.startBuildingExisting(workoutName)
        .pipe(
          map(workout => {
            if (workout) {
              this.workoutBuilderService.buildingWorkout = workout;
              return workout;
            } else {
              this.router.navigate(['/builder/workouts']);
              return null;
            }
          }),
          catchError(error => {
            console.log('An error occurred!');
            this.router.navigate(['/builder/workouts']);
            return of(null);
          })
        );
  }
}
```

As you can see, we have split out the behavior for a new workout (one where there is no workout name being passed as a parameter in the URL) and that for an existing workout. In the former case, we call `workoutBuilderService.startBuildingExisting`, which will return a new `WorkoutPlan`. In the latter case, we call `workoutBuilderService.startBuildingExisting` and pipe the results and then map them to return the `workout` unless it is not found, in which case we route the user back to the `Workouts` screen.

Fixing the Workout and Exercise components

Once we have fixed the `WorkoutBuilderService` and the `WorkoutResolver`, there are actually no further fixes needed in the `WorkoutComponent`. All the work to handle the Observables has been done further downstream and all we need to do at this stage is subscribe to the route data and retrieve the workout as we have already been doing:

```
ngOnInit() {
    this.sub = this.route.data
        .subscribe(
            (data: { workout: WorkoutPlan }) => {
                this.workout = data.workout;
            }
        );
}
```

To test the implementation, uncomment the following highlighted code contained in the `onSelect` method within `workouts.component.ts`:

```
onSelect(workout: WorkoutPlan) {
    this.router.navigate( ['./builder/workout', workout.name] );
}
```

Then click on any existing workout, such as *7 Minute Workout*, from the list of workouts displayed at `/builder/workouts/`. The workout data should load successfully.

The `ExerciseBuilderService` and `ExerciseResolver` also need fixing. `Checkpoint 5.2` contains those fixes. You can copy those files or do it yourself and compare the implementation. And don't forget to uncomment the code in the `onSelect` method in `exercises.component.ts`.

 `Checkpoint 5.2` in the GitHub repository contains the working implementation for what we have covered thus far. If you are not using Git, download the snapshot of Checkpoint 5.2 (a ZIP file) from the following GitHub location: `https://github.com/chandermani/angular6byexample/tree/checkpoint5.2`. Refer to the `README.md` file in the `trainer` folder when setting up the snapshot for the first time.

It is now time to fix, create, and update scenarios for the exercises and workouts.

Performing CRUD on exercises/workouts

When it comes to create, read, update, and delete (CRUD) operations, all save, update, and delete methods need to be converted to the Observable pattern.

Earlier in the chapter, we detailed the endpoint access pattern for CRUD operations in a MongoLab collection. Head back to the *Loading exercise and workout data* section and revisit the access patterns. We need this now as we plan to create/update workouts.

Before we start the implementation, it is important to understand how MongoLab identifies a collection item and what our ID generation strategy is. Each collection item in MongoDB is uniquely identified in the collection using the _id property. While creating a new item, either we supply an ID or the server generates one itself. Once _id is set, it cannot be changed. For our model, we will use the name property of the exercise/workout as the unique ID and copy the name into the _id field (hence, there is no autogeneration of _id). Also, remember that our model classes do not contain this _id field; it has to be created before saving the record for the first time.

Let's fix the workout creation scenario first.

Creating a new workout

Taking the bottom-up approach, the first thing that needs to be fixed is WorkoutService. Update the addWorkout method as shown in the following code:

```
addWorkout(workout: WorkoutPlan) {
    const workoutExercises: any = [];
    workout.exercises.forEach(
        (exercisePlan: any) => {
            workoutExercises.push({name: exercisePlan.exercise.name,
duration: exercisePlan.duration});
        }
    );

    const body = {
        '_id': workout.name,
        'exercises': workoutExercises,
        'name': workout.name,
        'title': workout.title,
        'description': workout.description,
        'restBetweenExercise': workout.restBetweenExercise
    };

    return this.http.post(this.collectionsUrl + '/workouts' +
```

```
this.params, body)
        .pipe(
          catchError(this.handleError<WorkoutPlan>())
        );
    }
```

In `getWorkout`, we had to map data from the server model to our client model; the reverse has to be done here. First, we create a new array for the exercises, `workoutExercises`, and then add to that array a version of the exercises that is more compact for server storage. We only want to store the exercise name and duration in the exercises array on the server (this array is of type `any` because in its compact format it does not conform to the `ExercisePlan` type).

Next, we set up the body of our post by mapping these changes into a JSON object. Note that as part of constructing this object, we set the `_id` property as the name of the workout to uniquely identify it in the database of the workouts collection.

The simplistic approach of using the *name* of the workout/exercise as a record identifier (or `id`) in MongoDB will break for any decent-sized app. Remember that we are creating a web-based application that can be accessed simultaneously by many users. Since there is always the possibility of two users coming up with the same name for a workout/exercise, we need a strong mechanism to make sure that names are not duplicated. Another problem with the MongoLab REST API is that if there is a duplicate `POST` request with the same `id` field, one will create a new document and the second will update it, instead of the second failing. This implies that any duplicate checks on the `id` field on the client side still cannot safeguard against data loss. In such a scenario, assigning auto generation of the `id` value is preferable. In standard cases where we are creating entities, unique ID generation is done on the server (mostly by the database). The response to when an entity is created then contains the generated ID. In such a case, we need to update the model object before we return data to the calling code.

Lastly, we call the `post` method of the `HTTPClient` module, passing the URL to connect to, an extra query string parameter (`apiKey`), and the data we are sending.

The last return statement should look familiar, as we use Observables to return the workout object as part of the Observable resolution. You need to be sure you add `.subscribe` to the Observable chain in order to make it work. We'll do that shortly by adding a subscription to the `save` method to `WorkoutComponent`.

Updating a workout

Why not try to implement the update operation? The `updateWorkout` method can be fixed in the same manner, the only difference being that the `HTTPClient` module's `put` method is required:

```
updateWorkout(workout: WorkoutPlan) {
    const workoutExercises: any = [];
    workout.exercises.forEach(
        (exercisePlan: any) => {
            workoutExercises.push({name: exercisePlan.exercise.name,
duration: exercisePlan.duration});
        }
    );

    const body = {
        '_id': workout.name,
        'exercises': workoutExercises,
        'name': workout.name,
        'title': workout.title,
        'description': workout.description,
        'restBetweenExercise': workout.restBetweenExercise
    };

    return this.http.put(this.collectionsUrl + '/workouts/' +
workout.name + this.params, body)
        .pipe(
            catchError(this.handleError<WorkoutPlan>())
        );
}
```

The preceding request URL now contains an extra fragment (`workout.name`) that denotes the identifier of the collection item that needs to be updated.

The MongoLab PUT API request creates the document passed in as the request body if the document is not found in the collection. While making the PUT request, make sure that the original record exists. We can do this by making a GET request for the same document first and confirming that we get a document before we update it. We'll leave that for you to implement.

Deleting a workout

The last operation that needs to be fixed is deleting the workout. Here is a simple implementation where we call the HTTPClient module's delete method to delete the workout referenced by a specific URL:

```
deleteWorkout(workoutName: string) {
    return this.http.delete(this.collectionsUrl + '/workouts/' +
workoutName + this.params)
        .pipe(
          catchError(this.handleError<WorkoutPlan>())
        );
}
```

Fixing the upstream code

With that, it's now time to fix the WorkoutBuilderService and Workout components. The save method of WorkoutBuilderService now looks as follows:

```
save() {
  const workout = this.newWorkout ?
     this.workoutService.addWorkout(this.buildingWorkout) :
     this.workoutService.updateWorkout(this.buildingWorkout);
  this.newWorkout = false;
  return workout;
}
```

Most of it looks the same as it was earlier because it is the same! We did not have to update this code because we effectively isolated the interaction with the external server in our WorkoutService component.

Finally, the save code for the Workout component is shown here:

```
save(formWorkout: any) {
  this.submitted = true;
  if (!formWorkout.valid) { return; }
  this.workoutBuilderService.save().subscribe(
    success => this.router.navigate(['/builder/workouts']),
    err => console.error(err)
  );
}
```

Here we have made a change so that we now subscribe to the save. As you may recall from our previous discussions, `subscribe` makes an Observable live so that we can complete the save.

And that's it! We can now create new workouts and update existing workouts (we'll leave completion of deleting workouts to you). That was not too difficult!

Let's try it out. Open the new `Workout Builder` page, create a workout, and save it. Also try to edit an existing workout. Both scenarios should work seamlessly.

 Check out `checkpoint 5.3` for an up-to-date implementation if you are having issues running your local copy. If you are not using Git, download the snapshot of Checkpoint 5.3 (a ZIP file) from the following GitHub location: `https://github.com/chandermani/angular6byexample/tree/checkpoint5.3`. Refer to the `README.md` file in the `trainer` folder when setting up the snapshot for the first time.

Something interesting happens on the network side while we make `POST` or `PUT` requests save data. Open the browser's network log console (*F12*) and see the requests being made. The log looks something like the following:

Name	Method	Status
7minworkout?apiKey=9...	OPTIONS	200
7minworkout?apiKey=...	PUT	200
workouts?apiKey=9...	GET	200

The network log

An `OPTIONS` request is made to the same endpoint before the actual `POST` or `PUT` is done. The behavior that we witness here is termed as a **prefight request**. This happens because we are making a cross-domain request to `api.mongolab.com`.

Using promises for HTTP requests

The bulk of this chapter has focused on how the Angular HTTPClient uses Observables as the default for XMLHttpRequests. This represents a significant change from the way things used to work. Many developers are familiar with using promises for asynchronous HTTP requests. With that being the case, Angular continues to support promises, but just not as the default choice. A developer has to opt for promises in an XMLHttpRequest in order to be able to use them.

For example, if we want to use promises with the getExercises method in WorkoutService, we will have to restructure the command as follows:

```
getExercises(): Promise<Exercise[]> {
    return this.http.get<Exercise[]>(this.collectionsUrl + '/exercises'
+ this.params)
    .toPromise()
    .then(res => res)
    .catch(err => {
        return Promise.reject(this.handleError('getExercises', []));
    });
}
```

In order to convert this method to use promises, all we have to do is add .toPromise() to the method chain, a success parameter, then, for the promise, and catch with a Promise.reject pointing to the existing handleError method.

For upstream components, we just have to switch to handling the return value as a promise rather than an Observable. So, to use promises in this case, we would have to change the code in Exercises.component.ts and LeftNavExercises.component.ts to first add a new property for the error message (we'll leave it to you as to how the error message is displayed on the screen):

```
errorMessage: any;
```

Then change the ngOnInit method that is calling WorkoutService to the following:

```
ngOnInit() {
  this.workoutService.getExercises()
  .then(exerciseList => this.exerciseList = exerciseList,
    error => this.errorMessage = <any>error
  );
}
```

Of course, the ease with which we can substitute promises for Observables in this simple example does not indicate that they are essentially the same. A then promise returns another promise, which means that you can create successively chained promises. In the case of an Observable, a subscription is essentially the end of the line and cannot be mapped or subscribed to beyond that point.

If you're familiar with promises, it may be tempting at this stage to stick with them and not give Observables a try. After all, much of what we have done with Observables in this chapter can be done with promises as well. For example, the mapping of two streams of Observables that we did with getWorkouts using the Observable's forkJoin operator can also be done with the promise's q, all function.

However, you would be selling yourself short if you took that approach. Observables open up an exciting new way of doing web development using what is called functional reactive programming. They involve a fundamental shift in thinking that treats an application's data as a constant stream of information to which the application reacts and responds. This shift allows applications to be built with a different architecture that makes them faster and more resilient. Observables are at the core of Angular in such things as event emitters and the new version of NgModel.

While promises are a useful tool to have in your toolkit, we encourage you to investigate Observables as you get into developing with Angular. They are part of the forward-looking philosophy of Angular and will be useful in future-proofing both your applications and your skill set.

Check out the checkpoint 5.3 file for an up-to-date implementation that includes the promises-related code that we covered previously. If you are not using Git, download the snapshot of Checkpoint 5.3 (a ZIP file) from the following GitHub location: https://github.com/chandermani/angular6byexample/tree/checkpoint5.3. Refer to the README.md file in the trainer folder when setting up the snapshot for the first time. Be aware that in the next section, we will be reverting to the use of Observables for this code. This code can be found in the checkpoint 5.4 file.

The async pipe

As we have seen with many of the data operations covered in this chapter, there is a fairly common pattern being repeated over and over again. When an Observable is returned from an HTTP request, we convert the response to JSON and subscribe to it. The subscription then binds the Observable output to a UI element. Wouldn't it be nice if we could eliminate this repetitive coding and replace it with a simpler way to accomplish what we are wanting to do?

Not surprisingly, Angular provides us with just the right way to do that. It's called the **async pipe**, and it can be used like any other pipe for binding to an element on the screen. However, the async pipe is a much more powerful mechanism than other pipes. It takes an Observable or a promise as an input and subscribes to it automatically. It also handles the teardown of the subscription for an Observable without necessitating any further lines of code.

Let's look at an example of this in our application. Let's go back to the `LeftNavExercises` component that we were just looking at in the previous section in connection with promises. Note that we have converted this component and the `Exercises` component from promises back to using Observables.

 Check out the `checkpoint 5.4` file for an up-to-date implementation that includes the conversion of this code to use Observables once again. If you are not using Git, download the snapshot of Checkpoint 5.4 (a ZIP file) from the following GitHub location: `https://github.com/ chandermani/angular6byexample/tree/checkpoint5.4`. Refer to the `README.md` file in the `trainer` folder when setting up the snapshot for the first time.

Then make the following changes in `LeftNavExercises`. First, import Observable from RxJs:

```
import { Observable } from 'rxjs/Observable';
```

Then change `exerciseList` from an array of exercises to an Observable of the same type:

```
public exerciseList:Observable<Exercise[]>;
```

Next modify the call to `WorkoutService` that gets the exercises to eliminate the subscription:

```
this.exerciseList = this.workoutService.getExercises();
```

Finally, open `left-nav-exercises.component.html` and add the `async` pipe to the `*ngFor` loop, as follows:

```
<div *ngFor="let exercise of exerciseList|async|orderBy:'title'">
```

Refresh the page and you will still see the Exercise list displaying. But this time, we have used the `async` pipe to eliminate the need to set up the subscription to the Observable. Pretty cool! This is a nice convenience that Angular has added, and since we have been spending time in this chapter understanding how Observables work with subscriptions, we have a clear idea of what the `async` pipe is now handling for us under the hood.

We'll leave it to you to implement the same change in the `Exercises` component.

It is important to understand the cross-domain behavior of the HTTP request and the constructs that Angular provides to make cross-domain requests.

Cross-domain access and Angular

Cross-domain requests are requests made for resources in a different domain. Such requests, when originated from JavaScript, have some restrictions imposed by the browser; these are called *same-origin policy* restrictions. Such a restriction stops the browser from making AJAX requests to domains that are different from the script's original source. The source match is done strictly based on a combination of protocol, host, and port.

For our own app, the calls to `https://api.mongolab.com` are cross-domain invocations as our source code hosting is in a different domain (most probably, something like `http://localhost/....`).

There are some workarounds and some standards that help relax/control cross-domain access. We will be exploring two of these techniques as they are the most commonly used ones. They are as follows:

- **JSON with Padding (JSONP)**
- **Cross-Origin Resource Sharing (CORS)**

A common way to circumvent this same-origin policy is to use the JSONP technique.

Using JSONP to make cross-domain requests

The JSONP mechanism of remote invocation relies on the fact that browsers can execute JavaScript files from any domain irrespective of the source of origin as long as the script is included via the `<script>` tag.

In JSONP, instead of making a direct request to a server, a dynamic `<script>` tag is generated, with the `src` attribute set to the server endpoint that needs to be invoked. This `<script>` tag, when appended to the browser's DOM, causes a request to be made to the target server.

The server then needs to send a response in a specific format, wrapping the response content inside a function invocation code (this extra padding around the response data gives this technique the name JSONP).

The Angular JSONP service hides this complexity and provides an easy API to make JSONP requests. The StackBlitz link, `https://stackblitz.com/edit/angular-nxeuxo`, highlights how JSONP requests are made. It uses the *IEX Free Stock API* (`https://iextrading.com/developer/`) to get quotes for any stock symbol.

> The Angular JSONP service only supports HTTP `GET` requests. Using any other HTTP request, such as `POST` or `PUT`, will generate an error.

If you look at the StackBlitz project, you will see the familiar pattern for component creation that we have followed throughout this book. We will not go over this pattern again, but will highlight a few details that are relevant to using the Angular JSONP service.

First, along with the imports for `FormsModule` and `HttpClientModule`, you will need to import `HttpClientJsonpModule` into `app.module.ts` as follows:

```
. . .
import { HttpClientModule, HttpClientJsonpModule } from
'@angular/common/http';
import { FormsModule } from '@angular/forms';
. . .
@NgModule({
. . .
  imports: [
    BrowserModule,
    FormsModule,
    HttpClientModule,
    HttpClientJsonpModule
  ],
```

```
. . .
})
```

Next, we need to add the following imports to `get-quote.component.ts`:

```
import { Component }from '@angular/core';
import { HttpClient } from '@angular/common/http';
import { Observable } from 'rxjs/Observable';
import { map } from 'rxjs/operators';
```

We are importing `HttpClient`, which contains the `JSONP` methods we will be using, as well as the RxJS `Observable` and the `map` operator. These imports will look familiar to you from what we have been building in this chapter.

 As you work with Angular JSONP, it is important to understand that by default, it returns Observables using RxJS. This means that we will have to follow the pattern for subscribing to those Observables and use the RxJS operators to manipulate the results. We can also use the async pipe to streamline these operations.

Then we inject `HttpClient` into the constructor:

```
constructor(public http: HttpClient) {}
```

Next we add several variables that we will be using in our JSONP call:

```
symbol: string;
quote: Observable<string>;
url: string = 'https://api.iextrading.com/1.0/stock/';
```

The `symbol` variable will hold the search string provided by the user. The `quote` variable will be used in our template to display the returned value from the JSONP call. And the `url` variable is the base URL for the call we will be making to the service.

Now we have everything in place for our `getQuote` method. Let's take a look at it:

```
getQuote (){
   let searchUrl = `${this.url}${this.symbol}/quote`;
   this.quote = this.http.jsonp(searchUrl, 'callback')
      .pipe(
       map( (res: string) => res)
     );
};
```

We first construct our `searchUrl` by concatenating the `url` with the `symbol` and adding `/quote`. The last part `quote` is what we need to pass to the quote service to return a stock quote.

We then use the HTTPClient's `jsonp` method to execute the remote call to the quote service. We pass the `searchUrl` as the first parameter of that method and a string `'callback'` as our second parameter. The latter parameter is used by Angular to augment the `searchUrl` with an extra query string parameter, `callback`. Internally, the Angular JSONP service then generates a dynamic `script` tag and a callback function and makes the remote request.

Open StackBlitz and enter symbols such as GOOG, MSFT, or FB to see the stock quote service in action. The browser network log for requests looks as follows:

```
https://api.iextrading.com/1.0/stock/MSFT/quote?callback=ng_jsonp_callback_
0
```

Here, `ng_jsonp_callback_0` is the dynamically generated function. And the response looks as follows:

```
typeof ng_jsonp_callback_0 === 'function' &&
ng_jsonp_callback_0({"quote"::{"symbol":"MSFT"..});
```

The response is wrapped in the callback function. Angular parses and evaluates this response, which results in the invocation of the `__ng_jsonp__.__req1` callback function. Then, this function internally routes the data to our function callback.

We hope this explains how JSONP works and what the underlying mechanism of a JSONP request is. However, JSONP has its limitations:

- First, we can make only GET requests (which is obvious as these requests originate due to script tags)
- Second, the server also needs to implement the part of the solution that involves wrapping the response in a function callback
- Third, there is always a security risk involved, as JSONP depends on dynamic script generation and injection
- Fourth, error handling is not reliable too because it is not easy to determine why a script load failed

Ultimately, we must recognize that JSONP is more of a workaround than a solution. As we move towards Web 2.0, where mashups become commonplace and more and more service providers decide to expose their API over the web, a far better solution/standard has emerged: CORS.

Cross-origin resource sharing

Cross-origin Resource Sharing (**CORS**) provides a mechanism for the web server to support cross-site access control, allowing browsers to make cross-domain requests from scripts. With this standard, a consumer application (such as *Personal Trainer*) is allowed to make some types of requests, termed **simple requests**, without any special setup requirements. These simple requests are limited to GET, POST (with specific MIME types), and HEAD. All other types of requests are termed **complex requests**.

For complex requests, CORS mandates that the request should be preceded by an HTTP OPTIONS request (also called a preflight request) that queries the server for HTTP methods allowed for cross-domain requests. And only on successful probing is the actual request made.

 You can learn more about CORS from the MDN documentation available at https://developer.mozilla.org/en-US/docs/Web/HTTP/Access_control_CORS.

The best part about CORS is that the client does not have to make any adjustment as in the case of JSONP. The complete handshake mechanism is transparent to the calling code and our Angular HTTPClient calls work without a hitch.

CORS requires configurations to be made on the server, and the MongoLab servers have already been configured to allow cross-domain requests. So the preceding POST and PUT requests that we made to the MongoLab to add and update Exercise and Workout documents all caused the preflight OPTIONS request.

Handling workouts not found

You might recall that in Chapter 2, *Personal Trainer*, we created the WorkoutResolver to not only retrieve a workout prior to navigation to the WorkoutComponent, but also prevent navigation to that component if a non-existent workout was in the route parameters. Now we would like to augment this functionality by displaying an error message on the workouts screen, indicating that the workout was not found.

In order to do this, we are going to modify `WorkoutResolver` so that it reroutes to the workouts screen if a workout is not found. To start, add the following child route to `WorkoutBuilderRoutingModule` (making sure it precedes the existing workouts route):

```
children: [
  {path: '', pathMatch: 'full', redirectTo: 'workouts'},
  {path: 'workouts/workout-not-found', component: WorkoutsComponent'},
  {path: 'workouts', component: 'WorkoutsComponent'},
   *** other child routes ***
  },
]
```

Next, modify the `resolve` method in the `WorkoutResolver` to redirect to this route in the event that a workout is not found:

```
resolve(
    route: ActivatedRouteSnapshot,
    state: RouterStateSnapshot): Observable<WorkoutPlan> {
    const workoutName = route.paramMap.get('id');

    if (!workoutName) {
        return this.workoutBuilderService.startBuildingNew();
    } else {
        this.isExistingWorkout = true;
        return
this.workoutBuilderService.startBuildingExisting(workoutName)
        .pipe(
          map(workout => {
            if (workout) {
                this.workoutBuilderService.buildingWorkout = workout;
                return workout;
            } else {
                this.router.navigate(['/builder/workouts/workout-not-
found']);
                return null;
            }
          }),
          catchError(error => {
            console.log('An error occurred!');
            this.router.navigate(['/builder/workouts']);
            return of(null);
          })
        );
    }
```

Then add a `notFound` boolean set to `false` to the variables in the `Workouts` component:

```
workoutList: Array<WorkoutPlan> = [];
public notFound = false;
```

And, in the `ngOnInit` method of that component, add the following code to check for the `workout-not-found` path and set the `notFound` value to `true`:

```
ngOnInit() {
  if(this.route.snapshot.url[1] && this.route.snapshot.url[1].path ===
  'workout-not-found') this.notFound = true;
  this.subscription = this.workoutService.getWorkouts()
  .subscribe(
    workoutList => this.workoutList = workoutList,
    (err:any) => console.error(err)
  );
}
```

Finally in the `Workouts.component.html` template, add the following `div` tag above the workout list that will display if the `notFound` is set to `true`:

```
<div *ngIf="notFound" class="not-found-msgbox">Could not load the specific
workout!</div>
```

If we find `workout-not-found` in the path when a user is returned to the `Workouts` page, then this displays the following message on the screen:

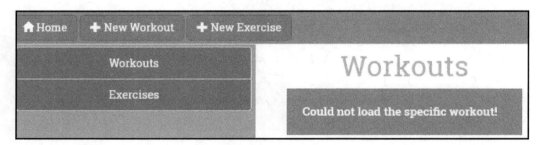

We have fixed routing failure for the Workout Builder page, but the exercise builder page is still pending. Again, we will leave it to you to fix it yourself.

Another major (and pending) implementation is fixing *7 Minute Workout*, as it currently caters to only one workout routine.

Fixing the 7 Minute Workout app

As it stands now, the *7 Minute Workout* (or *Workout Runner*) app can play only one specific workout. It needs to be fixed to support the execution of any workout plan built using *Personal Trainer*. There is an obvious need to integrate these two solutions. We already have the groundwork done to commence this integration. We've got the shared model services and `WorkoutService` to load data, enough to get us started.

Fixing *7 Minute Workout* and converting it into a generic *Workout Runner* roughly involves the following steps:

- Removing the hardcoded workout and exercises used in *7 Minute Workout*.
- Fixing the start page to show all available workouts and allowing users to select a workout to run.
- Fixing the workout route configuration to pass the selected workout name as the route parameter to the workout page.
- Loading the selected workout data using `WorkoutService` and starting the workout.
- And, of course, we need to rename the *7 Minute Workout* part of the app; the name is now a misnomer. I think the complete app can be called *Personal Trainer*. We can remove all references to *7 Minute Workout* from the view as well.

An excellent exercise to try out yourself! And that is why we are not going to walk you through the solution. Instead, go ahead and implement the solution. Compare your implementation with the one available at `checkpoint 5.4`.

It's time to end the chapter and summarize your learning.

Summary

We now have an app that can do a lot of stuff. It can run workouts, load workouts, save and update them, and track history. And if we look back, we have achieved this with minimal code. We bet that if we were to try this in standard jQuery or some other framework, it would require substantially more effort as compared to Angular.

We started the chapter by providing a *MongoDB* database on *MongoLab* servers. Since MongoLab provided a RESTful API to access the database, we saved some time by not setting up our own server infrastructure.

The first Angular construct that we touched upon was the HTTPClient, which is the primary service for connecting to any HTTP backend.

You also learned how the HTTPClient module uses Observables. For the first time, in this chapter, we created our own Observable and explained how to create subscriptions to those Observables.

We fixed our *Personal Trainer* app so that it uses the HTTPClient module to load and save workout data (note that data persistence for exercises is left for you to complete). In the process, you also learned about issues surrounding cross-domain resource access. You learned about JSONP, a workaround to circumvent a browser's *same-origin* restrictions, and how to issue JSONP requests using Angular. We also touched upon CORS, which has emerged as a standard when it comes to cross-domain communication.

We have now covered most of the building blocks of Angular, except the big one: Angular directives. We have used directives everywhere, but have not created one. The next chapter is exclusively dedicated to Angular directives. We will be creating a number of small directives, such as a remote validator, AJAX button, and a validation cues directive for the *Workout Builder* app.

Angular Directives in Depth 4

Directives are everywhere. They are the fundamental building blocks of Angular. Each extension to the application has resulted in us creating new **component directives**. These component directives have further consumed **attribute directives** (such as `NgClass` and `NgStyle`) and **structural directives** (such as `NgIf` and `NgFor`) to extend their behavior.

While we have built a number of component directives and a lone attribute directive, there are still some concepts of directive building that are worth exploring. This is especially true for attribute and structural directives, which we are yet to cover in detail.

The topics we will cover in this chapter include the following:

- **Building directives**: We build multiple directives and learn where directives are useful, how they differ from components, and how directives communicate with each other and/or their host component. We explore all directive types, including *component directives*, *attribute directives*, and *structural directives*.
- **Asynchronous validation**: Angular makes it easy to validate rules that require server interaction and hence are async in nature. We will build our first async validator in this chapter.
- **Using renderer for view manipulation**: Renderer allows view manipulation in a platform-agnostic way. We will utilize renderer for the busy indicator directive and learn about its API.
- **Host binding**: Host binding allows directives to communicate with their *host element*. This chapter covers how to utilize such bindings for directives.
- **Directive injection**: The Angular DI framework allows directive injection based on where in the HTML hierarchy the directives are declared. We will cover multiple scenarios pertaining to such injections.

- **Working with view children and content children**: Components have the capability to include external view templates into their own view. How to work with the injected content is something we will cover here.

- **Understanding the NgIf platform directive**: We will look under the hood of the `NgIf` platform directive and try to comprehend the working of *structural directives* such as `NgIf`.

- **View encapsulation of Angular components**: We will learn how Angular uses concepts derived from *web components* to support view and style encapsulation.

Building a remote validator directive

We ended `Chapter 3`, *Supporting Server Data Persistence*, with *Workout Runner* capable of managing workouts in the MongoDB store. Since each workout should have a unique name, we need to enforce the uniqueness constraint. Therefore, while creating/editing a workout, every time the user changes the workout name, we can query MongoDB to verify that the name already exists.

As is the case with any remote invocation, this check is asynchronous, and hence it requires a *remote validator*. We are going to build this remote validator using Angular's *async validator support*.

Async validators are similar to standard custom validators, except that instead of returning a key-value object map or null, the return value of a validation check is a **promise**. This promise is eventually resolved with the validation state being set (if there is an error), or null otherwise (on validation success).

We are going to create a validation directive that does workout name checks. There are two possible implementation approaches for such a directive:

- We can create a directive specifically for unique name validation
- We can create a generic directive that can perform any remote validation

Validation directives

While we are building a validation directive here, we could have built a standard custom validator class. The advantage of creating a directive is that it allows us to incorporate the directive in a template-driven form approach, where the directive can be embedded in the view HTML. Or, if the form has been generated using a model (reactive approach), we can directly use the validator class while creating the Control objects.

At first, the requirement of checking duplicate names against a data source (the *mLab* database) seems to be too a specific requirement and cannot be handled by a generic validator. But with some sensible assumptions and design choices, we can still implement a validator that can handle all types of remote validation, including workout name validation.

The plan is to create a validator that externalizes the actual validation logic. The directive will take the validation function as input. This implies that the actual validation logic is not a part of the validator, but a part of the component that actually needs to validate input data. The job of the directive is just to call the function and return the appropriate error keys based on the function's return value.

Let's put this theory into practice and build our remote validation directive, aptly named RemoteValidatorDirective.

The companion code base for the following section is Git branch checkpoint6.1. You can work along with us or check out the implementation available in the aforementioned folder. Or if you are not using Git, download the snapshot of checkpoint6.1 (a ZIP file) from GitHub location http://bit.ly/ng2be-checkpoint6-1. Refer to the README.md file in the trainer folder when setting up the snapshot for the first time.

Validating workout names using async validators

Like custom validators, async validators inherit from the same `Validator` class too; but this time, instead of returning an object map, async validators return a `Promise`.

Let's look at the definition of the validator. Copy the definition of the validator from the GitHub (`http://bit.ly/ng6be-6-1-remote-validator-directive-ts`) folder and add it to the `shared` module folder. The validator definition looks as follows:

```
import { Directive, Input } from '@angular/core';
import { NG_ASYNC_VALIDATORS, FormControl } from '@angular/forms';

@Directive({
  selector: '[abeRemoteValidator][ngModel]',
  providers: [{ provide: NG_ASYNC_VALIDATORS, useExisting:
RemoteValidatorDirective, multi: true }]
})
export class RemoteValidatorDirective {

  @Input() abeRemoteValidator: string;
  @Input() validateFunction: (value: string) => Promise<boolean>;

  validate(control: FormControl): { [key: string]: any } {
    const value: string = control.value;
    return this.validateFunction(value).then((result: boolean) => {
      if (result) {
        return null;
      }
      else {
        const error: any = {};
        error[this.abeRemoteValidator] = true;
        return error;
      }
    });
  }
}
```

Do remember to export this directive from the shared module, allowing us to use it in the workout builder module.

Since we are registering the validator as a directive instead of registering using a `FormControl` instance (generally used when building forms with a *reactive approach*), we need the extra provider configuration setting (added in the preceding `@Directive` metadata) by using this syntax:

```
providers:[{ provide: NG_ASYNC_VALIDATORS, useExisting:
RemoteValidatorDirective,  multi: true }]
```

This statement registers the validator with the existing async validators.

> The strange directive selector, `selector:`
> `` `[abeRemoteValidator][ngModel]` ``, used in the preceding code will be covered in the next section, where we will build a busy indicator directive.

Before we dig into the validator implementation, let's add it to the workout name input. This will help us correlate the behavior of the validator with its usage.

Update the workout name input (`workout.component.html`) with the validator declaration:

```
<input type="text" name="workoutName" ...
  abeRemoteValidator="workoutname"
[validateFunction]="validateWorkoutName">
```

Prefixing the directive selector
Always prefix your directives with an identifier (`abe` as you just saw) that distinguishes them from framework directives and other third-party directives.

Note: If the `ngModelOptions`, `updateOn` is set to `submit`, change it to `blur`.

The directive implementation takes two inputs: the *validation key* through directive property `abeRemoveValidator`, used to set the *error key*, and the *validation function* (`validateFunction`), called to validate the value of the control. Both inputs are annotated with the `@Input` decorator.

The input parameter `@Input("validateFunction")` `validateFunction: (value: string) => Promise<boolean>;`, binds to a function, not a standard component property. We are allowed to treat the function as a property due to the nature of the underlying language, TypeScript (as well as JavaScript).

When the async validation fires (on a change of `input`), Angular invokes the function, passing in the underlying `control`. As the first step, we pull the current input value and then invoke the `validateFunction` function with this input. The `validateFunction` returns a promise, which should eventually resolve to `true` or `false`:

- If the promise resolves to `true`, the validation is successful, the promise callback function returns `null`.
- If it is `false`, the validation has failed, and an error key-value map is returned. The *key* here is the string literal that we set when using the validator (`a2beRemoteValidator="workoutname"`).

This *key* comes in handy when there are multiple validators declared on the input, allowing us to identify validations that have failed.

To the workout component next add a validation message for this failure too. Add this label declaration after the existing validation `label` for *workout name*:

```
<label *ngIf="name.control.hasError('workoutname')" class="alert alert-
danger validation-message">A workout with this name already exists.</label>
```

And then wrap these two labels inside a `div`, as we do for *workout title* error labels.

The `hasError` function checks whether the `'workoutname'` validation key is present.

The last missing piece of this implementation is the actual validation function we assigned when applying the directive (`[validateFunction]="validateWorkoutName"`), but never implemented.

Add the `validateWorkoutName` function to `workout.component.ts`:

```
validateWorkoutName = (name: string): Promise<boolean> => {
    if (this.workoutName === name) { return Promise.resolve(true); }
    return this.workoutService.getWorkout(name).toPromise()
        .then((workout: WorkoutPlan) => {
            return !workout;
        }, error => {
            return true;
        });
}
```

Before we explore what the preceding function does, we need to do some more fixes on the `WorkoutComponent` class. The `validateWorkoutName` function is dependent on `WorkoutService` to get a workout with a specific name. Let's inject the service in the constructor and add the necessary import in the imports section:

```
import { WorkoutService }  from "../../core/workout.service";
...
constructor(... , private workoutService: WorkoutService) {
```

Then declare variables `workoutName` and `queryParamsSub`:

```
private workoutName: string;
queryParamsSub: Subscription
```

And add this statement to `ngOnInit`:

```
this.queryParamsSub = this.route.params.subscribe(params =>
this.workoutName = params['id']);
```

The preceding statement set the current workout name by watching (subscribing) over the observable `route.params` service. `workoutName` is used to skip workout name validation for an existing workout if the original workout name is used.

The subscription created previously needs to be clear to avoid memory leak, hence add this line to the `ngDestroy` function:

```
this.queryParamsSub.unsubscribe();
```

The reason for defining the `validateWorkoutName` function as an *instance function* (the use of the *arrow operator*) instead of defining it as a standard function (which declares the function on the *prototype*) is the `'this'` scoping issue.

Look at the validator function invocation inside `RemoteValidatorDirective` (declared using `@Input("validateFunction") validateFunction;`):

```
return this.validationFunction(value).then((result: boolean) => { ... });
```

When the function (named `validateFunction`) is invoked, the `this` reference is bound to `RemoteValidatorDirective` instead of the `WorkoutComponent`. Since `execute` is referencing the `validateWorkoutName` function in the preceding setup, any access to `this` inside `validateWorkoutName` is problematic.

This causes the `if (this.workoutName === name)` statement inside `validateWorkoutName` to fail, as `RemoteValiatorDirective` does not have a `workoutName` instance member. By defining `validateWorkoutName` as an instance function, the *TypeScript* compiler *creates a closure* around the value of `this` when the function is defined.

With the new declaration, `this` inside `validateWorkoutName` always points to the `WorkoutComponent` irrespective of how the function gets invoked.

We can also look at the compiled JavaScript for `WorkoutComponent` to know how the closure works with respect to `validateWorkoutName`. The parts of the generated code that interest us are as follows:

```
function WorkoutComponent(...) {
  var _this = this;
  ...
  this.validateWorkoutName = function (name) {
    if (_this.workoutName === name)
      return Promise.resolve(true);
```

If we look at the validation function implementation, we see that it involves querying *mLab* for a specific workout name. The `validateWorkoutName` function returns `true` when a workout with the same name is not found and `false` when a workout with the same name is found (actually a *promise* is returned).

 The `getWorkout` function on `WorkoutService` returns an *observable,* but we convert it into a *promise* by calling the `toPromise` function on the observable.

The validation directive can now be tested. Create a new workout and enter an existing workout name such as 7minworkout. See how the validation error message shows up eventually:

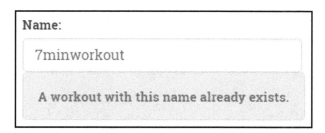

Excellent! It looks great, but there is still something missing. The user is not informed that we are validating the workout name. We can improve this experience.

Building a busy indicator directive

While the workout name is being validated remotely, we want the user to be aware of the activity in the background. A visual clue around the input box while the remote validation happens should serve the purpose.

Think carefully; there is an input box with an asynchronous validator (which does remote validation) and we want to adorn the input box with a visual clue during validation. Seems like a common pattern to solve? Indeed it is, so let's create another directive!

But before we start the implementation, it is imperative to understand that we are not in it alone. The busy indicator directive requires the help of another directive, NgModel. We have already used the NgModel directive on input elements in Chapter 2, *Personal Trainer*. NgModel helps us track the input element state. The following example is taken from Chapter 2, *Personal Trainer*, and it highlights how NgModel helps us validate inputs:

```
<input type="text" name="workoutName" #name="ngModel" class="form-control"
id="workout-name" ... [(ngModel)]="workout.name" required>
...
<label *ngIf="name.control.hasError('required') && (name.touched ||
submitted)" class="alert alert-danger">Name is required</label>
```

Even the unique workout name validation done in the previous section employs the same technique of using `NgModel` to check the validation state.

Let's begin with defining the outline of the directive. Create a `busy-indicator.directive.ts` file using the CLI generator in the `src/app/shared` folder:

```
ng generate directive busy-indicator
```

Also, export it by adding the directive to the `exports` array in the shared module file `shared.module.ts`.

Next, update the directive's constructor with `NgModel` injection and import the `NgModel` reference from `@angular/forms`:

```
constructor(private model: NgModel) { }
```

This instructs Angular to inject the `NgModel` instance of the element on which the directive is declared. Remember that the `NgModel` directive is already present on `input` (workoutname):

```
<input... name="workoutName" #name="ngModel" [(ngModel)]="workout.name"
...>
```

This is enough to integrate our new directive in the workout view, so let's do it quickly.

Open `workout.component.html` from `workout-builder` and add the busy indicator directive to the workout name `input`:

```
<input type="text" name="workoutName" ... abeBusyIndicator>
```

Create a new workout or open an existing one to see whether the `BusyIndicatorDirective` is loaded and the `NgModel` injection worked fine. This can be easily verified by putting a breakpoint inside the `BusyIndicatorDirective` constructor.

Angular injects the same `NgModel` instance into `BusyIndicatorDirective` that it created when it encountered `ngModel` on the input HTML.

You may be wondering what happens if we apply this directive on an input element that does not have the `ngModel` attribute, or as a matter of fact on any HTML element/component, such as this:

```
<div abeBusyIndicator></div>
<input type="text" abeBusyIndicator>
```

Will the injection work?

Of course not! We can try it in the create workout view. Open `workout.component.html` and add the following `input` above the workout name `input`. Refresh the app:

```
<input type="text" name="workoutName1" a2beBusyIndicator>
```

Angular throws an exception, as follows:

EXCEPTION: No provider for NgModel! (BusyIndicatorDirective -> NgModel)

How to avoid this? Well, Angular's DI can rescue us here as it allows us to declare an optional dependency.

> Remove the `input` control that you just added before proceeding further.

Injecting optional dependencies with the @Optional decorator

Angular has an `@Optional` decorator, which when applied to a constructor argument instructs the Angular *injector* to inject `null` if the dependency is not found.

Hence, the busy indicator constructor can be written as follows:

```
constructor(@Optional() private model: NgModel) { }
```

Problem solved? Not really; as stated previously, we require the `NgModel` directive for `BusyIndicatorDirective` to work. So, while we have learned something new, it is not very useful in the current scenario.

> Before proceeding further, remember to revert the `workoutnameinput` to its original state, with `abeBusyIndicator` applied.

`BusyIndicatorDirective` should only be applied if there is an `NgModel` directive already present on the element.

The `selector` directive is going to save our day this time. Update the `BusyIndicatorDirective` selector to this:

```
selector: `[abeBusyIndicator][ngModel]`
```

This selector creates the `BusyIndicatorDirective` only if the combination of `a2beBusyIndicator` with the `ngModel` attribute is present on the element. Problem solved!

It's now time to add the actual implementation.

Implementation one – using renderer

For `BusyIndicatorDirective` to work, it needs to know when the async validation on the `input` fires and when it is over. This information is only available with the `NgModel` directive. `NgModel` has a property, `control`, which is an instance of the `Control` class. It is this `Control` class that tracks the current state of the input, including the following:

- Currently assigned validators (sync and async)
- The current value
- The input element state, such as `pristine`, `dirty`, and `touched`
- The input validation state, which could be any one of `valid`, `invalid`, or `pending` in the case of validation being performed asynchronously
- Events that track when the value changes or the validation state changes

`Control` seems to be a useful class, and it's the `pending` state that interests us!

Let's add our first implement for the `BusyIndicatorDirective` class. Update the class with this code:

```
private subscriptions: Array<any> = [];
ngAfterViewInit(): void {
    this.subscriptions.push(
        this.model.control.statusChanges.subscribe((status: any) => {
            if (this.model.control.pending) {
                this.renderer.setElementStyle(this.element.nativeElement,
'border-width', '3px');
                this.renderer.setElementStyle(this.element.nativeElement,
'border-color', 'gray');
            }
            else {
                this.renderer.setElementStyle(this.element.nativeElement,
'border-width', null);
```

```
        this.renderer.setElementStyle(this.element.nativeElement,
'border-color', null);
        }
      }));
  }
```

Two new dependencies need to be added to the constructor, as we use them in the
`ngAfterViewInit` function. Update the `BusyIndicatorDirective` constructor to look as
follows:

```
constructor(private model: NgModel,
    private element: ElementRef, private renderer: Renderer) { }
```

And also add imports for `ElementRef` and `Renderer` in `'@angular/core'`.

`ElementRef` is a wrapper object over the underlying HTML element (`input` in this case).
The `MyAudioDirective` directive used `ElementRef` to get hold of the underlying `Audio`
element.

The `Renderer` injection deserves a bit of attention. Calling `setElementStyle` is a dead
giveaway that `Renderer` is responsible for managing the DOM. But before we delve more
deeply into the role of `Renderer`, let's try to understand what the preceding code is doing.

In the preceding code, the `control` property on the model (the `NgModel` instance) defines
an event (an `Observable`), `statusChanges`, which we can subscribe to in order to know
when the control validation state changes. The available validation states are `valid`,
`invalid`, and `pending`.

The subscription checks whether the control state is `pending` or not, and accordingly
adorns the underlying element using the `Renderer` API function, `setElementStyle`. We
set the `border-width` and `border-color` of the input.

The preceding implementation is added to the `ngAfterViewInit` directive lifecycle hook,
which is called after the view has initialized.

Let's try it out. Open the create workout page or the existing *7 Minute Workout*. As soon as
we leave workout name input, the `input` style changes and reverts once the remote
validation of the workout name is complete. Nice!

Name:

7MinWorkou

Before moving forward, also add the un-subscription code to the
`BusyIndicatorDirective` to avoid a memory leak. Add this function (life cycle hook) to
`BusyIndicatorDirective`:

```
ngOnDestroy() {
    this.subscriptions.forEach((s) => s.unsubscribe());
}
```

Always unsubscribe from observables
Always remember to unsubscribe from any `Observable/EventEmitter`
subscription done in the code to avoid memory leaks.

The implementation looks good. The `Renderer` is doing its job. But there are some
unanswered questions.

Why not just get hold of the underlying DOM object and use the standard DOM API to
manipulate the input styles? Why do we need the *renderer*?

Angular renderer, the translation layer

One of the primary design goals of Angular 2 was to make it run across environments,
frameworks, and devices. Angular enabled this by dividing the core framework
implementation into an **application layer** and a **rendering layer**. The application layer has
the API we interact with, whereas the rendering layer provides an abstraction that the
application layer can use without worrying about how and where the actual view is being
rendered.

By separating the rendering layer, Angular can theoretically run in various setups. These
include (but are not limited to):

- Browser
- Browser main thread and web worker thread, for obvious performance reasons
- Server-side rendering
- Native app frameworks; efforts are underway to integrate Angular with
  `NativeScript` with `ReactNative`
- Testing, allowing us to test the app UI outside the web browser

The `Renderer` implementation that Angular uses inside our browser is `DOMRenderer`. It is responsible for translating our API calls into browser DOM updates. In fact, we can verify the renderer type by adding a breakpoint in the `BusyIndicatorDirective`'s constructor and seeing the value of `renderer`.

For this precise reason, we avoid direct manipulation of DOM elements inside `BusyIndicatorDirective`. You never know where the code will end up running. We could have easily done this:

```
this.element.nativeElement.style.borderWidth="3px";
```

Instead, we used the `Renderer` to do the same in a platform-agnostic way.

Look at the `Renderer` API function, `setElementStyle`:

```
this.renderer.setElementStyle(
        this.element.nativeElement, "border-width", "3px");
```

It takes the element on which the style has to be set, the style property to update, and the value to set. The `element` references the `input` element injected into `BusyIndicatorDirective`.

 Resetting styles
Styles set by calling `setElementStyle` can be reset by passing a `null` value in the third argument. Check out the `else` condition in the preceding code.

The `Renderer` API has a number of other methods that can be used to set attributes, set properties, listen to events, and even create new views. Whenever you build a new directive, remember to evaluate the `Renderer` API for DOM manipulation.

 A more detailed explanation of `Renderer` and its application is available as part of Angular's design documents here: `http://bit.ly/ng2-render`

We are not done yet! With Angular's awesomeness, we can improve the implementation. Angular allows us to do *host binding* in directive implementation, helping us avoid a lot of boilerplate code.

Host binding in directives

In the Angular realm, the component/element that a directive gets attached to is termed the **host element**: a container that hosts our directive/component. For the `BusyIndicatorDirective`, the `input` element is the *host*.

While we can use the `Renderer` to manipulate the host (and we did too), the Angular data binding infrastructure can reduce the code further. It provides a declarative way to manage directive-host interaction. Using the host binding concepts, we can manipulate an element's *properties* and *attributes* and subscribe to its *events*.

Let's understand each of the host binding capabilities, and in the end, we will fix our `BusyIndicatorDirective` implementation.

Property binding using @HostBinding

Use **host property binding** to bind a *directive property* to a *host element property*. Any changes to the directive property will be synced with the linked host property during the change detection phase.

We just need to use the `@HostBinding` decorator on the directive property that we want to sync with. For example, consider this binding:

```
@HostBinding("readOnly") get busy() {return this.isbusy};
```

When applied to `input`, it will set the `input` `readOnly` property to `true` when the `isbusy` directive property is `true`.

 Note that `readonly` is also an *attribute* on `input`. What we are referring to here is the input *property* `readOnly`.

Attribute binding

Attribute binding binds a directive property to a host component attribute. For example, consider a directive with binding like the following:

```
@HostBinding("attr.disabled") get canEdit(): string
  { return !this.isAdmin ? "disabled" : null };
```

If applied to input it will add the `disabled` attribute on `input` when the `isAdmin` flag is `false`, and clear it otherwise. We follow the same attribute binding notation used in the HTML template here too. The attribute name is prefixed with string literal `attr`.

We can do something similar with *class* and *style binding* too. Consider the following line:

```
@HostBinding('class.valid')
    get valid { return this.control.valid; }
```

This line sets up a class binding, and the following line creates a style binding:

```
@HostBinding("style.borderWidth")
    get focus(): string { return this.focus?"3px": "1px"};
```

Event binding

Lastly, **event binding** is used to subscribe to the events raised by the host component/element. Consider this example:

```
@Directive({ selector: 'button, div, span, input' })
class ClickTracker {
  @HostListener('click', ['$event.target'])
  onClick(element: any) {
    console.log("button", element, "was clicked");
  }
}
```

This sets up a listener on the host event `click`. Angular will instantiate the preceding directive for every *button*, *div*, *span*, and *input* on the view and set up the host binding with the `onClick` function. The `$event` variable contains the event data for the event raised, and `target` refers to the element/component that was clicked on.

Event bindings work for components too. Consider the following example:

```
@Directive({ selector: 'workout-runner' })
class WorkoutTracker {
  @HostListener('workoutStarted', ['$event'])
  onWorkoutStarted(workout: any) {
    console.log("Workout has started!");
  }
}
```

With this directive, we track the `workoutStarted` event defined on the `WorkoutRunner` component. The `onWorkoutStarted` function is called when the workout starts, with the details of the started workout.

Now that we understand how these bindings work, we can improve our `BusyIndicatorDirective` implementation.

Implementation two - BusyIndicatorDirective with host bindings

You may have already guessed it! We will use *host property binding* instead of `Renderer` to set styles. Want to give it a try? Go ahead! Clear the existing implementation and try to set up a host binding for the `borderWidth` and `borderColor` style attributes without looking at the following implementation.

This is how the directive will look after the host binding implementation:

```
import {Directive, HostBinding} from '@angular/core';
import {NgModel} from '@angular/forms';

@Directive({ selector: `[abeBusyIndicator][ngModel]`})
export class BusyIndicatorDirective {
  private get validating(): boolean {
    return this.model.control != null && this.model.control.pending;
  }
  @HostBinding('style.borderWidth') get controlBorderWidth():
        string { return this.validating ? '3px' : null; }
  @HostBinding('style.borderColor') get controlBorderColor():
        string { return this.validating ? 'gray' : null; }

  constructor(private model: NgModel) { }
}
```

We have moved the `pending` state check into a directive property called `validating` and then used the `controlBorderWidth` and `controlBorderColor` properties for style binding. This is definitely more succinct than our earlier approach! Go test it out.

And if we tell you that this can be done without the need for a custom directive, don't be surprised! This is how we do it, just by using style bindings on the workout name `input`:

```
<input type="text" name="workoutName" ...
[style.borderColor]="name.control.pending ? 'gray' : null"
[style.borderWidth]="name.control.pending ? '3px' : null">
```

We get the same effect!

No, our effort did not go to waste. We did learn about **renderer** and **host binding**. These concepts will come in handy while building directives that provide complex behavior extension instead of just setting element styles.

 If you are having a problem with running the code, look at the Git branch `checkpoint6.1` for a working version of what we have done thus far. Or if you are not using Git, download the snapshot of `checkpoint6.1` (a ZIP file) from `http://bit.ly/ng6be-checkpoint-6-1`. Refer to the `README.md` file in the `trainer` folder when setting up the snapshot for the first time.

The next topic that we are going to take up is *directive injection*.

Directive injection

Go back a few pages and look at the `BusyIndicatorDirective` implementation that uses the *renderer*, specifically the constructor:

```
constructor(private model: NgModel ...) { }
```

Angular automatically locates the `NgModel` directive created for the directive element and injects it into `BusyIndicatorDirective`. This is possible because both directives are declared on the same *host element*.

The good news is that we can influence this behavior. Directives created on a parent HTML tree or child tree can also be injected. The next few sections talk about how to inject directives across the component tree, a very handy feature that allows cross-directive communication for directives that have a *common lineage* (in a view).

We will use StackBlitz (`https://stackblitz.com/edit/angular-pzljm3`) to demonstrate these concepts. SlackBlitz is an online IDE to run Angular applications!

To start with, look at the file `app.component.ts`. It has three directives: `Relation`, `Acquaintance`, and `Consumer` and this view hierarchy is defined:

```
<div relation="grand-parent" acquaintance="jack">
    <div relation="parent">
      <div relation="me" consumer>
        <div relation="child-1">
          <div relation="grandchild-1"></div>
        </div>
        <div relation="child-2"></div>
      </div>
    </div>
</div>
```

In the next few sections, we will describe the various ways in which we can inject the different `relation` and `Acquaintance` directives into the `consumer` directive. Check out the browser console for the injected dependencies that we log during the `ngAfterViewInit` lifecycle hook.

Injecting directives defined on the same element

Constructor injection by default supports injecting directives defined on the same element. The constructor function just needs to declare the directive type variable that we want to inject:

```
variable:DirectiveType
```

The `NgModel` injection that we did in `BusyIndicatorDirective` falls under this category. If the directive is not found on the current element, the Angular DI will throw an error, unless we mark the dependency as `@Optional`.

Optional dependency

The `@Optional` decorator is not limited to directive injection. It's there to mark any type of dependency optional.

From the plunk example, the first injection (in `Consumer` directive implementation) injects the `Relation` directive with the `me` attribute (`relation="me"`) into the consumer directive:

```
constructor(private me:Relation ...
```

Injecting directive dependency from the parent

Prefixing a constructor argument with the @Host decorator instructs Angular to search for the dependency on the *current element, its parent,* or its *parents* until it reaches the component boundaries (a component with the directive present somewhere in its view hierarchy). Check the second consumer injection:

```
constructor(..., @Host() private myAcquaintance:Acquaintance
```

This statement injects the Acquaintance directive instance declared two levels up the hierarchy.

 Like the @Option decorator described previously, the usage of @Host() is not limited to directives too. Angular service injection also follows the same pattern. If a service is marked with @Host, the search stops at the host component. It does not continue further up the component tree.

The @Skipself decorator can be used to skip the current element for a directive search.

From the StackBlitz example, this injection injects the Relation directive with the relation attribute value parent (relation="parent") into consumer:

```
@SkipSelf() private myParent:Relation
```

Injecting a child directive (or directives)

If there is a need to inject directive(s) defined on nested HTML into a parent directive/component, there are four decorators that can help us:

- @ViewChild/@ViewChildren
- @ContentChild/@ContentChildren

As these naming conventions suggest, there are decorators to inject a single child directive or multiple children directives:

To understand the significance of @ViewChild/@ViewChildren versus @ContentChild/@ContentChildren, we need to look at what view and content children are, a topic that we will take up soon. But for now, it's enough to understand that view children are part of a component's own view and content children are external HTML injected into the component's view.

Look how, in the StackBlitz example, the `ContentChildren` decorator is used to inject the child `Relation` directive into `Consumer`:

```
@ContentChildren(Relation) private children:QueryList<Relation>;
```

Surprisingly, the data type of the variable `children` is not an array, but a custom class- `QueryList`. The `QueryList` class is not a typical array, but a collection that is kept up to date by Angular whenever dependencies are added or removed. This can happen if the DOM tree is created/destroyed when using structural directives such as `NgIf` or `NgFor`. We will also talk more about `QueryList` in the coming sections.

You may have observed that the preceding injection is not a constructor injection as were the earlier two examples. This is for a reason. The injected directive(s) will not be available until the underlying component/element's content has initialized. For this precise reason, we have the `console.log` statements inside the `ngAfterViewInit` lifecycle hook. We should only access the content children post this life cycle hook execution.

The preceding sample code injects in all three child `relation` objects into the `consumer` directive.

Injecting descendant directive(s)

The standard `@ContentChildren` decorator (or as a matter of fact `@ViewChildren` too) only injects the immediate children of a directive/component and not its descendants. To include all its descendants, we need to provide an argument to `Query`:

```
@ContentChildren(Relation, {descendants: true}) private
allDescendents:QueryList<Relation>;
```

Passing the `descendants: true` parameter will instruct Angular to search for all descendants.

If you look at the console log, the preceding statement injects in all four descendants.

The Angular DI, while it seems simple to use, packs a lot of functionality. It manages our services, components, and directives and provides us with the right stuff in the right place at the right time. Directive injection in components and other directives provides a mechanism for directives to communicate with each other. Such injections allow one directive to access the public API (public functions/properties) of another directive.

It's now time to explore something new. We are going to build an Ajax button component that allows us to inject an external view into the component, a process also known as **content transclusion**.

Building an Ajax button component

When we save/update an exercise or workout, there is always the possibility of duplicate submission (or duplicate POST requests). The current implementation does not provide any feedback as to when the save/update operation started and when it is completed. The user of an app can knowingly or unknowingly click on the **Save** button multiple times due to the lack of visual clues.

Let's try to solve this problem by creating a specialized button—an *Ajax button* that gives some visual clues when clicked on and also stops duplicate Ajax submissions.

The button component will work on these lines. It takes a function as input. This input function (input parameter) should return a promise pertaining to the remote request. On clicking on the button, the button internally makes the remote call (using the input function), tracks the underlying promise, waits for it to complete, and shows some busy clues during this activity. Also, the button remains disabled until the remote invocation completes to avoid duplicate submission.

The companion code base for the following section is Git branch checkpoint6.2. You can work along with us, or check out the implementation available in the branch. Or if you are not using Git, download the snapshot of checkpoint6.2 (a ZIP file) from the GitHub location http://bit.ly/ng6be-checkpoint-6-2. Refer to the README.md file in the trainer folder when setting up the snapshot for the first time.

Let's create the component outline to make things clearer. Use the following command to create an ajax-button component under the application's shared module (src/app/shared) and **then export the component** from the SharedModule:

```
ng generate component ajax-button -is
```

Update the component definition too and import them from @angular/core:

```
export class AjaxButtonComponent implements OnInit {
  busy: boolean = null;
  @Input() execute: any;
  @Input() parameter: any;
}
```

And add the following HTML template to `ajax-button.component.html`:

```
<button [attr.disabled]="busy" class="btn btn-primary">
    <span [hidden]="!busy">
        <div class="ion-md-cloud-upload spin"></div>
    </span>
    <span>Save</span>
</button>
```

The component (`AjaxButtonComponent`) takes two property bindings, `execute` and `parameter`. The `execute` property points to the function that is invoked on the Ajax button click. The `parameter` is the data that can be passed to this function.

Look at the usage of the `busy` flag in the view. We disable the button and show the spinner when the `busy` flag is set. Let's add the implementation that makes everything work. Add this code to the `AjaxButtonComponent` class:

```
@HostListener('click', ['$event'])
onClick(event: any) {
    const result: any = this.execute(this.parameter);
    if (result instanceof Promise) {
      this.busy = true;
      result.then(
        () => { this.busy = null; },
        (error: any) => { this.busy = null; });
    }
}
```

We set up a *host event binding* to the click event on `AjaxButtonComponent`. Anytime the `AjaxButtonComponent` component is clicked on, the `onClick` function is invoked.

The `HostListener` import needs to be added to the `'@angular/core'` module.

The `onClick` implementation calls the input function with a lone parameter as `parameter`. The result of the invocation is stored in the `result` variable.

The `if` condition checks whether the `result` is a `Promise` object. If yes, the `busy` indicator is set to `true`. The button then waits for the promise to get resolved, using the `then` function. Irrespective of whether the promise is resolved with *success* or *error*, the busy flag is set to `null`.

The reason the busy flag is set to `null` and not `false` is due to this attribute binding `[attr.disabled]="busy"`. The `disabled` attribute will not be removed unless `busy` is null. Remember that in HTML, `disabled="false"` does not enable the button. The attribute needs to be removed before the button becomes clickable again.

If we are confused about this line:

```
const result: any = this.execute(this.parameter);
```

Then you need to look at how the component is used. Open `workout.component.html` and replace the `Save` button HTML with the following:

```
<abe-ajax-button [execute]="save" [parameter]="f"></abe-ajax-button>
```

The `Workout.save` function binds to `execute`, and `parameter` takes the `FormControl` object `f`.

We need to change the `save` function in the `Workout` class to return a promise for `AjaxButtonComponent` to work. Change the `save` function implementation to the following:

```
save = (formWorkout: any): Promise<Object | WorkoutPlan> => {
    this.submitted = true;
    if (!formWorkout.valid) { return; }
    const savePromise = this.workoutBuilderService.save().toPromise();

    savePromise.then(
      result => this.router.navigate(['/builder/workouts']),
      err => console.error(err)
    );
    return savePromise;
}
```

The `save` function now returns a *promise* that we build by calling the `toPromise` function on the *observable* returned from the call to `workoutBuilderService.save()`.

Make note of how we define the `save` function as an *instance function* (with the use of the arrow operator) to create a closure over *this*. It's something we did earlier while building the *remote validator directive*.

Time to test our implementation! Refresh the application and open the create/edit workout view. Click on the **Save** button and see the Ajax button in action:

The preceding animation may be short-lived as we navigate back to the workout list page post save. We can temporarily disable the navigation to see the new changes.

We started this section with the aim of highlighting how external elements/components can be transcluded into a component. Let's do it now!

Transcluding external components/elements into a component

From the very start, we need to understand what **transclusion** means. And the best way to understand this concept would be to look at an example.

No component that we have built thus far has borrowed content from outside. Not sure what this means?

Consider the preceding `AjaxButtonComponent` example in `workout.component.html`:

```
<ajax-button [execute]="save" [parameter]="f"></ajax-button>
```

What if we change the `ajax-button` usage to the following?

```
<ajax-button [execute]="save" [parameter]="f">Save Me!</ajax-button>
```

Will the `Save Me!` text show up on the button? It will not try it!

The `AjaxButtonComponent` component already has a template, and it rejects the content we provide in the preceding declaration. What if we can somehow make the content (`Save Me!` in the preceding example) load inside the `AjaxButtonComponent`? This act of injecting an external view fragment into the component's view is what we call **transclusion**, and the framework provides the necessary constructs to enable transclusions.

It's time to introduce two new concepts, *content children* and *view children*.

Content children and view children

To define it succinctly, the HTML structure that a component defines internally (using `template or templateUrl`) is the **view children** of the component. However, the HTML view provided as part of the component usage added to the host element (such as `<ajax-button>`**Save Me!**`</ajax-button>`), defines the **content children** of the component.

By default, Angular does not allow *content children* to be embedded as we saw before. The `Save Me!` text was never emitted. We need to explicitly tell Angular where to emit the *content children* inside the *component view template*. To understand this concept, let's fix the `AjaxButtonComponent` view. Open `ajax-button.component.ts` and update the view template definition to the following:

```
<button [attr.disabled]="busy" class="btn btn-primary">
    <span [hidden]="!busy">
        <ng-content select="[data-animator]"></ng-content>
    </span>
    <ng-content select="[data-content]"></ng-content>
</button>
```

The two `ng-content` elements in the preceding view define the *content injection locations*, where the content children can be injected/transcluded. The `selector` property defines the *CSS selector* that should be used to locate the content children when injected into the main host.

It starts to make more sense as soon as we fix the `AjaxButtonComponent` usage in `workout.component.html`. Change it to the following:

```
<ajax-button [execute]="save" [parameter]="f">
    <div class="ion-md-cloud-upload spin" data-animator></div>
    <span data-content>Save</span>
</ajax-button>
```

The `span` with `data-animator` is injected into the `ng-content` with the `select=[data-animator]` property and the other `span` (with the `data-content` attribute) is injected into the second `ng-content` declaration.

Refresh the application again and try to save a workout. While the end result is the same, the resultant view is a combination of multiple view fragments: one part for component definition (*view children*) and another part for component usage (*content children*).

The following diagram highlights this difference for the rendered `AjaxButtonComponent`:

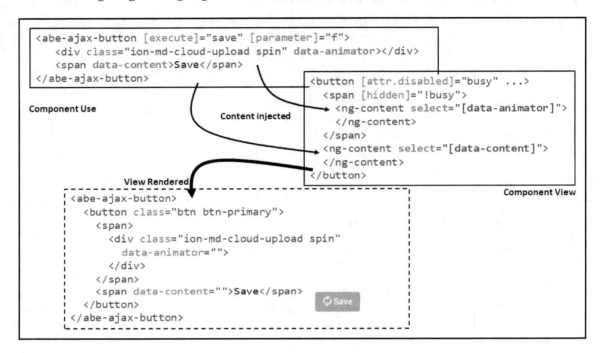

The `ng-content` can be declared without the `selector` attribute. In such a scenario, the complete content defined inside the component tag is injected.

Content injection into an existing component view is a very powerful concept. It allows the component developer to provide extension points that the component consumer can readily consume and customize the behavior of the component, that too in a controlled manner.

The content injections that we defined for the `AjaxButtonComponent` allow the consumer to change the busy indicator animation and the button content, keeping the behavior of the button intact.

Angular's advantages do not end here. It has the capability to inject *content children* and *view children* into the *component code/implementation*. This allows the component to interact with its content/view children and control their behavior too.

Injecting view children using @ViewChild and @ViewChildren

Let's look at the relevant parts of the `WorkoutAudioComponent` implementation. The view definition looked as follows:

```
<audio #ticks="MyAudio" loop src="/assets/audic/tick10s.mp3"></audio>
<audio #nextUp="MyAudio" src="/assets/audio/nextup.mp3"></audio>
<audio #nextUpExercise="MyAudio" [src]="'/assets/audio/' +
nextupSound"></audio>
// Some other audio elements
```

And the injection looked as follows:

```
@ViewChild('ticks') private _ticks: MyAudioDirective;
@ViewChild('nextUp') private _nextUp: MyAudioDirective;
@ViewChild('nextUpExercise') private _nextUpExercise: MyAudioDirective;
```

The directive (`MyAudioDirective`) associated with the `audio` tag was injected into the `WorkoutAudio` implementation using the `@ViewChild` decorator. The parameters passed to `@ViewChild` are the *template variable* names (such as `tick`) used to locate the element in the view definition. The `WorkoutAudio` component then used these audio directives to control the audio playback for *7 Minute Workout*.

While the preceding implementation injects `MyAudioDirective`, even child components can be injected. For example, instead of using `MyAudioDirective`, suppose we build a `MyAudioComponent`, something like the following:

```
@Component({
  selector: 'my-audio',
  template: '<audio ...></audio>',
})
export class MyAudioComponent {
  ...
}
```

We can then use it instead of the `audio` tag:

```
<my-audio #ticks loop
   src="/static/audio/tick10s.mp3"></my-audio>
```

The injection would still work.

What happens if there is more than one directive/component of the same type defined on the component view? Use the @ViewChildren decorator. It allows you to query injections of one type. The syntax for the use of @ViewChildren is as follows:

```
@ViewChildren(directiveType) children: QueryList<directiveType>;
```

This injects all the view children of type directiveType. For the WorkoutAudio component example stated previously, we can use the following statement to get hold of all MyAudioDirective:

```
@ViewChildren(MyAudioDirectives) private all: QueryList<MyAudioDirectives>;
```

The ViewChildren decorator can also take a list of comma-separated selectors (*template variable names*) instead of type. For example, to select multiple MyAudioDirective instances in the WorkoutAudio component, we can use the following:

```
@ViewChildren('ticks, nextUp, nextUpExercise, halfway, aboutToComplete')
private all: QueryList<MyAudioDirective>;
```

The QueryList class is a special class provided by Angular. We introduced QueryList in the *Injecting descendant directive(s)* section earlier in the chapter. Let's explore QueryList further.

Tracking injected dependencies with QueryList

For components that require multiple components/directives to be injected (using either @ViewChildren or @ContentChildren), the dependency injected is a QueryList object.

The QueryList class is a *read-only collection* of injected components/directives. Angular keeps this collection in sync based on the current state of the user interface.

Consider, for example, the WorkoutAudio directive view. It has five instances of MyAudioDirective. Hence, for the following collection, we will have five elements:

```
@ViewChildren(MyAudioDirective) private all: QueryList<MyAudioDirective>;
```

While the preceding example does not highlight the syncing part, Angular can track components/directives being added or removed from the view. This happens when we use content generation directives such as `ngFor`.

Take this hypothetical template for example:

```
<div *ngFor="let audioData of allAudios">
  <audio [src]="audioData.url"></audio>
</div>
```

The number of `MyAudioDirective` directives injected here equals the size of the `allAudios` array. During the program's execution, if elements are added to or removed from the `allAudios` array, the directive collection is also kept in sync by the framework.

While the `QueryList` class is not an array, it can be iterated over (as it implements the **ES6 iterable interface**) using the `for (var item in queryListObject)` syntax. It also has some other useful properties, such as `length`, `first`, and `last`, which can come in handy. Check out the framework documentation (`http://bit.ly/ng2-querylist-class`) for more details.

From the preceding discussion, we can conclude that `QueryList` saves the component developer a lot of boilerplate code that would be required if tracking had to be done manually.

View children access timing

View children injections are not available when the component/directive initializes. Angular makes sure that the view children injections are available to the component no later than the `ngAfterViewInit` life cycle event. Make sure you access the injected components/directives only when (or after) the `ngAfterViewInit` event has fired.

Let's now look at content children injection, which is almost similar, except for a few minor differences.

Injecting content children using @ContentChild and @ContentChildren

Angular allows us to inject *content children* too, using a parallel set of attributes: `@ContentChild` to inject a specific content child and `@ContentChildren` to inject content children of a specific type.

If we look back at the usage of `AjaxButtonComponent`, its content children spans can be injected into `AjaxButtonComponent` implementation by doing this:

```
@ContentChild('spinner') spinner:ElementRef;
@ContentChild('text') text:ElementRef;
```

And adding template variables onto the corresponding spans in `workout.component.html`:

```
<div class="ion-md-cloud-upload spin" data-animator #spinner></div>
<span data-content #text>Save</span>
```

While the preceding injection is `ElementRef`, it could have been a component too. Had we defined a component for spinner, such as:

```
<ajax-button>
    <busy-spinner></busy-spinner>
    ...
</ajax-button>
```

We could have injected it too using the following:

```
@ContentChild(BusySpinner) spinner: BusySpinner;
```

The same holds true for directives too. Any directive declared on `AjaxButtonComponent` can be injected into the `AjaxButtonComponent` implementation. For the preceding case, since the transcluded elements are standard HTML elements, we injected `ElementRef`, a wrapper that Angular creates for any HTML element.

 Like *view children*, Angular makes sure that the content children references are bound to the variables injected before the `ngAfterContentInit` life cycle event.

While we are on the subject of injecting dependencies, let's talk about some variations around *injecting services into components*.

Dependency injection using viewProvider

We are already familiar with the mechanism of DI registration in Angular, where we register a dependency at the global level by adding it to any module declaration.

Or we can do it at a component level using the `providers` property on the `@Component` decorator:

```
providers:[WorkoutHistoryTracker, LocalStorage]
```

 Just to avoid confusion, we are now talking about injecting dependencies other than directive/component objects. Directives/components are registered in the `declarations` array of a module before they can be injected using decorator hints such as `@Query`, `@ViewChild`, `@ViewChildren`, and a few others.

Dependencies registered at the component level are available for its *view children* and *content children* and their descendants.

 Before we proceed, we hope that the distinction between *view* and *content children* is crystal clear to everyone. If in doubt, refer to the *Content children and view children* section again.

Let's take an example from `Chapter 2`, *Personal Trainer*. The `WorkoutBuilderService` service was registered at the app level in the workout builder module (`WorkoutBuilderModule`):

```
providers: [ExerciseBuilderService, ...
        WorkoutBuilderService]);
```

This allows us to inject `WorkoutBuilderService` across the app in order to build workouts and while running workouts. Instead, we could have registered the service at the `WorkoutBuilderComponent` level since it is the parent of all workout/exercise creation components, something like the following:

```
@Component({
    template: `...`
    providers:[ WorkoutBuilderService ]
})
export class WorkoutBuilderComponent {
```

This change would disallow injecting `WorkoutBuilderService` in `WorkoutRunner` or any component related to workout execution.

What if the `WorkoutBuilderService` service is registered at the app level as well as at the component level (as shown in the preceding example)? How does the injection happen? From our experience, we know that Angular will inject a different instance of the `WorkoutBuilderService` service into `WorkoutBuilderComponent` (and its descendants), while other parts of the application (*Workout runner*) will get the global dependency. Remember **hierarchical injectors**!

Angular does not stop here. It provides some further scoping of dependencies using the `viewProviders` property. The `viewProviders` property, available on the `@Component` decorator, allows the registering of dependencies that can be injected only in the view children.

Let's consider the `AjaxButtonComponent` example again, and a simple directive implementation called `MyDirective`, to elaborate on our discussion:

```
@Directive({
  selector: '[myDirective]',
})
export class MyDirective {
  constructor(service:MyService) { }
  ...
}
```

The `MyDirective` class depends upon a service, `MyService`.

To apply this directive to the *button element* in the `AjaxButtonComponent` template, we need to register the `MyService` dependency too (assuming that `MyService` has not been registered globally):

```
@Component({
  selector: 'ajax-button',
  template:` <button [attr.disabled]="busy" ...
          myDirective>
          ...
          <button>`
  providers:[MyService],
  ...
```

Since `MyService` is registered with `AjaxButtonComponent`, `MyDirective` can be added to its content children too. Hence the `myDirective` application on *spinner HTML* will also work (the code in `workout.component.html`):

```
<div class="ion-md-cloud-upload spin" data-animator myDirective></div>
```

But changing the `providers` property to `viewProviders`:

```
viewProviders:[MyService]
```

Will fail the `MyService` injection for the `AjaxButtonComponent`'s content children (the `div` in the preceding code), with a DI error in the console.

 Dependencies registered with `viewProviders` are invisible to its content children.

This dependency scoping for *the view* and *content children* may not seem useful at first sight, but it does have its benefits. Imagine we are building a reusable component that we want to package and deliver to developers for consumption. If the component has a service dependency that it prepackages too, we need to be extra cautious. If such a component allows *content injection* (content children), the dependent service is widely exposed if *provider-based* registration is used on the component. Any content children can get hold of the service dependency and use it, leading to undesirable consequences. By registering the dependency using `viewProvider`, only the component implementation and its child views have access to the dependency, providing the necessary layer of encapsulation.

Yet again, we are amazed by the flexibility and level of customization that the DI framework provides. While it may be intimidating for starters, once we start building more and more components/directives with Angular, we will always find areas where these concepts make our implementation simpler.

Let's shift our focus to the third classification of directives: *structural directives*.

Understanding structural directives

While we will often be using structural directives, such as `NgIf` and `NgFor`, there is seldom a need to creating a structural directive. Think carefully. If we need a new view, we create a *component*. If we need to extend an existing element/component, we use a *directive*. Whereas the most common use of structural directives is to clone a piece of a view (also called a *template view*) and then, based on some conditions:

- Either inject/destroy these templates (`NgIf` and `NgSwitch`)
- Or duplicate these templates (`NgFor`)

Any behavior implemented using structure directives will inadvertently fall into either of these two categories.

Given this fact, instead of building our own structural directive, let's look at the source code of the `NgIf` implementation.

The following is an excerpt from the `NgIf` directive that is of interest to us. We have ignored the `ngIfElse` parts from the excerpt intentionally:

```
@Directive({selector: '[ngIf]'})
export class NgIf {
 constructor(private _viewContainer: ViewContainerRef, templateRef:
TemplateRef<NgIfContext>) {
    this._thenTemplateRef = templateRef;
 }

 @Input()
  set ngIf(condition: any) {
    this._context.$implicit = this._context.ngIf = condition;
    this._updateView();
 }
 private _updateView() {
    if (this._context.$implicit) {
      if (!this._thenViewRef) {
        this._viewContainer.clear();
        this._elseViewRef = null;
        if (this._thenTemplateRef) {
          this._thenViewRef =
              this._viewContainer.createEmbeddedView(this._thenTemplateRef,
this._context);
        }
      }
    }
    ...
 }
```

No magic here, just a simple structural directive that checks a Boolean condition (`this._context.$implicit`) to create/destroy the view!

The first if condition above check, if the condition `this._context.$implicit` is `true`. The next condition makes sure that the view is already not rendered by checking the variable _thenViewRef. We only want to flip the view if `this._context.$implicit` translates from `false` to `true`. If both if's conditions are true the existing view is cleared (`this._viewContainer.clear()`) and the reference to the else view is cleared. The innermost if condition makes sure that the if's template reference is available. Finally, the code calls _viewContainer.`createEmbeddedView` to render (or re-render) the view.

It's not difficult to understand how the directive works. What needs to be detailed are the two new injections, `ViewContainerRef` (_viewContainer) and `TemplateRef` (_templateRef).

TemplateRef

The `TemplateRef` class (_templateRef) stores the reference to the template that the structural directive is referring to. Remember the discussion on structural directives from Chapter 1, *Building Our First App - 7 Minute Workout*? All structural directives take a template HTML that they work on. When we use a directive such as `NgIf`:

```
<h3 *ngIf="currentExercise.exercise.name=='rest'">
    . . .
</h3>
```

Angular internally translates this declaration to the following:

```
<ng-template [ngIf]="currentExercise.exercise.name=='rest'">
  <h3> ... </h3>
</ng-template>
```

This is the template that structural directives work with, and _templateRef points to this template.

The other injection is `ViewContainerRef`.

ViewContainerRef

The `ViewContainerRef` class points to the container where templates are rendered. This class has a number of handy methods for managing views. The two functions that `NgIf` implementation uses, `createEmbeddedView` and `clear`, are there to add and remove the template HTML.

The `createEmbeddedView` function takes the template reference (again injected into the directive) and renders the view.

The `clear` function destroys the element/component already injected and clears the view container. Since every component and its children referenced inside the template (`TemplateRef`) are destroyed, all the associated bindings also cease to exist.

Structural directives have a very specific area of application. Still, we can do a lot of nifty tricks using the `TemplateRef` and `ViewContainerRef` classes.

We can implement a structural directive that, depending on the user role, shows/hides the view template.

Consider this example of a hypothetical structural directive, `forRoles`:

```
<button *forRoles="admin">Admin Save</button>
```

The `forRoles` directive will not render the button if the user does not belong to the *admin* role. The core logic would look something like the following:

```
if(this.loggedInUser.roles.indexOf(this.forRole) >=0){
    this.viewContainer.createEmbeddedView(this.templateRef);
}
else {
    this.viewContainer.clear();
}
```

The directive implementation will need some sort of service that returns the logged-in user's details. We will leave the implementation for such a directive to the readers.

What the `forRoles` directive does can also be done using `NgIf`:

```
<button *ngIf="loggedInUser.roles.indexOf('admin')>=0">Admin Save</button>
```

But the `forRoles` directive just adds to the template's readability with clear intentions.

A fun application of structural directives may involve creating a directive that just duplicates the template passed to it. It would be quite easy to build one; we just need to call `createEmbeddedView` twice:

```
ngOnInit() {
  this.viewContainer.createEmbeddedView(this._templateRef);
  this.viewContainer.createEmbeddedView(this._templateRef);
}
```

Another fun exercise!

The `ViewContainerRef` class also has some other functions that allow us to inject *components*, get the number of embedded views, reorder the view, and so on and so forth. Look at the framework documentation for `ViewContainerRef` (`http://bit.ly/view-container-ref`) for more details.

That completes our discussion on structural directives and it's time to start something new!

The components that we have built thus far derive their styles (CSS) from the common *bootstrap style sheet* and some custom styles defined in `app.css`. Angular has much more to offer in this area. A truly reusable component should be completely self-contained, in terms of both behavior and user interface.

Component styling and view encapsulation

A longstanding problem with web app development is the lack of encapsulation when it comes to DOM element behavior and styles. We cannot segregate one part of the application HTML from another through any mechanism.

In fact, we have too much power at our disposal. With libraries such as jQuery and powerful *CSS selectors*, we can get hold of any DOM element and change its behavior. There is no distinction between our code and any external library code in terms of what it can access. Every single piece of code can manipulate any part of the rendered DOM. Hence, the encapsulation layer is broken. A badly written library can cause some nasty issues that are hard to debug.

The same holds true for CSS styling too. Any UI library implementation can override global styles if the library implementation wants to do so.

These are genuine challenges that any library developer faces when building reusable libraries. Some emerging web standards have tried to address this issue by coming up with concepts such as **web components**.

Web components, in simple terms, are reusable user interface widgets that encapsulate their *state, style, user interface,* and *behavior*. Functionality is exposed through well-defined APIs, and the user interface parts are encapsulated too.

The *web component* concept is enabled by four standards:

- HTML templates
- Shadow DOM
- Custom elements
- HTML imports

For this discussion, the technology standard we are interested in is **Shadow DOM.**

Overview of Shadow DOM

Shadow DOM is like a parallel DOM tree hosted inside a component (*an HTML element, not to be confused with Angular components*), hidden away from the main DOM tree. No part of the application has access to this shadow DOM other than the component itself.

It is the implementation of the Shadow DOM standard that allows view, style, and behavior encapsulation. The best way to understand Shadow DOM is to look at HTML5 `video` and `audio` tags.

Have you ever wondered how this `audio` declaration:

```
<audio src="/static/audio/nextup.mp3" controls></audio>
```

Produces the following?

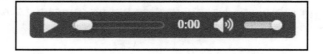

It is the browser that generates the underlying Shadow DOM to render the audio player. Surprisingly, we can even look at the generated DOM! Here is how we do it:

- Take the preceding HTML, create a dummy HTML page, and open it in Chrome.
- Then open the **Developer tools** window (*F12*). Click on the **Setting** icon on the upper-left corner.
- On the **General** settings, click on the checkbox, as highlighted in the following screenshot, to enable the inspection of Shadow DOM:

Refresh the page, and if we now inspect the generated `audio` HTML, the Shadow DOM shows up:

```
▼<audio controls src="/static/audio/nextup.mp3">
 ▼#shadow-root (user-agent)
  ▼<div pseudo="-webkit-media-controls">
   ▼<div pseudo="-webkit-media-controls-overlay-enclosure">
    ▶<input type="button" style="display: none;">…</input>
    </div>
   ▼<div pseudo="-webkit-media-controls-enclosure">
    ▼<div pseudo="-webkit-media-controls-panel">
     ▶<input type="button" pseudo="-webkit-media-controls-play-button">…</input>
     ▶<input type="range" step="any" pseudo="-webkit-media-controls-timeline" max="0.972">…</input>
      <div pseudo="-webkit-media-controls-current-time-display" style>0:00</div>
      <div pseudo="-webkit-media-controls-time-remaining-display" style="display: none;">0:00</div>
     ▶<input type="button" pseudo="-webkit-media-controls-mute-button">…</input>
     ▶<input type="range" step="any" max="1" pseudo="-webkit-media-controls-volume-slider" style>…</input>
     ▶<input type="button" pseudo="-webkit-media-controls-toggle-closed-captions-button" style="display: none;">…</input>
     ▶<input type="button" style="display: none;">…</input>
     ▶<input type="button" pseudo="-webkit-media-controls-fullscreen-button" style="display: none;">…</input>
     </div>
    </div>
   </div>
 </audio>
```

Under `shadow-root`, there is a whole new world that the other part of the page and script do not have access to.

> In the Shadow DOM realm, **shadow-root** (`#shadow-root` in the preceding code) is the root node for the generated DOM, hosted inside a **shadow host** (in this case the `audio` tag). When the browser renders this element/component, what gets rendered is the content from the *shadow root* and not the *shadow host*.

From this discussion, we can conclude that Shadow DOM is a parallel DOM created by the browser that encapsulates the *markup*, *style*, and *behavior* (DOM manipulation) of an HTML element.

> This was a gentle introduction to Shadow DOM. To learn more about how Shadow DOM works, we recommend this series by Rob Dodson: `http://bit.ly/shadow-dom-intro`

But what has all this got to do with Angular? As it turns out, Angular components support some sort of view encapsulation too! This allows us to isolate styles for Angular components too.

Shadow DOM and Angular components

To understand how Angular employs the concept of Shadow DOM, we will first have to learn about styling Angular components.

When it comes to styling the apps built as part of this book, we have taken a conservative approach. Be it *Workout Builder* or the *Workout Runner* (*7 Minute Workout*) app, all the components that we built derive their style from *bootstrap CSS* and from custom styles defined in `app.css`. No component has defined its own style.

While this adheres to the standard practices of web app development, sometimes we do need to deviate. This is especially true when we are building self-contained, packaged, and reusable components.

Angular allows us to define styles specific to a component by using the `style` (for inline style) and `styleUrl` (external style sheet) properties on the `@Component` decorator. Let's play around with the `style` property and see what Angular does.

We will use the `AjaxButtonComponent` implementation as our playground for the next exercise. But before doing that, let's look at the `AjaxButtonComponent` HTML as it stands now. The HTML tree for `AjaxButtonComponent` looks as follows:

```
<abe-ajax-button>
  <button class="btn btn-primary">
    <span hidden>
      <div class="ion-md-cloud-upload spin"
        data-animator="">
      </div>
    </span>
    <span data-content="">Save</span>
  </button>
</abe-ajax-button>
```

Let's override some styles using the `styles` property:

```
@Component({
  ...
  styles:[`
    button {
      background: green;
    }`]
})
```

The preceding *CSS selector* sets the `background` property to `green` for all HTML buttons. Save the preceding style and refresh the work builder page. The button style has been updated. No surprises here? Not true, there are some! Look at the generated HTML:

```
▼<abe-ajax-button _nghost-c1 ng-reflect-execute="function (formWorkout) {
    " ng-reflect-parameter="[object Object]">
  ▼<button _ngcontent-c1 class="btn btn-primary">
    ▶<span _ngcontent-c1 hidden>...</span>
      <span data-content>Save</span>
    </button>
</abe-ajax-button>
```

There are some new attributes added to a number of HTML elements. And where have the recently defined styles landed? At the very top, inside the `head` tag:

```
<style>button[_ngcontent-c1] {
    background: green;
}</style>
```

The style defined in the `head` section has an extra scope with the `_ngcontent-c1` attribute (the attribute name may differ in your case). This scoping allows us to style `AjaxButtonComponent` independently and it cannot override any global styles.

 Angular does the same even if we use the `styleUrls` property. Suppose we had embedded the same CSS in an external CSS file and used this: `styleUrls:['static/css/ajax-button.css']` Angular would have still in-lined the styles into the `head` section, by fetching the CSS, parsing it, and then injecting it.

The styles that by definition, should have affected the appearance of all the buttons in the application, have had no effect. Angular has scoped these styles.

 This scoping makes sure that the component styles do not mess with the already defined style, but the reverse is not true. Global styles will still affect the component unless overridden in the component itself.

This scoped style is the result of Angular trying to emulate the Shadow DOM paradigm. The styles defined on the component never leak into the global styles. All this awesomeness without any effort!

 If you are building components that define their own styles and want a degree of isolation, use the component's `style/styleUrl` property instead of using the old-school approach of having a common CSS file for all styles.

We can further control this behavior by using a `@Component` decorator property called **encapsulation**. The API documentation for this property mentions:

encapsulation: `ViewEncapsulation` Specify how the template and the styles should be encapsulated. The default is `ViewEncapsulation.Emulated` if the view has styles, otherwise `ViewEncapsulation.None`.

As we can see, as soon as we set the style on the component, the encapsulation effect is `Emulated`. Otherwise, it is `None`.

 If we explicitly set `encapsulation` to `ViewEncapsulation.None`, the scoping attributes are removed and the styles are embedded in the head section as normal styles.

And then there is a third option, `ViewEncapsulation.Native`, in which Angular actually creates Shadow DOM for the components view. Set the `encapsulation` property on the `AjaxButtonComponent` implementation to `ViewEncapsulation.Native`, and now look at the rendered DOM:

```
▼<abe-ajax-button ng-reflect-execute="function (formWorkout) {
    " ng-reflect-parameter="[object Object]">
  ▼#shadow-root (open)
    <style></style>
    <style>
      button {
        background: green;
      }</style>
    ▼<button class="btn btn-primary">
      ▼<span hidden>
          <div class="ion-md-cloud-upload spin" data-animator></div>
        </span>
        <span data-content>Save</span>
      </button>
  </abe-ajax-button>
```

`AjaxButtonComponent` now has a shadow DOM! This also implies that the complete styling of the button is lost (style derived from bootstrap CSS) and the button needs to now define its own style.

Angular goes to great lengths to make sure that the components we develop can work independently and are reusable. Each component already has its own template and behavior. In addition to that, we can also encapsulate component styles, allowing us to create robust, standalone components.

This brings us to the end of the chapter, and it's time to wrap up the chapter with what we've learned.

Summary

As we conclude this chapter, we now have a better understanding of how directives work and how to use them effectively.

We started the chapter by building a `RemoteValidatorDirective`, and learned a lot about Angular's support for *asynchronous validations*.

Next in line was `BusyIndicatorDirective`, again an excellent learning ground. We explored the **renderer** service, which allows component view manipulation in a platform-agnostic way. We also learned about **host bindings**, which let us bind to a host element's *events*, *attributes*, and *properties*.

Angular allows directives declared across the view lineage to be injected into the lineage. We dedicated a few sections to understanding this behavior.

The third directive (component) that we created was `AjaxButtonComponent`. It helped us understand the critical difference between *content children* and *view children* for a component.

We also touched upon structural directives, where we explored the `NgIf` platform directive.

Lastly, we looked at Angular's capabilities in terms of view encapsulation. We explored the basics of Shadow DOM and learned how the framework employs the Shadow DOM paradigm to provide view plus style encapsulation.

All of this is interesting from an educational standpoint. It doesn't describe the elephant in the room, how do we manage our data when things get complicated? The concerns we have to deal with are:

- Bidirectional data flow
- Lack of predictability (a change can lead to cascading changes)
- Spread out state (there is no one source of truth and our components can sit on a state that is partially updated)

Let's keep these concerns in mind as we move on to Chapter 5, *1.21 Gigawatt - Flux Pattern Explained*.

1.21 Gigawatt - Flux Pattern Explained

5

Your application has grown and in that process, you slowly feel you are losing track of what your application knows at a given point, what we call the state of the application. There might be other issues, such as parts of your application not being in agreement with what they know. An update that happened in one part may not have been applied to some other part and you scratch your head, thinking should it be this hard and is there a better answer?

It's entirely possible you are just picking up this book as you have heard about NgRx as the way to structure your application and you are curious and want to know more.

Let's first explain our title. What do we mean by 1.21 Gigawatt? I'm going to quote the character Doc Brown from the movie *Back to the Future* (`http://www.imdb.com/name/nm0000502/?ref_=tt_trv_qu`):

> *"Marty, I'm sorry, but the only power source capable of generating 1.21 gigawatts of electricity is a bolt of lightning."*

Why are we talking about the movie Back to the Future? This is where the name Flux comes from. It's time for another quote from the same movie:

> *"Yes! Of course! November 5, 1955! That was the day I invented time-travel. I remember it vividly. I was standing on the edge of my toilet hanging a clock, the porcelain was wet, I slipped, hit my head on the sink, and when I came to I had a revelation! A vision! A picture in my head! A picture of this! This is what makes time travel possible: the **flux** capacitor!"*

So as you can see, there is an explanation for the name Flux. It obviously allows us to travel in time. At least for Redux, which we will write about later in this book, time travel is possible through something called time-travel debugging. Whether that needs a bolt of lightning is for you to find out dear reader.

Flux is an architectural pattern created by Facebook. It came about as it was perceived that the MVC pattern simply did not scale. It did not scale for large code bases as they tended to become fragile, generally complicated as more and more features were added, and most of all, unpredictable. Now let's hang on that word for a second, unpredictable.

Large systems were thought to become unpredictable due to their bidirectional data flow between models and views when the number of models and views really grew, as depicted in the following diagram:

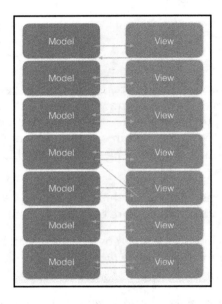

Here, we can see that the number of models and views is starting to grow. Everything is somewhat under control as long as one model talks to one view and vice versa. This is, however, seldom the case. In the preceding diagram, we see that suddenly a view can talk to more than one model and vice versa, which means we have a cascading effect on the system and we suddenly lose control. Sure, it doesn't look so bad with just one deviating arrow, but imagine that this one is suddenly ten arrows, then we have a real problem on our hands.

It is the very fact that we allow bidrectional data flows to happen that things get complicated and we lose predictability. The medicine or cure for that is thought to be a simpler type of data flow, a unidirectional flow. Now, there are some key players involved in enabling undirectional data flow, which brings us to what this chapter is meant to teach us.

In this chapter, we will learn:

- What an action and an action creator are
- How the dispatcher plays a central role in your application as a hub for messages
- State management with a store
- How to put our knowledge of Flux into practice by coding up a Flux application flow

Core concepts overview

At the core of the Flux pattern is a unidirectional data flow. It uses some core concepts to achieve this flow. The main idea is when an event is created on a UI, through the interaction of a user, an action is created. This action consists of an intent and a payload. The intent is what you are trying to achieve. Think of the intent as a verb. Add an item, remove an item, and so on. The payload is the data change that needs to happen to achieve our intent. If we are trying to add an item, then the payload is the newly created item. The action is then propagated in the flow with the help of a dispatcher. The action and its data eventually end up in a store.

The concepts that make up the Flux pattern are:

- Action and action creators, where we set up an intention and a payload of data
- The dispatcher, our spider in the web that is able to send messages left and right
- The store, our central place for state and state management

All these together form the Flux pattern and promote unidirectional data flow. Consider the following diagram:

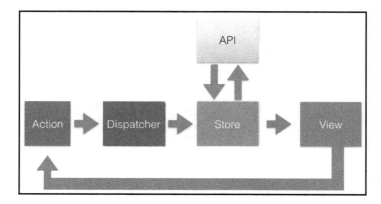

What is depicted here is an undirectional data flow. The data flows from **View** to **Action**, from **Action** to **Dispatcher**, from **Dispatcher** to **Store**. There are two possible ways that the flow is triggered:

- The application is loaded a first time, in which the data is pulled from the **Store** to populate the view.
- A user interaction happens in the view that leads to an intent to change something. The intent is encapsulated in an **Action**, and thereafter sent to the **Store**, via the **Dispatcher**. At the **Store**, it may be persisted in a database, through an **API** or saved as an application state, or both.

Let's dive into each concept in more detail, together with highlighting some code examples, in the upcoming sections.

A uniform data flow

Let's introduce all parties involved in our uniform data flow by starting from the very top and slowly work our way down, concept by concept. We will build an application consisting of two views. In the first view, the user will select an item from a list. This should result in an action being created. This action will then be dispatched, by the dispatcher. The action and its payload will end up in a store. The other view meanwhile listens to changes from the store. When an item is selected, the second view will be made aware and can, therefore, indicate in its UI that a specific item has been selected. On a high level, our application and its flow will look like the following:

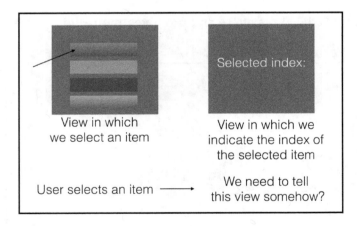

View in which we select an item

Selected index:

View in which we indicate the index of the selected item

User selects an item ⟶ We need to tell this view somehow?

Action – capture the intent

An action is something as simple as an intent with accompanying data, that is, a message. How does an action come about though? An action comes about when a user interacts with a UI. The user may select a specific item in a list or a press a button with the intention of submitting a form. Submitting the form should, in turn, lead to a product being created.

Let's look at two different actions:

- Selecting an item in a list, here we are interested in saving the index of our selected item
- Saving a todo to a todo list

An action is represented by an object. The object has two properties of interest:

- The type: This is a unique string that tells us the intention of the action, for example, SELECT_ITEM
- The data: This is the data we mean to persist, for example, the numerical index of a selected item

Given our first example action, a code representation of that action would look like the following:

```
{
  type: 'SELECT_ITEM',
  data: 3 // selected index
}
```

OK, so we have prepared our action, which we can also think of as a message. We want the message to be sent so that the selected item is highlighted in the UI. As this is a undirectional flow, we need to follow a charted course and pass our message over to the next party, which is the dispatcher.

Dispatcher – the spider in the web

Think of the dispatcher as the spider in the web that handles messages being passed to it. You can also think of the dispatcher as a mailman who promises that your message will reach its target destination. A dispatcher lives, for one thing, to dispatch messages to anyone who will listen. There is usually just one dispatcher in a Flux architecture and a typical usage looks something like this:

```
dispatcher.dispatch(message);
```

Listening to the dispatcher

We have established that the dispatcher dispatches a message to anyone who will listen. Now it is time to be that listener. The dispatcher needs a `register` or `subscribe` method so that you, who listens, have the ability to listen for incoming messages. The setup for that usually looks something like this:

```
dispatcher.register(function(message){});
```

Now, when you set up a listener this way, it will have the capability to listen to any message type being sent. You want to narrow this down; usually, a listener is specified to only handle a few message types around a certain theme. Your listener most likely looks something like this:

```
dispatcher.register((message) => {
  switch(message.type) {
    case 'SELECT_ITEM':
      // do something
  }
});
```

OK, so we are able to filter out only the message types we care about, but before actually filling in some code we need to think about who this listener is. The answer is simple: it is the store.

The store – managing state, data retrieval, and callbacks

It's easy to think of the store as the place where our data lives. That is, however, not all it is. What the store's responsibilities are can be expressed by this list:

- Holder of state
- Manages the state, able to update it if need be
- Able to handle side effects such as fetching/persisting data through HTTP
- Handles callbacks

As you can see, that is a bit more than just storing the state. Let's now reconnect to what we were doing when we set up a listener with the `dispatcher`. Let's move that code into our store file, `store.js`, and let's persist our message content in our store:

```
// store.js
```

```
let store = {};

function selectIndex(index) {
  store["selectedIndex"] = index;
}

dispatcher.register(message => {
  switch (message.type) {
    case "SELECT_INDEX":
      selectIndex(message.data);
      break;
  }
});
```

OK, so now the store is being told about the new index, but an important piece is missing, how do we tell the UI? We need a way to tell the UI that something has changed. A change means that the UI should reread its data.

The view

To tell the view that something has happened and act on it, three things need to happen:

- The view needs to register with the store as a listener
- The store needs to send off an event conveying that a change has happened
- The view needs to reload its data

Starting with the store, we need to build it out so that you can register as a listener to its events. We, therefore, add the `addListener()` method:

```
// store-with-pubsub.js

function selectIndex(index) {
  store["selectedIndex"] = index;
}

// registering with the dispatcher
dispatcher.register(message => {
  switch (message.type) {
    case "SELECT_INDEX":
      selectIndex(message.data);
      // signals to the listener that a change has happened
      store.emitChange();
      break;
  }
});
```

```
class Store {
  constructor() {
    this.listeners = [];
  }

  addListener(listener) {
    if (!this.listeners["change"]) {
      this.listeners["change"] = [];
    }
    this.listeners["change"].push(listener);
  }

  emitChange() {
    if (this.listeners["change"]) {
      this.listeners["change"].forEach(cb => cb());
    }
  }

  getSelectedItem() {
    return store["selectedIndex"];
  }
}

const store = new Store();
export default store;
```

In the preceding code, we also add the ability to emit an event with the addition of the emitChange() method. You can easily switch out this implementation to use an EventEmitter or similar. So now is the time to hook up our view to the store. We do so by calling the addListener() method like so:

```
// view.js

import store from "./store-with-pubsub";

class View {
  constructor(store) {
    this.index = 0;
    store.addListener(this.notifyChanged);
  }

  // invoked from the store
  notifyChanged() {
    // rereads data from the store
    this.index = store.getSelectedItem();
    // reloading the data
    render();
  }
```

```
  render() {
    const elem = document.getElementById('view');
    elem.innerHTML = `Your selected index is: ${this.index}`;
  }
}

let view = new View();

// view.html
<html>
  <body>
    <div id="view"></div>
  </body>
</html>
```

In the preceding code, we implement the `notifyChanged()` method, which when called invokes the `getSelectedItem()` method from the store and thereby receives the new value.

At this point, we have described the whole chain: how one view receives a user interaction, turns that into an action, which is then dispatched to a store, which updates the store's state. The store then emits an event that the other view is listening to. When the event is received, in the view the state from the store is reread and the view is then free to render this state, which it just read in, the way it sees fit.

We have described two things here:

- How to set up the flow
- How the information flows in Flux

Setting up the flow can be depicted with the following diagram:

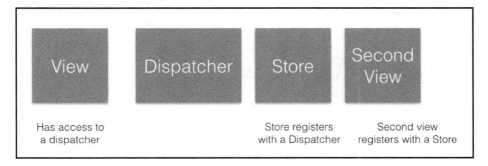

As for the second scenario, how the information flows through the system, it can be depicted in the following way:

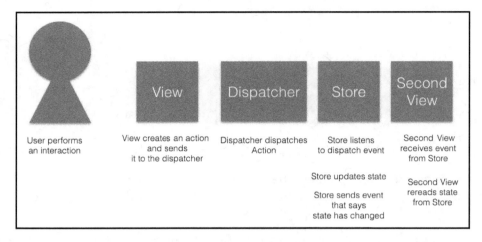

Demoing a uniform data flow

Ok, so we have described the parts our application consists of:

- A view where a user is able to select an index
- A dispatcher that allows us to send a message
- A store that contains our selected index
- A second view where the selected index is read from the store

Let's build a real app from all of this. The following code is found in the code repository under `Chapter2/demo`.

Creating a selection view

First off we need our view in which we will perform the selection:

```
// demo/selectionView.js

import dispatcher from "./dispatcher";

console.log('selection view loaded');

class SelectionView {
```

```
  selectIndex(index) {
    console.log('selected index ', index);
    dispatcher.dispatch({
      type: "SELECT_INDEX",
      data: index
    });
  }
}

const view = new SelectionView();
export default view;
```

We have bolded the `selectIndex()` method above that we intend to use.

Adding the dispatcher

Next off we need a dispatcher that is able to take our message, like so:

```
// demo/dispatcher.js

class Dispatcher {
  constructor() {
    this.listeners = [];
  }

  dispatch(message) {
    this.listeners.forEach(listener => listener(message));
  }

  register(listener) {
    this.listeners.push(listener);
  }
}

const dispatcher = new Dispatcher();
export default dispatcher;
```

Adding the store

The store will act as the data source for our state but will also be able tell any listeners when a change to the store happens:

```
// demo/store.js

import dispatcher from './dispatcher';

function selectIndex(index) {
  store["selectedIndex"] = index;
}

// 1) store registers with dispatcher
dispatcher.register(message => {
  switch (message.type) {
    // 3) message is sent by dispatcher ( that originated from the first
view)
    case "SELECT_INDEX":
      selectIndex(message.data);
      // 4) listener, a view, is being notified of the change
      store.emitChange();
      break;
  }
});

class Store {
  constructor() {
    this.listeners = [];
  }

  // 2) listener is added by a view
  addListener(listener) {
    if (!this.listeners["change"]) {
      this.listeners["change"] = [];
    }

    this.listeners["change"].push(listener);
  }

  emitChange() {
    if (this.listeners["change"]) {
      this.listeners["change"].forEach(cb => cb());
    }
  }

  getSelectedItem() {
    return store["selectedIndex"];
```

```
    }
  }

const store = new Store();
export default store;
```

Adding a selected view

This view will register itself with the store and ask for updates to its content. If there are any updates it will be notified and the data from the store will be read and this view will communicate what the store value now is:

```
// demo/selectedView.js

import store from "./store";

console.log('selected view loaded');

class SelectedView {
  constructor() {
    this.index = 0;
    store.addListener(this.notifyChanged.bind(this));
  }

  notifyChanged() {
    this.index = store.getSelectedItem();
    console.log('new index is ', this.index);
  }
}

const view = new SelectedView();
export default SelectedView;
```

Running the demo

Before we can run our demo we need an application file, app.js. The app.js file should require in our views and also carry out the selection:

```
// demo/app.js

import selectionView from './selectionView';
import selectedView from './selectedView';

// carry out the selection
```

```
selectionView.selectIndex(1);
```

To run our demo we need to compile it. Above we are using ES2015 modules. To compile those we will use `webpack`. We need to install `webpack` by typing the following in our terminal:

```
npm install webpack webpack-cli --save-dev
```

Once we have done so we need to create `webpack.config.js` file where we tell Webpack how to compile our files and where to place the resulting bundle. That file looks like the following:

```
// webpack.config.js

module.exports = {
  entry: "./app.js",
  output: {
    filename: "bundle.js"
  },
  watch: false
};
```

This tells Webpack that `app.js` is the entry point to our application and it should crawl all the dependencies when creating the output file, `bundle.js`. Webpack will by default place `bundle.js` in the `dist` directory.

One more thing, we need an HTML file that we will name `index.html`. We will place under the `dist` folder. It should look like this:

```
// demo/dist/index.html

<html>
  <body>
    <script src="bundle.js"></script>
  </body>
</html>
```

Finally, to run our application, we need to compile it with Webpack and start a HTTP server and start up a browser. We will do all that with the following command from the `demo` directory:

```
webpack && cd dist && http-server -p 5000
```

Now, start a browser and navigate to `http://localhost:5000`. You should see the following:

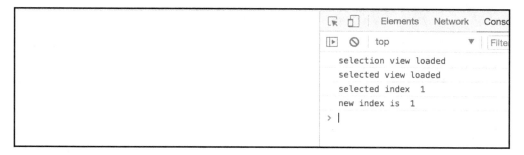

All of this demonstrates how to views can be made to communicate using a dispatcher and a store.

Adding more actions to our flow

Let's do a reality check here. We haven't built the Flux flow as prettily as we could make it. The overall picture is correct but it'd be nice if we can clean it up a bit to make room for more actions so we get a real sense of how the application should grow from here.

Cleaning up the view

The first order of business is to have a look at our first view and how it reacts to user interactions. It looks like this currently:

```
// first.view.js

import dispatcher from "./dispatcher";

class FirstView {
  selectIndex(index) {
    dispatcher.dispatch({
      type: "SELECT_INDEX",
      data: index
    });
  }
}

let view = new FirstView();
```

Adding a few more actions into the mix means we would extend the view with a few methods like this:

```javascript
// first.viewII.js

import dispatcher from "./dispatcher";

class View {
  selectIndex(data) {
    dispatcher.dispatch({
      type: "SELECT_INDEX",
      data
    });
  }

  createProduct(data) {
    dispatcher.dispatch({
      type: "CREATE_PRODUCT",
      data
    });
  }

  removeProduct(data) {
    dispatcher.dispatch({
      type: "REMOVE_PRODUCT",
      data
    });
  }
}

let view = new View();
```

OK, so now we get how we can add actions. It looks a little ugly though with all these calls to the `dispatcher` and magic strings, so we clean this up a bit by creating a file with constants, called `product.constants.js`, which consists of the following code:

```javascript
// product.constants.js

export const SELECT_INDEX = "SELECT_INDEX",
export const CREATE_PRODUCT = "CREATE_PRODUCT",
export const REMOVE_PRODUCT = "REMOVE_PRODUCT"
```

Let's do one more thing. Let's move the `dispatcher` into a `product.actions.js`; this is generally known as an action creator. This will contain the `dispatcher` and refer to our `product.constants.js` file. So let's create said file:

```
// product.actions.js

import {
  SELECT_INDEX,
  CREATE_PRODUCT,
  REMOVE_PRODUCT
} from "./product-constants";
import dispatcher from "./dispatcher";
import ProductConstants from "./product.constants";

export const selectIndex = data =>
  dispatcher.dispatch({
    type: SELECT_INDEX,
    data
  });

export const createProduct = data =>
  dispatcher.dispatch({
    type: CREATE_PRODUCT,
    data
  });

export const removeProduct = data =>
  dispatcher.dispatch({
    type: REMOVE_PRODUCT,
    data
  });
```

With these constructs, we can clean up our view considerably to look like this:

```
// first.viewIII.js

import {
  selectIndex,
  createProduct,
  removeProduct
} from 'product.actions';

function View() {
  this.selectIndex = index => {
    selectIndex(index);
  };

  this.createProduct = product => {
```

```
    createProduct(product);
  };

  this.removeProduct = product => {
    removeProduct(product)
  };
}

var view = new View();
```

Cleaning up the store

There are improvements we can make to on the store. There is no need to write all the code we do currently. In fact, there are libraries out there that do a better job of handling certain functionality.

Before we apply all those changes we have in mind, let's recap what our store can do and what features still need to be in place after the cleanup work.

Let's remind ourselves, what our store is capable of so far:

- Handles state changes: It handles the state changes; the store is able to change the state regardless of whether it is creating, updating, listing, or removing state.
- Subscribable: It lets you subscribe to it; it's important for the store to have a subscription functionality so a view, for example, can listen to the store's state when it changes. A suitable reaction by the view is, for example, rerendering based on new data.
- Can communicate a state change: It can send an event that its state has been changed; this goes together with being able to subscribe to the store, but this is the very act of actually notifying a listener that a state has changed.

Adding EventEmitter

The two last bullets can really be condensed into one theme, namely eventing, or the ability to register to and fire off events.

So what does a cleanup of the store look like, and why would we need to clean it up? The reason for cleaning it up is it makes for simpler code. There is a standard library that is often used when constructing a store, called `EventEmitter`. The library handles just what we mentioned previously, namely it is able to register and fire off events. It is a simple implementation of the pub-sub pattern. Basically, `EventEmitter` allows you to subscribe to certain events and also allows you to trigger events. For more information on the pattern itself, have a look at the following link: `https://en.wikipedia.org/wiki/Publish%E2%80%93subscribe_pattern`.

You could definitely write your own code for this, but it's nice to be able to use a dedicated library so you can focus on other things that matter, such as solving business problems.

We decided to use the `EventEmitter` library and we do so in the following way:

```
// store-event-emitter.js

export const Store = (() => {
  const eventEmitter = new EventEmitter();
  return {
    addListener: listener => {
      eventEmitter.on("changed", listener);
    },
    emitChange: () => {
      eventEmitter.emit("changed");
    },
    getSelectedItem: () => store["selectedItem"]
  };
})();
```

This makes our code a little cleaner because we no longer need to hold an internal list of subscribers. There are more changes we can make though, so let us talk about that in the next section.

Adding to and cleaning up the register method

One of the store's jobs has been to handle eventing, especially when the store wants to convey to a view that a change has happened to its state. In the `store.js` file, other things were happening as well, things like registering ourselves with the `dispatcher` and being able to receive dispatched actions. We used these actions to alter the state of the store. Let's remind ourselves what that looked like:

```
// store.js

let store = {};
```

```
function selectIndex(index) {
  store["selectedIndex"] = index;
}

dispatcher.register(message => {
  switch (message.type) {
    case "SELECT_INDEX":
      selectIndex(message.data);
      break;
  }
});
```

Here, we are only supporting one action, namely SELECT_INDEX. There are two things we need to do here:

- Add the other two actions, CREATE_PRODUCT and REMOVE_PRODUCT, and the accompanying functions createProduct() and removeProduct()
- Stop using magic strings and start using our constants file
- Use the store we created in the store-event-emitter.js file

Let's implement the suggested changes from our preceding list:

```
// store-actions.js

import dispatcher from "./dispatcher";
import {
  SELECT_INDEX,
  CREATE_PRODUCT,
  REMOVE_PRODUCT
} from "./product.constants";

let store = {};

function selectIndex(index) {
  store["selectedIndex"] = index;
}

export const Store = (() => {
  var eventEmitter = new EventEmitter();
  return {
    addListener: listener => {
      eventEmitter.on("changed", listener);
    },
    emitChange: () => {
      eventEmitter.emit("changed");
    },
    getSelectedItem: () => store["selectedItem"]
```

```
  };
})();

dispatcher.register(message => {
  switch (message.type) {
    case "SELECT_INDEX":
      selectIndex(message.data);
      break;
  }
});

const createProduct = product => {
  if (!store["products"]) {
    store["products"] = [];
  }
  store["products"].push(product);
};

const removeProduct = product => {
  var index = store["products"].indexOf(product);
  if (index !== -1) {
    store["products"].splice(index, 1);
  }
};

dispatcher.register(({ type, data }) => {
  switch (type) {
    case SELECT_INDEX:
      selectIndex(data);
      break;
    case CREATE_PRODUCT:
      createProduct(data);
      break;
    case REMOVE_PRODUCT:
      removeProduct(data);
  }
});
```

Further improvements

There are definitely more improvements we can make to this code. We did use ES2015 imports to import other files, but most of our code was written in ES5 so why not use most of what ES2015 gives us? Another improvement we can make is introducing immutability and making sure our store is not mutated but transitions from one state to another.

Let's have a look at the store file, primarily because that is where we can add the most ES2015 syntax. Our revealing module pattern looks like this currently:

```js
// store-event-emitter.js

var Store = (function(){
  const eventEmitter = new EventEmitter();

  return {
    addListener: listener => {
      eventEmitter.on("changed", listener);
    },
    emitChange: () => {
      eventEmitter.emit("changed");
    },
    getSelectedItem: () => store["selectedItem"]
  };
})();
```

It can be replaced with a simple class and instead of instantiating an EventEmitter, we can inherit from it. In all fairness, we could have used ES2015 inheritance or the merge library to not have to create a separate EventEmitter instance, but this shows how elegant ES2015 can make things:

```js
// store-es2015.js

import { EventEmitter } from "events";
import {
SELECT_INDEX,
CREATE_PRODUCT,
REMOVE_PRODUCT
} from "./product.constants";

let store = {};

class Store extends EventEmitter {
  constructor() {}
    addListener(listener) {
    this.on("changed", listener);
  }
```

```
    emitChange() {
      this.emit("changed");
    }

    getSelectedItem() {
      return store["selectedItem"];
    }
}

const storeInstance = new Store();

function createProduct(product) {
  if (!store["products"]) {
    store["products"] = [];
  }
  store["products"].push(product);
}

function removeProduct(product) {
  var index = store["products"].indexOf(product);
  if (index !== -1) {
    store["products"].splice(index, 1);
  }
}

dispatcher.register(({ type, data }) => {
  switch (type) {
    case SELECT_INDEX:
      selectIndex(data);
      storeInstance.emitChange();
      break;
    case CREATE_PRODUCT:
      createProduct(data);
      storeInstance.emitChange();
      break;
    case REMOVE_PRODUCT:
      removeProduct(data);
      storeInstance.emitChange();
  }
});
```

Adding immutability

The other thing we can undertake is adding immutability. The reasons for using immutability in the first place are to make your code more predictable, and some frameworks can use this for simpler change detection and can rely on reference checking over dirty checking. This was the case when AngularJS got its whole change detection mechanism changed when Angular was written. From a practical standpoint, this means that there are functions we can target in our store and apply immutable principles on. The first principle is to not mutate but create an entirely new state, instead of where the new state is *the old state + the state change*. A simple example of this is the following:

```
var oldState = 3;
var newState = oldState + 2
```

Here, we are creating a new variable, newState, rather than mutating our oldState variable. There are functions that will help us with this, called Object.assign and the function filter. We can use these for updating scenarios, as well as adding or removing things from a list. Let us use these and rewrite part of our store code. Let's highlight the code we mean to change:

```
// excerpt from store-actions.js

const createProduct = product => {
  if (!store["products"]){
    store["products"] = [];
  }
  store["products"].push(product);
};

const removeProduct = product => {
  var index = store["products"].indexOf(product);
  if (index !== -1) {
    store["products"].splice(index, 1);
  }
};
```

Let's apply Object.assign and filter(), and remember to not mutate things. The end result should look like this:

```
// excerpt from our new store-actions-immutable.js

const createProduct = product => {
  if (!store["products"]) {
    store["products"] = [];
  }
  store.products = [...store.products, Object.assign(product)];
```

```
};

const removeProduct = product => {
  if (!store["products"]) return;

  store["products"] = products.filter(p => p.id !== product.id);
};
```

We can see that the `createProduct()` method uses an ES2015 construct, namely the spread parameter, `. . .`, which takes a list and turns its members into a comma-separated list of items. `Object.assign()` is used to copy over all the values from an object so we store the value of an object rather than its reference. The `removeProduct()` method becomes very simple when we use the filter method. We simply create a projection that does not include the product that we should remove; removing has never been this easy or elegant. We haven't mutated anything.

Summarizing

Our cleanup started with the view; we wanted to remove a direct connection to the dispatcher and also stop having to use magic strings as this is quite error prone, and it's easy to misspell. Instead, we can rely on constants. To remedy this, we created an action creator class that talked to the dispatcher instead.

We also created a constants module to remove the magic strings.

Furthermore, we improved the store by starting to use `EventEmitter`. Finally, we further improved the store by adding more actions to it and also started to refer to the constants.

At this point, our solution is ready for more actions to be added to it and we should feel pretty clear on what files we need to add to, as we support more and more user interactions.

Lastly, we added improvements around ES2015 and immutability, which made our code look a lot cleaner. With this foundation, we are now ready to go from static data to involve working with side effects and Ajax in the upcoming section.

Let us summarize all our improvements in a diagram showing the constructs added to our flow:

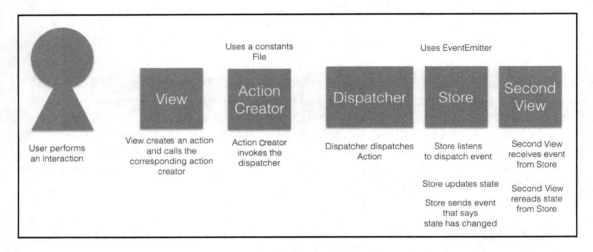

It is clear that using an action creator isn't strictly necessary but it does clean up the code quite a bit, and the same goes for using an `EventEmitter` in the store; it's nice but not necessary.

Adding AJAX calls

So far, we have only been dealing with static data in our Flux flow. The time has now come to add real data connections to the flow and thereby real data. It is time to start talking to APIs through AJAX and HTTP. Fetching data is quite easy nowadays, thanks to the fetch API and libraries such as RxJS. What you need to think about when incorporating it in the flow is:

- Where to place the HTTP call
- How to ensure that the store is updated and interested views are notified

We have a point at which we register the store to the `dispatcher`, with this piece of code:

```
// excerpt from store-actions-immutable.js

const createProduct = (product) => {
  if (!store["products"]) {
    store["products"] = [];
  }
```

```
    store.products = [...store.products, Object.assign(product)];
}

dispatcher.register(({ type, data }) => {
  switch (type) {
    case CREATE_PRODUCT:
      createProduct(data);
      store.emitChange();
      break;
      /* other cases below */
  }
})
```

If we do this for real, that is, call an API to persist this product, `createProduct()` would be where we would do the API call, like so:

```
// example use of fetch()

fetch(
  '/products' ,
  { method : 'POST', body: product })
  .then(response => {
   // send a message to the dispatcher that the list of products should be
reread
}, err => {
  // report error
});
```

Calling `fetch()` returns a `Promise`. Let's use async/await however, as it makes the call much more readable. The difference in code can be seen in the following example:

```
// contrasting example of 'fetch() with promise' vs 'fetch with
async/await'

fetch('url')
 .then(data => console.log(data))
 .catch(error => console.error(error));

 // using async/await
 try {
   const data = await fetch('url');
   console.log(data);
 } catch (error) {
   console.error(error);
 }
```

Replacing what happens in `createProduct()` with this adds code with a lot of noise so it is a good idea to wrap your HTTP interactions in an API construct like so:

```
// api.js

export class Api {
  createProduct(product) {
    return fetch("/products", { method: "POST", body: product });
  }
}
```

Now let us replace the `createProduct()` method content with the call to our API construct like so:

```
// excerpt from store-actions-api.js

import { Api } from "./api";

const api = new Api();

createProduct() {
  api.createProduct();
}
```

That's not really enough though. Because we created a product through an API call, we should dispatch an action that forces the product list to be reread. We don't have such an action or supporting method in a store to handle it, so let's add one:

```
// product.constants.js

export const SELECT_INDEX = "SELECT_INDEX";
export const CREATE_PRODUCT = "CREATE_PRODUCT";
export const REMOVE_PRODUCT = "REMOVE_PRODUCT";
export const GET_PRODUCTS = "GET_PRODUCTS";
```

Now let's add the required method in the store and the case to handle it:

```
// excerpt from store-actions-api.js

import { Api } from "./api";
import {
  // other actions per usual
  GET_PRODUCTS,
} from "./product.constants";

const setProducts = (products) => {
  store["products"] = products;
}
```

```
const setError = (error) => {
  store["error"] = error;
}

dispatcher.register( async ({ type, data }) => {
  switch (type) {
    case CREATE_PRODUCT:
      try {
        await api.createProduct(data);
        dispatcher.dispatch(getProducts());
      } catch (error) {
        setError(error);
        storeInstance.emitError();
      }
      break;
    case GET_PRODUCTS:
      try {
        const products = await api.getProducts();
        setProducts(products);
        storeInstance.emitChange();
      }
      catch (error) {
        setError(error);
        storeInstance.emitError();
      }
      break;
  }
});
```

We can see that the CREATE_PRODUCT case will call the corresponding API method createProduct(), which on completion will dispatch the GET_PRODUCTS action. The reason for doing so is that when we successfully manage to create a product, we need to read from the endpoint to get an updated version of the products list. We don't see that in detail, but it is being invoked through us calling getProducts(). Again, it is nice to have a wrapper on everything being dispatched, that wrapper being an action creator.

The full file looks like this:

```
// store-actions-api.js

import dispatcher from "./dispatcher";
import { Action } from "./api";
import { Api } from "./api";
import {
  CREATE_PRODUCT,
  GET_PRODUCTS,
  REMOVE_PRODUCT,
  SELECT_INDEX
} from "./product.constants";

let store = {};

class Store extends EventEmitter {
  constructor() {}
  addListener(listener) {
    this.on("changed", listener);
  }

  emitChange() {
    this.emit("changed");
  }

  emitError() {
    this.emit("error");
  }

  getSelectedItem() {
    return store["selectedItem"];
  }
}

const api = new Api();
const storeInstance = new Store();

const selectIndex = index => {
  store["selectedIndex"] = index;
};

const createProduct = product => {
  if (!store["products"]) {
    store["products"] = [];
  }
  store.products = [...store.products, Object.assign(product)];
};
```

```
const removeProduct = product => {
  if (!store["products"]) return;
  store["products"] = products.filter(p => p.id !== product.id);
};

const setProducts = products => {
  store["products"] = products;
};

const setError = error => {
  store["error"] = error;
};

dispatcher.register(async ({ type, data }) => {
  switch (type) {
    case "SELECT_INDEX":
      selectIndex(message.data);
      storeInstance.emitChange();
      break;
    case CREATE_PRODUCT:
      try {
        await api.createProduct(data);
        storeInstance.emitChange();
      } catch (error) {
        setError(error);
        storeInstance.emitError();
      }
      break;
    case GET_PRODUCTS:
      try {
        const products = await api.getProducts();
        setProducts(products);
        storeInstance.emitChange();
      } catch (error) {
        setError(error);
        storeInstance.emitError();
      }
      break;
  }
});
```

An even bigger solution

So far, we have been describing a solution that consists of only a product's topic and communication has only taken place from one view to another. In a more realistic application, we would have a lot of topics such as user management, orders, and so on; exactly what they are called is dependent on the domain of your application. As for views, it is quite possible that you will have a ton of views listening to another view, as in this example:

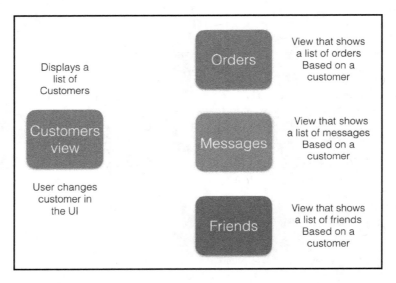

This describes an application that contains four different view components around their own topic. The **Customers view** contains a list of customers and it allows us to alter which customer we currently want to focus on. The other three supporting views show **Orders**, **Messages**, and **Friends** and their content depends on which customer is currently highlighted. From a Flux standpoint, the **Orders**, **Messages**, and **Friends** views can easily register with the store to know when things gets updated so they can fetch/refetch the data they need. However, imagine that the supporting views themselves want to support CRUD actions; then they would need their own set of constants, action creator, API, and store. So now your application would need to look something like this:

```
/customers
  constants.js
  customer-actions.js
  customer-store.js
  customer-api.js
/orders
```

```
    constants.js
    orders-actions.js
    orders-store.js
    orders-api.js
/messages
    constants.js
    messages-actions.js
    messages-store.js
    messages-api.js
/friends
    constants.js
    friends-actions.js
    friends-store.js
    friends-api.js
/common
    dispatcher.js
```

Two interesting situations exist here:

- You have a self-contained view; all CRUD actions happen within it
- You have a view that needs to listen to other views

For the first situation, a good rule of thumb is to create its own set of constants, action creator, API, and store.

For the second situation, ensure your view registers itself with the store of that topic. For example, if the friends view needs to listen to the customer view, then it needs to register itself with the customer store.

Summary

We set out trying only to explain the Flux architecture pattern. It would have been very easy to start mentioning how it fits with React and how there are nice libraries and tools that support Flux and React. That would, however, have taken our focus away from explaining the pattern from a more framework-agnostic viewpoint. Therefore, the rest of this chapter set out to explain core concepts such as actions, action creator, dispatcher, store, and uniform data flow. Little by little, we improved the code to start using constants, action creators, and a nice supporting library such as `EventEmitter`. We explained how HTTP fits into this and, lastly, we discussed how we could build out our application. There is a lot more that can be said about Flux, but we chose to limit the scope to understand the fundamentals so we can compare its approach as we dive into Redux and NgRx in later chapters.

The next chapter will build on that foundation by introducing the concept of **Functional Reactive Programming** (**FRP**). It deals more with how to reason around the fact that data arrives seemingly when it wants to. As messy as that sounds, even that can be modeled to create a sense of structure and order if we think of our data as a stream. More on that in the next chapter.

6
Functional Reactive Programming

According to Wikipedia, **Functional Reactive Programming** (**FRP**) is a programming paradigm for reactive programming, which uses the building blocks of functional programming. OK, that sounds fancy, but what does it mean? To understand the whole sentence we need to break it apart a bit. Let's try to define the following:

- A **programming paradigm** is an overarching theory, or way of working, centered around how a program should be organized and structured. Object-oriented programming and functional programming are examples of programming paradigms.
- **Reactive programming**, in short, is programming with asynchronous data streams. Asynchronous data streams are streams of data whose values can arrive at any point in time.
- **Functional programming** is a programming paradigm that takes a more mathematical approach, in that it sees a functional call as a mathematical computation and thereby avoids changing states or dealing with mutable data.

So, in short, our Wikipedia definition means we have a functional programming approach to values that might arrive at any point in time. That doesn't really mean much, but hopefully things will have been cleared up a bit by the end of this chapter.

In this chapter, we will learn about:

- Asynchronous data streams
- How these streams can be manipulated

Recursion

"To understand the word recursion see the word recursion."

This is a standing joke at most engineering schools and it explains what it is in a very short way. Recursion is a mathematical concept. Let's explain it a bit more. The official definition says the following:

Recursion is the process a procedure goes through when one of the steps of the procedure involves invoking the procedure itself. A procedure that goes through recursion is said to be 'recursive'.

Ok, what does that mean in human speak? It says that at some point in running our function, we will call ourselves. This means we have a function that looks something like this:

```
function something() {
  statement;
  statement;
  if(condition) {
    something();
  }
  return someValue;
}
```

We can see that the function `something()` at some point in its body calls itself. A recursive function should abide to the following rules:

- Should call itself
- Should eventually meet an exit condition

If a recursive function doesn't have an exit condition, we will run out of memory as the function will call itself for all eternity. There are certain types of problems that are more suitable than others to apply recursive programming to. Examples of these are:

- Traversing trees
- Compiling code
- Writing algorithms for compression
- Sort lists

There are many more examples, but it's important to remember that, although it's a great tool, it shouldn't be used everywhere. Let's look at an example where recursion really shines. Our example is a linked list. A linked list consists of nodes that know about the node they are connected to. The code for the `Node` structure looks like this:

```
class Node {
  constructor(
    public left,
    public value
  ) {}
}
```

Using such a structure as a `Node`, we can construct a linked list consisting of several linked nodes. We can connect a set of node instances in the following way:

```
const head = new Node(null, 1);
const firstNode = new Node(head, 2);
const secondNode = new Node(firstNode, 3);
```

A graphical representation of the preceding code would be the following diagram. Here, we can clearly see what our nodes consist of and how they are connected:

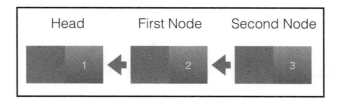

Here, we have a linked list where we have three connected node instances. The head node is not connected to the node to the left. The second node however is connected to the first node and the first node is connected to the head node. The following type of operations on a list might be interesting to do:

- Find the head node, given any node in the list
- Insert a node at a given point in the list
- Remove a node from a given point in the list

Let's have a look at how we can solve the first bullet point. Firstly, we will use an imperative approach and thereafter we will use a recursive approach to see how they differ. More importantly, let's discuss why the recursive approach might be preferred:

```
// demo of how to find the head node, imperative style

const head = new Node(null, 1);
const firstNode = new Node(head, 2);
const secondNode = new Node(firstNode, 3);

function findHeadImperative (startNode)  {
  while (startNode.left !== null) {
    startNode = startNode.left;
  }
  return startNode;
}

const foundImp = findHeadImperative(secondNode);
console.log('found', foundImp);
console.log(foundImp === head);
```

As we can see here, we are using a `while` loop to traverse through the list until we find the node instance whose `left` property is null. Now, let's show the recursive approach:

```
// demo of how to find head node, declarative style using recursion

const head = new Node(null, 1);
const firstNode = new Node(head, 2);
const secondNode = new Node(firstNode, 3);

function findHeadRecursive(startNode) {
  if(startNode.left !== null) {
    return findHeadRecursive(startNode.left);
  } else {
    return startNode;
  }
}

const found = findHeadRecursive(secondNode);
console.log('found', found);
console.log(found === head);
```

In the preceding code, we check whether `startNode.left` is null. If that is the case, we have reached our exit condition. If we haven't reached the exit condition yet, we keep on calling ourselves.

Ok, so we have an imperative approach and a recursive approach. Why is the latter so much better? Well, with the recursive approach, we start off with a long list and we make the list shorter every time we call ourselves: a bit of a *divide and conquer* approach. One thing that clearly stands out with the recursive approach is that we defer execution by saying, no, our exit condition isn't met yet, keep processing. Keep processing means we call ourselves as we do in our `if` clause. Is the point of recursive programming that we get fewer lines of code? Well, that could be the result, but more importantly: it changes our mindset toward how we go about solving problems. In imperative programming, we have a *let's solve the problem from top to bottom mindset*, whereas in recursive programming, our mindset is more, define when we are done and slice down the problem to make it easier to deal with. In the preceding case, we discarded the part of our linked list that wasn't interesting anymore.

No more loops

One of the more significant changes when starting to code in a more functional way is that we get rid of `for` loops. Now that we know about recursion, we can just use that instead. Let's have look at a simple imperative piece of code that prints an array:

```
// demo of printing an array, imperative style

let array = [1, 2, 3, 4, 5];

function print(arr) {
  for(var i = 0, i < arr.length; i++) {
    console.log(arr[i]);
  }
}

print(arr);
```

The corresponding code using recursion looks like this:

```
// print.js, printing an array using recursion

let array = [1, 2, 3, 4, 5];

function print(arr, pos, len) {
  if (pos < len) {
    console.log(arr[pos]);
```

```
      print(arr, pos + 1, len);
   }
   return;
}

print(array, 0, array.length);
```

As we can see, our imperative code is still there in spirit. We still start at 0. Moreover, we keep going until we come to the last position of our array. Once we hit our break condition, we exit the method.

Reoccurring pattern

We haven't really sold recursion as a concept at this point. We kind of get it, but are probably not convinced why good old `while` or `for` loops can't be used in its place. Recursion shines when it solves problems that look like a reoccurring pattern. An example of that is a tree. A tree has some similar concepts to it such as consisting of nodes. A node without children connected to it is called a leaf. A node with children but that has no connection to an upward node is called a root node. Let's illustrate this with a diagram:

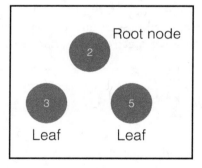

There are a few interesting operations that we would want to carry out on a tree:

- Summarise the node values
- Count the number of nodes
- Calculate the width
- Calculate the depth

To attempt to solve that, we need to think about how to store a tree as a data structure. The most common way of modeling it is by creating a representation of a node as having a value, and a `left` property and a `right` property, then both those properties point to nodes in turn. Therefore, the code for said Node class might look like this:

```
class NodeClass {
  constructor(left, right, value) {
    this.left = left;
    this.right = right;
    this.value = value;
  }
}
```

The next step is thinking how to create the tree itself. This code shows how we can create a tree with a root node and two children, and how to bind these together:

```
// tree.js

class NodeClass {
  constructor(left, right, value) {
    this.left = left;
    this.right = right;
    this.value = value;
  }
}

const leftLeftLeftChild = new NodeClass(null, null, 7);
const leftLeftChild = new NodeClass(leftLeftLeftChild, null, 1);
const leftRightChild = new NodeClass(null, null, 2);
const rightLeftChild = new NodeClass(null, null, 4);
const rightRightChild = new NodeClass(null, null, 2);
const left = new NodeClass(leftLeftChild, leftRightChild, 3);
const right = new NodeClass(rightLeftChild, rightRightChild, 5);
const root = new NodeClass(left, right, 2);

module.exports = root;
```

Worth highlighting is how the instances `left` and `right` do not have children. We can see that because we set their values to `null` on creation. Our root node, on the other hand, has the object instances `left` and `right` as children.

Summarise

Thereafter, we need to think about how to summarise the nodes. Just looking at it, it looks like we should summarise the top node and its two children. So, a code implementation would start off like this:

```
// tree-sum.js

const root = require('./tree');

function summarise(node) {
  return node.value + node.left.value + node.right.value;
}

console.log(summarise(root)) // 10
```

What happens if our tree grows and suddenly looks like this:

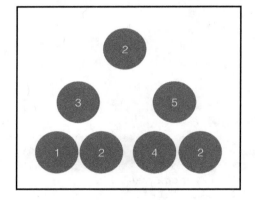

Let's add to the preceding code so it looks like this:

```
// example of a non recursive code

function summarise(node) {
  return node.value +
    node.left.value +
    node.right.value +
    node.right.left.value +
    node.right.right.value +
    node.left.left.value +
    node.left.right.value;
}

console.log(summarise(root)) // 19
```

This is technically working code, but it can be improved. What we should see at this point, looking at the tree, are reoccurring patterns in the tree. We have the following triangles:

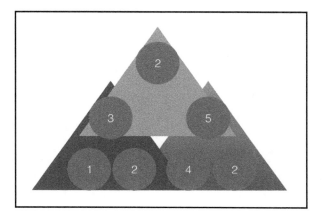

One triangle is made up of **2**, **3**, **5**, another one is made up of **3**, **1**, **2**, and the last one is made up of **5**, **4**, **2**. Every triangle computes its sum by taking the node itself, plus its left child and its right child. Recursion is all about this: discovering a reoccurring pattern and codifying it. We can now implement our `summarise()` function with recursion, like so:

```
function summarise(node) {
  if(node === null) {
    return 0;
  }
  return node.value + summarise(node.left) + summarise(left.right);
}
```

What we are doing here is expressing our reoccurring pattern as *node + left node + right node*. When we call `summarise(node.left)` we simply run through `summarise()` again for that node. The preceding implementation is short and elegant, and is able to traverse the entire tree. Recursion is truly elegant once you find that your problem can be seen as a repeating pattern. The full code looks like this:

```
// tree.js

class NodeClass {
  constructor(left, right, value) {
    this.left = left;
    this.right = right;
    this.value = value;
  }
}
```

```
const leftLeftLeftChild = new NodeClass(null, null, 7);
const leftLeftChild = new NodeClass(leftLeftLeftChild, null, 1);
const leftRightChild = new NodeClass(null, null, 2);
const rightLeftChild = new NodeClass(null, null, 4);
const rightRightChild = new NodeClass(null, null, 2);
const left = new NodeClass(leftLeftChild, leftRightChild, 3);
const right = new NodeClass(rightLeftChild, rightRightChild, 5);
const root = new NodeClass(left, right, 2);

module.exports = root;

// tree-sum.js

const root = require("./tree");

function sum(node) {
  if (node === null) {
    return 0;
  }
  return node.value + sum(node.left) + sum(node.right);
}

console.log("sum", sum(root));
```

Count

Implementing a function that counts all the nodes in the trees is quite trivial now that we are beginning to grasp the nature of recursion. We can reuse our summary function from before and simply count every non-null node as 1 and null as 0. So, we simply take the existing summary function and modify it to this:

```
//tree-count.js

const root = require("./tree");

function count(node) {
  if (node === null) {
    return 0;
  } else {
    return 1 + count(node.left) + count(node.right);
  }
}

console.log("count", count(root));
```

The preceding code ensures we traverse each and every node successfully. Our exit condition happens when we reach null. That is, we are trying to go from a node to one of its non-existing children.

Width

To create a width function, we first need to define what we mean by width. Let's have a look at our tree again:

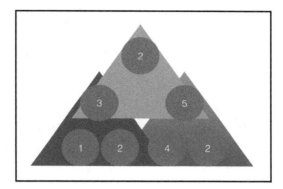

This tree has a width of **4**. How is that? For every step down in the tree, our nodes expand one step to the left and one step to the right. This means that to calculate the width correctly, we need to traverse the edges of our tree. Every time we have to traverse a node to the left or to the right, we increment the width. What we are interested in doing from a calculation standpoint is to traverse the tree like this:

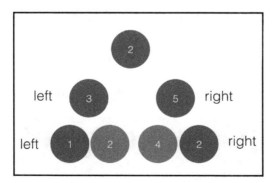

The code should therefore reflect this fact. We can implement this like this:

```javascript
// tree-width.js

const root = require("./tree");

function calc(node, direction) {
  if (node === null) {
    return 0;
  } else {
    return (
      1 + (direction === "left" ?
      calc(node.left, direction) :
      calc(node.right, direction))
    );
  }
}

function calcWidth(node) {
  return calc(node.left, "left") + calc(node.right, "right");
}

console.log("width", calcWidth(root));
```

Note especially how, in the `calcWidth()` function, we call `calc()` with `node.left` and `node.right`, respectively, as arguments. We also add a `left` and `right` argument which, in the method `calc()`, means that we will keep going in that direction. Our exit condition is when we eventually hit null.

Asynchronous data streams

An asynchronous data stream is a stream of data where values are emitted, one after another, with a delay between them. The word asynchronous means that the data emitted can appear anywhere in time, after one second or even after two minutes, for example. A way to model asynchronous streams is to place the emitted values on a time axis, like so:

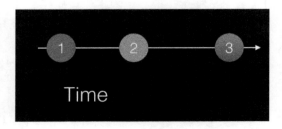

There are a lot of things that can be considered asynchronous. One such thing is fetching data through AJAX. When the data arrives depends on a number of factors, such as:

- The speed of your connection
- The responsiveness of the backend API
- The size of the data, and many more factors.

The point is the data isn't arriving right at this very second.

Other things that can be considered asynchronous are user initiated events, such as scrolling or mouse clicks. These are events that can happen at any point in time, depending on the user's interaction. As such, we can consider these UI events as a continuous stream of data on a time axis. The following diagram depicts a stream of data representing a user clicking several times. Each click leads to a click event, **c**, which we place on a time axis:

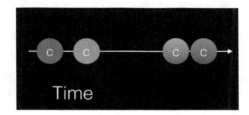

At first glance, our diagram depicts four click events. Taking a closer look, we see that the click events seem grouped. The preceding diagram contains two pieces of information:

- That a number of click events have occurred
- That the click events have occurred with a certain delay in between events

Here, we can see that the two first clicks seem to happen very close together in time; when two events happen very close in time, this will be interpreted as a double-click. Therefore, our image above thus tells us about the events that occurred; it also tells us when and how often they occurred. Looking at the previous diagram, it is quite easy to distinguish between a single-click and a double-click.

We can assign different actions to each click behavior. A double-click might mean that we want to zoom-in, whereas a single-click might mean we want to select something; exactly what is up to the application you are writing.

A third example is that of input. What if we have a situation where the user is typing and stops typing after a while? After a certain amount of time has passed, the user expects the UI to react. This is the case with a search field. In that case, the user might enter something in a search field and press a search button when done. Another way to model that situation in a UI is to just provide a search field and wait for the user to stop typing as a sign of when to start searching for what the user wants. The final example is known as **autocomplete** behavior. It can be modeled in the following way:

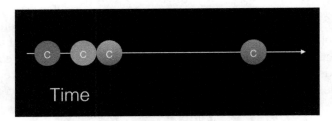

The first three characters entered seem to belong to the same search query, whereas the fourth character entered occurs a lot later and probably belongs to another query.

The point of this section has been to highlight that different things lend themselves to being modeled as streams, and that the time axis and the placement of the emitted values on it can come to mean something.

Comparing lists to async streams – preparing for RxJS

We have discussed so far how we can model asynchronous events as a continuous stream of data on a time axis, or stream modeling. Events can be AJAX data, mouse clicks, or some other type of event. Modeling things this way makes for an interesting perspective on things but, looking at a double-click situation for example, doesn't mean much unless we are able to dig out the data. There might be another case where there is data that we need to filter out. What we are discussing here is how to manipulate streams. Without that ability, stream modeling itself has no practical value.

There are different ways to manipulate data: sometimes we want to change the data emitted to some other data and sometimes we might want to change how often the data is being emitted to a listener. Sometimes, we want our stream of data to become a totally different stream. We will try to model the following situations:

- **Projection**: Changing the data of the value being emitted
- **Filtering**: Changing what gets emitted

Combining the functional programming paradigm with streams

This chapter has covered functional programming and asynchronous data streams. Working with RxJS doesn't require a deep understanding of functional programming, but you do need to understand what declarative means, in order to focus on the right things. Your focus should be on what you want done, not how you want it done. RxJS, as a library, will take care of the how.

These might seem like two different topics. Combining the two, however, gives us the ability to manipulate streams. A stream can be seen as a list of data, where the data is available at a certain point in time. If we start treating our streams as lists, especially immutable lists, then there are operations that go with lists that manipulate lists by applying operators to them. The result of the manipulation is a new list, not a mutated list. So let's start applying our list philosophy and its operators to the following situations.

Projection

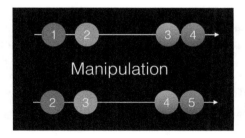

Here, we can see that our stream is emitting the values **1**, **2**, **3**, and **4**, and then a manipulation happens that changes every value by incrementing it by one. This is quite a simple situation. If we consider this as a list, we can see that what we do here is simply a projection, which we would code like this:

```
let newList = list.map(value => value + 1)
```

Filtering

There might be some items in a list, as well as in a stream, that you do not want. What you do to fix that is to create a filter that filters out the unwanted data. Modeling our initial array, the manipulation, and the resulting array, we get the following:

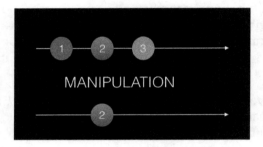

In JavaScript, we can accomplish this by writing the following code:

```
let array = [1,2,3];
let filtered = array.filter(data => data % 2 === 0);
```

Combining mindsets

So, what are we trying to say with this section. Clearly, we have shown examples of how to manipulate lists. Well, what we have done is shown how we can display items on an axis. In that sense, we can see how it is easy to think of asynchronous events and lists of values in the same way, as we are graphically picturing them in the same way. The question is, why do we want to do that? The reason is that this is the mindset the RxJS library wants you to have when you start manipulating and crafting streams.

Summary

This chapter has established that we can model asynchronous events as values on a time axis. We introduced the idea of comparing these streams to lists and thereby applying functional methods to them that would not change the lists themselves but merely create a new list. The benefit of applying the functional paradigm is that we can focus on *what* to achieve rather than *how* to achieve it, thereby having a declarative approach. We realize it's not easy to combine async and lists and create readable code from it. Fortunately, this is what the RxJS library does for us.

It is this realization that prepares us for `Chapter 8`, *RxJS Advanced*, which will cover more operators, and some more advanced concepts.

Manipulating Streams and Their Values

7

Operators are functions we can call on our streams to perform manipulation in many different ways. Operators are immutable, which makes the stream easy to reason about and will also make it quite easy to test. As you will see throughout this chapter, we will seldom deal with just one stream, but many streams, and it is understanding how to forge and control these streams that allow you to go from thinking it's *dark magic* to actually being able to apply RxJS when and where you need it.

In this chapter, we will cover:

- How to use basic operators
- Debugging streams with operators as well as with existing tools
- Digging deeper into different operator categories
- Developing the mindset to solve a problem the Rx way

Starting out

You almost always start out coding with RxJS by creating a stream of static values. Why static values? Well, there is no need to make it unnecessarily complex, and all you really need to start reasoning is an `Observable`. As you gradually progress in your problem solving, you might replace the static values with a more appropriate call to an AJAX call, or from another asynchronous source that your values originate from.

You then start thinking about what you want to achieve. This leads you to consider which operators you might need and in which order you need to apply them. You might also think about how to divide your problem up; this usually means creating more than one stream, where each stream solves a specific problem that connects to the larger problem you are trying to solve.

Let's start with stream creation and see how we can take our first steps working with streams.

The following code creates a stream of static values:

```
const staticValuesStream$ = Rx.Observable.of(1, 2, 3, 4);

staticValuesStream$.subscribe(data => console.log(data));
// emits 1, 2, 3, 4
```

That is a very basic example of how we can create a stream. We use the `of()` creation operator, which takes any number of arguments. All the arguments are emitted, one by one, as soon as there is a subscriber. In the preceding code, we also subscribe to `staticValuesStream$` by calling the `subscribe()` method and passing a function that takes the emitted value as a parameter.

Let's introduce an operator, `map()`, which acts like a projection and allows you to change what is being emitted. The `map()` operator gets called on each value in the stream before it is emitted.

You use the map() operator by supplying it with a function and carrying out a projection, like so:

```
const staticValuesStream$ =
Rx.Observable
  .of(1, 2, 3, 4)
  .map(data => data + 1);

staticValuesStream$.subscribe(data => console.log(data))
// emits 2, 3, 4, 5
```

In the preceding code, we have appended the map() operator to staticValuesStream$ and we apply it to each value before emitting it and incrementing it by one. The resulting data is therefore changed. This is how you append operators to a stream: simply create the stream, or take an existing one, and append the operators one by one.

Let's add another operator, filter(), to ensure that we really understand how to work with operators. What does filter() do. Well, just like the map() operator, it is applied to each value, but instead of creating a projection, it decides which values will be emitted. filter() takes a Boolean. Any expression evaluated to true means the value will be emitted; if false, the expression will not be emitted.

You use the filter() operator in the following way:

```
const staticValuesStream$ =
Rx.Observable
  .of(1, 2, 3, 4)
  .map(data => data + 1)
  .filter(data => data % 2 === 0 );

staticValuesStream$.subscribe(data => console.log(data));
// emits 2, 4
```

We add the filter() operator by chaining it to the existing map() operator. The condition we give our filter() operator says to only return true for values that are divisible by 2, that's what the modulus operator does. We know from before that the map() operator alone ensures that the values 2, 3 , 4, and 5 are emitted. These are the values that are now being evaluated by the filter() operator. Out of those four values, only 2 and 4 fulfill the condition set out by the filter() operator.

Of course, when working on a stream and applying operators, things might not always be as simple as the preceding code. It might not be possible to anticipate exactly what gets emitted. For those occasions, we have a few tricks we can use. One such trick is to use the `do()` operator, which will allow us to inspect each value without changing it. This gives us ample opportunity to use it for debugging purposes. Depending on where we are in the stream, the `do()` operator will output different values. Let's look at different situations where it matters where the `do()` operator is applied:

```
const staticValuesStream$ =
Rx.Observable.of(1, 2, 3, 4)
  .do(data => console.log(data)) // 1, 2, 3, 4
  .map(data => data + 1)
  .do(data => console.log(data)) // 2, 3, 4, 5
  .filter(data => data % 2 === 0 )
  .do(data => console.log(data)); // 2, 4

// emits 2, 4
staticValuesStream$.subscribe(data => console.log(data))
```

As you can see, just by using the `do()` operator, we have a nice way to debug our streams, which becomes necessary as our streams grow in complexity.

Understanding operators

So far, we have shown how to create a stream and use some very basic operators on it to change what values get emitted. We also introduced how to inspect your stream without changing it by using the `do()` operator. Not all operators are as easy to understand as the `map()`, `filter()`, and `do()` operators. There are different tactics you can use to try to understand what each operator does so you know when to use them. Using the `do()` operator is one way, but there is a graphical approach you can take. This approach is known as a marble diagram. It consists of an arrow that represents time passing from left to right. There are circles, or marbles, on this arrow that represent emitted values. The marbles have a value in them, but the distance between the marbles might also describe what is happening over time. A marble diagram usually consists of at least two arrows with marbles on them, as well as an operator. The idea is to represent what happens to a stream when an operator is applied. The second arrow usually represents the resulting stream.

Here's an example of a marble diagram:

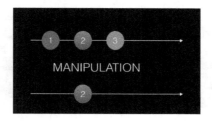

Most operators in RxJS are depicted by a marble diagram on the site RxMarbles: `http://rxmarbles.com/`. This is a truly great resource to quickly gain an understanding of what operators do. However, to truly understand RxJS you need to code; there is no getting around it. There are different ways of doing that of course. You can easily set up your own project and install RxJS from NPM, refer to it through a CDN link, or you can use a page such as JS Bin (`www.jsbin.com`), which gives you the ability to easily add RxJS as a library and allows you to start coding straight away. It looks something like this:

JS Bin makes it easy to start, but wouldn't it be great if we could combine marble diagrams and JS Bin, and get a graphical representation of what you code, when you code? You can get just that with RxFiddle: `http://rxfiddle.net/`. You can enter your code, click **Run**, and you are shown a marble diagram of what you just coded, which will look like this:

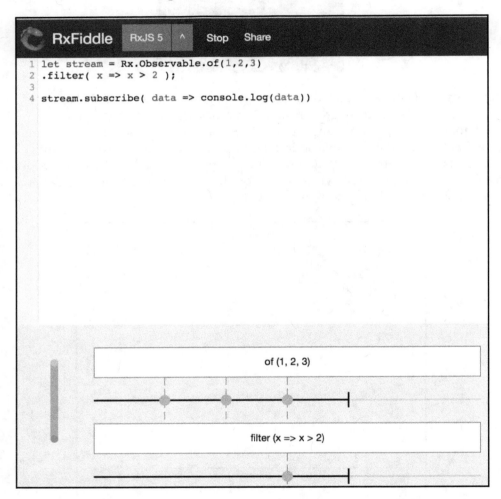

Stream in a stream

We have been looking at different operators that change the values being emitted. There is another different aspect to streams: what if you need to create a new stream from an existing stream? Another good question is: when does such a situation usually occur? There are plenty of situations, such as:

- Based on a stream of keyUp events, do an AJAX call.
- Count the number of clicks and determine whether the user single, double, or triple-clicked.

You get the idea; we are starting with one type of stream that needs to turn into another type of stream.

Let's first have a look at creating a stream and see what happens when we try to create a stream as the result of using an operator:

```
let stream$ = Rx.Observable.of(1,2,3)
   .map(data => Rx.Observable.of(data));

// Observable, Observable, Observable
stream$.subscribe(data => console.log(data));
```

At this point, every value that passes through the `map()` operator produces a new `Observable`. When you subscribe to `stream$`, each value that is emitted will be a stream. Your first instinct might be to attach a `subscribe()` to each of those values, like this:

```
let stream$ = Rx.Observable
   .of(1,2,3)
   .map(data => Rx.Observable.of(data))


stream$.subscribe(data => {
   data.subscribe(val => console.log(val))
});

// 1, 2, 3
```

Fight this urge. This will only create code that is hard to maintain. What you want to do is merge all these streams into one so, that you just need one `subscribe()`. There is an operator just for that, called `flatMap()`. What `flatMap()` does is to take your array of streams and turn them into one stream, a metastream.

It is used in the following way:

```
let stream$ = Rx.Observable.of(1,2,3)
  .flatMap(data => Rx.Observable.of(data))

stream$.subscribe(data => {
  console.log(val);
});

// 1, 2, 3
```

OK, we get it, we don't want a stream of Observables, but rather a stream of values. This operator seems really great. We still aren't quite certain when to use though. Let's make this a bit more realistic. Imagine you have a UI that consists of an input field. The user enters characters into that input field. Imagine that you want to react to one or more characters being entered and, for example, perform an AJAX request as the result of characters being entered. We focus on two things here: how to collect characters being entered and how to perform an AJAX request.

Let' start with the first thing, capturing characters entered into an input field. For this, we need an HTML page and a JavaScript page. Let's start with the HTML page:

```
<html>
  <body>
    <input id="input" type="text">
    <script src="https://unpkg.com/rxjs/bundles/Rx.min.js"></script>
    <script src="app.js"></script>
  </body>
</html>
```

This depicts our input element and a script reference to RxJS, as well as a reference to the app.js file. Then we have app.js file, where we get a reference to the input element and start listening to keystrokes as soon as they are entered:

```
let elem = document.getElementById('input');
let keyStream$ = Rx.Observable
  .fromEvent(elem, 'keyup')
  .map( ev => ev.key);

keyStream$.subscribe( key => console.log(key));

// emits entered key chars
```

Worth highlighting is the fact that we start listening to `keyup` events being emitted by calling the `fromEvent()` creation operator. Thereafter, we apply the `map()` operator to dig out the character value store on `ev.key`. Lastly, we subscribe to the stream. As expected, running this code will lead to characters being typed in the console as soon as you input values in the HTML page.

Let's make this more tangible by doing an AJAX request based on what we type. For this, we will be using the `fetch()` API and an online API called swapi (swapi.com), which contains a collection of APIs containing information on the Star Wars movies. Let's first define our AJAX call and then see how it fits into our existing stream of keys.

We said we would use `fetch()`. It lets us formulate a GET request as simple as this:

```
fetch('https://swapi.co/api/people/1')
  .then(data => data.json())
  .then(data => console.log('data', data));
```

Of course, we want to turn this request into an `Observable` so that it can play well with our `keyStream$`. Fortunately for us, this is easily accomplished through the use of the `from()` operator. Let's, however, first rewrite our `fetch()` call into a method that's easy to work with. The result of the rewrite looks like this:

```
function getStarwarsCharacterStream(id) {
  return fetch('https://swapi.co/api/people/' + id)
    .then(data => data.json());
}
```

This code allows us to provide an argument used to construct a URL which we use to fetch some data with AJAX. At this point, we are ready to connect our function to our existing stream. We do that by typing the following:

```
let keyStream$ = Rx.Observable.fromEvent(elem, 'keyup')
  .map(ev => ev.key)
  .filter(key => key !== 'Backspace')
  .flatMap( key =>
    Rx.Observable
      .from(getStarwarsCharacterStream(key))
  );
```

We highlight the usage of the `flatmap()` operator in bold using our `from()` conversion operator. The operator mentioned last takes our `getStarwarsCharacterStream()` function as a parameter. The `from()` operator converts said function into a stream.

Here, we have learned how to connect two different streams, but also how to convert a `Promise` into a stream. As good as this approach seems on paper, using `flatMap()` has its limitations and it is important to understand what they are. For that reason, let's talk about the `switchMap()` operator next. The benefits of using a `switchMap()` operator will become clearer when we execute long-running tasks. For argument's sake, let's define such a task, like so:

```
function longRunningTask(input) {
  return new Promise(resolve => {
    setTimeout(() => {
      resolve('response based on ' + input);
    }, 5000);
  });
}
```

In this code, we have a function that takes 5 seconds to execute; enough time to show the point we are trying to make. Next, let's show what the effect is if we keep using the `flatMap()` operator in the following code:

```
let longRunningStream$ = keyStream$
  .map(ev => ev.key)
  .filter(key => elem.value.length >3)
  .filter( key => key !== 'Backspace')
  .flatMap( key =>
    Rx.Observable
      .from(longRunningTask(elem.value))
  );

longRunningStream$.subscribe(data => console.log(data));
```

The preceding code works in the following way: every time we hit a key, it generates an event. However, we have a `.filter()` operator in place that ensures an event is only generated when at least four keys are entered, `filter(key => elem.value.length >3)`. Let's talk about the user's expectation at this point. If a user enters keys in an input control, they most likely expect a request to be made when they are done typing. A user defines being done as entering a few characters and also that they should be able to remove characters if they were mistyped. So, therefore, we can assume the following input sequence:

```
// enters abcde
abcde
// removes 'e'
```

At this point, they have entered characters and, within a reasonable amount of time, edited their answer. The user expects to receive an answer based on abcd. Using the flatMap() operator, however, means the user will get two answers back because, in reality, they typed abcde and abcd. Imagine we get a results list based on these two inputs; it would most likely be two lists that looked somewhat different. The response based on our code would look like this:

```
response based on 1234
response based on 12345
```

Our code most likely would be able to handle the situation described by rerendering the results list as soon as a new response arrives. There are two problems with this though: firstly, we do an unnecessary network request for abcde, and secondly, if the backend is fast enough in responding, we will see a flickering in the UI as the result list is rendered once and then, shortly after, is rendered again, based on the second response. This is not good, and we want to have a situation where the first request will be abandoned if we keep on typing. This is where the switchMap() operator comes in. It does exactly that. Let's therefore alter the preceding code to the following:

```
let longRunningStream$ = keyStream$
  .map(ev => ev.key)
  .filter(key => elem.value.length >3)
  .filter( key => key !== 'Backspace')
  .switchMap( key =>
    Rx.Observable
    .from(longRunningTask(elem.value))
  );
```

In this code, we simply switched our flatMap() to a switchMap(). When we now execute the code in the exact same way, that is, the user firstly typing 12345 and shortly altering that to 1234, the end result is:

```
response based on abcde
```

As we can see, we get one request only. The reason for this is that the previous event is aborted when a new event happens—switchMap() is doing its magic. The user is happy and we are happy.

AJAX

We have already touched upon the topic of making AJAX requests. There are many ways to make AJAX requests; the two most common approaches are:

- Using the fetch API; the fetch API is a web standard and is thus built into most browsers
- Using the `ajax()` method, nowadays built into the RxJS library; it used to exist in a library called Rx.Dom

fetch()

The `fetch()` API is a web standard. You can find the official documentation at the following link: `https://developer.mozilla.org/en-US/docs/Web/API/Fetch_API`. The `fetch()` API is `Promise`-based, which means we need to convert it to an `Observable` before use. The API exposes a `fetch()` method, which takes a mandatory URL parameter as the first argument, with the second argument being an optional object that allows you to control which body to send, if any, which HTTP verb to use, and so on.

We have already mentioned how to best deal with it in the context of RxJS. It is worth repeating though. It is not as simple as just taking our fetch and sticking it into the `from()` operator though. Let's write some code and see why:

```
let convertedStream$ =
Rx.Observable.from(fetch('some url'));

convertedStream$.subscribe(data => 'my data?', data);
```

We get our data right? Sorry, no, we get a `Response` object back. But that's easy, just call a `json()` method in the `map()` operator and surely then we have our data? Again, sorry no, the `json()` method returns a `Promise` when you type the following:

```
let convertedStream$ = Rx.Observable.from(fetch('some url'))
  .map( r=> r.json());

// returns PromiseObservable
convertedStream$.subscribe(data => 'my data?', data);
```

We have already shown a possible solution to this in the previous section, and that is the following construct:

```
getData() {
  return fetch('some url')
    .then(r => r.json());
}

let convertedStream$ = Rx.Observable.from(getData());
convertedStream$.subscribe(data => console.log('data', data));
```

What we did in this code was to simply take care of digging out our data before handing it over to the `from()` operator. It doesn't feel quite RxJS to play around with Promises. There is a more stream-based approach you can take; we were almost there before, we just needed to make a minor adjustment:

```
let convertedStream$ = Rx.Observable.from(fetch('some url'))
  .flatMap( r => Rx.Observable.from(r.json()));

// returns data
convertedStream$.subscribe(data => console.log('data'), data);
```

And there it is: our `fetch()` call is now providing us data like a stream. So what did we do? Well, we changed our `map()` call to a `flatMap()` call. The reason for that was that when we called `r.json()`, we got a `Promise`. We fixed that by wrapping it in a `from()` call, `Rx.Observable.from(r.json())`. That would make the stream emit a `PromiseObservable` unless we changed from `map()` to `flatMap()`. As we learned in the previous section, if we risk creating a stream within a stream, we need `flatMap()` to come to our rescue, which it did.

ajax() operator

Unlike the `fetch()` API, which is `Promise`-based, the `ajax()` method is actually `Observable`-based, which makes our job a little easier. Using it is quite straightforward, like so:

```
Rx.Observable
  .ajax('https://swapi.co/api/people/1')
  .map(r => r.response)
  .subscribe(data => console.log('from ajax()', data));
```

As we can see, the preceding code calls the `ajax()` operator with a URL as an argument. The second thing worthy of mentioning is the call to the `map()` operator, which digs out our data from the `response` property. Because it is an `Observable`, we just have to subscribe to it as usual by calling the `subscribe()` method and providing it with a listener function as an argument.

This covers a simple case when you want to fetch data using the HTTP verb `GET`. Fortunately for us, it is quite easy to create, update, or delete by using an overloaded version of the `ajax()` operator which takes an `AjaxRequest` object instance which has the following fields:

```
url?: string;
body?: any;
user?: string;
async?: boolean;
method?: string;
headers?: Object;
timeout?: number;
password?: string;
hasContent?: boolean;
crossDomain?: boolean;
withCredentials?: boolean;
createXHR?: () => XMLHttpRequest;
progressSubscriber?: Subscriber<any>;
responseType?: string;
```

As we can see from this object specification, all the fields are optional and there are also quite a few things we can configure with our request, such as `headers`, `timeout`, `user`, `crossDomain`, and so on; pretty much what we would expect from a nice AJAX wrapping functionality. Except for the overload of the `ajax()` operator, a few shorthand options also exist:

- `get()`: Fetches data using the `GET` verb
- `put()`: Updates data using the `PUT` verb
- `post()`: Creates data using the `POST` verb
- `patch()`: The idea with using the `PATCH` verb is to update a partial resource
- `delete()`: Removes data using the `DELETE` verb
- `getJSON()`: Fetches data using the `GET` verb and sets the response type to `application/json`

Cascading calls

So far, we have covered the two main ways you will use AJAX to send or receive data. When it comes to receiving data, it's usually not as simple as fetching the data and rendering it. In fact, you will most likely have a dependency on when you can fetch which data. A typical example of this is needing to perform a login call before you can fetch the remaining data. In some cases, it might be that you need to first log in, then fetch the data of the logged in user, and once you have that you can fetch messages, orders, or whichever kind of data you need that might be specific to a certain user. This whole phenomenon of fetching data in this way is called cascading calls.

Let's have a look at how we use cascading calls with Promises and gradually learn how to do the same with RxJS. We are taking this little detour as we assume that most of you reading this book are familiar with Promises.

Let's look at the dependent case we first mentioned, where we need to perform the following steps in this order:

1. The user first logs in to the system
2. Then we fetch information about the user
3. Then we fetch information about the user's orders

Using promises, it would look something like this in code:

```
// cascading/cascading-promises.js

login()
  .then(getUser)
  .then(getOrders);

// we collect username and password from a form
const login = (username, password) => {
  return fetch("/login", {
    method: "POST",
    body: { username, password }
  })
  .then(r => r.json())
  .then(token => {
    localStorage.setItem("auth", token);
  });
};

const getUser = () => {
  return fetch("/users", {
    headers: {
```

```
        Authorization: "Bearer " + localStorage.getToken("auth")
      }
   }).then(r => r.json());
};

const getOrders = user => {
   return fetch(`/orders/user/${user.id}`, {
      headers: {
         Authorization: "Bearer " + localStorage.getToken("auth")
      }
   }).then(r => r.json());
};
```

This code describes how we first log in to the system, using the `login()` method, and obtain a token. We use this token in any future calls to ensure we make authenticated calls. We also see how we perform the `getUser()` call and obtain a user instance. We use that same user instance to perform our last call, `getOrders()`, whereby the user ID is used as a routing parameter: `` `/orders/user/${user.id}` ``.

We have shown how to perform cascading calls using promises; we did this to establish a common ground for the problem we are trying to solve. The RxJS approach is very similar: we have shown that the `ajax()` operator exists and makes our lives easier when dealing with AJAX calls. To achieve the cascading calls effect with RxJS, we simply need to use the `switchMap()` operator. This will lead to our code looking like this:

```
// cascading/cascading-rxjs.js

let user = "user";
let password = "password";

login(user, password)
  .switchMap(getUser)
  .switchMap(getOrders);

// we collect username and password from a form
const login = (username, password) => {
  return Rx.Observable.ajax("/login", {
    method: "POST",
    body: { username, password }
  })
  .map(r => r.response)
  .do(token => {
    localStorage.setItem("auth", token);
  });
};
```

```
const getUser = () => {
  return Rx.Observable.ajax("/users", {
    headers: {
      Authorization: "Bearer " + localStorage.getToken("auth")
    }
  }).map(r => r.response);
};

const getOrders = user => {
  return Rx.Observable.json(`/orders/user/${user.id}`, {
    headers: {
      Authorization: "Bearer " + localStorage.getToken("auth")
    }
  }).map(r => r.response);
};
```

We have highlighted the parts that need changing in the preceding code. In short, the changes are:

- `fetch()` is replaced by the `ajax()` operator
- We call `.map(r => r.response)` instead of `.then(r => r.json())`
- We do `.switchMap()` calls for each cascading call instead of `.then(getOrders)`

There is one more interesting aspect that we need to cover, namely that of parallel calls. When we fetched the user and the order, we waited for a previous call to fully complete before we initiated the next call. In a lot of cases, this might not be strictly necessary. Imagine that we have a similar case to the previous one, but there is a lot of interesting information surrounding the user that we want to fetch. Instead of just fetching orders, the user might have a friends collection or a collection of messages. The precondition for fetching that data is only that we fetched the user, so we know which collection of friends we should query for and which collection of messages we need. In the world of promises, we would use the `Promise.all()` construct to achieve parallelization. With that in mind, we update our `Promise` code to look like this:

```
// parallell/parallell-promise.js

// we collect username and password from a form
login(username, password) {
  return new Promise(resolve => {
    resolve('logged in');
  });
}

getUsersData(user) {
```

```
      return Promise.all([
        getOrders(user),
        getMessages(user),
        getFriends(user)
        // not implemented but you get the idea, another call in parallell
      ])
    }

    getUser() {
      // same as before
    }

    getOrders(user) {
      // same as before
    }

    login()
      .then(getUser)
      .then(getUsersData);
```

As we can see from the preceding code, we introduce the new
getUsersData() method, which fetches orders, messages, and friends collections in
parallel, making our app responsive sooner, as the data will arrive sooner than if we just
fetched it one after another.

We can easily achieve the same thing with RxJS by introducing the forkJoin() operator. It
takes a list of streams and fetches everything in parallel. We therefore update our RxJS code
to look like the following:

```
// parallell/parallell-rxjs.js

import Rx from 'rxjs/Rx';
// imagine we collected these from a form
let user = 'user';
let password = 'password';

login(user, password)
  .switchMap(getUser)
  .switchMap(getUsersData)

// we collect username and password from a form
login(username, password) {
  // same as before
}

getUsersData(user) {
  return Rx.Observable.forkJoin([
```

```
    getOrders(),
    getMessages(),
    getFriends()
  ])
}

getUser() {
  // same as before
}

getOrders(user) {
  // same as before
}

login()
  .then(getUser)
  .then(getUsersData);
```

A deeper look

So far, we have had a look at some operators that will let you create streams or change streams with the map() and filter() operators, we have learned how to manage different AJAX scenarios, and so on. The basics are there, but we haven't really approached the topic of operators in a structured way. What do we mean by that? Well, operators can be thought of as belonging to different categories. The number of operators at our disposal is a staggering 60 plus. It's going to take us time to learn all that, if we ever do. Here is the thing though: we just need to know which different types of operators exist so that we can apply them where appropriate. This reduces our cognitive load and our memory. Once we know which categories we have, we just have to drill down, and most likely we will end up knowing 10-15 operators in total and the rest we can just look up when we need them.

Currently, we have the following categories:

- **Creation operators**: These operators help us create streams in the first place. Almost anything can be converted into a stream with the help of these operators.
- **Combination operators**: These operators help us combine values as well as streams.
- **Mathematical operators**: These operators perform mathematical evaluations on the values being emitted.

- **Time-based operators**: These operators change at which speed values are emitted.
- **Grouping operators**: The idea with these operators is to operate on a group of values rather than individual ones.

Creation operators

We use creation operators to create the streams themselves, because let's face it: what we need to turn into a stream isn't always going to be a stream, but by making it into a stream, it will have to play nicely with other streams and, best of all, will get to leverage the full power of using operators.

So, what do these other non-streams consist of? Well, it could be anything asynchronous or synchronous. The important thing is that it is data that needs to be emitted at some point. Therefore, a range of creation operators exist. In the coming subsections, we will present a subset of all those that exist, enough for you to realize the power of turning anything into a stream.

of() operator

We have already had the chance to use this operator a few times. It takes an unknown number of comma-separated arguments, which can be integers, strings, or objects. This is an operator you want to use if you just want to emit a limited set of values. To use it, simply type:

```
// creation-operators/of.js

const numberStream$ = Rx.Observable.of(1,2, 3);
const objectStream$ = Rx.Observable.of({ age: 37 }, { name: "chris" });

// emits 1 2 3
numberStream$.subscribe(data => console.log(data));

// emits { age: 37 }, { name: 'chris' }
objectStream$.subscribe(data => console.log(data));
```

As can be seen from the code, it really doesn't matter what we place in our `of()` operator, it is able to emit it anyway.

from() operator

This operator can take arrays or a `Promise` as input and turn them into a stream. To use it, simply call it like this:

```
// creation-operators/from.js

const promiseStream$ = Rx.Observable.from(
  new Promise(resolve => setTimeout(() => resolve("data"),3000))
);

const arrayStream$ = Rx.Observable.from([1, 2, 3, 4]);

promiseStream$.subscribe(data => console.log("data", data));
// emits data after 3 seconds

arrayStream$.subscribe(data => console.log(data));
// emits 1, 2, 3, 4
```

This saves us a lot of headache by not having to deal with different types of asynchronous calls.

range() operator

This operator lets you specify a range, a number to start from and a number to end on. This is a nice shorthand that quickly lets you create a stream with a range of numbers. To use it, simply type:

```
// creation-operators/range.js

const stream$ = Rx.Observable.range(1,99);

stream$.subscribe(data => console.log(data));
// emits 1... 99
```

fromEvent() operator

Now it gets really interesting. The `fromEvent()` operator allows us to mix a UI event such as a `click` or a `scroll` event and turn it into a stream. So far, we have operated under the assumption that asynchronous calls is something that only has to do with AJAX calls. This is far from true. The fact that we can mix UI events with any type of asynchronous calls creates a really interesting situation that allows us to compose really powerful, expressive code. We will touch on this topic further in the coming section, *Thinking in streams*.

To use this operator, you need to provide it with two arguments: a DOM element and the name of an event, like so:

```
// creation-operators/fromEvent.js

// we imagine we have an element in our DOM looking like this <input
id="id" />
const elem = document.getElementById("input");
const eventStream$ = Rx.Observable
  .fromEvent(elem, "click")
  .map(ev => ev.key);

// outputs the typed key
eventStream$.subscribe(data => console.log(data));
```

Combination

Combination operators are about combining values from different streams. We have a few operators at our disposal that can help us out. This kind of operator makes sense when we, for some reason, don't have all the data in one place but need to acquire it from more than one place. Combining data structures from different sources could be tedious and error-prone work if it weren't for the powerful operators we are about to describe.

merge() operator

The `merge()` operator takes data from different streams and combines it. Here is the thing though: these streams can be of any kind as long as they are of type `Observable`. This means we can combine data from a timing operation, a promise, static data from an `of()` operator, and so on. What merging does is to interleave the emitted data. This means that it will emit from both streams at the same time in the following example. Using the operator comes in two flavors, as a static method but also as an instance method:

```
// combination/merge.js

let promiseStream = Rx.Observable
.from(new Promise(resolve => resolve("data")))

let stream = Rx.Observable.interval(500).take(3);
let stream2 = Rx.Observable.interval(500).take(5);

// instance method version of merge(), emits 0,0, 1,1 2,2 3, 4
stream.merge(stream2)
  .subscribe(data => console.log("merged", data));
```

```
// static version of merge(), emits 0,0, 1,1, 2, 2, 3, 4 and 'data'
Rx.Observable.merge(
  stream,
  stream2,
  promiseStream
)
.subscribe(data => console.log("merged static", data));
```

The takeaway here is that if you just need to combine one stream with another, then use the instance method version of this operator, but if you have several streams, then use the static version. Furthermore, the order in which the streams are specified matters.

combineLatest()

Imagine you have a situation where you have set up connections with several endpoints that serve you with data. What you care about is the latest data that was emitted from each endpoint. You might be in a situation where one or several endpoints stop sending data after a while and you want to know what the last thing that happened was. In this situation, we want the ability to combine all the latest values from all of the involved endpoints. That's where the `combineLatest()` operator comes in. You use it in the following way:

```
// combination/combineLatest.js

let firstStream$ = Rx.Observable
  .interval(500)
  .take(3);

let secondStream$ = Rx.Observable
  .interval(500)
  .take(5);

let combinedStream$ = Rx.Observable.combineLatest(
  firstStream$,
  secondStream$
)

// emits [0, 0] [1,1] [2,2] [2,3] [2,4] [2,5]
combinedStream$.subscribe(data => console.log(data));
```

What we can see here is that `firstStream$` stops emitting values after a while thanks to the `take()` operator, which limits the number of items. However, the `combineLatest()` operator ensures we are still given the very last value `firstStream$` emitted.

zip()

The point of this operator is to stitch as many values together as possible. We may be dealing with continuous streams, but also with streams that have a limit to the number of values they emit. You use this operator in the following way:

```js
// combination/zip.js

let stream$ = Rx.Observable.of(1, 2, 3, 4);
let secondStream$ = Rx.Observable.of(5, 6, 7, 8);
let thirdStream$ = Rx.Observable.of(9, 10);

let zippedStream$ = Rx.Observable.zip(
  stream$,
  secondStream$,
  thirdStream$
)

// [1, 5, 9] [2, 6, 10]
zippedStream$.subscribe(data => console.log(data))
```

As we can see, here, we stitch values together vertically, and by the least common denominator, `thirdStream$` is the shortest, calculating the number of emitted values. This means we will take values from left to right and zip them together. As `thirdStream$` only has two values, we end up with only two emits.

concat()

At first look, the `concat()` operator looks like another `merge()` operator, but this is not entirely true. The difference is that a `concat()` waits for other streams to be completed first before emitting a stream from the next stream in order. How you arrange your stream in your call to `concat()` matters. The operator is used in the following way:

```js
// combination/concat.js

let firstStream$ = Rx.Observable.of(1,2,3,4);
let secondStream$ = Rx.Observable.of(5,6,7,8);

let concatStream$ = Rx.Observable.concat(
  firstStream$,
  secondStream$
);

concatStream$.subscribe(data => console.log(data));
```

Mathematical

Mathematical operators are simply operators that carry out mathematical operations on values, such as finding the largest or smallest value, summarizing all values, and so on.

max

The `max()` operator finds the largest value. This comes in two flavors: we either just call the `max()` operator with no arguments, or we give it a `compare` function. The `compare` function then decides whether something is larger than, smaller than, or equal to an emitted value. Let's have a look at the two different versions:

```
// mathematical/max.js

let streamWithNumbers$ = Rx.Observable
  .of(1,2,3,4)
  .max();

// 4
streamWithNumbers$.subscribe(data => console.log(data));

function comparePeople(firstPerson, secondPerson) {
  if (firstPerson.age > secondPerson.age) {
    return 1;
  } else if (firstPerson.age < secondPerson.age) {
    return -1;
  }
  return 0;
}

let streamOfObjects$ = Rx.Observable
  .of({
    name : "Yoda",
    age: 999
  }, {
    name : "Chris",
    age: 38
  })
  .max(comparePeople);

// { name: 'Yoda', age : 999 }
streamOfObjects$.subscribe(data => console.log(data));
```

We can see in the preceding code that we get one result back and it is the largest one.

min

The `min()` operator is pretty much the opposite of the `max()` operator; it comes in two flavors: with parameter and without parameter. Its task is to find the smallest value. To use it, type:

```
// mathematical/min.js

let streamOfValues$ = Rx.Observable
  .of(1, 2, 3, 4)
  .min();

// emits 1
streamOfValues$.subscribe(data => console.log(data));
```

sum

There used to be an operator called `sum()`, but it hasn't existed for several versions. What there is instead is `.reduce()`. With the `reduce()` operator, we can easily achieve the same thing. The following is how you would write a `sum()` operator using `reduce()`:

```
// mathematical/sum.js

let stream = Rx.Observable.of(1, 2, 3, 4)
  .reduce((acc, curr) => acc + curr);

// emits 10
stream.subscribe(data => console.log(data));
```

What this does is to loop through all the emitted values and sum up the results. So, in essence, it sums up everything. Of course, this kind of operator can not only be applied to numbers, but to objects as well. The difference lies in how you carry out the `reduce()` operation. The following example covers such a scenario:

```
let stream = Rx.Observable.of({ name : "chris" }, { age: 38 })
  .reduce((acc, curr) => Object.assign({},acc, curr));

// { name: 'chris', age: 38 }
stream.subscribe(data => console.log(data));
```

As you can see from the preceding code, the `reduce()` operator ensures that all the object's properties get merged together into one object.

Time

Time is a very important concept when talking about streams. Imagine you have multiple streams that have different bandwidths, or one stream is just faster than the other, or you have a scenario where you want to retry an AJAX call within a certain time interval. In all of these situations, we need to control how fast the data is being emitted, and time plays an important role in all these scenarios. At our disposal, we have a ton of operators that, like a magician, enable us to craft and control our values as we see fit.

interval() operator

In JavaScript, there is a `setInterval()` function that enables you to execute code at regular intervals, up until the point that you choose to stop it. RxJS has an operator that behaves just like that, the `interval()` operator. It takes one parameter: normally, the number of milliseconds between emitted values. You use it in the following way:

```
// time/interval.js

let stream$ = Rx.Observable.interval(1000);

// emits 0, 1, 2, 3 ... n with 1 second in between emits, till the end of
time
stream$.subscribe(data => console.log(data));
```

A word of caution is that this operator will continue emitting until you stop it. The best way to stop it is to combine it with a `take()` operator. A `take()` operator takes a parameter that specifies how many emitted values it wants before stopping. The updated code looks like this:

```
// time/interval-take.js

let stream$ = Rx.Observable.interval(1000)
  .take(2);

// emits 0, 1, stops emitting thanks to take() operator
stream$.subscribe(data => console.log(data));
```

timer() operator

The `timer()` operator has the job of emitting values after a certain amount of time. It comes in two flavors: you either emit just one value after a number of milliseconds, or you keep on emitting values with a certain amount of delay between them. Let's look at the two different flavors available:

```
// time/timer.js

let stream$ = Rx.Observable.timer(1000);

// delay with 500 milliseconds
let streamWithDelay$ = Rx.Observable.timer(1000, 500)

// emits 0 after 1000 milliseconds, then no more
stream$.subscribe(data => console.log(data));

streamWithDelay$.subscribe(data => console.log(data));
```

delay() operator

The `delay()` operator delays all the values being emitted and is used in the following way:

```
// time/delay.js

let stream$ = Rx.Observable
.interval(100)
.take(3)
.delay(500);

// 0 after 600 ms, 1 after 1200 ms, 2 after 1800 ms
stream.subscribe(data => console.log(data));
```

sampleTime() operator

The `sampleTime()` operator is used to only emit values after the sample period has passed. A good use case for this is when you want to have a *cooldown* functionality. Imagine you have users that press a **Save** button way too often. It might be that saving takes a few seconds to complete. A way to approach this is to disable the **Save** button while saving. Another valid approach is to simply ignore any presses of the button until the operation has had the chance to complete. The following code does just that:

```
// time/sampleTime.js
```

```
let elem = document.getElementById("btn");
let stream$ = Rx.Observable
  .fromEvent(elem, "click")
  .sampleTime(8000);

// emits values every 8th second
stream$.subscribe(data => console.log("mouse clicks",data));
```

debounceTime() operator

The `sampleTime()` operator was able to ignore the user for a certain period of time, but the `debounceTime()` operator takes a different approach. Debounce as a concept means that we wait for things to calm down before emitting a value. Imagine an input element that the user types into. The user will stop typing eventually. We want to make sure the user has actually stopped, so we wait for a while before we actually do something. This is what the `debounceTime()` operator does for us. The following example shows how we can listen to the user typing into an input element, wait for the user to stop typing, and lastly, perform an AJAX call:

```
// time/debounceTime.js
const elem = document.getElementById("input");

let stream$ = Rx.Observable.fromEvent(elem, "keyup")
  .map( ev => ev.key)
  .filter(key => key !== "Backspace")
  .debounceTime(2000)
  .switchMap( x => {
    return new
Rx.Observable.ajax(`https://swapi.co/api/people/${elem.value}`);
  })
  .map(r => r.response);

stream$.subscribe(data => console.log(data));
```

When the user then types a number in the text box, the keyup event will be triggered after 2 seconds of inactivity. After that, an AJAX call will be carried out using our text box input.

Grouping

Grouping operators allow us to operate on a group of collected events rather than one emitted event at a time.

buffer() operator

The idea with the `buffer()` operator is that we can collect a bunch of events without them being emitted straight away. The operator itself takes an argument, an `Observable` that defines when we should stop collecting events. At that point in time, we can choose what to do with those events. Here is how you can use this operator:

```js
// grouping/buffer.js

const elem = document.getElementById("input");

let keyStream$ = Rx.Observable.fromEvent(elem, "keyup");
let breakStream$ = keyStream$.debounceTime(2000);
let chatStream$ = keyStream$
  .map(ev => ev.key)
  .filter(key => key !== "Backspace")
  .buffer(breakStream$)
  .switchMap(newContent => Rx.Observable.of("send text as I type",
newContent));

chatStream$.subscribe(data=> console.log(data));
```

What this does is to collect events until there has been 2 seconds of inactivity. At that point, we release all the key events we have buffered up. When we release all those events, we can, for example, send them somewhere via AJAX. This is a typical scenario in a chat application. Using the preceding code, we can always send the latest character that has been typed.

bufferTime() operator

A very similar operator to `buffer()` is `bufferTime()`. This one lets us specify how long we would like to buffer events for. It is a bit less flexible than `buffer()`, but can still be quite useful.

Thinking in streams

So far, we have gone through a bunch of scenarios that have shown us which operators are at our disposal and how they can be chained. We have also seen how operators such as `flatMap()` and `switchMap()` can really change things as we move from one type of observable to another. So, which approach should you take when working with Observables? Obviously, we need to express an algorithm using operators, but where do we start? The first thing we need to do is to think of the start and the end. Which types of events do we want to capture and what should the end result look like? That already gives us a hint as to the number of transformations we need to carry out to get there. If we want to transform the data only, then we can probably make do with a `map()` operator and a `filter()` operator. If we want to transform from one `Observable` to the next, then we need a `flatMap()` or a `switchMap()`. Do we have a specific behavior, such as waiting for the user to stop typing? If so, then we need to look at `debounceTime()` or similar. It's really the same as all problems: break it down, see which parts you have, divide, and conquer. Let's try to break this down into a list of steps though:

- What are the inputs? UI events or something else?
- What are the outputs? The end result?
- Given the second bullet, which transformations do I need to get there?
- Do I deal with more than one stream?
- Do I need to handle errors, and if so, how?

This has hopefully introduced you to how to think about streams. Remember, start small and work your way toward your goal.

Summary

We set out to learn more about basic operators. In doing so, we encountered the `map()` and `filter()` operators, which allowed us to control what was being emitted. Knowledge of the `do()` operator gave us a way to debug our streams. Furthermore, we learned about the existence of sandboxed environments, such as JS Bin and RxFiddle, and how they can help us to quickly get started with RxJS. AJAX was the next topic that we delved into, and we built an understanding of the different scenarios that might occur. Moving on deeper into RxJS, we looked at different operator categories. We barely scratched the surface on that one, but it offered us a way to approach how to learn which types of operators are in the library. Finally, we finished off this chapter by looking at how to change and develop our mindset to thinking about streams.

It is with all this acquired knowledge that we are now ready to venture into more advanced Rx topics in the next chapter. We know our basics, now the time has come to master them.

8
RxJS Advanced

We finished the last chapter that taught us more about what operators exist and how to utilize them effectively. Armed with this knowledge, we will now go into this subject in more depth. We will go from learning about what parts exist, to actually understanding the nature of RxJS. Knowing the nature of RxJS involves understanding more about what makes it tick. To uncover this, we need to cover topics such as what the differences are between hot, warm, and cold Observables; knowing about Subjects and what they are good for; and the sometimes ignored topic of Schedulers.

There are also other aspects of working with Observables that we want to cover, namely, how to deal with errors and how to test your Observables.

In this chapter, you will learn about:

- Hot, cold, and warm Observables
- Subjects: how they differ from Observables, and when to use them
- Pipeable operators, a recent addition to the RxJS library, and how they affect how you compose Observables
- Marble testing, the testing machinery in place that helps you with testing your Observables

Hot, cold, and warm Observables

There are hot, cold, and warm Observables. What do we actually mean by that? For starters, let's say that most things you will deal with are cold Observables. Not helping? If we say that cold Observables are lazy, does that help? No? OK, let's talk about Promises for a second. Promises are hot. They are hot because when we execute their code, it happens straight away. Let's see an example of that:

```
// hot-cold-warm/promise.js

function getData() {
  return new Promise(resolve => {
    console.log("this will be printed straight away");
    setTimeout(() => resolve("some data"), 3000);
  });
}

// emits 'some data' after 3 seconds
getData().then(data => console.log("3 seconds later", data));
```

If you come from a non-RxJS background, you will most likely, at this point, think: OK, yes, that's what I expected. This is the point we are trying to make, though:
Calling `getData()` makes your code run straight away. This differs from RxJS in the sense that similar RxJS code will actually not run until there is a listener/subscriber that cares about the result. RxJS answers the old philosophical question: Does a tree make a sound when it falls in the forest if no one is there to listen? In the case of Promises, it does. In the case of an Observable, it doesn't. Let's clarify what we just said with a similar code example using RxJS and Observables:

```
// hot-cold-warm/observer.js

const Rx = require("rxjs/Rx");

function getData() {
  return Rx.Observable(observer => {
    console.log("this won't be printed until a subscriber exists");
    setTimeout(() => {
      observer.next("some data");
      observer.complete();
    }, 3000);
  });
}

// nothing happens
getData();
```

In RxJS, code like this is considered cold, or lazy. We need a subscriber for something to actually happen. We can add a subscriber like so:

```
// hot-cold-warm/observer-with-subscriber

const Rx = require("rxjs/Rx");

function getData() {
  return Rx.Observable.create(observer => {
    console.log("this won't be printed until a subscriber exists");
    setTimeout(() => {
      observer.next("some data");
      observer.complete();
    }, 3000);
  });
}

const stream$ = getData();
stream$.subscribe(data => console.log("data from observer", data));
```

This is a major difference in how Observables behave versus Promises, and it's important to know. This is a cold Observable; so, what is a hot Observable? It would be easy to think, at this point, that a hot Observable is something that executes straight away; there is more to it than that, however. One of the official explanations of what a hot Observable is, is that anything that subscribes to it will share the Producer with other Subscribers. The Producer is what spouts out values internally inside the Observable. This means that the data is shared. Let's look at a cold Observable subscription scenario and contrast that with a hot Observable subscription scenario. We will start with the cold scenario:

```
// hot-cold-warm/cold-observable.js
const Rx = require("rxjs/Rx");

const stream$ = Rx.Observable.interval(1000).take(3);

// subscriber 1 emits 0, 1, 2
stream$.subscribe(data => console.log(data));

// subscriber 2, emits 0, 1, 2
stream$.subscribe(data => console.log(data));

// subscriber 3, emits 0, 1, 2, after 2 seconds
setTimeout(() => {
  stream$.subscribe(data => console.log(data));
}, 3000);
```

In the preceding code, we have three different subscribers that receive their own copy of emitted values. The values start from the beginning, every time we add a new subscriber. That might be expected when looking at the two first subscribers. As for the third one, it is added as a subscriber after two seconds. Yes, even that subscriber receives its own set of values. The explanation is that each subscriber receives its own Producer upon subscription.

With hot Observables, there is just one producer, which means the scenario above will play out differently. Let's write down the code for a hot Observable scenario:

```
// hot observable scenario

// subscriber 1 emits 0, 1, 2
hotStream$.subscribe(data => console.log(data));

// subscriber 2, emits 0, 1, 2
hotStream$.subscribe(data => console.log(data));

// subscriber 3, emits 2, after 2 seconds
setTimeout(() => {
  hotStream$.subscribe(data => console.log(data));
}, 3000);
```

The reason the third subscriber is outputting only the value 2 is that the other values have been emitted already. The third subscriber wasn't around to see that happen. On the third value emit, it is around, and that is the reason it receives the value 2.

Making a stream hot

This `hotStream$`, how can it be created? You did say that most of the streams being created are cold? We have an operator for doing just that, or two operators, in reality. We can make a stream go from cold to hot by using the operators `publish()` and `connect()`. Let's start with a cold Observable and add the mentioned operators, like so:

```
// hot-cold-warm/hot-observable.js

const Rx = require("rxjs/Rx");

let start = new Date();
let stream = Rx.Observable
  .interval(1000)
  .take(5)
  .publish();
```

```
setTimeout(() => {
  stream.subscribe(data => {
    console.log(`subscriber 1 ${new Date() - start}`, data);
  });
}, 2000);

setTimeout(() => {
  stream.subscribe(data => {
    console.log(`subscriber 2 ${new Date() - start}`, data)
  });
}, 3000);

stream.connect();
stream.subscribe(
  data => console.log(
    `subscriber 0 - I was here first ${new Date() - start}`,
    data
  )
);
```

We can see from the preceding code that we create our Observable and instruct it to emit values, one value per second. Furthermore, it should stop after five emitted values. We then call the operator `publish()`. This puts us in ready mode. We then set up a few subscriptions to happen after two seconds and three seconds, respectively. This is followed by us calling `connect()` on the stream. This will make the stream go from hot to cold. Thereby, our stream starts emitting values, and any subscriber, whenever it starts subscribing, will share a producer with any future subscriber. Lastly, we add a subscriber to happen straight after the call to `connect()`. Let's show what the output becomes with the following screenshot:

```
subscriber 0 - I was here first 1005 0
subscriber 0 - I was here first 2006 1
subscriber 1 2007 1
subscriber 0 - I was here first 3008 2
subscriber 1 3009 2
subscriber 2 3010 2
subscriber 0 - I was here first 4016 3
subscriber 1 4017 3
subscriber 2 4018 3
subscriber 0 - I was here first 5022 4
subscriber 1 5023 4
subscriber 2 5024 4
```

Our first subscriber is emitting values after one second. Our second subscriber kicks in after yet another second. This time its value is 1; it has missed out on the first value. After yet another second, the third subscriber has been attached. The first value that subscriber emits is 2; it missed out on the two first values. We clearly see how the operators `publish()` and `connect()` help to create our hot Observable, but also how it matters when you start subscribing to a hot Observable.

Why on earth would I want a hot Observable? What's the area for application? Well, imagine you have a live stream, a football game that you stream to many subscribers/viewers. They wouldn't want to see what happens from the first minute of the game when they arrive late, but, rather, where the match is right now, at the time of subscription (when they park themselves in front of the television). So, there definitely exist cases where hot Observables are the way to go.

Warm streams

So far, we have been describing and discussing cold Observables and hot Observables, but there is a third kind: the warm Observable. A warm Observable can be thought of as being created as a cold Observable, but turning into a hot Observable under certain conditions. Let's look at such a case by introducing the `refCount()` operator:

```
// hot-cold-warm/warm-observer.js

const Rx = require("rxjs/Rx");

let warmStream = Rx.Observable.interval(1000).take(3).publish().refCount();
let start = new Date();

setTimeout(() => {
  warmStream.subscribe(data => {
    console.log(`subscriber 1 - ${new Date() - start}`,data);
  });
}, 2000);
```

OK, so we started to use the operator `publish()`, and it looks like we are about to use our `connect()` operator and that we have a hot Observable, right? Well, yes, but instead of calling `connect()`, we call `refCount()`. This operator will warm our Observable up so that when the first subscriber arrives, it will act like a cold Observable. OK? That just sounds like a cold Observable, right? Let's have a look at the output first:

```
subscriber 1 - 3010 0
subscriber 1 - 4012 1
subscriber 1 - 5019 2
>
```

To answer the preceding question, yes, it's correct that it just behaves like a cold Observable; we aren't missing out on any emitted values. The interesting thing happens when we get a second subscriber. Let's add that second subscriber and see what the effects are:

```
// hot-cold-warm/warm-observable-subscribers.js

const Rx = require("rxjs/Rx");

let warmStream = Rx.Observable.interval(1000).take(3).publish().refCount();
let start = new Date();

setTimeout(() => {
  warmStream.subscribe(data => {
    console.log(`subscriber 1 - ${new Date() - start}`,data);
  });
}, 1000);

setTimeout(() => {
  warmStream.subscribe(data => {
    console.log(`subscriber 2 - ${new Date() - start}`,data);
  });
}, 3000);
```

Our second subscriber is added; now, let's have a look at what the result is:

```
subscriber 1 - 2008 0
subscriber 1 - 3009 1
subscriber 2 - 3010 1
subscriber 1 - 4014 2
subscriber 2 - 4015 2
```

What we can see from the results above is that the first subscriber is alone in receiving the number 0. When the second subscriber arrives, its first value is 1, which proves the stream has gone from acting like a cold Observable to a hot Observable.

There is another way we can do warm Observables, and that is through using the share() operator. The share() operator can be seen as more of a smart operator that allows our Observable to go from cold to hot, depending on the situation. That can be a really great idea sometimes. So, there are the following situations for Observables:

- Created as a hot Observable; the stream hasn't completed, and none of the subscribers are more than one
- Falls back into being a cold Observable; any previous subscription has had time to end before a new subscription arrives
- Created as a cold Observable; the Observable itself has had time to complete before the subscription happens

Let's try to show in code how the first bullet can happen:

```
// hot-cold-warm/warm-observable-share.js

const Rx = require("rxjs/Rx");

let stream$ = Rx.Observable.create((observer) => {
  let i = 0;
  let id = setInterval(() => {
    observer.next(i++);
  }, 400);

  return () => {
    clearInterval(id);
  };
}).share();

let sub0, sub;

// first subscription happens immediately
sub0 = stream$.subscribe(
  (data) => console.log("subscriber 0", data),
  err => console.error(err),
  () => console.log("completed"));

// second subscription happens after 1 second
setTimeout(() => {
  sub = stream$.subscribe(
  (data) => console.log("subscriber 1", data),
  err => console.error(err),
  () => console.log("completed"));
}, 1000);

// everything is unscubscribed after 2 seconds
```

```
setTimeout(() => {
  sub0.unsubscribe();
  sub.unsubscribe();
}, 2000);
```

The preceding code describes a situation where we defined a stream with a subscription that happens straight away. The second subscription happens after one second. Now, according to the definition of the `share()` operator, this means that the stream will be created as a cold Observable, but will, at the time of the second subscriber, be turned into a hot Observable, as there is a pre-existing subscriber and the stream has yet to complete. Let's inspect our output to verify that this is the case:

```
subscriber 0 0
subscriber 0 1
subscriber 0 2
subscriber 1 2
subscriber 0 3
subscriber 1 3
subscriber 0 4
subscriber 1 4
```

The first subscriber seems to be clearly alone in the values it gets. When the second subscriber arrives, it seems to share the producer, as it doesn't start from zero, but, rather, it starts listening where the first subscriber is.

Subjects

We are used to using Observables in a certain way. We construct them from something and we start listening to values that they emit. There is usually very little we can do to affect what is being emitted after the point of creation. Sure, we can change it and filter it, but it is next to impossible to add more to our `Observable` unless we merge it with another stream. Let's have a look at when we are really in control of what is being emitted when it comes to Observables, using the `create()` operator:

```
let stream$ = Rx.Observable.create(observer => {
  observer.next(1);
  observer.next(2);
});

stream$.subscribe(data => console.log(data));
```

We see the Observable acting as a wrapper around the thing that really emits our values, the Observer. In our Observer instance, the Observer is calling `next()`, with a parameter to emit values – values that we listen to in our `subscribe()` method.

This section is about the Subject. The Subject differs from the Observable in that it can affect the content of the stream after its creation. Let's have a look at just that with the following piece of code:

```
// subjects/subject.js

const Rx = require("rxjs/Rx");

let subject = new Rx.Subject();

// emits 1
subject.subscribe(data => console.log(data));

subject.next(1);
```

The first thing we notice is how we just call the constructor instead of using a factory method like `create()` or `from()` or similar, as we do on an Observable. The second thing we notice is how we subscribe to it on the second line, and only on the last line do we emit values by calling `next()`. Why is the code written in this order? Well, if we didn't write it this way and have the `next()` call happen as the second thing, our subscription wouldn't be there, and the value would have been emitted straight away. We know two things for sure, though: we are calling `next()`, and we are calling `subscribe()`, which makes `Subject` a double nature. We did mention another thing the `Subject` was capable of: changing the stream after creation. Our call to `next()` is literally doing that. Let's add a few more calls so we ensure we really get the idea:

```
// subjects/subjectII.js

const Rx = require("rxjs/Rx");

let subject = new Rx.Subject();

// emits 10 and 100 2 seconds after
subject.subscribe(data => console.log(data));
subject.next(10);

setTimeout(() => {
  subject.next(100);
}, 2000);
```

As we stated before, all the calls we make to the `next()` method enable us to affect the stream; we see in our `subscribe()` method that every call to `next()` leads to the `subscribe()` being hit, or, technically, the first function we pass into it.

Using Subject for cascading lists

So, what's the point? Why should we use Subjects over Observables? That's actually a quite deep question. There are many ways of solving most streaming-related problems; problems where it is tempting to use a Subject can often be solved through some other way. Let's have a look at what you could be using it for, though. Let's talk about cascading drop-down lists. What we mean by that is that we want to know what restaurants exist in a city. Imagine, therefore, that we have a drop-down list that allows us to select what country we are interested in. Once we select a country, we should select the city we are interested in from a drop-down list of cities. Thereafter, we get to select from a list of restaurants, and, finally, pick the restaurant that interests us. In the markup, it most likely looks like this:

```
// subjects/cascading.html

<html>
<body>
  <select id="countries"></select>
  <select id="cities"></select>
  <select id="restaurants"></select>

  <script src="https://unpkg.com/rxjs/bundles/Rx.min.js"></script>
  <script src="cascadingIV.js"></script>
</body>
</html>
```

At the start of the application, we haven't selected anything, and the only drop-down list that is selected is the first one, and it is filled with countries. Imagine that we therefore set up the following code in JavaScript:

```
// subjects/cascadingI.js

let countriesElem = document.getElementById("countries");
let citiesElem = document.getElementBtyId("cities");
let restaurantsElem = document.getElementById("restaurants");

// talk to /cities/country/:country, get us cities by selected country
let countriesStream = Rx.Observable.fromEvent(countriesElem, "select");

// talk to /restaurants/city/:city, get us restaurants by selected
restaurant
```

```
let citiesStream = Rx.Observable.fromEvent(citiesElem, "select");

// talk to /book/restaurant/:restaurant, book selected restaurant
let restaurantsElem = Rx.Observable.fromEvent(restaurantsElem, "select");
```

At this point, we have established that we want to listen to the selected events of each drop-down list, and we want, in the cases of countries or cities droplist, filter the upcoming droplist. Say we select a specific country then we want to repopulate/filter the cities droplist so that it only shows cities for the selected country. For the restaurant drop-down list, we want to perform a booking based on our restaurant selection. Sounds pretty simple, right? We need some subscribers. The cities drop-down list needs to listen to changes in the countries drop-down list. So we add that to our code:

```
// subjects/cascadingII.js

let countriesElem = document.getElementById("countries");
let citiesElem = document.getElementBtyId("cities");
let restaurantsElem = document.getElementById("restaurants");

fetchCountries();

function buildList(list, items) {
  list.innerHTML ="";
  items.forEach(item => {
    let elem = document.createElement("option");
    elem.innerHTML = item;
    list.appendChild(elem);
  });
}

function fetchCountries() {
  return Rx.Observable.ajax("countries.json")
    .map(r => r.response)
    .subscribe(countries => buildList(countriesElem, countries.data));
}

function populateCountries() {
  fetchCountries()
    .map(r => r.response)
    .subscribe(countries => buildDropList(countriesElem, countries));
}

let cities$ = new Subject();
cities$.subscribe(cities => buildList(citiesElem, cities));

Rx.Observable.fromEvent(countriesElem, "change")
  .map(ev => ev.target.value)
```

```
.do(val => clearSelections())
.switchMap(selectedCountry => fetchBy(selectedCountry))
.subscribe( cities => cities$.next(cities.data));

Rx.Observable.from(citiesElem, "select");

Rx.Observable.from(restaurantsElem, "select");
```

So, here, we have a behavior of performing an AJAX request when we select a country; we get a filtered list of cities, and we introduce the new subject instance `cities$`. We call the `next()` method on it with our filtered cities as a parameter. Finally, we listen to changes to the `cities$` stream by calling the `subscribe()` method on the stream. As you can see, when data arrives, we rebuild our cities drop-down list there.

We realize that our next step is to react to changes from us doing a selection in the cities drop-down list. So, let's set that up:

```
// subjects/cascadingIII.js

let countriesElem = document.getElementById("countries");
let citiesElem = document.getElementBtyId("cities");
let restaurantsElem = document.getElementById("restaurants");

fetchCountries();

function buildList(list, items) {
  list.innerHTML = "";
  items.forEach(item => {
    let elem = document.createElement("option");
    elem.innerHTML = item;
    list.appendChild(elem);
  });
}

function fetchCountries() {
  return Rx.Observable.ajax("countries.json")
    .map(r => r.response)
    .subscribe(countries => buildList(countriesElem, countries.data));
}

function populateCountries() {
  fetchCountries()
    .map(r => r.response)
    .subscribe(countries => buildDropList(countriesElem, countries));
}

let cities$ = new Subject();
```

```
cities$.subscribe(cities => buildList(citiesElem, cities));

let restaurants$ = new Rx.Subject();
restaurants$.subscribe(restaurants => buildList(restaurantsElem,
restaurants));

Rx.Observable.fromEvent(countriesElem, "change")
  .map(ev => ev.target.value)
  .do( val => clearSelections())
  .switchMap(selectedCountry => fetchBy(selectedCountry))
  .subscribe( cities => cities$.next(cities.data));

Rx.Observable.from(citiesElem, "select")
  .map(ev => ev.target.value)
  .switchMap(selectedCity => fetchBy(selectedCity))
  .subscribe( restaurants => restaurants$.next(restaurants.data));

// talk to /book/restaurant/:restaurant, book selected restaurant
Rx.Observable.from(restaurantsElem, "select");
```

In the preceding code, we added some code to react to a selection being made in our cities drop-down list. We also added some code to listen to changes in the `restaurants$` stream, which finally led to our restaurants drop-down list being repopulated. The last step is to listen to changes on us selecting a restaurant in the restaurants drop-down list. What should happen here is up to you, dear reader. A suggestion is that we query some API for the selected restaurant's opening hours, or its menu. Use your creativity. We will leave you with some final subscription code, though:

```
// subjects/cascadingIV.js

let cities$ = new Rx.Subject();
cities$.subscribe(cities => buildList(citiesElem, cities));

let restaurants$ = new Rx.Subject();
restaurants$.subscribe(restaurants => buildList(restaurantsElem,
restaurants));

function buildList(list, items) {
  list.innerHTML = "";
  items.forEach(item => {
    let elem = document.createElement("option");
    elem.innerHTML = item;
    list.appendChild(elem);
  });
}

function fetchCountries() {
```

```
    return Rx.Observable.ajax("countries.json")
      .map(r => r.response)
      .subscribe(countries => buildList(countriesElem, countries.data));
}

function fetchBy(by) {
  return Rx.Observable.ajax(`${by}.json`)
   .map(r=> r.response);
}

function clearSelections() {
  citiesElem.innerHTML = "";
  restaurantsElem.innerHTML = "";
}

let countriesElem = document.getElementById("countries");
let citiesElem = document.getElementById("cities");
let restaurantsElem = document.getElementById("restaurants");

fetchCountries();

Rx.Observable.fromEvent(countriesElem, "change")
  .map(ev => ev.target.value)
  .do(val => clearSelections())
  .switchMap(selectedCountry => fetchBy(selectedCountry))
  .subscribe(cities => cities$.next(cities.data));

Rx.Observable.fromEvent(citiesElem, "change")
  .map(ev => ev.target.value)
  .switchMap(selectedCity => fetchBy(selectedCity))
  .subscribe(restaurants => restaurants$.next(restaurants.data));

Rx.Observable.fromEvent(restaurantsElem, "change")
  .map(ev => ev.target.value)
  .subscribe(selectedRestaurant => console.log("selected restaurant",
selectedRestaurant));
```

This became a quite long code example, and it should be said that this is not the best way of solving a problem like this, but it does demonstrate how a Subject works: it can add value to the stream when it wants, and it can be subscribed to.

BehaviorSubject

So far, we have been looking at the default type of Subject, and we have uncovered a little of its secrets. However, there are many more types of Subjects. One such interesting type of Subject is the `BehaviorSubject`. So, why do we need a `BehaviorSubject`, and for what? Well, when dealing with a default Subject, we are able to add values to the stream, as well as subscribe to the stream. The `BehaviorSubject` gives us some added capabilities, in the form of:

- A starter value, which is great if we are able to show something to the UI while waiting for an AJAX call to finish
- We can query on the latest value; in some situations, it is interesting to know what the last emitted value was

To address the first bullet, let's write some code and showcase this capability:

```
// subjects/behavior-subject.js

let behaviorSubject = new Rx.BehaviorSubject("default value");

// will emit 'default value'
behaviorSubject.subscribe(data => console.log(data));

// long running AJAX scenario
setTimeout(() => {
  return Rx.Observable.ajax("data.json")
    .map(r => r.response)
    .subscribe(data => behaviorSubject.next(data));
}, 12000);
```

ReplaySubject

With a normal Subject, it matters when we start subscribing. If we start emitting values before our subscription is set up, those values are simply lost. If we have a `BehaviorSubject`, we have a somewhat better scenario. Even if we are late in subscribing, so a value has already been emitted, the very last emitted value is still possible to gain access to. Then the following question arises: What if two or more values are emitted before a subscription happens and we care about those values – what then?

Let's illustrate this scenario and see what happens with a Subject and `BehaviorSubject`, respectively:

```
// example of emitting values before subscription

const Rx = require("rxjs/Rx");

let subject = new Rx.Subject();
subject.next("subject first value");

// emits 'subject second value'
subject.subscribe(data => console.log("subscribe - subject", data));
subject.next("subject second value");

let behaviourSubject = new Rx.BehaviorSubject("behaviorsubject initial
value");
behaviourSubject.next("behaviorsubject first value");
behaviourSubject.next("behaviorsubject second value");

// emits 'behaviorsubject second value', 'behaviorsubject third value'
behaviourSubject.subscribe(data =>
  console.log("subscribe - behaviorsubject", data)
);

behaviourSubject.next("behaviorsubject third value");
```

What we can see from the preceding code is that Subject is not a good candidate if we care about values prior to us subscribing. The `BehaviorSubject` constructors are slightly better for that scenario, but if we really care about prior values, and a lot of them, then we should have a look at the `ReplaySubject`. The `ReplaySubject` has the ability to specify two things: a buffer size and a window size. A buffer size is simply the amount of values it should remember from the past, and the window size specifies for how long it should remember them for. Let us demonstrate this in code:

```
// subjects/replay-subject.js

const Rx = require("rxjs/Rx");

let replaySubject = new Rx.ReplaySubject(2);

replaySubject.next(1);
replaySubject.next(2);
replaySubject.next(3);

// emitting 2 and 3
replaySubject.subscribe(data => console.log(data));
```

In the preceding code, we can see how we emit 2 and 3, that is, the two latest emitted values. This is due to the fact that we specify the buffer size in the `ReplaySubject` constructor to be 2. The only value we loose out on is 1. Had we, on the other hand, specified a 3 in our constructor, all three values would have reached the subscriber. So much for the buffer size and how that works; what about the window size property? Let's illustrate how that works with the following code:

```
// subjects/replay-subject-window-size.js

const Rx = require("rxjs/Rx");

let replaySubjectWithWindow = new Rx.ReplaySubject(2, 2000);
replaySubjectWithWindow.next(1);
replaySubjectWithWindow.next(2);
replaySubjectWithWindow.next(3);

setTimeout(() => {
  replaySubjectWithWindow.subscribe(data =>
    console.log("replay with buffer and window size", data));
  },
2010);
```

Here, we specify the window size as 2,000 milliseconds; that is how long the values should be held in the buffer. We can see below that we delay the creation of our subscription to occur after 2,010 milliseconds. The end result of this is that no values will be emitted, as the buffer will have been emptied before the subscription has time to occur. A higher value of the window size would have fixed this issue.

AsyncSubject

The `AsyncSubject` has a capacity of one, which means we can emit a ton of values, but only the latest one is something that is stored. It isn't really lost, either, but you won't see it unless you complete the stream. Let's look at a piece of code that illustrates just this:

```
// subjects/async-subject.js

let asyncSubject = new Rx.AsyncSubject();
asyncSubject.next(1);
asyncSubject.next(2);
asyncSubject.next(3);
asyncSubject.next(4);

asyncSubject.subscribe(data => console.log(data), err =>
console.error(err));
```

Earlier, we had fours values being emitted, but nothing seems to reach the subscriber. At this point, we don't know whether this is because it just acts like a subject and throws away all emitted values that happen before a subscription or not. Let's therefore call the `complete()` method and see how that plays out:

```
// subjects/async-subject-complete.js

let asyncSubject = new Rx.AsyncSubject();
asyncSubject.next(1);
asyncSubject.next(2);
asyncSubject.next(3);
asyncSubject.next(4);

// emits 4
asyncSubject.subscribe(data => console.log(data), err =>
console.error(err));
asyncSubject.complete();
```

This will emit a 4 due to the fact that `AsyncSubject` only remembers the last value and we are calling the `complete()` method, thereby signaling the completion of the stream.

Error handling

Error handling is a very big topic. It is an area that is easy to underestimate. Normally, when coding, we could be led to believe we just need to do certain things, such as ensure we don't have syntax errors or runtime errors. With streams, we mostly think of runtime errors. The question is, how should we act when an error occurs? Should we pretend like it rains and just throw the error away? Should we hope for a different outcome if we try the same code some time in the future, or should we maybe just give up when a certain type of error exists? Let's try to collect our thoughts and look at the different error approaches that exist within RxJS.

Catch and continue

Sooner or later, we will have a stream that will throw an error. Let's see what that can look like:

```
// example of a stream with an error

let stream$ = Rx.Observable.create(observer => {
  observer.next(1);
  observer.error('an error is thrown');
```

```
    observer.next(2);
});

stream$.subscribe(
  data => console.log(data), // 1
  error => console.error(error) // 'error is thrown'
);
```

In the preceding code, we set up a scenario where we first emit a value, followed by emitting an error. The first value is captured in our first callback in our subscribe method. The second emitted thing, the error, is captured by our error callback. The third emitted value does not get emitted to our subscriber because our stream has been interrupted by the error. There is something we can do here, and that is to use the `catch()` operator. Let's apply that to our stream and see what happens:

```
// error-handling/error-catch.js
const Rx = require("rxjs/Rx");

let stream$ = Rx.Observable.create(observer => {
  observer.next(1);
  observer.error("an error is thrown");
  observer.next(2);
}).catch(err => Rx.Observable.of(err));

stream$.subscribe(
  data => console.log(data), // emits 1 and 'error is thrown'
  error => console.error(error)
);
```

Here, we capture our error with the `catch()` operator. In the `catch()` operator, we take our error and emit it as a normal Observable using the `of()` operator. What happens to the 2 we emit, though? Still no luck with that one. The `catch()` operator is able to take our error and turn it into a normal emitted value; instead of an error, we don't get all the values from the stream.

Let's have a look at a scenario when we are dealing with multiple streams:

```
// example of merging several streams

let merged$ = Rx.Observable.merge(
  Rx.Observable.of(1),
  Rx.Observable.throw("err"),
  Rx.Observable.of(2)
);

merged$.subscribe(data => console.log("merged", data));
```

In the scenario above, we merge three streams. The first stream emits the number 1 and nothing else gets emitted. This is due to our second stream tearing everything down, as it emits an error. Let's try to apply our newfound `catch()` operator and see what happens:

```
// error-handling/error-merge-catch.js

const Rx = require("rxjs/Rx");

let merged$ = Rx.Observable.merge(
  Rx.Observable.of(1),
  Rx.Observable.throw("err").catch(err => Rx.Observable.of(err)),
  Rx.Observable.of(2)
);

merged$.subscribe(data => console.log("merged", data));
```

We run the above code and we notice that the 1 is emitted, the error is emitted as a normal value, and, finally, even the 2 is emitted. Our conclusion here is that it is a good idea to apply a `catch()` operator to a stream before it is being merged with our streams.

As before, we can also conclude that the `catch()` operator is able to stop the stream from just erroring out, but that other values that would have been emitted after the error are effectively lost.

Ignoring the error

As we saw in the former section, the `catch()` operator does a good job of ensuring that a stream that errors out doesn't cause any problems when being merged with another stream. The `catch()` operator enables us to take the error, investigate it, and create a new Observable that will emit a value as though nothing happened. Sometimes, however, you don't want to even deal with streams that error out. For such a scenario, there is a different operator, called `onErrorResumeNext()`:

```
// error-handling/error-ignore.js
const Rx = require("rxjs/Rx");

let mergedIgnore$ = Rx.Observable.onErrorResumeNext(
  Rx.Observable.of(1),
  Rx.Observable.throw("err"),
  Rx.Observable.of(2)
);

mergedIgnore$.subscribe(data => console.log("merge ignore", data));
```

The implication of using the `onErrorResumeNext()` operator is that the second stream, the one that emits an error, gets completely ignored, and the values 1 and 2 get emitted. This is a very nice operator to use if your scenario is only about caring for the streams that do not error out.

Retry

There are different reasons why you would want to retry a stream. It's easier to imagine why you would want to if your stream is dealing with AJAX calls. Network connections may be unreliable at times with the local network you are on, or the service you are trying to hit may be temporarily down for some reason. Regardless of the reason, you have a situation where hitting that endpoint will some of the time reply with an answer, and some of the time return a 401 error. What we are describing here is the business case for adding retry logic to your streams. Let's have a look at a stream designed to fail:

```
// error-handling/error-retry.js
const Rx = require("rxjs/Rx");

let stream$ = Rx.Observable.create(observer => {
  observer.next(1);
  observer.error("err");
})
.retry(3);

// emits 1 1 1 1 err
stream$
  .subscribe(data => console.log(data));
```

The output of the code above is the value 1 being emitted four times, followed by our error. What happens is that our streams' values are retried three times before the error callback is hit in the subscribe. Using the `retry()` operator delays when the error is actually treated as an error. The preceding example doesn't make sense to retry, though, as the error will always occur. Therefore, let's take a better example – an AJAX call where the network connection may come and go:

```
// example of using a retry with AJAX

let ajaxStream$ = Rx.Observable.ajax("UK1.json")
  .map(r => r.response)
  .retry(3);
```

```
ajaxStream$.subscribe(
  data => console.log("ajax result", data),
  err => console.error("ajax error", err)
);
```

Here, we are attempting an AJAX request towards a file that doesn't seem to exist. Having a look at the console, we are faced with the following result:

```
⊗ ▶GET http://localhost:8080/UK1.json 404 (Not Found)
⊗ ▶GET http://localhost:8080/UK1.json 404 (Not Found)
⊗ ▶GET http://localhost:8080/UK1.json 404 (Not Found)
⊗ ▶GET http://localhost:8080/UK1.json 404 (Not Found)
⊗ ▶ajax error ▶AjaxError {message: "ajax error 404", xhr: XMLHttpRequest, request: {…}, status: 404, responseType: "json", …}
```

What we see in the above logging are four failed AJAX requests that lead to an error. We have essentially just switched our simple stream to a more credible AJAX request stream, with the same behavior. Should the file suddenly start to exist, we may have a scenario with two failed attempts and one successful attempt. Our approach has a flaw, though: we retry our AJAX attempts far too often. If we are actually dealing with an intermittent network connection, we need to have some kind of delay between attempts. It is reasonable to set a delay between attempts of at least 30 seconds or more. We can accomplish that by using a slightly different retry operator that takes milliseconds rather than a number of attempts as an argument. It looks like the following:

```
// retry with a delay

let ajaxStream$ = Rx.Observable.ajax("UK1.json")
  .do(r => console.log("emitted"))
  .map(r => r.response)
  .retryWhen(err => {
    return err.delay(3000);
  });
```

What we do here is use the operator `retryWhen()`. The `retryWhen()` operator's mission in life is to return a stream. At this point, you can manipulate the stream it returns by appending a `.delay()` operator that takes a number of milliseconds. The result from doing so is that it will retry the AJAX call for all eternity, which may not be what you want.

Advanced Retry

What we most likely want is to combine the delay between retry attempts with being able to specify how many times we want to retry the stream. Let's have a look at how we can accomplish that:

```
// error-handling/error-retry-advanced.js

const Rx = require("rxjs/Rx");

let ajaxStream$ = Rx.Observable.ajax("UK1.json")
  .do(r => console.log("emitted"))
  .map(r => r.response)
  .retryWhen(err => {
    return err
    .delay(3000)
    .take(3);
});
```

The interesting part here is that we use the operator `.take()`. We specify the number of emitted values we want from this inner Observable. We have now accomplished a nice approach in which we are able to control the number of retries and the delay between retries. There is an aspect to this that we haven't tried, namely, how we want all the retries to end when it finally gives up. In the preceding code, the stream just completes after the stream is retried after *x* number of times with no successful result. However, we may want the stream to error out instead. We can accomplish this by just adding an operator to the code, like this:

```
// error-handling/error-retry-advanced-fail.js

let ajaxStream$ = Rx.Observable.ajax("UK1.json")
  .do(r => console.log("emitted"))
  .map(r => r.response)
  .retryWhen(err => {
    return err
    .delay(3000)
    .take(3)
    .concat(Rx.Observable.throw("giving up"));
});
```

Here, we are adding a `concat()` operator that adds a stream that just fails. So we are guaranteed, after three failed attempts, to have an error happen. This is usually a better approach than having the stream silently complete after *x* number of failed attempts.

This isn't a perfect approach, though; imagine that you want to investigate what type of error you get back. In the case of AJAX requests being made, it matters whether we get a 400-something error or a 500-something error back as HTTP status code. They mean different things. With 500 errors, something is very wrong on the backend, and we probably want to give up straight away. With a 404 error, however, this implies the resource isn't there, but in the case with an intermittent network connection, this means the resource can't be reached due to our connection being offline. For that reason, a 404 error might be worth retrying. To solve that in code, we need to inspect the value being emitted to determine what to do. We can inspect values using the `do()` operator.

In the following code, we investigate the type of HTTP status of the response and determine how to handle it:

```
// error-handling/error-retry-errorcodes.js

const Rx = require("rxjs/Rx");

function isOkError(errorCode) {
  return errorCode >= 400 && errorCode < 500;
}

let ajaxStream$ = Rx.Observable.ajax("UK1.json")
  .do(r => console.log("emitted"))
  .map(r => r.response)
  .retryWhen(err => {
    return err
      .do(val => {
        if (!isOkError(val.status) || timesToRetry === 0) {
          throw "give up";
        }
      })
      .delay(3000);
  });
```

Marble testing

Testing asynchronous code can be challenging. For one, we have the time factor. The way we specify what operators to use for our crafted algorithm leads to the algorithm taking anywhere from 2 seconds to 30 minutes to execute. Therefore, it will at first feel like there is no point in testing it, because it can't be done within a reasonable time. We have a way to test RxJS, though; it is called Marble testing and it allows us to control how fast time passes so we have a test that can execute it in milliseconds.

The idea of a Marble is known to us. We can represent one or many streams and the effect an operator has one two or more streams. We do this by drawing the streams as a line and values as circles on the lines. The operator is shown as verb below the input streams. Following operator is a third stream, the result of taking the input streams and applying the operator, a so - called marble diagram. The line represents a continuous timeline. We take this concept and bring it to testing. What this means is that we can express our incoming values as a graphical representation and apply our algorithm to it and assert on the result.

Set up

Let's set up our environment correctly so we can write marble tests. We need the following:

- The NPM library jasmine-marbles
- A scaffolded Angular application

With that we scaffold our Angular project, like so:

```
ng new MarbleTesting
```

After the project has been scaffolded, it's time to add our NPM library, like so:

```
cd MarbleTesting
npm install jasmine-marbles --save
```

Now we have finished the setup, so the time has come to write tests.

Writing your first marble test

Let's create a new file `marble-testing.spec.ts`. It should look like the following:

```
// marble-testing\MarbleTesting\src\app\marble-testing.spec.ts

import { cold } from "jasmine-marbles";
import "rxjs/add/operator/map";

describe("marble tests", () => {
  it("map - should increase by 1", () => {
    const one$ = cold("x-x|", { x: 1 });
    expect(one$.map(x => x + 1)).toBeObservable(cold("x-x|", { x: 2 }));
  });
});
```

A lot of interesting things are happening here. We import the function `cold()` from the NPM library marble-testing. Thereafter we set up a test suite by calling `describe()`, followed by a test specification, by calling `it()`. Then we call our `cold()` function and provide it a string. Let's have a close look at that function call:

```
const stream$ = cold("x-x|", { x: 1 });
```

The above code set up a stream that expects to values to be emitted followed by the stream ending. How do we know that? It's time to explain what `x-x|` means. x is just any value, the hyphen – means time has passed. The pipe | means our stream has ended. The second argument in the cold function is a mapping object that tells us what the x means. In this case, it has come to mean the value 1.

Moving on, let's have a look at the next line:

```
expect(stream$.map(x => x + 1)).toBeObservable(cold("x-x|", { x: 2 }));
```

The preceding code applies the operator `.map()` and increased the value with one for each value emitted in the stream. Thereafter, we call the `.toBeObservable()` helper method and verify it against an expected condition,

```
cold("x-x|", { x: 2 })
```

The previous condition states that we expect the stream to should emit two values, but that the values should now have the number 2. This makes sense, as our `map()` function performs just that.

Fleshing out with more tests

Let's write one more test. This time we will be testing the `filter()` operator. This one is interesting, as it filters away values that does not fulfill a certain condition. Our test file should now look like the following:

```
import { cold } from "jasmine-marbles";
import "rxjs/add/operator/map";
import "rxjs/add/operator/filter";

describe("marble testing", () => {
  it("map - should increase by 1", () => {
    const one$ = cold("x-x|", { x: 1 });
    expect(one$.map(x => x + 1)).toBeObservable(cold("x-x|", { x: 2 }));
  });

  it("filter - should remove values", () => {
```

```
      const stream$ = cold("x-y|", { x: 1, y: 2 });
      expect(stream$.filter(x => x > 1)).toBeObservable(cold("--y|", { y: 2
}));
    });
  });
});
```

This test is set up in pretty much the same way as our first test. This time we use the `filter()` operator but what stands out is our expected stream:

```
cold("--y|", { y: 2 })
```

`--y`, means that our first values is removed. Based on how the filter condition is defined, we are not surprised. The reason for the double hyphen, –, though, is that time still passes, but instead of an emitted value a hyphen takes its place.

To learn more about Marble testing, have a look at the following link from the official documentation, `https://github.com/ReactiveX/rxjs/blob/master/doc/writing-marble-tests.md`

Pipeable operators

We haven't mentioned it much so far, but the RxJS library weighs in quite heavily when used in an app. In today's world of mobile first, every kilobyte counts when it comes to libraries that you include in your app. They count because the user may be on a 3G connection, and if it takes too long to load, your user may leave, or just may end up not liking your app, as it feels slow to load, and this may cause you to have bad reviews or lose users. So far, we have used two different ways of importing RxJS:

- Importing the whole library; this one is quite costly in terms of size
- Importing only the operators we need; this ensures that the bundle decreases significantly

The different options have looked like this, for importing the whole library and all its operators:

```
import Rx from "rxjs/Rx";
```

Or like this, to only import what we need:

```
import { Observable } from 'rxjs/Observable';
import "rxjs/add/operator/map";
import "rxjs/add/operator/take";

let stream = Observable.interval(1000)
  .map(x => x +1)
  .take(2)
```

That looks good, right? Well, yes, but it is a flawed approach. Let's explain what happens when you type:

```
import "rxjs/add/operator/map";
```

By typing the preceding, we add to the prototype of the Observable. Looking in the source code for RxJS, it looks like this:

```
var Observable_1 = require('../../Observable');
var map_1 = require('../../operator/map');

Observable_1.Observable.prototype.map = map_1.map;
```

As you can see from the preceding code, we import the Observable as well as the operator in question and we add the operator to the prototype by assigning it to a map property on the prototype. What's flawed with that, you might wonder? The problem is tree shaking, a process we use to get rid of unused code. Tree shaking has a hard time determining what you use and don't use, respectively. You may actually import a map() operator and it gets added to the Observable. As the code changes over time, you may end up not using it anymore. You may argue that you should remove the import at that point, but you might have a lot of code, and it is easy to overlook. It would be better if only used operators were included in the final bundle. It is, as we mentioned before, hard for the tree-shaking process to know what is used and what is not, with the current approach. For that reason, a big rewrite has happened in RxJS, adding something called pipeable operators, which help us with the above problem. There is also another downside to patching the prototype, and that is the fact that it creates a dependency. If the library changes and the operator is no longer added when we patch it (calling the import), then we have a problem. We won't detect the problem until runtime. We would rather be told that the operator has gone through us importing and explicitly using it, like so:

```
import { operator } from 'some/path';

operator();
```

Creating reusable operators with let()

The `let()` operator lets you have the whole operator and operate on it, rather than just manipulating the values as you would do with the `map()` operator, for example. Using the `let()` operator could look like this:

```
import Rx from "rxjs/Rx";

let stream = Rx.Observable.of(0,1,2);
let addAndFilter = obs => obs.map( x => x * 10).filter(x => x % 10 === 0);
let sub3 = obs => obs.map(x => x - 3);

stream
  .let(addAndFilter)
  .let(sub3)
  .subscribe(x => console.log('let', x));
```

In the preceding example, we were able to define a group of operators such as `addAndFilter` and `sub3` and use them on the stream with the `let()` operator. This enables us to create composable and reusable operators. It is with this very knowledge that we now move on to the concept of pipeable operators.

Shifting to pipeable operators

As we mentioned already, pipeable operators are here, and you can find them by importing the respective operators from the `rxjs/operators` directory, like so:

```
import { map } from "rxjs/operators/map";
import { filter } from "rxjs/operators/filter";
```

To use it, we are now relying on the `pipe()` operator that we use as the parent operator, if you will. Using the preceding operators will, therefore, look like this:

```
import { map } from "rxjs/operators/map";
import { filter } from "rxjs/operators";
import { of } from "rxjs/observable/of";
import { Observable } from "rxjs/Observable";

let stream = of(1,2);
stream.pipe(
  map(x => x + 1),
  filter(x => x > 1)
)
.subscribe(x => console.log("piped", x)); // emits 2 and 3
```

Summary

This chapter has taken us deep into RxJS by covering topics such as hot, cold, and warm Observables, and what that generally means in terms of when to subscribe to a stream and how they share their Producer under certain conditions. Next up, we covered Subjects, and the fact that Observable isn't the only thing you can subscribe to. Subjects also allow as to append values to the stream whenever we want, and we also learned that there exist different types of Subjects, depending on the situation at hand.

We ventured deeper into an important topic, testing, and tried to explain the difficulty in testing asynchronous code. We talked about the current state of the testing situation and what libraries to use here and now for your testing scenarios. Lastly, we covered pipeable operators, and our new preferred way of importing and composing operators to ensure we end up with the smallest possible bundle size.

In the next chapter, you will leverage Kanban using Waffle, build a simple web app with a full-stack architecture in mind, and get introduced to reactive programming with RxJS.

Create a Local Weather Web Application

9

We will be designing and building a simple Local Weather app with Angular and a third-party web API, using an iterative development methodology. You will focus on delivering value first while learning about the nuances and optimal ways of using Angular, TypeScript, Visual Studio Code, Reactive Programming, and RxJS.

In this chapter, you will learn the following:

- Planning out your roadmap using Waffle as a GitHub-connected Kanban board
- Crafting a new UI element to display current weather information using components and interfaces
- Using Angular Services and HttpClient to retrieve data from OpenWeatherMap APIs
- Leveraging observable streams to transform data using RxJS

The code samples provided in this book require Angular version 5 and 6. Angular 5 code is runtime compatible with Angular 6. Angular 6 will be supported in LTS until October 2019. The most up-to-date versions of the code repositories may be found at the following:

- LocalCast Weather, at: `Github.com/duluca/local-weather-app`
- LemonMart, at: `Github.com/duluca/lemon-mart`

Planning a feature road map using Waffle

Building a rough plan of action before you start coding is very important so that you and your colleagues or clients are aware of the road map you're planning to execute. Whether you're building an app for yourself or for someone else, a living backlog of features will always serve as a great reminder when you get back to a project after a break or serve as an information radiator that prevents constant requests for status updates.

In Agile development, you may have used various ticketing systems or tools that surface or Kanban boards. My favorite tool is Waffle.io, `https://waffle.io/`, because it directly integrates with your GitHub repository's issues and keeps track of the status of issues via labels. This way, you can keep using the tool of your choice to interact with your repository and still, effortlessly, radiate information. In the next section, you will set up a Waffle project to achieve this goal.

Setting up a Waffle project

We will now set up our Waffle project:

1. Go to Waffle.io `https://waffle.io/`.
2. Click on **Login** or **Get Started for Free**.
3. Select **Public & Private Repos** to allow access to all of your repositories.
4. Click on **Create Project**.
5. Search for the **local-weather-app** repository and select it.

6. Hit **Continue.**

You will get two starter layout templates, as shown in the following image:

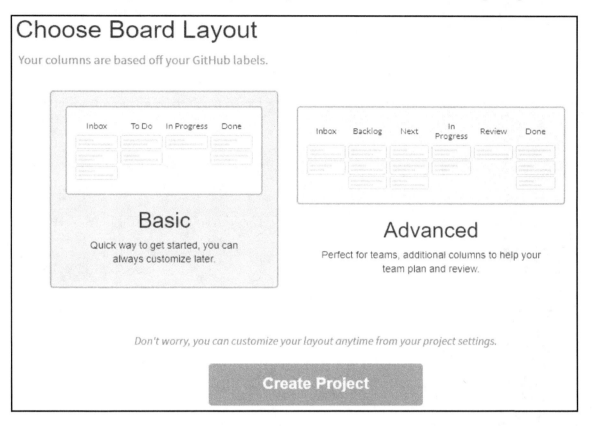

Waffle.io Default Board Layouts

For this simple project, you will be selecting **Basic**. However, the **Advanced** layout demonstrates how you can modify the default setup of Waffle, by adding additional columns such as **Review**, to account for testers or product owners participating in the process. You can further customize any board to fit your existing process.

7. Select the **Basic** layout and click on **Create Project**.
8. You will see a new board created for you.

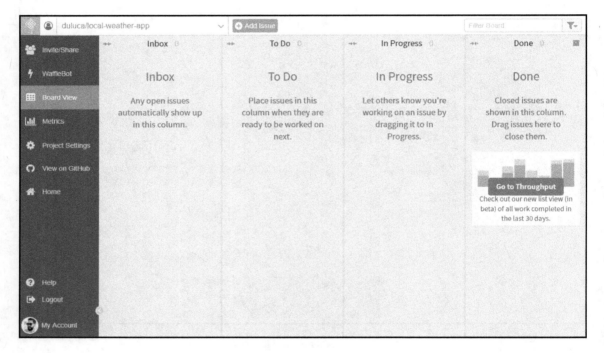

Empty Waffle Board

By default, Waffle will serve as a Kanban board. Allowing you to move a task from one state to another. However, the default view will show all the issues that are present on the repository. To use Waffle as a Scrum board, you need to assign issues to GitHub milestones that will represent sprints. You can then use the filtering functionality to only display issues from that milestone, or put another way from the current sprint.

On Waffle, you can attach story points to issues by clicking on the ⚖ scale icon. The columns will automatically show totals and card orders, which represent priority, and they will be retained from session to session. Furthermore, you can switch to the **Metrics** view to get **Milestone Burndown** and **Throughput** graphs and statistics.

Creating issues for your Local Weather app

We will now create a backlog of issues that you will use to keep track of your progress as you implement the design of your application. When creating issues, you should focus on delivering functional iterations that bring some value to the user. The technical hurdles you must clear to achieve those results are of no interest to your users or clients.

Here are the features we plan to be building in our first release:

- Display Current Location weather information for the current day
- Display forecast information for current location
- Add city search capability so that users can see weather information from other cities
- Add a preferences pane to store the default city for the user
- Improve the UX of the app with Angular Material

Go ahead with creating your issues on Waffle or on GitHub; whichever you prefer is fine. While creating the scope for **Sprint 1**, I had some other ideas for features, so I just added those issues, but I did not assign them to a person or a milestone. I also went ahead and added story points to the issues I intended to work on. The following is what the board looks like, as I'm to begin working on the first story:

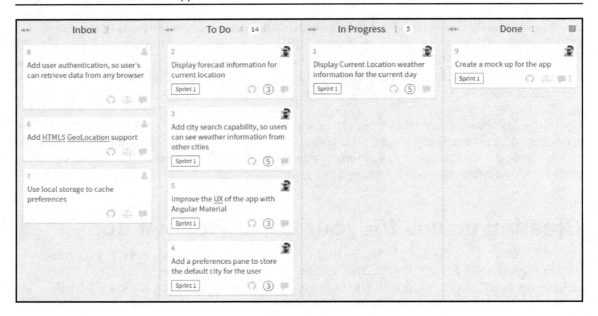

A snapshot of the initial state of the board at `https://waffle.io/duluca/local-weather-app`

Ultimately, Waffle provides an easy-to-use GUI so that non-technical people can easily interact with GitHub issues. By allowing non-technical people to participate in the development process on GitHub, you unlock the benefit of GitHub becoming the single source of information for your entire project. Questions, answers, and discussions around features and issues are all tracked as part of GitHub issues, instead of being lost in emails. You can also store wiki type documentation on GitHub, so by centralizing all project-related information, data, conversations, and artifacts on GitHub, you are greatly simplifying a potentially complicated interaction of multiple systems that require continued maintenance, at a high cost. For private repositories and on-premise Enterprise installations, GitHub has a very reasonable cost. If you're sticking with open source, as we are in this chapter, all these tools are free.

As a bonus, I created a rudimentary wiki page on my repository at `https://github.com/duluca/local-weather-app/wiki`. Note that you can't upload images to `README.md` or wiki pages. To get around this limitation, you can create a new issue, upload an image in a comment, and copy and paste the URL for it to embed images to `README.md` or wiki pages. In the sample wiki, I followed this technique to embed the wireframe design into the page.

With a concrete road map in place, you're now ready to start implementing your application.

Crafting UI elements using components and interfaces

You will be leveraging Angular components, interfaces, and services to build the current weather feature in a decoupled, cohesive, and encapsulated manner.

The landing page of an Angular app, by default, resides in `app.component.html`. So, start by editing the template of `AppComponent` with rudimentary HTML, laying out the initial landing experience for the application.

> We are now beginning the development of Feature 1: **Display Current Location weather information for the current day**, so, you can move the card in Waffle to the **In Progress** column.

We will add a header as an `h1` tag, followed by the tagline of our app as a `div` and placeholders for where we may want to display the current weather, as demonstrated as shown in the following code block:

src/app/app.component.html
```
<div style="text-align:center">
  <h1>
  LocalCast Weather
  </h1>
  <div>Your city, your forecast, right now!</div>
  <h2>Current Weather</h2>
  <div>current weather</div>
</div>
```

> At this point, you should run `npm start` and navigate to `http://localhost:5000` on your browser so that you can observe the changes you're making in real time.

Adding an Angular component

We need to display the current weather information, where `<div>current weather</div>` is located. In order to achieve this, you need to build a component that will be responsible for displaying the weather data.

The reason behind creating a separate component is an architectural best practice that is codified in the **Model-View-ViewModel** (**MVVM**) design pattern. You may have heard of the **Model-View-Controller** (**MVC**) pattern before. Vast majority of web-based code written circa 2005-2015 has been written following the MVC pattern. MVVM differs, in important ways, from the MVC pattern. As I have explained in my 2013 article on DevPro:

> *[An effective implementation of MVVM] inherently enforces proper separation of concerns. Business logic is clearly separated from presentation logic. So when a View is developed, it stays developed, because fixing a bug in one View's functionality doesn't impact other views. On the flip side, if [you use] visual inheritance effectively and [create] reusable user controls, fixing a bug in one place can fix issues throughout the application.*

Angular provides an effective implementation of MVVM.

> *ViewModels neatly encapsulate any presentation logic and allow for simpler View code by acting as a specialized version of the model. The relationship between a View and ViewModel is straightforward, allowing for more natural ways to wrap UI behavior in reusable user controls.*

You can read further about the architectural nuance, with illustrations, at `http://bit.ly/MVVMvsMVC`.

Next, you will create your very first Angular component, which will include the View and the ViewModel, using Angular CLI's `ng generate` command:

1. In the terminal, execute `npx ng generate component current-weather`

> Ensure that you are executing `ng` commands under the `local-weather-app` folder, and not under the `root` project folder. In addition, note that `npx ng generate component current-weather` can be rewritten as `ng g c current-weather`. Going forward, this book will utilize the shorthand format and expect you to prepend `npx`, if necessary.

2. Observe the new files created in your `app` folder:

```
src/app
├──── app.component.css
├──── app.component.html
├──── app.component.spec.ts
├──── app.component.ts
├──── app.module.ts
├──── current-weather
     ├──── current-weather.component.css
     ├──── current-weather.component.html
     ├──── current-weather.component.spec.ts
     └──── current-weather.component.ts
```

A generated component has four parts:

- `current-weather.component.css` contains any CSS that is specific to the component and is an optional file
- `current-weather.component.html` contains the HTML template that defines the look of the component and rendering of the bindings, and can be considered the View, in combination with any CSS styles used
- `current-weather.component.spec.ts` contains Jasmine-based unit tests that you can extend to test your component functionality
- `current-weather.component.ts` contains the `@Component` decorator above the class definition and is the glue that ties together the CSS, HTML, and JavaScript code together. The class itself can be considered the ViewModel, pulling data from services and performing any necessary transformations to expose sensible bindings for the View, as shown as follows:

```
src/app/current-weather/current-weather.component.ts
import { Component, OnInit } from '@angular/core'
@Component({
  selector: 'app-current-weather',
  templateUrl: './current-weather.component.html',
  styleUrls: ['./current-weather.component.css'],
})
export class CurrentWeatherComponent implements OnInit {
  constructor() {}

  ngOnInit() {}
}
```

If the component you're planning to write is a simple one, you can rewrite it using inline styles and an inline template, to simplify the structure of your code.

3. Update `CurrentWeatherComponent` with an inline template and styles:

src/app/current-weather/current-weather.component.ts
```
import { Component, OnInit } from '@angular/core'

@Component({
  selector: 'app-current-weather',
  template: `
  <p>
    current-weather works!
  </p>
  `,
  styles: ['']
})
export class CurrentWeatherComponent implements OnInit {
constructor() {}

ngOnInit() {}
}
```

When you executed the generate command, in addition to creating the component, the command also added the new module you created to `app.module.ts`, avoiding an otherwise tedious task of wiring up components together:

src/app/app.module.ts
```
...
import { CurrentWeatherComponent } from './current-weather/current-weather.component'
...
@NgModule({
declarations: [AppComponent, CurrentWeatherComponent],
...
```

The bootstrap process of Angular is, admittedly, a bit convoluted. This is the chief reason Angular CLI exists. `index.html` contains an element named `<app-root>`. When Angular begins execution, it first loads `main.ts`, which configures the framework for browser use and loads the app module. App module then loads all its dependencies and renders within the aforementioned `<app-root>` element. In `Chapter 12`, *Create a Router-First Line-of-Business App*, when we build a line-of-business app, we will create our own feature modules to take advantage of the scalability features of Angular.

Now, we need to display our new component on the initial `AppComponent` template, so it is visible to the end user:

4. Add the `CurrentWeatherComponent` to `AppComponent` by replacing `<div>current weather</div>` with `<app-current-weather></app-current-weather>`:

   src/app/app.component.html
   ```
   <div style="text-align:center">
   <h1>
    LocalCast Weather
    </h1>
    <div>Your city, your forecast, right now!</div>
    <h2>Current Weather</h2>
    <app-current-weather></app-current-weather>
   </div>
   ```

5. If everything worked correctly, you should see this:

Initial render of your local weather app

Note the icon and name in the tab of the browser window. As a web development norm, in the index.html file, update the <title> tag and the favicon.ico file with the name and icon of your application to customize the browser tab information. If your favicon doesn't update, append the href attribute with a unique version number, such as href="favicon.ico?v=2". As a result, your app will start looking like a real web app, instead of a CLI-generated starter project.

Define your model using interfaces

Now that your `View` and `ViewModel` are in place, you need to define your `Model`. If you look back on the design, you will see that the component needs to display:

- City
- Country
- Current date
- Current image
- Current temperature
- Current weather description

You will first create an interface that represents this data structure:

1. In the terminal, execute `npx ng generate interface ICurrentWeather`
2. Observe a newly generated file named `icurrent-weather.ts` with an empty interface definition that looks like this:

   src/app/icurrent-weather.ts
   ```
   export interface ICurrentWeather {
   }
   ```

   This is not an ideal setup, since we may add numerous interfaces to our app and it can get tedious to track down various interfaces. Over time, as you add concrete implementations of these interfaces as classes, then it will make sense to put classes and their interfaces in their own files.

    Why not just call the interface `CurrentWeather`? This is because later on we may create a class to implement some interesting behavior for `CurrentWeather`. Interfaces establish a contract, establishing the list of available properties on any class or interface that implements or extends the interface. It is always important to be aware of when you're using a class versus an interface. If you follow the best practice to always start your interface names with a capital `I`, you will always be conscious of what type of an object you are passing around. Hence, the interface is named `ICurrentWeather`.

3. Rename `icurrent-weather.ts` to `interfaces.ts`
4. Correct the capitalization of the interface name to `ICurrentWeather`

5. Also, implement the interface as follows:

src/app/interfaces.ts
```
export interface ICurrentWeather {
  city: string
  country: string
  date: Date
  image: string
  temperature: number
  description: string
}
```

This interface and its eventual concrete representation as a class is the Model in MVVM. So far, I have highlighted how various parts of Angular fit the MVVM pattern; going forward, I will be referring to these parts with their actual names.

Now, we can import the interface into the component and start wiring up the bindings in the template of CurrentWeatherComponent.

6. Import ICurrentWeather
7. Switch back to the templateUrl and styleUrls
8. Define a local variable called current with type ICurrentWeather

src/app/current-weather/current-weather.component.ts
```
import { Component, OnInit } from '@angular/core'
import { ICurrentWeather } from '../interfaces'

@Component({
  selector: 'app-current-weather',
  templateUrl: './current-weather.component.html',
  styleUrls: ['./current-weather.component.css'],
})
export class CurrentWeatherComponent implements OnInit {
  current: ICurrentWeather
  constructor() {}
  ngOnInit() {}
}
```

If you just type current: ICurrentWeather, you can use the auto-fixer to automatically insert the import statement.

In the constructor, you will temporarily populate the current property with dummy data to test your bindings.

9. Implement dummy data as a JSON object and declare its adherence to `ICurrentWeather` using the as operator:

src/app/current-weather/current-weather.component.ts
```
...
constructor() {
  this.current = {
    city: 'Bethesda',
    country: 'US',
    date: new Date(),
    image: 'assets/img/sunny.svg',
    temperature: 72,
    description: 'sunny',
  } as ICurrentWeather
}
...
```

In the `src/assets` folder, create a subfolder named `img` and place an image of your choice to reference in your dummy data.

You may forget the exact properties in the interface you created. You can get a quick peek at them by holding *Ctrl* + hover-over the interface name with your mouse, as shown:

```
current: ICurrentWeather

              export interface ICurrentWeather {
construct       city: string
  this.cu       country: string
    city:       date: Date
    count       image: string
                temperature: string
  }             description: string
}             }

ngOnInit(   import ICurrentWeather
```

Ctrl + hover-over the interface

Now you update the template to wire up your bindings with a rudimentary HTML-based layout.

10. Implement the template:

```
src/app/current-weather/current-weather.component.html
<div>
  <div>
    <span>{{current.city}}, {{current.country}}</span>
    <span>{{current.date | date:'fullDate'}}</span>
  </div>
  <div>
    <img [src]='current.image'>
    <span>{{current.temperature | number:'1.0-0'}}°F</span>
  </div>
  <div>
    {{current.description}}
  </div>
</div>
```

To change the display formatting of `current.date`, we used the `DatePipe` above, passing in `'fullDate'` as the format option. In Angular, various out-of-the-box and custom pipe | operators can be used to change the appearance of data without actually changing the underlying data. This is a very powerful, convenient, and flexible system to share such user interface logic without writing repetitive boilerplate code. In the preceding example, we could pass in `'shortDate'` if we wanted to represent the current date in a more compact form. For more information on various `DatePipe` options, refer to the documentation at `https://angular.io/api/common/DatePipe`. To format `current.temperature` so that no fractional values are shown, you can use `DecimalPipe`. The documentation is at `https://angular.io/api/common/DecimalPipe`.

Note that you can render °C and °F using their respective HTML codes: `&#8451;` for °C and `&#8457;` for °F.

11. If everything worked correctly, you app should be looking similar to this screenshot:

App after wiring up bindings with dummy data

Congratulations, you have successfully wired up your first component.

Using Angular Services and HttpClient to retrieve data

Now you need to connect your `CurrentWeather` component to the `OpenWeatherMap` APIs. In the upcoming sections, we will go over the following steps to accomplish this goal:

1. Create a new Angular Service
2. Import `HttpClientModule` and inject it into the service
3. Discover the `OpenWeatherMap` API

4. Create a new interface that conforms to the shape of the API
5. Write a `get` request
6. Inject the new service into the `CurrentWeather` component
7. Call the service from the `init` function of the `CurrentWeather` component
8. Finally, map the API data to the local `ICurrentWeather` type using RxJS functions so that it can be consumed by your component

Creating a new Angular Service

Any code that touches outside of the boundaries of a component should exist in a service; this includes inter-component communication, unless there's a parent-child relationship, and API calls of any kind and any code that cache or retrieve data from a cookie or the browser's localStorage. This is a critical architectural pattern that keeps your application maintainable in the long term. I expand upon this idea in my DevPro MVVM article at `http://bit.ly/MVVMvsMVC`.

To create an Angular service, do this:

1. In the terminal, execute `npx ng g s weather --flat false`
2. Observe the new `weather` folder created:

```
src/app
...
└── weather
    ├── weather.service.spec.ts
    └── weather.service.ts
```

A generated service has two parts:

- `weather.service.spec.ts` contains Jasmine-based unit tests that you can extend to test your service functionality.
- `weather.service.ts` contains the `@Injectable` decorator above the class definition, which makes it possible to inject this service into other components, leveraging Angular's provider system. This will ensure that our service will be a singleton, meaning only instantiated once, no matter how many times it is injected elsewhere.

The service is generated, but it's not automatically provided. To do this, follow these steps:

1. Open `app.module.ts`
2. Type in `WeatherService` inside the providers array
3. Use the auto-fixer to import the class for you:

src/app/app.module.ts

```
...
import { WeatherService } from './weather/weather.service'
...
@NgModule({
  ...
  providers: [WeatherService],
  ...
```

 If you installed the recommended extension **TypeScript Hero**, the import statement will be automatically added for you. You won't have to use the auto-fixer to do it. Going forward, I will not call out the need to import modules.

Inject dependencies

In order to make API calls, you will be leveraging the `HttpClient` module in Angular. The official documentation (`https://angular.io/guide/http`) explains the benefits of this module succinctly:

"With HttpClient, @angular/common/http provides a simplified API for HTTP functionality for use with Angular applications, building on top of the XMLHttpRequest interface exposed by browsers. Additional benefits of HttpClient include testability support, strong typing of request and response objects, request and response interceptor support, and better error handling via APIs based on Observables."

Let's start with importing the `HttpClientModule` in to our app, so we can inject the `HttpClient` within the module into the `WeatherService`:

1. Add `HttpClientModule` to `app.module.ts`, as follows:

   src/app/app.module.ts
   ```
   ...
   import { HttpClientModule } from '@angular/common/http'
   ...
   @NgModule({
     ...
     imports: [
       ...
       HttpClientModule,
       ...
   ```

2. Inject `HttpClient` provided by the `HttpClientModule` in the `WeatherService`, as follows:

   src/app/weather/weather.service.ts
   ```
   import { HttpClient } from '@angular/common/http'
   import { Injectable } from '@angular/core'

   @Injectable()
   export class WeatherService {
     constructor(private httpClient: HttpClient) {}
   }
   ```

Now, `httpClient` is ready for use in your service.

Discover OpenWeatherMap APIs

Since `httpClient` is strongly typed, we need to create a new interface that conforms to the shape of the API we'll call. To be able to do this, you need to familiarize yourself with the Current Weather Data API.

1. Read documentation by navigating to `http://openweathermap.org/current`:

OpenWeatherMap Current Weather Data API Documentation

You will be using the API named **By city name**, which allows you to get current weather data by providing the city name as a parameter. So, your web request will look like this:

```
api.openweathermap.org/data/2.5/weather?q={city name},{country code}
```

2. On the documentation page, click on the link under **Example of API calls**, and you will see a sample response like the following:

```
http://samples.openweathermap.org/data/2.5/weather?q=London,uk&appid=b1b15e88fa797225412429c1c50c122a1
{
  "coord": {
    "lon": -0.13,
    "lat": 51.51
  },
  "weather": [
    {
      "id": 300,
      "main": "Drizzle",
      "description": "light intensity drizzle",
      "icon": "09d"
    }
  ],
  "base": "stations",
  "main": {
    "temp": 280.32,
    "pressure": 1012,
    "humidity": 81,
    "temp_min": 279.15,
    "temp_max": 281.15
  },
  "visibility": 10000,
  "wind": {
    "speed": 4.1,
    "deg": 80
  },
  "clouds": {
    "all": 90
  },
  "dt": 1485789600,
  "sys": {
    "type": 1,
    "id": 5091,
    "message": 0.0103,
    "country": "GB",
    "sunrise": 1485762037,
```

```
    "sunset": 1485794875
  },
  "id": 2643743,
  "name": "London",
  "cod": 200
}
```

Given the existing `ICurrentWeather` interface that you have already created, this response contains more information than you need. So you will write a new interface that conforms to the shape of this response, but only specify the pieces of data you will use. This interface will only exist in the `WeatherService` and we won't export it, since the other parts of the application don't need to know about this type.

3. Create a new interface named `ICurrentWeatherData` in `weather.service.ts` between the `import` and `@Injectable` statements

4. The new interface should like this:

src/app/weather/weather.service.ts
```
interface ICurrentWeatherData {
  weather: [{
    description: string,
    icon: string
  }],
  main: {
    temp: number
  },
  sys: {
    country: string
  },
  dt: number,
  name: string
}
```

With the `ICurrentWeatherData` interface, we are defining new anonymous types by adding children objects to the interface with varying structures. Each of these objects can be individually extracted out and defined as their own named interface. Especially, note that `weather` will be an array of the anonymous type that has the `description` and `icon` properties.

Storing environment variables

It's easy to miss, but the sample URL from previous sections contains a required `appid` parameter. You must store this key in your Angular app. You can store it in the weather service, but in reality, applications need to be able to target different sets of resources as they move from development to testing, staging, and production environments. Out of the box, Angular provides two environments: one `prod` and the other one as the default.

 Before you can continue, you need to sign up for a free `OpenWeatherMap` account and retrieve your own `appid`. You can read the documentation for `appid` at `http://openweathermap.org/appid` for more detailed information.

1. Copy your `appid`, which will have a long string of characters and numbers
2. Store your `appid` in `environment.ts`
3. Configure `baseUrl` for later use:

```
src/environments/environment.ts
export const environment = {
  production: false,
  appId: 'xxxxxxxxxxxxxxxxxxxxxxxxxxxxxxxx',
  baseUrl: 'http://',
}
```

 In code, we use a camel-case `appId` to keep our coding style consistent. Since URL parameters are case-insensitive, `appId` will work as well as `appid`.

Implementing an HTTP GET operation

Now, we can implement the GET call in the Weather service:

1. Add a new function to the `WeatherService` class named `getCurrentWeather`
2. Import the `environment` object
3. Implement the `httpClient.get` function

4. Return the results of the HTTP call:

src/app/weather/weather.service.ts
```
import { environment } from '../../environments/environment'
...
export class WeatherService {
  constructor(private httpClient: HttpClient) { }

  getCurrentWeather(city: string, country: string) {
    return this.httpClient.get<ICurrentWeatherData>(
`${environment.baseUrl}api.openweathermap.org/data/2.5/weather?` +
        `q=${city},${country}&appid=${environment.appId}`
    )
  }
}
```

Note the use of ES2015's String Interpolation feature. Instead of building your string by appending variables to one another like `environment.baseUrl + 'api.openweathermap.org/data/2.5/weather?q=' + city + ',' + country + '&appid=' + environment.appId`, you can use the backtick syntax to wrap `` `your string` ``. Inside the backticks, you can have newlines and also directly embed variables into the flow of your string by wrapping them with the `${dollarbracket}` syntax. However, when you introduce a newline in your code, it will be interpreted as a literal newline—\n. In order to break up the string in your code, you may add a backslash \, but then the next line of your code can have no indentation. It is easier to just concatenate multiple templates, as shown in the preceding code sample.

Note the use TypeScript Generics with the get function using the caret syntax like `<TypeName>`. Using generics is development-time quality of life feature. By providing the type information to the function, input and/or return variables types of that function will be displayed as you write your code and validated during development and also at compile time.

Retrieving service data from a component

To be able to use the `getCurrentWeather` function in the `CurrentWeather` component, you need to inject the service into the component:

1. Inject the `WeatherService` into the constructor of the `CurrentWeatherComponent` class

2. Remove the existing code that created the dummy data in the constructor:

   src/app/current-weather/current-weather.component.ts
   ```
   constructor(private weatherService: WeatherService) { }
   ```

3. Call the `getCurrentWeather` function inside the `ngOnInit` function:

   src/app/current-weather/current-weather.component.ts
   ```
   ngOnInit() {
     this.weatherService.getCurrentWeather('Bethesda', 'US')
       .subscribe((data) => this.current = data)
   }
   ```

Fair warning, do not expect this code to be working just yet. You should see an error, so let's understand what's going in the next segment.

Angular components have a rich collection of lifecycle hooks that allow you to inject your custom behavior when a component is being rendered, refreshed, or destroyed. `ngOnInit()` is the most common lifecycle hook you will be using. It is only called once when a component is first instantiated or visited. This is where you will want to perform your service calls. For a deeper understanding of component lifecycle hooks, check out the documentation at `https://angular.io/guide/lifecycle-hooks`.

Note that the anonymous function you have passed to `subscribe` is an ES2015 arrow function. If you're not familiar with arrow functions, it may be confusing at first. Arrow functions are actually quite elegant and simple.

Consider the following arrow function:
```
(data) => { this.current = data }
```
You can rewrite it simply as:
```
function(data) { this.current = data }
```

There's a special condition—when you write an arrow function that simply transforms a piece of data, such as this:
```
(data) => { data.main.temp }
```
This function effectively takes `ICurrentWeatherData` as an input and returns the temp property. The return statement is implicit. If you rewrite it as a regular function, it will look like this:
```
function(data) { return data.main.temp }
```

When the `CurrentWeather` component loads, `ngOnInit` will fire once, which will call the `getCurrentWeather` function that returns an object with a type of `Observable<ICurrentWeatherData>`. An Observable, as described in the official documentation, *is the most basic building block of RxJS* that represents an event emitter, which will emit any data received over time with the type of `ICurrentWeatherData`. The `Observable` object by itself is benign and will not cause a network event to be fired unless it is being listened to. You can read more about Observables at `reactivex.io/rxjs/class/es6/Observable.js~Observable.html`.

By calling `.subscribe` on the Observable, you're essentially attaching a listener to the emitter. You've implemented an anonymous function within the `subscribe` method, which will get executed whenever a new piece of data is received and an event is emitted. The anonymous function takes a data object as a parameter, and, the specific implementation in this case, assigns the piece of data to the local variable named current. Whenever current is updated, the template bindings you implemented earlier will pull in the new data and render it on the view. Even though `ngOnInit` executes only once, the subscription to the Observable persists. So whenever there's new data, the current variable will be updated and the view will re-render to display the latest data.

The root cause of the error at hand is that the data that is being emitted is of type
ICurrentWeatherData; however, our component only understands data that is shaped as
described by the ICurrentWeather interface. In the next section, you will need to dig
deeper into RxJS to understand how best to accomplish that task.

Beware, VS Code and CLI sometimes stop working. As previously noted,
as you code, the npm start command is running in the integrated
terminal of VS Code. Angular CLI, in combination with the Angular
Language Service plug-in, continuously watches for code changes and
transpiles your TypeScript code to JavaScript, so you can observe your
changes with live-reloading in the browser. The great thing is that when
you make coding errors, in addition to the red underlining in VS
Code, you will also see some red text in the terminal or even the browser,
because the transpilation has failed. In most cases, when correcting the
error, the red underlining will go away and Angular CLI will
automatically retranspile your code and everything will work. However,
under certain scenarios, you will note that VS Code will fail to pick typing
changes in the IDE, so you won't get autocompletion help or the CLI tool
will get stuck with message saying webpack: **Failed to compile.**
You have two main strategies to recover from such conditions:

1. Click on the terminal and hit *Ctrl + C* to stop running the CLI
   task and restart by executing npm start
2. If **#1** doesn't work, quit VS Code with *Alt + F4* for Windows or
   ⌘ + *Q* for macOS and restart it

Given Angular and VS Code's monthly releases cycles, I'm confident that
in time the tooling can only improve.

Transform data using RxJS

RxJS stands for Reactive Extensions, which is a modular library that enables reactive
programming, which itself is an asynchronous programming paradigm and allows for
manipulation of data streams through transformation, filtering, and control functions. You
can think of reactive programming as an evolution of event-based programming.

Understanding Reactive programming

In Event-Driven programming, you would define an event handler and attach it to an event source. In more concrete terms, if you had a **save** button, which exposes an `onClick` event, you would implement a `confirmSave` function, which when triggered, would show a popup to ask the user **Are you sure?**. Look at the following figure for a visualization of this process.

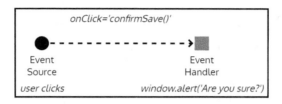

Event-Driven Implementation

In short, you would have an event firing once per user action. If the user clicks on the **save** button many times, this pattern would gladly render as many popups as there are clicks, which doesn't make much sense.

The publish-subscribe (pub/sub) pattern is a different type of event-driven programming. In this case, we can write multiple handlers to act on the result of a given event all simultaneously. Let's say that your app just received some updated data. The publisher will go through its list of subscribers and pass on the updated data to each of them. Refer to the following diagram, how can updated data event trigger an `updateCache` function that can update your local cache with new data, a `fetchDetails` function that can retrieve further details about the data from the server, and also a `showToastMessage` function that can inform the user that the app just received new data. All these events can happen asynchronously; however, the `fetchDetails` and `showToastMessage` functions will be receiving more data than they really need, and it can get really convoluted to try to compose these events in different ways to modify application behavior.

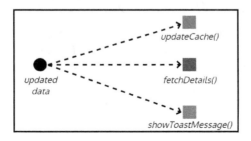

Pub/Sub Pattern Implementation

In reactive programming, everything is treated as a stream. A stream will contain events that happen over time and these events can contain some data or no data. The following diagram visualizes a scenario where your app is listening for mouse clicks from the user. Uncontrolled streams of user clicks are meaningless. You exert some control over this stream by applying the `throttle` function to it, so you only get updates every 250 **milliseconds (ms)**. If you subscribe to this new event, every 250 ms, you will receive a list of click events. You may try to extract some data from each click event, but in this case, you're only interested in the number of click events that happened. We can shape the raw event data into number of clicks using the `map` function.

Further down the stream, we may only be interested in listening for events with two or more clicks in it, so we can use the `filter` function to only act on what is essentially a double-click event. Every time our filter event fires, it means that the user intended to double-click, and you can act on that information by popping up an alert. The true power for streams comes from the fact that you can choose to act on the event at any time as it passes through various control, transformation, and filter functions. You can choose to display click data on an HTML list using `*ngFor` and Angular's `async` pipe, so the user can monitor the types of click data being captured every 250ms.

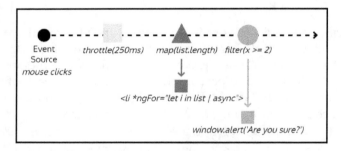

A Reactive Data Stream Implementation

Implementing Reactive transformations

To avoid future mistakes in returning the unintended type of data from your service, you need to update the `getCurrentWeather` function to define the return type to be `Observable<ICurrentWeather>` and import the `Observable` type, as shown:

```
src/app/weather/weather.service.ts
import { Observable } from 'rxjs'
import { ICurrentWeather } from '../interfaces'
...
```

```
export class WeatherService {
  ...
  getCurrentWeather(city: string, country: string):
Observable<ICurrentWeather> {
  }
  ...
}
```

Now, VS Code will let you know that Type `Observable<ICurrentWeatherData>` is not assignable to type `Observable<ICurrentWeather>`:

1. Write a transformation function named `transformToICurrentWeather` that can convert `ICurrentWeatherData` to `ICurrentWeather`

2. Also, write a helper function named `convertKelvinToFahrenheit` that converts the API provided Kelvin temperature to Fahrenheit:

   src/app/weather/weather.service.ts

```
export class WeatherService {
  ...
  private transformToICurrentWeather(data: ICurrentWeatherData):
ICurrentWeather {
    return {
      city: data.name,
      country: data.sys.country,
      date: data.dt * 1000,
      image:
`http://openweathermap.org/img/w/${data.weather[0].icon}.png`,
      temperature: this.convertKelvinToFahrenheit(data.main.temp),
      description: data.weather[0].description
    }
  }

  private convertKelvinToFahrenheit(kelvin: number): number {
    return kelvin * 9 / 5 - 459.67
  }
}
```

Note that you need to be converting the icon property to an image URL at this stage. Doing this in the service helps preserve encapsulation, binding the icon value to the URL in the view template will break the **Separation of concerns** (**SoC**) principle. If you wish to create truly modular, reusable, and maintainable components, you must remain vigilant and strict in terms of enforcing SoC. The documentation for Weather Icons and details of how the URL should be formed, including all the available icons can be found at `http://openweathermap.org/weather-conditions`.

On a separate note, the argument can be made that Kelvin to Fahrenheit conversion is actually a view concern, but we have implemented it in the service. This argument holds water, especially considering that we have a planned feature to be able to toggle between Celsius and Fahrenheit. A counter argument would be that at this time, we only need to display in Fahrenheit and it is part of the job of the weather service to be able to convert the units. This argument makes sense as well. The ultimate implementation will be to write a custom Angular Pipe and apply it in the template. A pipe can easily bind with the planned toggle button as well. However, at this time, we only need to display in Fahrenheit and I would err on the side of *not* over-engineering a solution.

3. Update `ICurrentWeather.date` to the `number` type

While writing the transformation function, you will note that the API returns the date as a number. This number represents time in seconds since the UNIX epoch (timestamp), which is January 1st, 1970 00:00:00 UTC. However, `ICurrentWeather` expects a `Date` object. It is easy enough to convert the timestamp by passing it into the constructor of the `Date` object like `new Date(data.dt)`. This is fine, but also unnecessary, since Angular's `DatePipe` can directly work with the timestamp. In the name of relentless simplicity and maximally leveraging the functionality of the frameworks we use, we will update `ICurrentWeather` to use `number`. There's also a performance and memory benefit to this approach if you're transforming massive amounts of data, but that concern is not applicable here. There's one caveat—JavaScript's timestamp is in milliseconds, but the server value is in seconds, so a simple multiplication during the transformation is still required.

4. Import the RxJS `map` operator right below the other import statements:

src/app/weather/weather.service.ts
```
import { map } from 'rxjs/operators'
```

It may seem odd to have to manually import the `map` operator. RxJS is a very capable framework with a wide API surface. Observable alone has over 200 methods attached to it. Including all of these methods by default creates development time issues with too many functions to choose from and also, it negatively impacts the size of the final deliverable, including app performance and memory use. So you must add each operator you intend to use individually.

5. Apply the `map` function to data stream returned by `httpClient.get` method through a `pipe`

6. Pass the `data` object into the `transformToICurrentWeather` function:

src/app/weather/weather.service.ts
```
. . .
return this.httpClient
  .get<ICurrentWeatherData>(
`http://api.openweathermap.org/data/2.5/weather?q=${city},${country
}&appid=${environment.appId}`
  ).pipe(
    map(data =>
      this.transformToICurrentWeather(data)
    )
  )
. . .
```

Now incoming data can be transformed as it flows through the stream, ensuring that the `OpenWeatherMap` Current Weather API data is in the correct shape, so it can be consumed by the `CurrentWeather` component.

7. Ensure that your app compiles successfully
8. Inspect the results in the browser:

LocalCast Weather

Your city, your forecast, right now!

Current Weather

Bethesda, US Friday, September 22, 2017

67°F

mist

Displaying Live Data from OpenWeatherMap

Finally, you should see that your app is able to pull live data from `OpenWeatherMap` and correctly transform server data into the format you expect.

You have completed the development of Feature 1: **Display Current Location weather information for the current day.** Commit your code and move the card in Waffle to the **Done** column.

9. Finally, we can move this task to the **Done** column:

Waffle.io Kanban Board Status

Summary

Congratulations, in this chapter, you created your first Angular application with a flexible architecture while avoiding over-engineering. This was possible because we first built a road map and codified it in a Kanban board that is visible to your peers and colleagues. We stayed focused on implementing the first feature we put in progress and didn't deviate from the plan.

You can now use Angular CLI and an optimized VS Code development environment to help you reduce the amount of coding you need to do. You can leverage TypeScript anonymous types and observable streams to accurately reshape complicated API data into a simple format without having to create one-use interfaces.

You learned to avoid coding mistakes by proactively declaring input and return types of functions and working with generic functions. You used the date and decimal pipes to ensure that the data is formatted as desired, while keeping formatting-related concerns mostly in the template, where this kind of logic belongs.

Finally, you used interfaces to communicate between components and services without leaking the external data structure to internal components. By applying all these techniques in combination, which Angular, RxJS, and TypeScript have allowed us to do, you have ensured proper separation of concerns and encapsulation. As a result, the `CurrentWeather` component is now a truly reusable and composable component; this is not an easy feat to achieve.

If you don't ship it, it never happened. In the next chapter, we will prepare this Angular app for a production release by troubleshooting application errors, and containerizing the Angular app with Docker, so it can be published on the web.

10
Prepare Angular App for Production Release

If you don't ship it, it never happened. In the previous chapter, you created a local weather application that can retrieve current weather data. You have created some amount of value; however, if you don't put your app on the web, you end up creating zero value. Delivering something is difficult, delivering something to production is even more difficult. You want to follow a strategy that results in a reliable, high quality, and flexible release.

The app we created in Chapter 9, *Create a Local Weather Web Application*, is fragile. We need to be able to deliver the frontend app separately from the backend app, which is a very important decoupling to retain the flexibility of being able to push separate app and server updates. In addition, decoupling will ensure that as the various tools and technologies in your application stack inevitably fall out of support or favor, you will be able to replace your frontend or backend without a full rewrite of your system.

In this chapter, you will learn to do the following:

- Guard against null data
- Containerize the app using Docker
- Deploy the app on the web using Zeit Now

Required software is as listed:

- Docker Community Edition Version 17.12
- Zeit Now Account

Null guarding in Angular

In JavaScript, the `undefined` and `null` values are a persistent issue that must be proactively dealt with every step of the way. There are multiple ways to guard against `null` values in Angular:

1. Property Initialization
2. Safe Navigation Operator `?.`
3. Null Guarding with `*ngIf`

Property initialization

In statically-typed languages such as Java, it is drilled into you that proper variable initialization/instantiation is the key to error free operation. So let's try that in `CurrentWeatherComponent` by initializing current with default values:

src/app/current-weather/current-weather.component.ts
```
constructor(private weatherService: WeatherService) {
  this.current = {
    city: '',
    country: '',
    date: 0,
    image: '',
    temperature: 0,
    description: '',
  }
}
```

The outcome of these changes will reduce console errors from 12 to 3, at which point you will only be seeing API call related errors. However, the app itself will not be in a presentable state, as you can see below:

LocalCast Weather

Your city, your forecast, right now!

Current Weather

, Wednesday, December 31, 1969
0°F

Results of Property Initialization

To make this view presentable to user, we will have to code for default values on every property on the template. So by fixing the null guarding issue by initialization, we created a default value handling issue. Both the initialization and the default value handling are $O(n)$ scale tasks for developers. At its best, this strategy will be annoying to implement and at its worst, highly ineffective and error prone, requiring, at minimum, $O(2n)$ effort per property.

Safe navigation operator

Angular implements the safe navigation operation `?.` to prevent unintended traversals of undefined objects. So, instead of writing initialization code and having to deal with template values, let's just update the template:

src/app/current-weather/current-weather.component.html
```
<div>
  <div>
    <span>{{current?.city}}, {{current?.country}}</span>
    <span>{{current?.date | date:'fullDate'}}</span>
  </div>
  <div>
    <img [src]='current?.image'>
    <span>{{current?.temperature}}°F</span>
  </div>
  <div>
    {{current?.description}}
  </div>
</div>
```

This time, we didn't have to make up defaults, and we let Angular deal with displaying undefined bindings. You will note that just like the initialization fix, the errors have been reduced from 12 to 3. The app itself is in a somewhat better shape. There's no more confusing data being displayed; however, it still is not in a presentable state, as shown below:

Results of Safe Navigation Operator

You can probably imagine ways where the safe navigation operator can come in handy, in far more complicated scenarios. However, when deployed at scale, this type of coding still requires, at minimum, *O(n)* level of effort to implement.

Null guarding with *ngIf

The idea strategy will be to use `*ngIf`, which is a structural directive, meaning Angular will stop traversing DOM tree elements beyond a falsy statement.

In the `CurrentWeather` component, we can easily check to see whether the `current` variable is null or undefined before attempting to render the template:

1. Update the topmost `div` element with `*ngIf` to check whether `current` is an object, as shown:

   src/app/current-weather/current-weather.component.html
   ```
   <div *ngIf="current">
     ...
   </div>
   ```

Now observe the console log and that no errors are being reported. You always ensure that your Angular application reports zero console errors. If you're still seeing errors in the console log, ensure that you have correctly reverted the `OpenWeather` URL to its correct state or kill and restart your `npm start` process. I highly recommend that you resolve any console errors before moving on. Once you've fixed all errors, ensure that you commit your code again.

2. Commit your code.

Containerizing the app using Docker

Docker `docker.io` is an *open platform* for developing, shipping, and running applications. Docker combines a *lightweight* container virtualization platform with workflows and tooling that help manage and deploy applications. The most obvious difference between **Virtual Machines** (**VMs**) and Docker containers are that VMs usually are dozens of gigabytes in size and require gigabytes of memory, whereas containers are megabytes in disk and memory size requirements. Furthermore, the Docker platform abstracts away host **operating system** (**OS**) level configuration settings, so every piece of configuration that is needed to successfully run an application is encoded within the human-readable Dockerfile format, as demonstrated here:

```
Dockerfile
FROM duluca/minimal-node-web-server:8.11.1
WORKDIR /usr/src/app
COPY dist public
```

The preceding file describes a new container that inherits from a container named `duluca/minimal-node-web-server`, changes the working directory to `/usr/src/app`, and then copies the contents of `dist` folder from your development environment into the container's `public` folder. In this case, the parent image is configured with an Express.js server to act as a web server to serve the content inside the `public` folder.

Refer to the following diagram for a visual representation of what's happening:

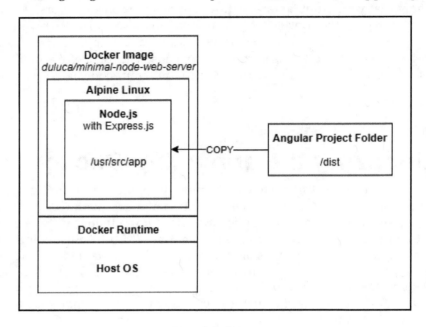

Context of a Docker Image

At the base layer is our host OS, such as Windows or macOS that runs the Docker runtime, which will be installed in the next section. The Docker runtime is capable of running self-contained Docker images, which is defined by the aforementioned `Dockerfile`. `duluca/minimal-node-web-server` is based off of the lightweight Linux operating system Alpine. Alpine is a completely pared down version of Linux that doesn't come with any GUI, drivers or even most CLI tools you may expect from a Linux system. As a result, the OS is around only ~5 MB in size. The base package then installs Node.js, which itself is around ~10 MB in size and my custom Node.js-based Express.js web server, resulting in a tiny ~15 MB image. The Express server is configured to serve the contents of the `/usr/src/app` folder. In the preceding `Dockerfile`, we merely copy the contents of the `/dist` folder in our development environment and place it into the `/usr/src/app` folder. We will later build and execute this image, which will run our Express web server containing the output of our `dist` folder.

The beauty of Docker is that you can navigate to `https://hub.docker.com`, search for `duluca/minimal-node-web-server`, read its `Dockerfile`, and trace its origins all the way back to the original base image that is the foundation of the web server. I encourage you to vet every Docker image you use in this manner to understand what exactly it brings to the table for your needs. You may find it either overkill or has features you never knew about that can make your life a lot easier. Note that the parent images require a specific version of `duluca/minimal-node-web-server` at `8.11.1`. This is quite intentional, and as the reader, you should choose the latest available version of a Docker image you find. However, if you don't specify a version number, you will always get the latest version of the image. As more versions of an image is published, you may pull a future version that may break your application. For this reason, always specify a version number for images you're depending on.

One such case is the HTTPS redirection support that is baked into `duluca/minimal-node-web-server`. You can spend countless hours trying to set up a nginx proxy to do the same thing, when all you need to do is add the following line to your Dockerfile:

```
ENV ENFORCE_HTTPS=xProto
```

Just like npm packages, Docker can bring great convenience and value, but you must take care to understand the tools you are working with.

> In `Chapter 16`, *Highly-Available Cloud Infrastructure on AWS*, we mention the use of a lower footprint docker image based on Nginx. If you're comfortable configuring `nginx`, you can use `duluca/minimal-nginx-web-server` as your base image.

Installing Docker

In order to be able to build and run containers, you must first install the Docker execution environment on your computer.

> Windows support of Docker can be challenging. You must have a PC with a CPU that supports virtualization extensions, which is not a guarantee on laptops. You must also have a Pro version of Windows with Hyper-V enabled. On the flip side, Windows Server 2016 has native support for Docker, which is an unprecedented amount of support shown by Microsoft toward the industry initiative to adopt Docker and containerization.

1. Install Docker by executing the following command:

For Windows:

```
PS> choco install docker docker-for-windows -y
```

For macOS:

```
$ brew install docker
```

2. Execute `docker -v` to verify the installation.

Setting up Docker scripts

Now, let's configure some Docker scripts that you can use to automated the building, testing, and publishing of your container. I have developed a set of scripts called **npm Scripts for Docker** that work on Windows 10 and macOS. You can get the latest version of these scripts at `bit.ly/npmScriptsForDocker`:

1. Sign up for a Docker Hub account on `https://hub.docker.com/`
2. Create a public (free) repository for your application

> Unfortunately, at the time of publication, Zeit doesn't support private Docker Hub repositories, so your only alternative is to publish your container publicly. If your image must remain private, I encourage you to set up an AWS ECS environment as described in Chapter 16, *Highly-Available Cloud Infrastructure on AWS*. You can keep tabs on the issue by visiting Zeit Now's documentation at `zeit.co/docs/deployment-types/docker`.

3. Update `package.json` to add a new config property with the following configuration properties:

package.json
```
...
  "config": {
    "imageRepo": "[namespace]/[repository]",
    "imageName": "custom_app_name",
    "imagePort": "0000"
  },
...
```

The namespace will be your DockerHub username. You will be defining what your repository is called during creation. An example image repository variable should look like `duluca/localcast-weather`. The image name is for easy identification of your container, while using Docker commands such as `docker ps`. I will call mine just `localcast-weather`. The port will define which port should be used to expose your application from inside the container. Since we use `5000` for development, pick a different one, like `8080`.

4. Add Docker scripts to `package.json` by copy-pasting the scripts from `bit.ly/npmScriptsForDocker`. Here's an annotated version of the scripts that explains each function.

Note that with npm scripts, the `pre` and `post` keywords are used to execute helper scripts, respectively, before or after the execution of a given script and scripts are intentionally broken into smaller pieces to make it easier to read and maintain them:

package.json
```
...
  "scripts": {
    ...
    "predocker:build": "npm run build",
    "docker:build": "cross-conf-env docker image build . -t
$npm_package_config_imageRepo:$npm_package_version",
    "postdocker:build": "npm run docker:tag",
    ...
```

`npm run docker:build` will build your Angular application in `pre`, then build the Docker image using the `docker image build` command and tag the image with a version number in post:

package.json
```
    ...
    "docker:tag": " cross-conf-env docker image tag
$npm_package_config_imageRepo:$npm_package_version
$npm_package_config_imageRepo:latest",
    ...
```

`npm run docker:tag` will tag an already built Docker image using the version number from the `version` property in `package.json` and the `latest` tag:

package.json

```
...
    "docker:run": "run-s -c docker:clean docker:runHelper",
    "docker:runHelper": "cross-conf-env docker run -e
NODE_ENV=local --name $npm_package_config_imageName -d -p
$npm_package_config_imagePort:3000 $npm_package_config_imageRepo",
    ...
```

`npm run docker:run` will remove any existing, prior version of an image and run the already built image using the `docker run` command. Note that the `imagePort` property is used as the external port of the Docker image, which is mapped to the internal port of the image that the Node.js server listens to, port 3000:

package.json

```
...
    "predocker:publish": "echo Attention! Ensure `docker login` is
correct.",
    "docker:publish": "cross-conf-env docker image push
$npm_package_config_imageRepo:$npm_package_version",
    "postdocker:publish": "cross-conf-env docker image push
$npm_package_config_imageRepo:latest",
    ...
```

`npm run docker:publish` will publish a built image to the configured repository, in this case, Docker Hub, using the `docker image push` command. First, the versioned image is published, followed by one tagged with `latest` in post:

package.json

```
...
    "docker:clean": "cross-conf-env docker rm -f
$npm_package_config_imageName",
    ...
```

`npm run docker:clean` will remove a previously built version of the image from your system, using the `docker rm -f` command:

package.json
```
    . . .
    "docker:taillogs": "cross-conf-env docker logs -f
$npm_package_config_imageName",
    . . .
```

`npm run docker:taillogs` will display the internal console logs of a running Docker instance using the `docker log -f` command, a very useful tool when debugging your Docker instance:

package.json
```
    . . .
    "docker:open:win": "echo Trying to launch on Windows && timeout
2 && start http://localhost:%npm_package_config_imagePort%",
    "docker:open:mac": "echo Trying to launch on MacOS && sleep 2
&& URL=http://localhost:$npm_package_config_imagePort && open
$URL",
    . . .
```

`npm run docker:open:win` or `npm run docker:open:mac` will wait for 2 seconds and then launch the browser with the correct URL to your application using the `imagePort` property:

package.json
```
    . . .
    "predocker:debug": "run-s docker:build docker:run",
    "docker:debug": "run-s -cs docker:open:win docker:open:mac
docker:taillogs"
  },
. . .
```

`npm run docker:debug` will build your image and run an instance of it in `pre`, open the browser, and then start displaying the internal logs of the container.

5. Install two development dependencies that are needed to ensure cross-platform functionality of the scripts:

```
$ npm i -D cross-conf-env npm-run-all
```

6. Customize the pre-build script to execute unit and e2e tests before building the image:

package.json
```
"predocker:build": "npm run build -- --prod --output-path dist &&
npm test -- --watch=false && npm run e2e",
```

Note that `npm run build` is provided the `--prod` argument, which achieves two things:
1. Development time payload of ~2.5 MB is optimized down to ~73kb or less
2. The configuration items defined in `src/environments/environment.prod.ts` is used at runtime

7. Update `src/environments/environment.prod.ts` to look like using your own `appId` from `OpenWeather`:

```
export const environment = {
  production: true,
  appId: '01ffxxxxxxxxxxxxxxxxxxxxxxxxxxxx',
  baseUrl: 'https://',
}
```

We are modifying how `npm test` is executed, so the tests are run only once and the tool stops executing. The `--watch=false` option is provided to achieve this behavior, as opposed to the development-friendly default continuous execution behavior. In addition `npm run build` is provided with `--output-path dist` to ensure that `index.html` is published at the root of the folder.

8. Create a new file named `Dockerfile` with no file-extensions

9. Implement the `Dockerfile`, as shown:

Dockerfile
```
FROM duluca/minimal-node-web-server:8.11.1
WORKDIR /usr/src/app
COPY dist public
```

Be sure to inspect the contents of your `dist` folder. Ensure that `index.html` is at the root of `dist`. Otherwise ensure that your `Dockerfile` copies the folder that has `index.html` at its root.

10. Execute `npm run predocker:build` to ensure that your application changes have been successful

11. Execute `npm run docker:build` to ensure that your image builds successfully

While you can run any of the provided scripts individually, you really only need to remember two of them going forward:

- **npm run docker:debug** will test, build, tag, run, tail and launch your containerize app in a new browser window for testing
- **npm run docker:publish** will publish the image you just built and test to the online Docker repository

12. Execute `docker:debug` in your terminal:

```
$ npm run docker:debug
```

You will note that the scripts display errors in the Terminal window. These are not necessarily indicators of a failure. The scripts are not polished, so they attempt both Windows and macOS compatible scripts parallelly, and during a first build, the clean command fails, because there's nothing to clean. By the time you read this, I may have published better scripts; if not, you're more than welcome to submit a pull request.

A successful `docker:debug` run should result in a new in-focus browser window with your application and the server logs being tailed in the terminal, as follows:

```
Current Environment: local.
Server listening on port 3000 inside the container
Attenion: To access server, use http://localhost:EXTERNAL_PORT
EXTERNAL_PORT is specified with 'docker run -p EXTERNAL_PORT:3000'.
See 'package.json->imagePort' for th
e default port.
GET / 304 12.402 ms - -
GET /styles.d41d8cd98f00b204e980.bundle.css 304 1.280 ms - -
GET /inline.202587da3544bd761c81.bundle.js 304 11.117 ms - -
GET /polyfills.67d068662b88f84493d2.bundle.js 304 9.269 ms - -
GET /vendor.c0dc0caeb147ad273979.bundle.js 304 2.588 ms - -
GET /main.9e7f6c5fdb72bb69bb94.bundle.js 304 3.712 ms - -
```

You should always run `docker ps` to check whether your image is running, when it was last updated, or if it is clashing with the existing images claiming the same port.

13. Execute `docker:publish` in your terminal:

    ```
    $ npm run docker:publish
    ```

    You should observe a successful run in the Terminal window like this:

    ```
    The push refers to a repository [docker.io/duluca/localcast-
    weather]
    60f66aaaaa50: Pushed
    ...
    latest: digest:
    sha256:b680970d76769cf12cc48f37391d8a542fe226b66d9a6f8a7ac81ad77be4
    f58b size: 2827
    ```

Over time, your local Docker cache may grow to a significant size, that is, on my laptop, roughly 40 GB over two years. You can use the `docker image prune` and `docker container prune` commands to reduce the size of your cache. For more detailed information, refer to the documentation at `https://docs.docker.com/config/pruning`.

Let's look into an easier way to interact with Docker next.

Docker extension in VS Code

Another way to interact with Docker images and containers is through VS Code. If you have installed the `PeterJausovec.vscode-docker` Docker extension, as suggested in Chapter 9, *Create a Local Weather Web Application*, you will see an expandable title named **DOCKER** in the **Explorer** pane of VS Code, as pointed out with an arrow in the following screenshot:

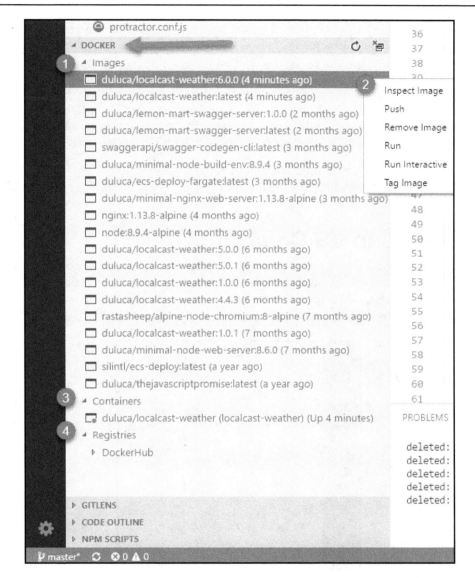

Docker extension in VS Code

Let's go through some of the functionality provided by the extension:

1. **Images** contains a list of all the container snapshots that exist on your system
2. Right-clicking on a Docker image brings up a context menu to run various operations on it, like run, push and tag

3. **Containers** list all executable Docker containers that exist on your system, which you start, stop or attach to
4. **Registries** display the registries that you're configured to connect to, like DockerHub or AWS Elastic Container Registry

While the extension makes it easier to interact with Docker, **npm Scripts for Docker** automate a lot of the chores related to building, tagging and testing and image. They are cross-platform and will work equally well in a continuous integration environment.

You may find it confusing to interact with npm scripts in general through the CLI. Let's look at VS Code's npm script support next.

NPM Scripts in VS Code

VS Code provides support for npm scripts out of the box. In order to enable npm script explorer, open VS Code settings and ensure that the `"npm.enableScriptExplorer":` `true` property is present. Once you do, you will see an expandable title named **NPM SCRIPTS** in the **Explorer** pane, as pointed out with an arrow here:

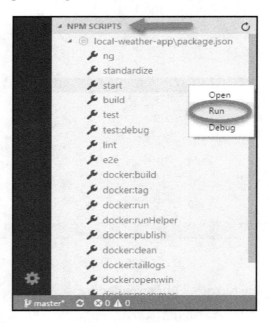

NPM Scripts in VS Code

You can click on any script to launch the line that contains the script in `package.json` or right-click and select **Run** to execute the script.

Deploying containerized app

If delivering something to production is difficult from a coding perspective, it is extremely difficult to do it right from an infrastructure perspective. In the later chapters, I will cover how to provision a world-class AWS **Elastic Container Service** (**ECS**) infrastructure for your applications, but that won't help if you need to quickly demonstrate an idea. Enter, Zeit Now.

Zeit Now

Zeit Now, `https://zeit.co/now`, is a multi-cloud service that enables real-time global deployments of applications directly from the CLI. Now works with applications that either correctly implement `package.json` or a `Dockerfile`. Even though we have done both, we will prefer to deploy our Docker image, because a lot more magic is applied behind the scenes to make a `package.json` deployment work, whereas your Docker image can be deployed anywhere, including AWS ECS.

Configuring the Now CLI tool

Now, let's configure Zeit Now to work on your repository:

1. Install Zeit Now by executing `npm i -g now`
2. Ensure correct installation by executing `now -v`
3. Create a new folder under `local-weather-app` called `now`
4. Create a new `Dockerfile` under the new `now` folder
5. Implement the file to pull from the image you just published:

now/Dockerfile
```
FROM duluca/localcast-weather:6.0.1
```

6. Finally, execute the now command in your terminal and follow the instructions to the finish configuration:

```
$ now
> No existing credentials found. Please log in:
> We sent an email to xxxxxxxx@gmail.com. Please follow the steps provided
   inside it and make sure the security code matches XXX XXXXX.
√ Email confirmed
√ Fetched your personal details
> Ready! Authentication token and personal details saved in
"~\.now"
```

Deploying

Deploying on Zeit Now is very easy:

1. Change your working directory to now and execute the command:

```
$ now --docker --public
```

2. In the Terminal window, the tool will report its progress and the URL from which you can access your now published app:

```
> Deploying C:\dev\local-weather-app\web-app\now under duluca
> Ready! https://xxxxxxxxxxxxx.now.sh [3s]
> Initializing...
> Building
> ▲ docker build
Sending build context to Docker daemon 2.048 kBkB
> Step 1 : FROM duluca/localcast-weather
> latest: Pulling from duluca/localcast-weather
...
> Deployment complete!
```

3. Navigate to the URL listed on the second line and verify the publication of your app.

Note that if you've made a configuration error along the way, your browser may display an error saying **This page is trying to load unsafe scripts**, allow and reload to see your app.

You can explore Zeit Now's paid features, which allow for advanced features such as automated scaling for your application.

Congratulations, you are app is live on the internet!

Summary

In this chapter, you learned how to best avoid Angular console errors by guarding against null data. You configured your system to work with Docker and successfully containerized your web application with its own dedicated web server. You configured your project with npm scripts for Docker that can be leveraged by any team member. Finally, you have successfully delivered a web application in the cloud.

Now you know what takes to build a production-ready Angular application that is reliable, resilient, and containerized to allow for a flexible deployment strategy. In the next chapter, we will improve the apps feature set and make it look great using Angular Material.

11
Enhance Angular App with Angular Material

In `Chapter 10`, *Prepare Angular App for Production Release*, we mentioned the need to deliver a high-quality application. Currently, the app has a terrible look and feel to it, which is only fit for a website created in the late 1990s. The first impression a user or a client will get about your product or your work is very important, so we must be able to create a great looking application that also delivers a great user experience across mobile and desktop browsers.

As full-stack developers, it is difficult to focus on the polish of your application. This gets worse, as the feature set of an application rapidly grows. It is no fun to write great and modular code backing your views, but then revert to CSS hacks and inline styles in a rush to improve your application.

Angular Material is an amazing library that is developed in close coordination with Angular. If you learn how to leverage Angular Material effectively, the features you create will look and work great from the get-go, whether you're working on small or large applications. Angular Material will make you a far more effective web developer because it ships with a wide variety of user controls that you can leverage, and you won't have to worry about browser compatibility. As an added bonus, writing custom CSS will become a rarity.

In this chapter, you will learn the following:

- How to configure Angular Material
- Upgrade the UX with Angular Material

Adding Material Components to your app

Now that we have all the various dependencies installed, we can start modifying our Angular app to add Material components. We will add a toolbar, material design card element, and cover accessibility and typography concerns alongside basic layout techniques.

Angular Material schematics

With Angular 6 and the introduction of schematics, libraries like Material can provide their own code generators. At time of publication, Angular Material ships with three rudimentary generators to create Angular components with a side navigation, a dashboard layout, or a data table. You can read more about generator schematics at `https://material.angular.io/guide/schematics`.

For example, you can create a side navigation layout by executing this:

```
$ ng generate @angular/material:material-nav --name=side-nav

CREATE src/app/side-nav/side-nav.component.css (110 bytes)
CREATE src/app/side-nav/side-nav.component.html (945 bytes)
CREATE src/app/side-nav/side-nav.component.spec.ts (619 bytes)
CREATE src/app/side-nav/side-nav.component.ts (489 bytes)
UPDATE src/app/app.module.ts (882 bytes)
```

This command updates `app.module.ts`, directly importing Material modules into that file, breaking my suggested `material.module.ts` pattern from earlier. Further, a new `SideNavComponent` is added to the app as a separate component, but as mentioned in the *Side Navigation* section in `Chapter 14`, *Design Authentication and Authorization,* such a navigation experience needs to be implemented at the very root of your application.

In short, Angular Material Schematics hold a promise of making it a lot less cumbersome to add various Material modules and components to your Angular app; however, as provided, these schematics are not suitable for the purposes of creating a flexible, scalable, and well-architected code base, as pursued by this book.

For the time being, I would recommend using these schematics for rapid prototyping or experimentation purposes.

Now, let's start manually adding some components to LocalCast Weather.

Modifying landing page with Material Toolbar

Before we start making further changes to `app.component.ts`, let's switch the component to use inline templates and inline styles, so we don't have to switch back and forth between file for a relatively simple component.

1. Update `app.component.ts` to use an inline template
2. Remove `app.component.html` and `app.component.css`

src/app/app.component.ts
```
import { Component } from '@angular/core'

@Component({
  selector: 'app-root',
  template: `
    <div style="text-align:center">
      <h1>
      LocalCast Weather
      </h1>
      <div>Your city, your forecast, right now!</div>
      <h2>Current Weather</h2>
      <app-current-weather></app-current-weather>
    </div>
    `
})
export class AppComponent {}
```

Let's start improving our app by implementing an app-wide toolbar:

3. Observe the h1 tag in `app.component.ts`:

   src/app/app.component.ts
   ```
   <h1>
     LocalCast Weather
   </h1>
   ```

4. Update the h1 tag with `mat-toolbar`:

   src/app/app.component.ts
   ```
   <mat-toolbar>
     <span>LocalCast Weather</span>
   </mat-toolbar>
   ```

5. Observe the result; you should see a toolbar, as illustrated:

LocalCast Weather Toolbar

6. Update `mat-toolbar` with a more attention-grabbing color:

src/app/app.component.ts
```
<mat-toolbar color="primary">
```

For a more native feeling, it is important that the toolbar touches the edges of the browser. This works well both on large- and small-screen formats. In addition, when you place clickable elements such as a hamburger menu or a help button on the far-left or far-right side of the toolbar, you'll avoid the potential that the user will click on empty space. This is why Material buttons actually have a larger hit-area than visually represented. This makes a big difference in crafting frustration-free user experiences:

src/styles.css
```css
body {
  margin: 0;
}
```

This won't be applicable to this app, however, if you're building a dense application; you'll note that your content will go all the way to the edges of the application, which is not a desirable outcome. Consider wrapping your content area in a div and apply the appropriate margins using css, as shown:

src/styles.css
```css
.content-margin {
  margin-left: 8px;
  margin-right: 8px;
}
```

In the next screenshot, you can see the edge-to-edge toolbar with the primary color applied to it:

LocalCast Weather with Improved Toolbar

Representing weather in Material Card

Material card is a great container to represent the current weather information. The card element is surrounded by a drop-shadow that delineates the content from its surroundings:

1. Import `MatCardModule` in `material.module`:

   src/app/material.module.ts
   ```
   import { ..., MatCardModule} from '@angular/material'
   ...
   @NgModule({
     imports: [..., MatCardModule],
     exports: [..., MatCardModule],
   })
   ```

2. In `app.component`, surround `<app-current-weather>` with `<mat-card>`:

   src/app/app.component.ts
   ```
   <div style="text-align:center">
     <mat-toolbar color="primary">
       <span>LocalCast Weather</span>
     </mat-toolbar>
     <div>Your city, your forecast, right now!</div>
     <mat-card>
       <h2>Current Weather</h2>
       <app-current-weather></app-current-weather>
     </mat-card>
   </div>
   ```

3. Observe the barely distinguishable card element, as shown:

LocalCast Weather with Indistinguishable Card

In order to lay out the screen better, we need to switch to the Flex Layout engine. Start by removing the training-wheels from the component template:

4. Remove `style="text-align:center"` from the surrounding `<div>`:

To center an element in a page, we need to create row, assign a width to the center element, and create two additional columns on either side that can flex to take the empty space, such as this:

src/app/app.component.ts
```
<div fxLayout="row">
  <div fxFlex></div>
  <div fxFlex="300px">

    ...
  </div>
  <div fxFlex></div>
</div>
```

5. Surround `<mat-card>` with the preceding HTML
6. Observe that the card element is properly centered, as follows:

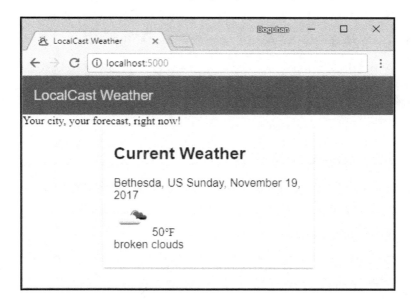

LocalCast Weather with Centered Card

Reading through the Card documentation and looking through the examples on Material's documentation site at `https://material.angular.io/components/card/overview`, you'll note that `mat-card` provides elements to house title and content. We will implement this in the upcoming sections.

 On `material.angular.io`, you can view the source code of any example by clicking on the brackets icons or launch a working example in Plunker by clicking on the arrow icon.

Accessibility

Leveraging such Material features may feel unnecessary; however, you must consider responsiveness, styling, spacing, and accessibility concerns when designing your app. The Material team has put in a lot of effort so that your code works correctly under most circumstances and can serve the largest possible user base with a high-quality user experience. This can include visually-impaired or keyboard-primary users, who must rely on specialized software or keyboard features such as tabs to navigate your app. Leveraging Material elements provides crucial metadata for these users to be able to navigate your app.

Material claims support for the following screen reader software:

- NVDA and JAWS with IE / FF / Chrome (on Windows)
- VoiceOver with Safari on iOS and Safari / Chrome on OSX
- TalkBack with Chrome on Android

Card header and content

Now, let's implement the title and content elements of `mat-card`, as shown:

```
src/app/app.component.ts
<mat-toolbar color="primary">
  <span>LocalCast Weather</span>
</mat-toolbar>
<div>Your city, your forecast, right now!</div>
<div fxLayout="row">
  <div fxFlex></div>
  <mat-card fxFlex="300px">
    <mat-card-header>
      <mat-card-title>Current Weather</mat-card-title>
    </mat-card-header>
    <mat-card-content>
```

```
      <app-current-weather></app-current-weather>
    </mat-card-content>
  </mat-card>
  <div fxFlex></div>
</div>
```

With Material, less is always more. You'll note that we were able to remove the center `div` and directly apply the `fxFlex` on the center card. All material elements have native support for the Flex Layout engine, and this has tremendous positive maintainability implications in complicated UIs.

After we apply `mat-card-header`, you can see this result:

LocalCast Weather Card with Title and Content

Note that fonts within the card now match Material's Roboto font. However, **Current Weather** is no longer attention grabbing, like before. If you add back in the `h2` tag inside `mat-card-title`, **Current Weather** will visually look bigger; however, the font won't match the rest of your application. To fix this issue, you must understand Material's typography features.

Material typography

Material's documentation aptly puts it as follows:

> *Typography is a way of arranging type to make text legible, readable, and appealing when displayed.*

Material offers a different level of typography that has different font-size, line-height, and font-weight characteristics that you can apply to any HTML element, not just the components provided out of the box.

In the following table are CSS classes that you can use to apply Material's typography, such as `<div class="mat-display-4">Hello, Material world!</div>`:

Class Name	Usage
`display-4`, `display-3`, `display-2` and `display-1`	Large, one-off headers, usually at the top of the page (for example, a hero header)
`headline`	Section heading corresponding to the `<h1>` tag
`title`	Section heading corresponding to the `<h2>` tag
`subheading-2`	Section heading corresponding to the `<h3>` tag
`subheading-1`	Section heading corresponding to the `<h4>` tag
`body-1`	Base body text
`body-2`	Bolder body text
`caption`	Smaller body and hint text
`button`	Buttons and anchors

You can read more about Material Typography at `https://material.angular.io/guide/typography`.

Applying typography

There are multiple ways to apply typography. One way is to leverage the `mat-typography` class and use the corresponding HTML tag like `<h2>`:

src/app/app.component.ts
```
<mat-card-header class="mat-typography">
  <mat-card-title><h2>Current Weather</h2></mat-card-title>
</mat-card-header>
```

Another way is to apply the specific typography directly on an element, like `class="mat-title"`:

src/app/app.component.ts
```
<mat-card-title><div class="mat-title">Current Weather</div></mat-card-title>
```

 Note that `class="mat-title"` can be applied to `div`, `span` or an `h2` with the same results.

As a general rule of thumb, it is usually a better idea to implement the more specific and localized option, which is the second implementation.

Updating the tagline as center-aligned caption

We can center the tagline of the application using `fxLayoutAlign` and give it a subdued `mat-caption` typography, as follows:

1. Implement the layout changes and caption typography:

   src/app/app.component.ts
   ```
   <div fxLayoutAlign="center">
     <div class="mat-caption">Your city, your forecast, right now!</div>
   </div>
   ```

2. Observe the results, as shown:

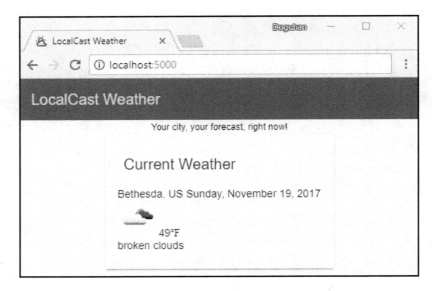

LocalCast Weather Centered Tagline

Updating Current Weather card layout

There's still more work to do to make the UI look like the design, particularly the contents of the Current Weather card, which looks like this:

To design the layout, we'll leverage Angular Flex.

You'll be editing `current-weather.component.html`, which uses the `<div>` and `<span>` tags to establish elements that live on separate lines or on the same line, respectively. With the switch over to Angular Flex, we need switch all elements to `<div>` and specify rows and columns using `fxLayout`.

Implementing Layout Scaffolding

We need to start by implementing the rough scaffolding.

Consider the current state of the template:

```
src/app/current-weather/current-weather.component.html
1  <div *ngIf="current">
2   <div>
3    <span>{{current.city}}, {{current.country}}</span>
4    <span>{{current.date | date:'fullDate'}}</span>
5   </div>
6   <div>
7    <img [src]='current.image'>
8    <span>{{current.temperature | number:'1.0-0'}}°F</span>
9   </div>
10  <div>
11   {{current.description}}
12  </div>
13 </div>
```

Let's go through the file step by step and update it:

1. Update `<span>` elements to `<div>` on lines 3, 4, and 8
2. Wrap the `<img>` element with a `<div>`
3. Add the `fxLayout="row"` property to the `<div>` element that has multiple child elements on lines 2 and 6
4. The City and Country column takes roughly 2/3rds of the screen, so add `fxFlex="66%"` to the `<div>` element on line 3
5. Add `fxFlex` to the next `<div>` element on line 4 to ensure that it takes up the rest of the horizontal space
6. Add `fxFlex="66%"` to the new `<div>` element, surrounding the `<img>` element
7. Add `fxFlex` to the next `<div>` element on line 4

The final state of the template should look like this:

src/app/current-weather/current-weather.component.html

```
1  <div *ngIf="current">
2    <div fxLayout="row">
3      <div fxFlex="66%">{{current.city}},
   {{current.country}}</div>
4      <div fxFlex>{{current.date | date:'fullDate'}}</div>
5    </div>
6    <div fxLayout="row">
7      <div fxFlex="66%">
8        <img [src]='current.image'>
9      </div>
10     <div fxFlex>{{current.temperature | number:'1.0-0'}}°F</div>
11   </div>
12   <div>
13     {{current.description}}
14   </div>
15 </div>
```

You can be more verbose in adding Angular Flex attributes; however, the more code you write, the more you'll need to maintain, making future changes more difficult. For example, the `<div>` element on line 12 doesn't need `fxLayout="row"`, since a `<div>` implicitly gets a new line. Similarly, on line 4 and line 7, the right-hand side column doesn't need an explicit `fxFlex` attribute, since it'll automatically be squeezed by the left-hand side element.

From a grid placement perspective, all your elements are now in the correct *cell*, as shown:

LocalCast Weather with layout scaffolding

Aligning elements

Now, we need to align and style each individual cell to match the design. The date and temperature needs to be right aligned and the description centered:

1. To right align the date and temperature, create a new css class named `.right` in `current-weather.component.css`:

   src/app/current-weather/current-weather.component.css
   ```
   .right {
     text-align: right
   }
   ```

2. Add `class="right"` to the `<div>` elements on lines 4 and 10
3. Center the `<div>` element for description in the same way you centered the app's tagline earlier in the chapter
4. Observe that the elements are aligned correctly, as follows:

LocalCast Weather with correct alignments

Styling elements

Finalizing the styling of elements is usually the most time-consuming part of frontend development. I recommend doing multiple passes to achieve a close enough version of the design with minimal effort first and then have your client or team decide whether it's worth the extra resources to spend more time to polish the design:

1. Add a new css property:

   src/app/current-weather/current-weather.component.css
   ```
   .no-margin {
     margin-bottom: 0
   }
   ```

2. For the city name, on line 3, add `class="mat-title no-margin"`

3. For the date, on line 4, add `"mat-subheading-2 no-margin"` to `class="right"`

4. Change the format of the date from `'fullDate'` to `'EEEE MMM d'` to match the design

5. Modify `<img>`, on line 8 to add `style="zoom: 175%"`

6. For the temperature, on line 10, append `"mat-display-3 no-margin"`

7. For the description, on line 12, add `class="mat-caption"`

   This is the final state of the template:

   src/app/current-weather/current-weather.component.html
   ```html
   <div *ngIf="current">
     <div fxLayout="row">
       <div fxFlex="66%" class="mat-title no-margin">{{current.city}},
   {{current.country}}</div>
       <div fxFlex class="right mat-subheading-2 no-
   margin">{{current.date | date:'EEEE MMM d'}}</div>
     </div>
     <div fxLayout="row">
       <div fxFlex="66%">
         <img style="zoom: 175%" [src]='current.image'>
       </div>
       <div fxFlex class="right mat-display-3 no-
   margin">{{current.temperature | number:'1.0-0'}}°F</div>
     </div>
     <div fxLayoutAlign="center" class="mat-caption">
       {{current.description}}
     </div>
   </div>
   ```

8. Observe that the styled output of your code changes, as illustrated:

LocalCast Weather with styling

Fine-tuning styles

The tagline can benefit from some top and bottom margins. This is common CSS that we're likely to use across the application, so let's put it in `styles.css`:

1. Implement `vertical-margin`:

   src/styles.css
   ```
   .vertical-margin {
     margin-top: 16px;
     margin-bottom: 16px;
   }
   ```

2. Apply `vertical-margin`:

   src/app/app.component.ts
   ```
   <div class="mat-caption vertical-margin">Your city, your forecast,
   right now!</div>
   ```

Current Weather has the same style as the City Name; we need to distinguish between the two.

3. In `app.component.ts`, update Current Weather with a `mat-headline` typography:

src/app/app.component.ts
```
<mat-card-title><div class="mat-headline">Current
Weather</div></mat-card-title>
```

4. The image and the temperature aren't centered, so add `fxLayoutAlign="center center"` to the row surrounding those elements on line 6:

src/app/current-weather/current-weather.component.html
```
<div fxLayout="row" fxLayoutAlign="center center">
```

5. Observe the final design of your app, which should look like this:

LocalCast Weather final design

Tweaking to match design

This is an area where you may spend a significant amount of time. If we were following the 80-20 principal, pixel-perfect tweaks usually end up being the last 20% that takes 80% of the time to complete. Let's examine the differences between our implementation and the design and what it would take to bridge the gap:

The date needs further customization. The numeric ordinal *th* is missing; to accomplish this, we will need to bring in a third-party library such as moment or implement our own solution and bind it next to the date on the template:

1. Update `current.date` to append an ordinal to it:

   src/app/current-weather/current-weather.component.html
   ```
   {{current.date | date:'EEEE MMM d'}}{{getOrdinal(current.date)}}
   ```

2. Implement a `getOrdinal` function:

   src/app/current-weather/current-weather.component.ts
   ```
   export class CurrentWeatherComponent implements OnInit {
   ...
     getOrdinal(date: number) {
       const n = new Date(date).getDate()
       return n > 0
         ? ['th', 'st', 'nd', 'rd'][(n > 3 &amp;&amp; n < 21) || n %
   10 > 3 ? 0 : n % 10]
         : ''
     }
     ...
   }
   ```

Note that the implementation of `getOrdinal` boils down to a complicated one-liner that isn't very readable and is very difficult to maintain. Such functions, if critical to your business logic, should be heavily unit tested.

 Angular 6, at the time of writing, doesn't support new line breaks in the date template; ideally, we should be able to specify the date format as `'EEEE\nMMM d'` to ensure that the line break is always consistent.

The temperature implementation needs to separate the digits from the unit with a `<span>` element, surrounded with a `<p>`, so the superscript style can be applied to the unit, such as `<span class="unit">°F</span>`, where unit is a CSS class to make it look like a superscript element.

3. Implement a `unit` CSS class:

    src/app/current-weather/current-weather.component.css
    ```
    .unit {
      vertical-align: super;
    }
    ```

4. Apply `unit`:

    src/app/current-weather/current-weather.component.html
    ```
    ...
     7 <div fxFlex="55%">
    ...
    10 <div fxFlex class="right no-margin">
    11    <p class="mat-display-3">{{current.temperature |
    number:'1.0-0'}}
    12      <span class="mat-display-1 unit">°F</span>
    13    </p>
    ```

We need to experiment with how much of space the forecast image should have, by tweaking the `fxFlex` value on line 7. Otherwise, the temperature overflows to the next line and your setting can further be affected by the size of your browser window. For example, `60%` works well with a small browser window, but when maximized, it forces an overflow. However, `55%` seems to satisfy both conditions:

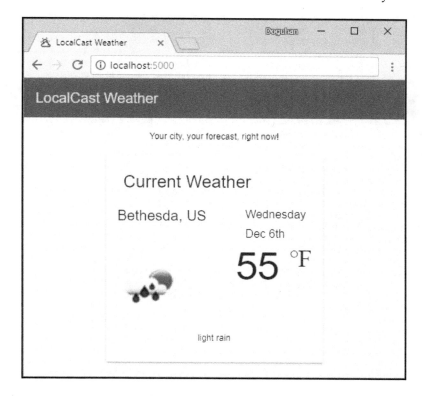

LocalCast Weather after tweaks

As always, it is possible to further tweak margins and paddings to further customize the design. However, each deviation from the library will have maintainability consequences down the line. Unless you're truly building a business around displaying weather data, you should defer any further optimizations to the end of the project, as time permits, and if experience is any guide, you will not be making this optimization.

With two negative margin-bottom hacks, you can attain a design fairly close to the original, but I will not include those hacks here and leave it as an exercise for the reader to discover on the GitHub repository. Such hacks are sometimes necessary evils, but in general, they point to a disconnect between design and implementation realities. The solution leading up to the tweaks section is the sweet spot, where Angular Material thrives:

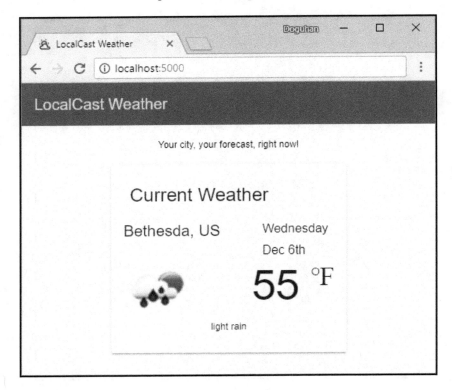

LocalCast Weather after tweaks and hacks

Updating unit tests

In order to keep your unit tests running, you will need to import `MaterialModule` to any component's `spec` file that uses Angular material:

`*.component.spec.ts`

```
...
  beforeEach(
    async(() => {
      TestBed.configureTestingModule({
        ...
        imports: [..., MaterialModule, NoopAnimationsModule],
      }).compileComponents()
    })
  )
```

You will also need to update any test, including e2e tests, that search for a particular HTML element.

For example, since the app's title, LocalCast Weather, is not in an `h1` tag anymore, you must update the `spec` file to look for it in a `span` element:

`src/app/app.component.spec.ts`

```
expect(compiled.querySelector('span').textContent).toContain('LocalCast
Weather')
```

Similarly, in e2e tests, you will need to update your page object function to retrieve the text from the correct location:

`e2e/app.po.ts`

```
getParagraphText() {
  return element(by.css('app-root mat-toolbar span')).getText()
}
```

Updating Angular Material

You can use `ng update` for a quick and painless upgrade experience, which should look like below:

```
$ npx ng update @angular/material
    Updating package.json with dependency @angular/cdk @ "6.0.0" (was
"5.2.2")...
    Updating package.json with dependency @angular/material @ "6.0.0" (was
"5.2.2")...
UPDATE package.json (5563 bytes)
```

In addition, I have discovered the `material-update-tool` published by the Angular team at `https://github.com/angular/material-update-tool`. In its current form this tool is advertised as a specific Angular Material 5.x to 6.0 updater tool, so it may perhaps become part of `ng update` like the `rxjs-tslint` tool in the future. You may run the tool as shown below:

```
$ npx angular-material-updater -p .\src\tsconfig.app.json

√ Successfully migrated the project source files. Please check above output
for issues that couldn't be automatically fixed.
```

If you're lucky and everything goes well, feel free to skip the rest of this section. For the rest of the section I will go over a specific scenario involving release candidates and beta versions that I ran into during the development of this example, which highlights the need for a manual update. First, we will establish awareness of the current versions, then discover latest available versions, and, finally, update and test the upgrade, like we did while updating Angular manually.

Updating Angular Material

Now that we know what version to upgrade to, let's go ahead and do it:

1. Execute the following command to update Material and its related components to their target versions:

```
$ npm install @angular/material@^5.0.0 @angular/cdk@^5.0.0
@angular/animations@^5.0.0 @angular/flex-layout@^2.0.0-rc.1
```

2. Verify your `package.json` to ensure that the versions match the expected version
3. Address any NPM Warnings

In this specific instance, we receive impossible-to-meet peer dependency warnings from the `@angular/flex-layout` package. Further investigation on GitHub (`https://github.com/angular/flex-layout/issues/508`) reveals that this is a known issue and in general to be expected from a Beta or RC package. This means it is safe to ignore these warnings.

Summary

In this chapter, you learned to apply specific Angular Material components to your application. You became aware of the pitfalls of overly-optimizing UI design. We also went over how you can keep Angular Material up-to-date.

In the next chapter, we will update the weather app to respond to user input with reactive forms and keep our components decoupled, while also enabling data exchange between them using `BehaviorSubject`. After the next chapter, we will be done with the weather app and shift our focus on building larger, line-of-business applications.

12
Create a Router-First Line-of-Business App

Line-of-Business (**LOB**) applications are the bread and butter of the software development world. As defined in Wikipedia, LOB is a general term, which refers to a product or a set of related products that serve a particular customer transaction or business need. LOB apps present a good opportunity to demonstrate a variety of features and functionality without getting into contorted or specialized scenarios that large enterprise applications usually require. In a sense, they are the 80-20 learning experience. I must, however, point out a curious thing about LOB apps—if you end up building a semi-useful LOB app, the demand for it will grow uncontrollably, and you will quickly become the victim of your own success. This is why you should treat the start of every new project as an opportunity, a coding-kata if you will, to get better at creating more flexible architectures.

In this chapter and the remaining chapters, we'll set up a new application with rich features that can meet the demands of a LOB application with a scalable architecture and engineering best practices that will help you start small and be able to grow your solution quickly if there's demand. We will follow the Router-first design pattern, relying on reusable components to create a grocery store LOB named LemonMart.

In this chapter, you will learn to do the following:

- Effectively use CLI to create major Angular Components and CLI Scaffolds
- Learn how to build Router-first Apps
- Branding, Custom and Material Iconography
- Debug complicated apps with Augury
- Enable lazy loading
- Create a walking skeleton

The code samples provided in this book require Angular version 5 and 6. Angular 5 code is runtime compatible with Angular 6. Angular 6 will be supported in LTS until October 2019. The most up-to-date versions of the code repositories may be found at the following URLs:

- LocalCast Weather at `Github.com/duluca/local-weather-app`
- LemonMart at `Github.com/duluca/lemon-mart`

Angular cheat sheet

Before we dive in to creating our LOB app, I have included a cheat sheet for you to familiarize yourself with common Angular syntax and CLI commands, because going forward, this syntax and these commands will be used without their purpose explicitly explained. Take some time to review and orient yourself with new Angular syntax, major components, CLI scaffolds, and common pipes. You may find the list especially useful if your background is with AngularJS, since you will need to unlearn some old syntax.

Binding

Binding, or data binding, refers to an automatic, one or two-way connection between a variable in code and a value displayed or input in an HTML template or another component:

Type	Syntax	Data direction

Interpolation
Property
Attribute
Class
Style
	`{{expression}}`
	`[target]="expression"`
	`bind-target="expression"`
		One-way
		from data source
		to view target

Event	`(target)="statement"` `on-target="statement"`	One-way from view target to data source
Two-way	`[(target)]="expression"` `bindon-target="expression"`	Two-way

Source: `https://angular.io/guide/template-syntax#binding-syntax-an-overview`

Built-in directives

Directives encapsulate coded behaviors that can be applied as attributes to HTML elements or other components:

Name	Syntax	Purpose
Structural Directives	`*ngIf` `*ngFor` `*ngSwitch`	Controls structural layout of the HTML and if elements get added or removed from the DOM
Attribute Directives	`[class]` `[style]` `[(model)]`	Listens to and modifies the behavior of other HTML elements, attributes, properties, and components, such as CSS classes, HTML styles, and HTML form elements

Structural Directives Source: `https://angular.io/guide/structural-directives`

Attribute Directives Source: `https://angular.io/guide/template-syntax#built-in-attribute-directives`

Common pipes

Pipes modify how a data-bound value is displayed in the HTML template.

Name	Purpose	Usage
Date	Formats a date according to locale rules	`{{date_value	date[:format]}}`
Text Transformation	Transforms text to uppercase, lowercase, or title case	`{{value	uppercase}}` `{{value	lowercase}}` `{{value	titlecase }}`
Decimal	Formats a number according to locale rules	`{{number	number[:digitInfo]}}`
Percent	Formats a number as a percentage according to locale rules	`{{number	percent[:digitInfo]}}`
Currency	Formats a number as currency with currency code and symbol according to locale rules	`{{number	currency[:currencyCode [:symbolDisplay[:digitInfo]]]}}`

Pipes Source: `https://angular.io/guide/pipes`

Starter commands, major components, and CLI scaffolds

Starter commands help generate new projects or add dependencies. Angular CLI commands help create major components by automatically generating boilerplate scaffolding code with ease. For the list of full set of commands, visit `https://github.com/angular/angular-cli/wiki`:

Name	Purpose	CLI Command
New	Creates a new Angular application with initialized git repository, package.json, and routing already configured. Run from parent folder.	`npx @angular/cli new project-name --routing`
Update	Updates Angular, RxJS, and Angular Material dependencies. Rewrites code, if necessary, to maintain compatibility.	`npx ng update`
Add Material	Installs and configures Angular Material dependencies.	`npx ng add @angular/material`
Module	Creates a new `@NgModule` class. Uses `--routing` to add routing for submodules. Optionally, import new module into a parent module using `--module`.	`ng g module new-module`
Component	Creates a new `@Component` class. Uses `--module` to specify parent module. Optionally, use `--flat` to skip directory creation, `-t` for an inline template, and `-s` for an inline style.	`ng g component new-component`
Directive	Creates a new `@Directive` class. Optionally, uses `--module` to scope directives for a given submodule.	`ng g directive new-directive`
Pipe	Creates a new `@Pipe` class. Optionally, use `--module` to scope pipes for a given submodule.	`ng g pipe new-pipe`

Service	Creates a new @Injectable class. Uses --module to provide a service for a given submodule. Services are not automatically imported to a module. Optionally use --flat false to create service under a directory.	ng g service new-service
Guard	Creates a new @Injectable class, which implements the Route lifecycle hook CanActivate. Uses --module to provide a guard for a given submodule. Guards are not automatically imported to a module.	ng g guard new-guard
Class	Creates a bare-bones class.	ng g class new-class
Interface	Creates a bare-bones interface.	ng g interface new-interface
Enum	Creates a bare-bones enum.	ng g enum new-enum

In order to properly scaffold some of the components listed earlier under a custom module, such as my-module, you can prepend the module name before the name of what you intend to generate, for example, ng g c my-module/my-new-component. Angular CLI will properly wire up and place the new component under the my-module folder.

Configure Angular CLI autocomplete

You get an autocomplete experience when working with Angular CLI. Execute the appropriate command for your *nix environment:

- For bash shell:

```
$ ng completion --bash >> ~/.bashrc
$ source ~/.bashrc
```

- For zsh shell:

```
$ ng completion --zsh >> ~/.zshrc
$ source ~/.zshrc
```

- For Windows users using git bash shell:

```
$ ng completion --bash >> ~/.bash_profile
$ source ~/.bash_profile
```

Router-first architecture

The Angular router, shipped in the `@angular/router` package, is a central and critical part of building **single-page-applications** (**SPAs**) that act and behave like regular websites that are easy to navigate using browser controls or the zoom or microzoom controls.

Angular Router has advanced features such as lazy loading, router outlets, auxiliary routes, smart active link tracking, and the ability to be expressed as an `href`, which enables a highly flexible Router-first app architecture leveraging stateless data-driven components using RxJS `SubjectBehavior`.

Large teams can work against a single-code base, with each team responsible of a module's development, without stepping on each other's toes, while enabling easy continuous integration. Google, with its billions of lines of code, works against a single code base for a very good reason. Integration, after the fact, is very expensive.

Small teams can remix their UI layouts on the fly to quickly respond to changes without having to rearchitect their code. It is easy to underestimate the amount of time wasted due to late game changes in layout or navigation. Such changes are easier to absorb by larger teams but a costly endeavor for small teams.

With lazy-loading, all developers benefit from sub-second first meaningful paints, because the file size of the core user experience that's delivered to the browser is kept at a minimum at build time. The size of a module impacts download and loading speed, because the more a browser has to do, the longer it will take for a user to see the first screen of the app. By defining lazy-loaded modules, each module can be packaged as separated files, which can be downloaded and loaded individually and as needed. Smart active link tracking results in a superior developer and user experience, making it very easy to implement highlighting features to indicate to the user the current tab or portion of the app that is currently active. Auxiliary routes maximize the reuse of components and help pull off complicated state transitions with ease. With auxiliary routes, you can render multiple master and detail views using only a single outer template. You can also control how the route is displayed to the user in the browser's URL bar and compose routes using `routerLink`, in templates, and `Router.navigate`, in code, driving complicated scenarios.

In order to pull off a router-first implementation, you need to do this:

1. Define user roles early on
2. Design with lazy loading in mind
3. Implement a walking-skeleton navigation experience
4. Design around major data components
5. Enforce a decoupled component architecture
6. Differentiate between user controls and components
7. Maximize code reuse

User roles normally indicate the job function of a user, such as a manager or data-entry specialist. In technical terms, they can be thought of as a group of actions that a particular class of user is allowed to execute. Defining user roles help identify sub modules that can then be configured to be lazy loaded. After all, a data-entry specialist won't ever see most of the screens that a manager can, so why deliver those assets to those users and slow down their experience? Lazy loading is critical in creating a scalable application architecture, not only from an application perspective, but also from a high-quality and efficient development perspective. Configuring lazy loading can be tricky, which is why it is important to nail down a walking-skeleton navigation experience early on.

Identifying major data components that your users will work with, such as invoice or people objects, will help you avoid over-engineering your application. Designing around major data components will inform API design early on and help define `BehaviorSubject` data anchors that you will use to achieve a stateless, data-driven design to ensure a decoupled component architecture.

Finally, identify self-contained user controls that encapsulate unique behaviors that you wish to create for your app. User controls will likely be created as directives or components that have data-binding properties and tightly-coupled controller logic and templates. Components, on the other hand, will leverage router lifecycle events to parse parameters and perform CRUD operations on data. Identifying these component reuses early on will result in creating more flexible components that can be reused in multiple contexts as orchestrated by the router, maximizing code reuse.

Creating LemonMart

LemonMart will be a mid-sized line-of-business application with over 90 code files. We will start our journey by creating a new Angular app with routing and Angular Material configured from the get go.

Creating a Router-first app

With the Router-first approach, we will want to enable routing early on in our application:

1. You can create the new application with routing already configured by executing this command:

   Ensure that `@angular/cli` is not installed globally, or you may run into errors:

   ```
   $ npx @angular/cli new lemon-mart --routing
   ```

2. A new `AppRoutingModule` file has been created for us:

   ```
   src/app/app-routing.modules.ts
   import { NgModule } from '@angular/core';
   import { Routes, RouterModule } from '@angular/router';

   const routes: Routes = [];

   @NgModule({
     imports: [RouterModule.forRoot(routes)],
     exports: [RouterModule]
   })
   export class AppRoutingModule { }
   ```

We will be defining routes inside the routes array. Note that routes array is passed in to be configured as the root routes for the application, the default root route being /.

When configuring your `RouterModule`, you can pass in additional options to customize the default behavior of the Router, such as when you attempt to load a route that is already being displayed, instead of taking no action, you can force a reload of the component. To enable this behavior, create your router like `RouterModule.forRoot(routes, { onSameUrlNavigation: 'reload' })`.

3. Finally, `AppRoutingModule` is registered with `AppModule`, as shown:

src/app/app.module.ts
```
...
import { AppRoutingModule } from './app-routing.module';

@NgModule({
  ...
  imports: [
    AppRoutingModule
    ...
  ],
  ...
```

Configuring Angular.json and Package.json

You should complete these steps before moving forward:

1. Modify `angular.json` and `tslint.json` to enforce your settings and coding standards
2. Install `npm i -D prettier`
3. Add `prettier` settings to `package.json`
4. Configure your development serve port to other than `4200`, such as `5000`
5. Add the `standardize` script and update `start` and `build` scripts
6. Add **npm Scripts for Docker** to `package.json`
7. Establish dev norms and document it in your project, `npm i -D dev-norms` then `npx dev-norms create`
8. If you use VS Code, set up the `extensions.json` and `settings.json` files

You may configure the TypeScript Hero extension to auto organize and prune import statements, but adding `"typescriptHero.imports.organizeOnSave": true` to `settings.json`. If combined with the setting `"files.autoSave": "onFocusChange"` you may find that the tool aggressively cleans unused imports as you are trying to type them out. Ensure that this setting works for you and doesn't collide with any other tools or VS Code's own import organization feature.

9. Execute `npm run standardize`

Refer to `Chapter 10`, *Prepare Angular App for Production Release*, for further configuration details.

You can get the npm Scripts for Docker at `bit.ly/npmScriptsForDocker` and npm Scripts for AWS at `bit.ly/npmScriptsForAWS`.

Configuring Material and Styles

We will also need to set up Angular Material and configure a theme to use, as covered in `Chapter 11`, *Enhance Angular App with Angular Material*:

1. Install Angular Material:

```
$ npx ng add @angular/material
$ npm i @angular/flex-layout hammerjs
$ npx ng g m material --flat -m app
```

2. Import and export `MatButtonModule`, `MatToolbarModule`, and `MatIconModule`

3. Configure your default theme and register other Angular dependencies

4. Add common css to `styles.css` as shown below,

src/styles.css

```
body {
  margin: 0;
}

.margin-top {
  margin-top: 16px;
```

```
  }

  .horizontal-padding {
    margin-left: 16px;
    margin-right: 16px;
  }

  .flex-spacer {
    flex: 1 1 auto;
  }
```

Refer to `Chapter 11`, *Enhance Angular App with Angular Material,* for further configuration details.

Designing LemonMart

It is important to build a rudimentary road map to follow, from the database to the frontend, while also avoiding over-engineering. This initial design phase is critical to the long-term health and success of your project, where any existing silos between teams must be broken down and an overall technical vision well understood by all members of the team. This is easier said than done, and there are volumes of books written on the topic.

In engineering, there's no one right answer to a problem, so it is important to remember that no one person can ever have all the answers nor a crystal clear vision. It is important that technical and non-technical leaders create a safe space with opportunities for open discussion and experimentation as part of the culture. The humility and empathy that comes along with being able to court such uncertainty as a team is as important as any single team member's technical capabilities. Every team member must be comfortable with checking their egos out at the door because our collective goal will be to grow and evolve an application to ever-changing requirements during the development cycle. You will know that you have succeeded if individual parts of the software you created is easily replaceable by anyone.

Identifying user roles

The first step of our design will be to think about you using the application and why.

We envision four user states or roles for LemonMart:

- Authenticated, any authenticated user would have access to their profile
- Cashier, whose sole role is to check out customers
- Clerk, whose sole role is to perform inventory-related functions
- Manager, who can perform all actions a cashier and a clerk can perform but also have access to administrative functions

With this in mind, we can start a high-level design of our app.

Identifying high-level modules with site map

Develop a high-level site map of your application, as shown:

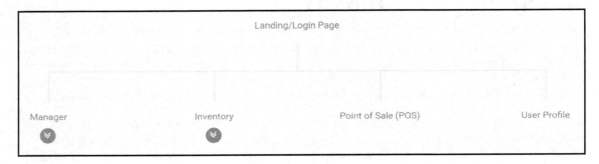

Landing pages for users

 I used MockFlow.com's SiteMap tool to create the site map shown at `https://sitemap.mockflow.com`.

Upon first examination, three high-level modules emerge as lazy-loading candidates:

1. **Point of Sale (POS)**
2. **Inventory**
3. **Manager**

Cashier will only have access to the POS module and component. The Clerk will only have access to the **Inventory** module, which will include additional screen for **Stock Entry**, **Products**, and **Categories** management components.

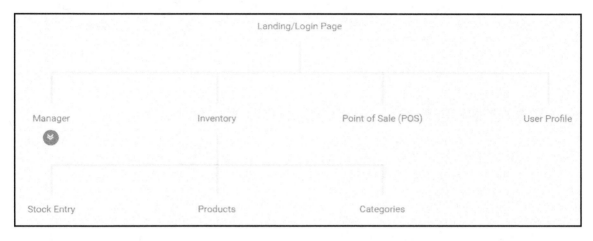

Inventory pages

Finally, the **Manager** will be able to access all three modules with the **Manager** module, including User management and Receipt lookup components.

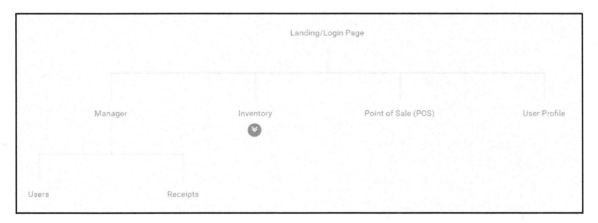

Manager pages

There's a great benefit to enable lazy-loading for all three modules since cashiers and clerks will never use components belonging to other user roles, there's no reason to send those bytes down to their devices. This means as the **Manager** module gains more advanced reporting features or new roles are added to the application, the **POS** module will be unaffected by the bandwidth and memory impact of an otherwise growing application. This means fewer support calls and consistent performance on the same hardware for a much longer period of time.

Generating router-enabled modules

Now that we have our high-level components defined as **Manager**, **Inventory**, and **POS**, we can define them as modules. These modules will be different from the ones you've created so far, for routing and Angular Material. We can create the user profile as a component on the app module; however, note that user profile will only ever be used for already authenticated users, so it makes sense to define a fourth module only meant for authenticated users in general. This way, you will ensure that your app's first payload remains as minimal as possible. In addition, we will create a Home component to contain the landing experience for our app so that we can keep implementation details out of `app.component`:

1. Generate `manager`, `inventory`, `pos`, and `user` modules, specifying their target module and routing capabilities:

    ```
    $ npx ng g m manager -m app --routing
    $ npx ng g m inventory -m app --routing
    $ npx ng g m pos -m app --routing
    $ npx ng g m user -m app --routing
    ```

    If you have configured `npx` to automatically recognize `ng` as a command, you can save some more keystrokes so that you won't have to append `npx` to your commands every time. Do not globally install `@angular/cli`. Note the abbreviate command structure, where `ng generate module manager` becomes `ng g m manager`, and similarly, `--module` becomes `-m`.

2. Verify that you don't have CLI errors.

    Note that using `npx` on Windows may encounter an error such as **Path must be a string. Received undefined**. This error doesn't seem to have any effect on the successful operation of the command, which is why it is critical to always inspect what the CLI tool generated.

3. Verify the folder and the files are created:

    ```
    /src/app
    |    app-routing.module.ts
    |    app.component.css
    |    app.component.html
    |    app.component.spec.ts
    |    app.component.ts
    |    app.module.ts
    |    material.module.ts
    |--------inventory
    |            inventory-routing.module.ts
    |            inventory.module.ts
    |--------manager
    |            manager-routing.module.ts
    |            manager.module.ts
    |--------pos
    |            pos-routing.module.ts
    |            pos.module.ts
    |--------user
                user-routing.module.ts
                user.module.ts
    ```

4. Examine how `ManagerModule` has been wired.

    A child module implements an `@NgModule` similar to `app.module`. The biggest difference is that a child module does not implement the `bootstrap` property, which is required for your root module, to initialize your Angular app:

    src/app/manager/manager.module.ts
    ```
    import { NgModule } from '@angular/core'
    import { CommonModule } from '@angular/common'

    import { ManagerRoutingModule } from './manager-routing.module'

    @NgModule({
      imports: [CommonModule, ManagerRoutingModule],
      declarations: [],
    ```

```
})
export class ManagerModule {}
```

Since we have specified the −m option, the module has been imported into
app.module:

src/app/app.module.ts
```
...
import { ManagerModule } from './manager/manager.module'
...
@NgModule({
  ...
  imports: [
    ...
    ManagerModule
  ],
  ...
```

In addition, because we also specified the --routing option, a routing module
has been created and imported into ManagerModule:

src/app/manager/manager-routing.module.ts
```
import { NgModule } from '@angular/core'
import { Routes, RouterModule } from '@angular/router'

const routes: Routes = []

@NgModule({
  imports: [RouterModule.forChild(routes)],
  exports: [RouterModule],
})
export class ManagerRoutingModule {}
```

Note that RouterModule is being configured using forChild, as opposed to forRoot,
which was the case for the AppRouting module. This way, the router understands the
proper relationship between routes defined in different modules' contexts and can correctly
prepend /manager to all child routes in this example.

The CLI doesn't respect your tslint.json settings. If you have correctly
configured your VS Code environment with prettier, your Code Styling
preferences will be applied as you work on each file or, globally, when
you run the prettier command.

Designing the home route

Consider the following mock-up as the landing experience for LemonMart:

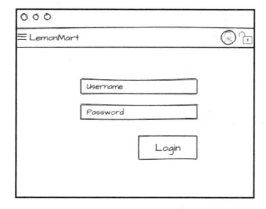

LemonMart Landing Experience

Unlike the `LocalCastWeather` app, we don't want all this markup to be in the `App` component. The `App` component is the root element of your entire application; therefore, it should only contain elements that will persistently appear throughout your application. In the following annotated mock-up, the toolbar marked as **1** will be persistent throughout the app.

The area marked as **2** will house the home component, which itself will contain a login user control, marked as **3**:

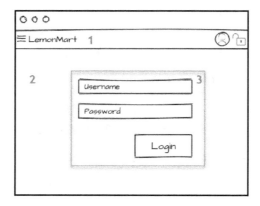

LemonMart Layout Structure

It is a best practice to create your default or landing component as a separate element in Angular. This helps reduce the amount of code that must be loaded and logic executed in every page, but it also results in a more flexible architecture when utilizing the router:

Generate the `home` component with inline template and styles:

```
$ npx ng g c home -m app --inline-template --inline-style
```

Now, you are ready to configure the router.

Setting up default routes

Let's get started with setting up a simple route for LemonMart:

1. Configure your `home` route:

    src/app/app-routing.module.ts
    ```
    ...
    const routes: Routes = [
      { path: '', redirectTo: '/home', pathMatch: 'full' },
      { path: 'home', component: HomeComponent },
    ]
    ...
    ```

    We first define a path for `'home'` and inform the router to render `HomeComponent` by setting the component property. Then, we set the default path of the application `''` to be redirected to `'/home'`. By setting the `pathMatch` property, we always ensure that this very specific instance of the home route will be rendered as the landing experience.

2. Create a `pageNotFound` component with an inline template
3. Configure a wildcard route for `PageNotFoundComponent`:

    src/app/app-routing.module.ts
    ```
    ...
    const routes: Routes = [
      ...
      { path: '**', component: PageNotFoundComponent }
    ]
    ...
    ```

This way, any route that is not matched will be directed to the `PageNotFoundComponent`.

RouterLink

When a user lands on the `PageNotFoundComponent`, we would like them to be redirected to the `HomeComponent` using the `RouterLink` direction:

1. Implement an inline template to link back to home using `routerLink`:

   src/app/page-not-found/page-not-found.component.ts
   ```
   ...
   template: `
       <p>
          This page doesn't exist. Go back to <a
   routerLink="/home">home</a>.
       </p>
       `,
   ...
   ```

 This navigation can also be done via an `<a href>` tag implementation; however, in more dynamic and complicated navigation scenarios, you will lose features such as automatic active link tracking or dynamic link generation.

The Angular bootstrap process will ensure that `AppComponent` is inside the `<app-root>` element in your `index.html`. However, we must manually define where we would like `HomeComponent` to render, to finalize the router configuration.

Router outlet

`AppComponent` is considered a root element for the root router defined in `app-routing.module`, which allows us to define outlets within this root element to dynamically load any content we wish using the `<router-outlet>` element:

1. Configure `AppComponent` to use inline template and styles
2. Add the toolbar for your application
3. Add the name of your application as a button link so that it takes the user to the home page when clicked on

4. Add `<router-outlet>` for the content to render:

src/app/app.component.ts
```
...
template: `
    <mat-toolbar color="primary">
      <a mat-button routerLink="/home"><h1>LemonMart</h1></a>
    </mat-toolbar>
    <router-outlet></router-outlet>
    `,
```

Now, the contents of home will render inside `<router-outlet>`.

Branding, Custom, and Material Icons

In order to construct an attractive and intuitive toolbar, we must introduce some iconography and branding to the app so that the users can easily navigate through the app with the help of familiar icons.

Branding

In terms of branding, you should ensure that your web app should have custom color palette and integrate with desktop and mobile browser features to bring forward your app's name and iconography.

Color palette

Pick a color palette using the Material Color tool, as discussed in Chapter 11, *Enhance Angular App with Angular Material*. Here's the one I picked for LemonMart:

```
https://material.io/color/#!/?view.left=0&view.right=0&primary.color=2E7D32
&secondary.color=C6FF00
```

Implementing browser manifest and icons

You need to ensure that the browser shows the correct title text and icon in a **Browser** tab. Further, a manifest file should be created that implements specific icons for various mobile operating systems, so that if a user pins your website, a desirable icon is displayed similar to other app icons on a phone. This will ensure that if a user favorites or pin your web app on their mobile device's home screen, they'll get a native-looking app icon:

1. Create or obtain an SVG version of your website's logo from a designer or site like `https://www.flaticon.com`

2. In this case, I will be using a particular lemon image:

LemonMart's signature logo

When using images you find on the internet, pay attention to applicable copyrights. In this case, I have purchased a license to be able to publish this lemon logo, but you may grab your own copy at the following URL, given that you provide the required attribution to the author of the image: `https://www.flaticon.com/free-icon/lemon_605070`.

3. Generate `favicon.ico` and manifest files using a tool such as `https://realfavicongenerator.net`

4. Adjust settings for iOS, Android, Windows Phone, macOS, and Safari to your liking

5. Ensure that you set a version number, favicons can be notorious with caching; a random version number will ensure that users always get the latest version

6. Download and extract the generated `favicons.zip` file into your `src` folder

7. Edit the `angular.json` file to include the new assets in your app:

```
angular.json
"apps": [
  {
    ...
      "assets": [
        "src/assets",
        "src/favicon.ico",
        "src/android-chrome-192x192.png",
        "src/favicon-16x16.png",
        "src/mstile-310x150.png",
```

```
        "src/android-chrome-512x512.png",
        "src/favicon-32x32.png",
        "src/mstile-310x310.png",
        "src/apple-touch-icon.png",
        "src/manifest.json",
        "src/mstile-70x70.png",
        "src/browserconfig.xml",
        "src/mstile-144x144.png",
        "src/safari-pinned-tab.svg",
        "src/mstile-150x150.png"
    ]
```

8. Insert the generated code in the `<head>` section of your `index.html`:

    src/index.html
    ```
    <link rel="apple-touch-icon" sizes="180x180" href="/apple-touch-
    icon.png?v=rMlKOnvxlK">
    <link rel="icon" type="image/png" sizes="32x32"
    href="/favicon-32x32.png?v=rMlKOnvxlK">
    <link rel="icon" type="image/png" sizes="16x16"
    href="/favicon-16x16.png?v=rMlKOnvxlK">
    <link rel="manifest" href="/manifest.json?v=rMlKOnvxlK">
    <link rel="mask-icon" href="/safari-pinned-tab.svg?v=rMlKOnvxlK"
    color="#b3ad2d">
    <link rel="shortcut icon" href="/favicon.ico?v=rMlKOnvxlK">
    <meta name="theme-color" content="#ffffff">
    ```

9. Ensure that your new favicon displays correctly

To further your branding, consider configuring a custom Material theme and leveraging
`https://material.io/color`

Custom icons

Now, let's add your custom branding inside your Angular app. You will need the svg icon you used to create your favicon:

1. Place the image under `src/app/assets/img/icons`, named `lemon.svg`
2. Import `HttpClientModule` to `AppComponent` so that the `.svg` file can be requested over HTTP

3. Update `AppComponent` to register the new svg file as an icon:

src/app/app.component.ts
```
import { DomSanitizer } from '@angular/platform-browser'
...
export class AppComponent {
  constructor(iconRegistry: MatIconRegistry, sanitizer:
DomSanitizer) {
    iconRegistry.addSvgIcon(
      'lemon',
sanitizer.bypassSecurityTrustResourceUrl('assets/img/icons/lemon.sv
g')
    )
  }
}
```

4. Add the icon to the toolbar:

src/app/app.component.ts
```
template: `
    <mat-toolbar color="primary">
      <mat-icon svgIcon="lemon"></mat-icon>
      <a mat-button routerLink="/home"><h1>LemonMart</h1></a>
    </mat-toolbar>
    <router-outlet></router-outlet>
  `,
```

Now let's add the remaining icons for menu, user profile, and logout.

Material icons

Angular Material works out of the box with Material Design icons, which can be imported into your app as a web font in your `index.html`. It is possible to self-host the font; however, if you go down that path, you also don't get the benefit of the user's browser having already cached the font when they visited another website, saving the speed and latency of downloading a 42-56 KB file in the process. The complete list of icons can be found at `https://material.io/icons/`.

Now let's update the toolbar with some icons and setup the home page with a minimal template for a fake login button:

1. Ensure Material icons `<link>` tag has been added to `index.html`:

   src/index.html
   ```
   <head>
     ...
     <link
   href="https://fonts.googleapis.com/icon?family=Material+Icons"
   rel="stylesheet">
   </head>
   ```

> Instructions on how to self-host can be found under the **Self Hosting** section at `http://google.github.io/material-design-icons/#getting-icons`.

   Once configured, working with Material icons is easy.

2. Update the toolbar to place a **Menu** button to the left of the title.
3. Add an `fxFlex` so that the remaining icons are right aligned.
4. Add user profile and logout icons:

   src/app/app.component.ts
   ```
   template: `
       <mat-toolbar color="primary">
         <button mat-icon-button><mat-icon>menu</mat-icon></button>
         <mat-icon svgIcon="lemon"></mat-icon>
         <a mat-button routerLink="/home"><h1>LemonMart</h1></a>
         <span class="flex-spacer"></span>
         <button mat-icon-button><mat-icon>account_circle</mat-
   icon></button>
         <button mat-icon-button><mat-icon>lock_open</mat-
   icon></button>
       </mat-toolbar>
       <router-outlet></router-outlet>
     `,
   ```

5. Add a minimal template for a login:

src/app/home/home.component.ts
```
styles: [`
  div[fxLayout] {margin-top: 32px;}
`],
template: `
  <div fxLayout="column" fxLayoutAlign="center center">
    <span class="mat-display-2">Hello, Lemonite!</span>
    <button mat-raised-button color="primary">Login</button>
  </div>
`
```

Your app should look similar to this screenshot:

LemonMart with minimal login

There's still some work to be done, in terms of implementing and showing/hiding the menu, profile, and logout icons, given the user's authentication status. We will cover this functionality in `Chapter 14`, *Design Authentication and Authorization*. Now that you've set up basic routing for your app, you need to learn how to debug your Angular app before we move on to setting up lazily loaded modules with subcomponents.

Angular Augury

Augury is a Chrome Dev Tools extension for debugging and profiling Angular applications. It is a purpose-built tool to help developers visually navigate the component tree, inspect the state of the router, and enable break point debugging by source-mapping between the generated JavaScript code and the TypeScript code that the developer coded in. You can download Augury from `augury.angular.io`. Once installed, when you open Chrome Dev Tools for your Angular app, you'll note a new tab for Augury, as illustrated:

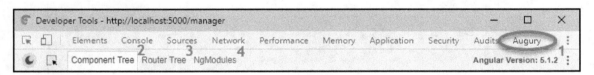

Chrome Dev Tools Augury

Augury provides useful and critical information in understanding how your Angular app is behaving at runtime:

1. Current Angular version is listed, in this case, as version **5.1.2**
2. **Component Tree**
3. **Router Tree** shows all the routes that have been configured in the app
4. **NgModules** shows the `AppModule` and Sub-Modules of the app

Component Tree

The **Component Tree** tab shows how all app components are related and how they interact with each other:

1. Select a particular component, such as HomeComponent, as follows:

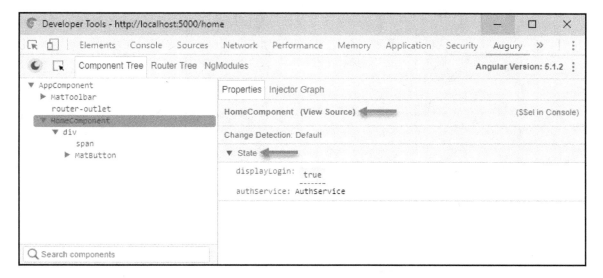

Augury Component Tree

The **Properties** tab on the right-hand side will display a link called **View Source**, which you can use to debug your component. Further below, you will be able to observe the state of properties of the component, such as the **displayLogin** boolean, including services that you have injected into the component and their state.

You can change the value of any property by double-clicking on the value. For example, if you would like to change the value of **displayLogin** to false, simply double-click on the blue box that contains the true value and type in false. You will be able to observe the effects of your changes in your Angular app.

In order to observe the runtime component hierarchy of HomeComponent, you can observe the Injector Graph.

2. Click on the **Injector Graph** tab, as shown:

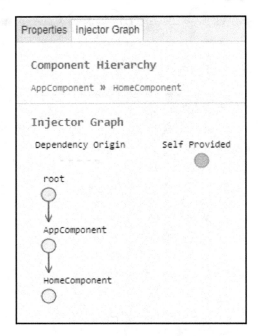

Augury Injector Graph

This view shows how your selected component came to be rendered. In this case, we can observe that HomeComponent was rendered within AppComponent. This visualization can be very helpful in tracking down the implementation of a particular component in an unfamiliar code base or where a deep component tree exists.

Break point debugging

Let me restate, for the record, that console.log statements shall never be checked in to your repository. In general, they are a waste of your time, because it requires editing code and later cleaning up your code. Furthermore, Augury already provides the state of your components, so in straightforward cases, you should be able to leverage it observe or coerce state.

There are some niche use cases, where `console.log` statements can be useful. These are mostly asynchronous workflows that operate in parallel and are dependent on timely user interaction. In these cases, console logs can help you better understand the flow of events and interaction between various components.

Augury is not yet sophisticated enough to resolve asynchronous data or data returned via functions. There are other common cases, where you would like to observe the state of properties as they are being set, and even be able to change their values on the fly to force your code to execute branching logic in `if-else` or `switch` statements. For these cases, you should be using break point debugging.

Let's presume that some basic logic exists on `HomeComponent`, which sets a `displayLogin` boolean, based on an `isAuthenticated` value retrieved from an `AuthService`, as demonstrated:

```
src/app/home/home.component.ts
...
import { AuthService } from '../auth.service'
...
export class HomeComponent implements OnInit {
  displayLogin = true
  constructor(private authService: AuthService) {}

  ngOnInit() {
    this.displayLogin = !this.authService.isAuthenticated()
  }
}
```

Now observe the state of the value of `displayLogin` and the `isAuthenticated` function as they are being set, then observe the change in the value of `displayLogin`:

1. Click on the **View Source** link on `HomeComponent`
2. Drop a break point on the first line inside the `ngOnInit` function
3. Refresh the page

4. Chrome Dev Tools will switch over to the **Source** tab, and you'll see your break point hit, as highlighted in blue here:

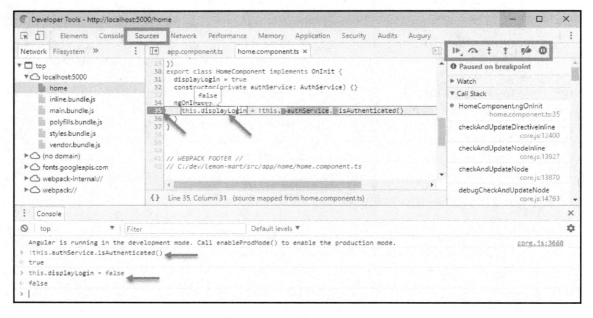

Chrome Dev Tools break point debugging

5. Hover over `this.displayLogin` and observe that its value is set to `true`
6. If hovering over `this.authService.isAuthenticated()`, you will not be able to observe its value

    While your break point is hit, you can access the current scope of the state in the console, which means you can execute the function and observe its value.

7. Execute `isAuthenticated()` in the console:

```
> !this.authService.isAuthenticated()
true
```

You'll observe that it returns `true`, which is what `this.displayLogin` is set to. You can still coerce the value of `displayLogin` in the console.

8. Set `displayLogin` to `false`:

```
> this.displayLogin = false
false
```

If you observe the value of `displayLogin`, either by hovering over it or retrieving it from the control, you'll see that the value is set to `false`.

Leveraging break point debugging basics, you can debug complicated scenarios without changing your source code at all.

Router Tree

The **Router Tree** tab will display the current state of the router. This can be a very helpful tool in visualizing the relationship between routes and components, as shown:

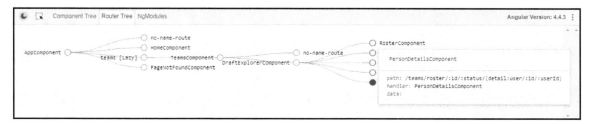

Augury Router Tree

The preceding router tree demonstrates a deeply nested routing structure with master-detail views. You can see the absolute path and parameters required to render a given component by clicking on the circular node.

As you can see, for `PersonDetailsComponent`, it can get complicated to determine, exactly, the set of parameters needed to render this detail portion of a master-detail view.

NgModules

The **NgModules** tab displays the `AppModule` and any other submodule that is currently loaded into memory:

1. Launch the `/home` route of the app
2. Observe the **NgModules** tab, as follows:

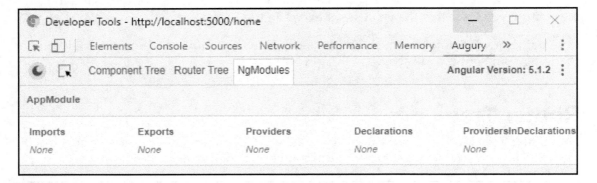

Augury NgModules

You'll note that only the `AppModule` is loaded. However, since our application has a lazy-loaded architecture, none of our other modules are yet loaded.

3. Navigate to a page in the `ManagerModule`
4. Then, navigate to a page in the `UserModule`
5. Finally, navigate back to the `/home` route

6. Observe the **NgModules** tab, as shown:

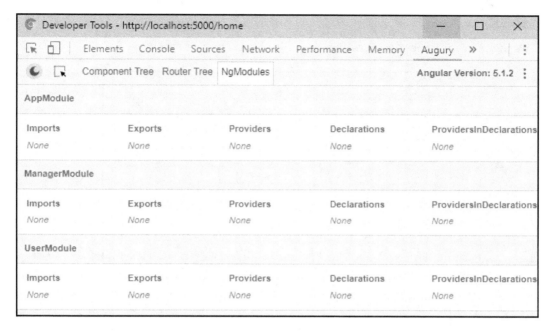

Augury NgModules with Three Modules

7. Now, you'll observe that three modules have been loaded into memory.

NgModules is an important tool to visualize the impact of your design and architecture.

Submodules with lazy loading

Lazy loading allows the Angular build process, powered by webpack, to separate our web application into different JavaScript files called chunks. By separating out portions of the application into separate submodules, we allow these modules and their dependencies to be bundled into separate chunks, thus keeping the initial JavaScript bundle size to a minimum. As the application grows, the time to first meaningful paint remains a constant, instead of consistently increasing over time. Lazy loading is critical to achieving a scalable application architecture.

We will now go over how to set up a submodule with components and routes. We will also use Augury to observe the effects of our various router configurations.

Configuring submodules with components and routes

The manager module needs a landing page, as shown in this mock-up:

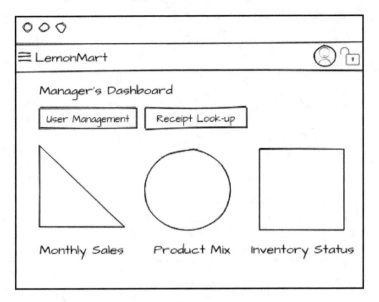

Manager's Dashboard

Let's start by creating the home screen for the `ManagerModule`:

1. Create the `ManagerHome` component:

```
$ npx ng g c manager/managerHome -m manager -s -t
```

In order to create the new component under the `manager` folder, we must prefix `manager/` in front of the component name. In addition, we specify that the component should be imported and declared with the `ManagerModule`. Since this is another landing page, it is unlikely to be complicated enough to require separate HTML and CSS files. You can use `--inline-style` (alias `-s`) and/or `--inline-template` (alias `-t`) to avoid creating additional files.

2. Verify that your folder structure looks as follows:

```
/src
├───────app
│   │
│   ├────────manager
│   │   │   manager-routing.module.ts
│   │   │   manager.module.ts
│   │   │
│   │   └────────manager-home
│   │   manager-home.component.spec.ts
│   │   manager-home.component.ts
```

3. Configure the `ManagerHome` component's route with `manager-routing.module`, similar to how we configured the `Home` component with `app-route.module`:

src/app/manager/manager-routing.module.ts
```
import { ManagerHomeComponent } from './manager-home/manager-
home.component'
import { ManagerComponent } from './manager.component'

const routes: Routes = [
  {
    path: '',
    component: ManagerComponent,
    children: [
      { path: '', redirectTo: '/manager/home', pathMatch: 'full' },
      { path: 'home', component: ManagerHomeComponent },
    ],
  },
]
```

You will note that `http://localhost:5000/manager` doesn't actually resolve to a component yet, because our Angular app isn't aware that `ManagerModule` exists. Let's first try the brute-force, eager-loading approach to import `manager.module` and register the manager route with our app.

Eager loading

This section is purely an exercise to demonstrate how the concepts we have learned so far in importing and registering routes doesn't result in a scalable solution, regardless of eagerly or lazily loading components:

1. Import the `manager.module` to `app.module`:

   src/app/app.module.ts
   ```
   import { ManagerModule } from './manager/manager.module'
   ...
     imports: [
   ...
       ManagerModule,
     ]
   ```

   You will note that `http://localhost:5000/manager` still doesn't render its home component.

2. Use **Augury** to debug the router state, as shown:

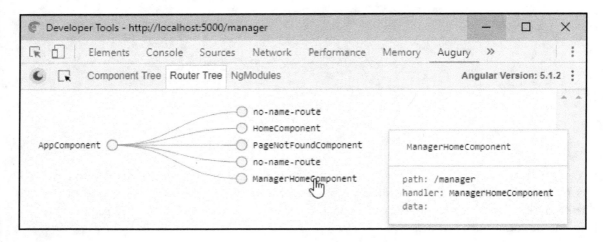

Router Tree with Eager Loading

3. It seems as if the `/manager` path is correctly registered and pointed at the correct component, `ManagerHomeComponent`. The issue here is that the `rootRouter` configured in `app-routing.module` isn't aware of the `/manager` path, so the `**` path is taking precedence and rendering the `PageNotFoundComponent` instead.

4. As a final exercise, implement the `'manager'` path in `app-routing.module` and assign `ManagerHomeComponent` to it as you would normally:

src/app/app-routing.module.ts
```
import { ManagerHomeComponent } from './manager/manager-
home/manager-home.component'
...
const routes: Routes = [
  ...
  { path: 'manager', component: ManagerHomeComponent },
  { path: '**', component: PageNotFoundComponent },
]
```

You'll now note that `http://localhost:5000/manager` renders correctly, by displaying `manager-home works!`; however, if you debug the router state through Augury, you will note that the `/manager` is registered twice.

This solution doesn't scale well, because it forces all developers to maintain a single master file to import and configure every module. It is ripe for merge conflicts and frustration, hoping that team members do not register the same route multiple times.

It is possible to engineer a solution to divide up the modules into multiple files. Instead of the standard `*-routing.module`, you can implement the Route array in `manager.module` and export it. Consider the following example:

example/manager/manager.module
```
export const managerModuleRoutes: Routes = [
  { path: '', component: ManagerHomeComponent }
]
```

These files will then need to be individually imported into `app-routing.module` and configured using the `children` attribute:

example/app-routing.module
```
import { managerModuleRoutes } from './manager/manager.module'
...
{ path: 'manager', children: managerModuleRoutes },
```

This solution will work and it is a correct solution, as demonstrated by the Augury Router tree here:

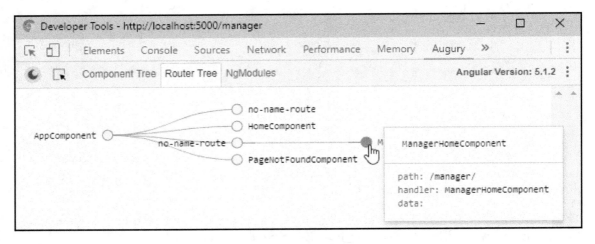

Router Tree with children routes

There are no duplicate registrations, because we removed `manager-routing.module`. In addition, we don't have to import `ManagerHomeComponent` outside of `manager.module`, resulting in a much better scalable solution. However, as the app grows, we must still register modules with `app.module`, and the submodules are still coupled to the parent `app.module` in potentially unpredictable ways. Further, this code can't be chunked, because any code that is imported using import is viewed as a hard dependency.

Lazy loading

Now that you understand how eager-loading of modules work, you will be able to better understand the code we are about to write, which may otherwise seem like black-magic, and magical (aka misunderstood) code always leads to spaghetti architectures.

We will now evolve the eager-loading solution to be a lazy-loading one. In order to load routes from a different module, we know we can't simply import them, otherwise they will be eagerly loaded. The answer lies in configuring a route using the `loadChildren` attribute with string informing the Router how to load a submodule in `app-routing.module.ts`:

1. Ensure that any module you intend to lazy load is *not* imported in `app.module`

2. Remove any routes added to `ManagerModule`
3. Ensure that `ManagerRoutingModule` is imported into `ManagerModule`
4. Implement or update the manager path with the `loadChildren` attribute:

src/app/app-routing.module.ts
```
import {
  ...
  const routes: Routes = [
    ...
    { path: 'manager', loadChildren:
'./manager/manager.module#ManagerModule' },
    { path: '**', component: PageNotFoundComponent },
  ]
  ...
```

 Lazy loading is achieved via a clever trick that avoids using an `import` statement. A string literal with two parts is defined, where the first part defines the location of the module file, such as `app/manager/manager.module`, and the second part defines the class name of the module. A string can be interpreted during the build process and at runtime, to dynamically create chunks, load the right module and instantiate the correct class. `ManagerModule` then acts as if its own Angular app and manages all of its children dependencies and routes.

5. Update the `manager-routing.module` routes, considering that manager is now their root route:

src/app/manager/manager-routing.module.ts
```
const routes: Routes = [
  { path: '', redirectTo: '/manager/home', pathMatch: 'full' },
  { path: 'home', component: ManagerHomeComponent },
]
```

We can now update the route for `ManagerHomeComponent` to a more meaningful `'home'` path. This path won't clash with the one found in `app-routing.module`, because in this context, `'home'` resolves to `'manager/home'` and, similarly, where path is empty, the URL will look like `http://localhost:5000/manager`.

6. Confirm that lazy loading is working by looking at Augury, as follows:

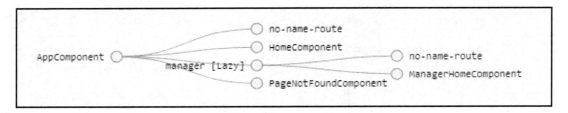

Router Tree with lazy loading

 The root node for ManagerHomeComponent is now named manager [Lazy].

Completing the walking skeleton

Using the sitemap, we have created for LemonMart, from earlier in the chapter, we need to complete the walking skeleton navigation experience for the app. In order to create this experience, we will need to create some buttons to link all modules and components together. We will go to this module by module:

- Before we start, update the login button on home.component to link to the Manager module:

src/app/home/home.component.ts

```
...
<button mat-raised-button color="primary"
routerLink="/manager">Login as Manager</button>
...
```

Manager module

Since we already enabled lazy loading for ManagerModule, let's go ahead and complete the rest of the navigational elements for it.

In the current setup, `ManagerHomeComponent` renders in the `<router-outlet>` defined in `app.component`, so when the user navigates from `HomeComponent` to `ManagerHomeComponent`, the toolbar implemented in `app.component` remains a constant. If we implement a similar toolbar that persists throughout `ManagerModule`, we can create a consistent UX for navigating subpages across modules.

For this to work, we need to replicate the parent-child relationship between `app.component` and `home/home.component`, where the parent implements the toolbar and a `<router-outlet>` so that children elements can be rendered in there:

1. Start by creating the base `manager` component:

   ```
   $ npx ng g c manager/manager -m manager --flat -s -t
   ```

   The `--flat` option skips directory creation and places the component directly under the `manager` folder, just like `app.component` residing directly under the `app` folder.

2. Implement a navigational toolbar with `activeLink` tracking:

   src/app/manager/manager.component.ts
   ```
   styles: [`
     div[fxLayout] {margin-top: 32px; }
     `,`
     .active-link {
       font-weight: bold;
       border-bottom: 2px solid #005005;
     }`
   ],
   template: `
     <mat-toolbar color="accent">
       <a mat-button routerLink="/manager/home"
   routerLinkActive="active-link">Manager's Dashboard</a>
       <a mat-button routerLink="/manager/users"
   routerLinkActive="active-link">User Management</a>
       <a mat-button routerLink="/manager/receipts"
   routerLinkActive="active-link">Receipt Lookup</a>
     </mat-toolbar>
     <router-outlet></router-outlet>
     `
   ```

It must be noted that submodules don't automatically have access to services or components created in parent modules. This is an important default behavior to preserve a decoupled architecture. However, there are certain cases where it is desirable to share some amount of code. In this case, `mat-toolbar` needs to be reimported. Since the `MatToolbarModule` is already loaded in `src/app/material.module.ts`, we can just import this module into `manager.module.ts` and there will not be a performance or memory penalty for doing so.

3. `ManagerComponent` should be imported into `ManagerModule`:

src/app/manager/manager.module.ts
```
import { MaterialModule } from '../material.module'
import { ManagerComponent } from './manager.component'
...
imports: [... MaterialModule, ManagerComponent],
```

4. Create components for the subpages:

```
$ npx ng g c manager/userManagement -m manager
$ npx ng g c manager/receiptLookup -m manager
```

5. Create the parent/children routing. We know that we need the following routes to be able to navigate to our subpages, as follows:

example
```
{ path: '', redirectTo: '/manager/home', pathMatch: 'full' },
{ path: 'home', component: ManagerHomeComponent },
{ path: 'users', component: UserManagementComponent },
{ path: 'receipts', component: ReceiptLookupComponent },
```

In order to target the `<router-outlet>` defined in `manager.component`, we need to create a parent route first and then specify routes for the subpages:

src/app/manager/manager-routing.module.ts
```
...
const routes: Routes = [
  {
    path: '', component: ManagerComponent, children: [
      { path: '', redirectTo: '/manager/home', pathMatch: 'full' },
      { path: 'home', component: ManagerHomeComponent },
```

```
            { path: 'users', component: UserManagementComponent },
            { path: 'receipts', component: ReceiptLookupComponent },
        ]
    },
]
```

You should now be able to navigate through the app. When you click on the **Login as Manager** button, you will be taken to the page shown here. The clickable targets are highlighted, as shown:

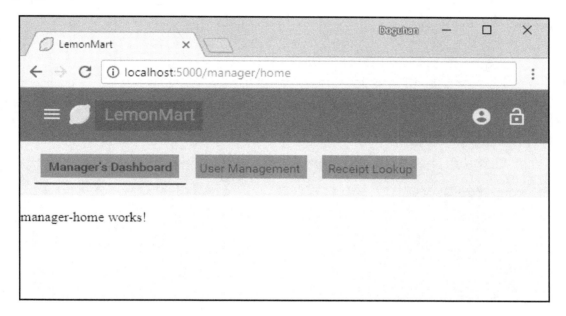

Manager's Dashboard with clickable targets highlighted

If you click on **LemonMart**, you will be taken to the home page. If you click on **Manager's Dashboard**, **User Management** or **Receipt Lookup**, you will be navigated to the corresponding subpage, while active link will be bold and underlined on the toolbar.

User module

Upon login, users will be able to access their profiles and view a list of actions they can access in the LemonMart app through a side navigation menu. In Chapter 14, *Design Authentication and Authorization*, when we implement authentication and authorization, we will be receiving the role of the user from the server. Based on the role of the user, we will be able to automatically navigate or limit the options users can see. We will implement these components in this module so that they will only be loaded once a user is logged in. For the purpose of completing the walking skeleton, we will ignore authentication-related concerns:

1. Create the necessary components:

```
$ npx ng g c user/profile -m user
$ npx ng g c user/logout -m user -t -s
$ npx ng g c user/navigationMenu -m user -t -s
```

2. Implement routing:

Start with implementing the lazy loading in app-routing:

src/app/app-routing.module.ts
```
...
  { path: 'user', loadChildren: 'app/user/user.module#UserModule' },
```

 Ensure that PageNotFoundComponent route is always the last route in app-routing.module.

Now implement the child routes in user-routing:

src/app/user/user-routing.module.ts
```
...
const routes: Routes = [
  { path: 'profile', component: ProfileComponent },
  { path: 'logout', component: LogoutComponent },
]
```

We are implementing routing for `NavigationMenuComponent`, because it'll be directly used as an HTML element. In addition, since `userModule` doesn't have a landing page, there's no default path defined.

3. Wire up the user and logout icons:

   src/app/app.component.ts
   ```
   ...
   <mat-toolbar>
     ...
     <button mat-mini-fab routerLink="/user/profile"
   matTooltip="Profile" aria-label="User Profile"><mat-
   icon>account_circle</mat-icon></button>
     <button mat-mini-fab routerLink="/user/logout"
   matTooltip="Logout" aria-label="Logout"><mat-icon>lock_open</mat-
   icon></button>
   </mat-toolbar>
   ```

 Icon buttons can be cryptic, so it's a good idea to add tooltips to them. In order for tooltips to work, switch from the `mat-icon-button` directive to the `mat-mini-fab` directive and ensure that you import `MatTooltipModule` in `material.module`. In addition, ensure that you add `aria-label` for icon only buttons so that users with disabilities relying on screen readers can still navigate your web application.

4. Ensure that the app works.

   You'll note that the two buttons are too close to each other, as follows:

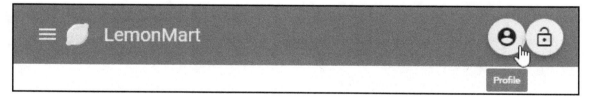

Toolbar with icons

5. You can fix the icon layout issue by adding `fxLayoutGap="8px"` to `<mat-toolbar>`; however, now the lemon logo is too far apart from the app name, as shown:

Toolbar with padded icons

6. The logo layout issue can be fixed by merging the icon and the button:

src/app/app.component.ts

```
...
<mat-toolbar>
  ...
  <a mat-icon-button routerLink="/home"><mat-icon
svgIcon="lemon"></mat-icon><span class="mat-
h2">LemonMart</span></a>
  ...
</mat-toolbar>
```

As shown in the following screenshot, the grouping fixes the layout issue:

Toolbar with grouped and padded elements

This is a more desirable from a UX perspective as well; now users can go back to the home page by clicking on the lemon as well.

POS and inventory modules

Our walking skeleton presumes the role of the manager. To be able to access all components we are about to create, we need to enable the manager to be able to access pos and inventory modules.

Update `ManagerComponent` with two new buttons:

```
src/app/manager/manager.component.ts
<mat-toolbar color="accent" fxLayoutGap="8px">
   ...
  <span class="flex-spacer"></span>
  <button mat-mini-fab routerLink="/inventory"
matTooltip="Inventory" aria-label="Inventory"><mat-icon>list</mat-
icon></button>
    <button mat-mini-fab routerLink="/pos" matTooltip="POS" aria-
label="POS"><mat-icon>shopping_cart</mat-icon></button>
</mat-toolbar>
```

Note that these router links will navigate use out of `ManagerModule`, so it is normal for the toolbar to disappear.

Now, it'll be up to you to implement the last two remaining modules.

POS module

POS module is very similar to the user module, except that `PosComponent` will be the default route. This will be a complicated component with some subcomponents, so ensure that it is created with a directory:

1. Create the `PosComponent`
2. Register `PosComponent` as the default route
3. Configure lazy loading for `PosModule`
4. Ensure that the app works

Inventory module

Inventory module is very similar to `ManagerModule`, as shown:

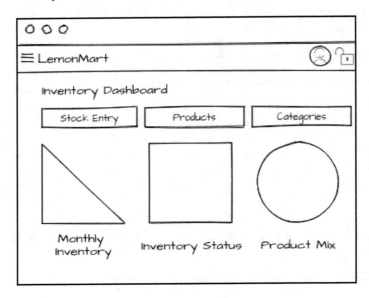

Inventory Dashboard mock-up

1. Create a base `Inventory` component
2. Register the `MaterialModule`
3. Create **Inventory Dashboard**, **Stock Entry**, **Products**, and **Categories** components
4. Configure parent-children routes in `inventory-routing.module`
5. Configure lazy loading for `InventoryModule`

6. Ensure that app works, as shown:

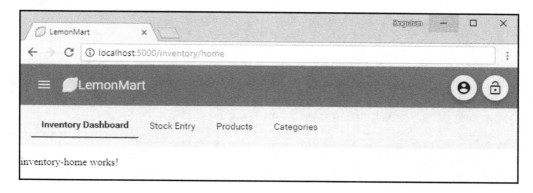

LemonMart Inventory Dashboard

Now that the walking skeleton of the app is completed, it is important to inspect the router tree to ensure that lazy loading has been configured correctly and module aren't unintentionally being eager loaded.

Inspect router tree

Navigate to the base route of the app and use Augury to inspect the router tree, as illustrated:

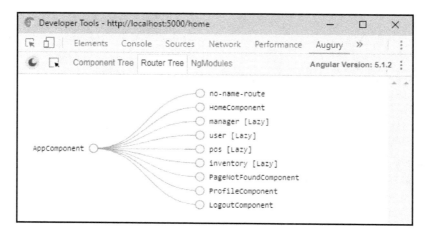

Router Tree with eager loading mistakes

Everything, but initially required components, should be denoted with the **[Lazy]** attribute. If, for some reason, routes are not denoted with **[Lazy]**, chances are that they are mistakenly being imported in `app.module` or some other component.

In the preceding screenshot, you may note that `ProfileComponent` and `LogoutComponent` are eagerly loaded, whereas the `user` module is correctly labeled as **[Lazy]**. Even multiple visual inspections through the tooling and the code base may leave you searching for the culprit. However, if you run a global search for `UserModule`, you'll quickly discover that it was being imported into `app.module`.

To be on the safe side make sure to remove any import statements for modules in `app.module` and your file should look like the one below:

src/app/app.module.ts
```
import { FlexLayoutModule } from '@angular/flex-layout'
import { BrowserModule } from '@angular/platform-browser'
import { NgModule } from '@angular/core'

import { AppRoutingModule } from './app-routing.module'
import { AppComponent } from './app.component'
import { BrowserAnimationsModule } from '@angular/platform-
browser/animations'
import { MaterialModule } from './material.module'
import { HomeComponent } from './home/home.component'
import { PageNotFoundComponent } from './page-not-found/page-not-
found.component'
import { HttpClientModule } from '@angular/common/http'

@NgModule({
  declarations: [AppComponent, HomeComponent, PageNotFoundComponent],
  imports: [
    BrowserModule,
    AppRoutingModule,
    BrowserAnimationsModule,
    MaterialModule,
    HttpClientModule,
    FlexLayoutModule,
  ],
  providers: [],
  bootstrap: [AppComponent],
})
export class AppModule {}
```

The next screenshot shows the corrected router tree:

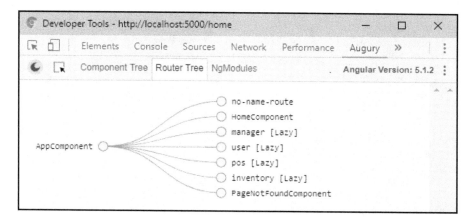

Router Tree with lazy loading

Ensure that `npm test` and `npm run e2e` executes without errors before moving on.

Common Testing Module

Now that we have a lot of modules to deal with, it becomes tedious to configure the imports and providers for each spec file individually. For this purpose, I recommend creating a common testing module to contain generic configuration that you can reuse across the board.

First start by creating a new `.ts` file.

1. Create `common/common.testing.ts`
2. Populate it with common testing providers, fakes and modules, shown as follows:

I have provided fake implementations of `ObservableMedia`, `MatIconRegistry`, `DomSanitizer`, along with arrays for `commonTestingProviders` and `commonTestingModules`.

```
src/app/common/common.testing.ts
import { HttpClientTestingModule } from '@angular/common/http/testing'
import { MediaChange } from '@angular/flex-layout'
import { FormsModule, ReactiveFormsModule } from '@angular/forms'
import { SafeResourceUrl, SafeValue } from '@angular/platform-browser'
import { NoopAnimationsModule } from '@angular/platform-browser/animations'
```

```
// tslint:disable-next-line:max-line-length
import { SecurityContext } from '@angular/platform-
browser/src/security/dom_sanitization_service'
import { RouterTestingModule } from '@angular/router/testing'
import { Observable, Subscription, of } from 'rxjs'
import { MaterialModule } from '../material.module'

const FAKE_SVGS = {
  lemon: '<svg><path id="lemon" name="lemon"></path></svg>',
}

export class ObservableMediaFake {
  isActive(query: string): boolean {
    return false
  }

  asObservable(): Observable<MediaChange> {
    return of({} as MediaChange)
  }

  subscribe(
    next?: (value: MediaChange) => void,
    error?: (error: any) => void,
    complete?: () => void
  ): Subscription {
    return new Subscription()
  }
}

export class MatIconRegistryFake {
  _document = document
  addSvgIcon(iconName: string, url: SafeResourceUrl): this {
    // this.addSvgIcon('lemon', 'lemon.svg')
    return this
  }

  getNamedSvgIcon(name: string, namespace: string = ''):
Observable<SVGElement> {
    return of(this._svgElementFromString(FAKE_SVGS.lemon))
  }

  private _svgElementFromString(str: string): SVGElement {
    if (this._document || typeof document !== 'undefined') {
      const div = (this._document || document).createElement('DIV')
      div.innerHTML = str
      const svg = div.querySelector('svg') as SVGElement
      if (!svg) {
        throw Error('<svg> tag not found')
```

```
        }
        return svg
      }
    }
  }
}

export class DomSanitizerFake {
  bypassSecurityTrustResourceUrl(url: string): SafeResourceUrl {
    return {} as SafeResourceUrl
  }
  sanitize(context: SecurityContext, value: SafeValue | string | null):
string | null {
    return value ? value.toString() : null
  }
}

export const commonTestingProviders: any[] = [
  // intentionally left blank
]

export const commonTestingModules: any[] = [
  FormsModule,
  ReactiveFormsModule,
  MaterialModule,
  NoopAnimationsModule,
  HttpClientTestingModule,
  RouterTestingModule,
]
```

Now let's see a sample use of this shared configuration file:

src/app/app.component.spec.ts
```
import {
  commonTestingModules,
  commonTestingProviders,
  MatIconRegistryFake,
  DomSanitizerFake,
  ObservableMediaFake,
} from './common/common.testing'
import { ObservableMedia } from '@angular/flex-layout'
import { MatIconRegistry } from '@angular/material'
import { DomSanitizer } from '@angular/platform-browser'

...
TestBed.configureTestingModule({
    imports: commonTestingModules,
    providers: commonTestingProviders.concat([
      { provide: ObservableMedia, useClass: ObservableMediaFake },
```

```
            { provide: MatIconRegistry, useClass: MatIconRegistryFake },
            { provide: DomSanitizer, useClass: DomSanitizerFake },
        ]),
        declarations: [AppComponent],
    ...
```

Most other modules will just need `commonTestingModules` to be imported.

Don't move on until all your tests are passing!

Summary

In this chapter, you mastered how to effectively use Angular CLI to create major Angular components and scaffolds. You created the branding of your app, leveraging custom and built-in Material iconography. You learned how to debug complicated Angular apps with Augury. Finally, you began building Router-first apps, defining user roles early on, designing with lazy loading in mind and nailing down a walking-skeleton navigation experience early on.

To recap, in order to pull off a Router-first implementation, you need to do this:

1. Define user roles early on
2. Design with lazy loading in mind
3. Implement a walking-skeleton navigation experience
4. Design around major data components
5. Enforce a decoupled component architecture
6. Differentiate between user controls and components
7. Maximize code reuse

In this chapter, you executed steps 1-3; in the next three chapters, you will execute steps 4-7. In Chapter 13, *Continuous Integration and API Design,* we will go over designing around major data components and enable Continuous Integration to ensure a high-quality deliverable. In Chapter 14, *Design Authentication and Authorization*, we will deep dive into security considerations and design a conditional navigation experience. In Chapter 15, *Angular App Design and Recipes*, we will tie everything together by sticking to a decoupled component architecture, smartly choosing between creating user controls versus components and maximizing code reuse with various TypeScript, RxJS, and Angular coding techniques.

Continuous Integration and API Design
13

Before we start building more complicated features for our LOB app, LemonMart, we need to ensure that every code push we create has passing tests, adheres to the coding standards, and is an executable artifact that team members can run tests against, as we continue to further develop our application. Simultaneously, we need to start thinking about how our application will communicate with a backend server. Whether you, your team or another team will be creating the new APIs, it will be important that the API design accommodates the needs of both the frontend and backend architectures. To ensure a smooth development process, a robust mechanism is needed to create an accessible, living piece of documentation for the API. **Continuous Integration** (**CI**) can solve the first problem and Swagger is perfect to address API design, documentation, and testing needs.

Continuous Integration is critical to ensuring a quality deliverable by building and executing tests on every code push. Setting up a CI environment can be time consuming and requires specialized knowledge of the tool being used. CircleCI is an established, cloud-based CI service with a free tier and helpful articles to get you started with as little configuration as possible. We will go over a Docker-based approach that can be run on most CI services, keeping your specific configuration knowledge relevant and CI service knowledge down to a minimum.

Another aspect of full-stack development is that you will likely be developing the frontend and backend of your application around the same time. Whether you work by yourself, as a team, or with multiple teams, it is critical to establish a data contract to ensure that you won't run into eleventh-hour integration challenges. We will use Swagger to define a data contract for a REST API and then create a mock server that your Angular application can make HTTP calls to. For backend development, Swagger can act as a great starting point to generate boilerplate code and can go forward as living documentation and testing UI for your API.

In this chapter, you will learn how to do the following:

- CI with CircleCI
- API design with Swagger

This chapter requires the following:

- A free CircleCI account
- Docker

Continuous Integration

The aim of Continuous Integration is to enable a consistent and repeatable environment to build, test, and generate deployable artifacts of your application with every code push. Before a pushing code, a developer should have a reasonable expectation that their build will pass; therefore creating a reliable CI environment that automates commands that developers can also run in their local machines is paramount.

Containerizing build environment

In order to ensure a consistent build environment across various OS platforms, developer machines, and Continuous Integration environments, you may containerize your build environment. Note that there are at least half-a-dozen common CI tools currently in use. Learning the ins and outs of each tool is almost an impossible task to achieve. Containerization of your build environment is an advanced concept that goes above and beyond of what is currently expected of CI tools. However, containerization is a great way to standardize over 90% of your build infrastructure, and can be executed in almost any CI environment. With this approach, the skills you learn and the build configuration you create becomes far more valuable, because both your knowledge and the tools you create become transferable and reusable.

There are many strategies to containerize your build environment with different levels of granularity and performance expectations. For the purpose of this book, we will focus on reusability and ease of use. Instead of creating a complicated, interdependent set of Docker images that may allow for more efficient fail-first and recovery paths, we will focus on a single and straightforward workflow. Newer versions of Docker have a great feature called multi-stage builds, which allow you to define a multi image process in an easy-to-read manner and maintain a singular `Dockerfile`.

At the end of the process, you can extract an optimized container image as our deliverable artifact, shedding the complexity of images used previously in the process.

As a reminder your single `Dockerfile` would look like the sample below:

```
Dockerfile
FROM duluca/minimal-node-web-server:8.11.1
WORKDIR /usr/src/app
COPY dist public
```

Multi-stage works by using multiple `FROM` statements in a single `Dockerfile`, where each stage can perform a task and make any resources within its instance available to other stages. In a build environment, we can implement various build-related tasks as their own stages, and then copy the end result, such as the `dist` folder of an Angular build to the final image, which contains a web server. In this case, we will implement three stages of images:

- **Builder**: Used to build a production version of your Angular app
- **Tester**: Used to run unit and e2e tests against a headless Chrome instances
- **Web Server**: The final result only containing the optimized production bits

 Multi-stage builds require Docker version 17.05 or higher. To read more about multi-stage builds, read the documentation at `https://docs.docker.com/develop/develop-images/multistage-build/`.

Start by creating a new file to implement the multi-stage configuration, named `Dockerfile.integration`, at the root of your project.

Builder

The first stage is `builder`. We need a lightweight build environment that can ensure consistent builds across the board. For this purpose, I've created a sample Alpine-based Node build environment complete with npm, bash, and git tools. For more information on why we're using Alpine and Node, refer to `Chapter 10`, *Prepare Angular App for Production Release*, in the *Containerizing the App using Docker* section:

1. Implement a new npm script to build your Angular app:

```
"scripts": {
  "build:prod": "ng build --prod",
}
```

2. Inherit from a Node.js based build environment like `node:10.1`
   or `duluca/minimal-node-build-env:8.11.2`

3. Implement your environment specific build script, as shown here:

Note that at the time of publishing a bug in low-level npm tooling is preventing `node` based images from successfully installing Angular dependencies. This means that the sample `Dockerfile` below is based on an older version of Node and npm with `duluca/minimal-node-build-env:8.9.4`. In the future, when the bugs are sorted out an updated build environment will be able to leverage `npm ci` to install dependencies, which brings significant speed gains over the `npm install` command.

`Dockerfile.integration`

```
FROM duluca/minimal-node-build-env:8.9.4 as builder

# project variables
ENV SRC_DIR /usr/src
ENV GIT_REPO https://github.com/duluca/lemon-mart.git
ENV SRC_CODE_LOCATION .
ENV BUILD_SCRIPT build:prod

# get source code
RUN mkdir -p $SRC_DIR
WORKDIR $SRC_DIR
# if necessary, do SSH setup here or copy source code from local or
CI environment
RUN git clone $GIT_REPO .
# COPY $SRC_CODE_LOCATION .

RUN npm install
RUN npm run $BUILD_SCRIPT
```

In the preceding example, the source code is being pulled from GitHub by the container. I have chosen to do that for the sake of keeping the sample simple, because it works the same way in both local and remote continuous integration environments. However, your CI server will already have a copy of the source code, which you'll want to copy from your CI environment and then into the container.

Instead of the `RUN git clone $GIT_REPO` . command, you can copy source code with the `COPY $SRC_CODE_LOCATION` . command from your CI server or your local machine. If you do this, you will have to implement a `.dockerignore` file that somewhat resembles your `.gitignore` file to ensure that secrets aren't leaked, `node_modules` is not copied and the configuration is repeatable in other environments. In a CI environment, you will want to override the environment variable `$SRC_CODE_LOCATION` so that the source directory of the `COPY` command is correct. Feel free to create multiple versions of the `Dockerfile` that may fit your various needs.

In addition, I have built a minimal Node build environment `duluca/minimal-node-build-env` based on `node-alpine`, which you can observe on Docker Hub at `https://hub.docker.com/r/duluca/minimal-node-build-env`. This image is about ten times smaller than `node`. The size of Docker images have a real impact on build times, since the CI server or your team members will spend extra time pulling a larger image. Choose the environment that best fits your needs.

Debugging build environment

Depending on your particular needs, your initial setup of the builder portion of the `Dockerfile` may be frustrating. To test out new commands or debug errors, you may need to directly interact with the build environment.

To interactively experiment and/or debug within the build environment, execute the following:

```
$ docker run -it duluca/minimal-node-build-env:8.9.4 /bin/bash
```

You can test or debug commands within this temporary environment before baking them into your `Dockerfile`.

Tester

The second stage is `tester`. By default, the Angular CLI generates a testing requirement that is geared toward a development environment. This will not work in a continuous integration environment; we must configure Angular to work against a headless browser that can execute without the assistance of a GPU and further, a containerized environment to execute the tests against.

Configuring a headless browser for Angular

The protractor testing tool officially supports running against Chrome in headless mode. In order to execute Angular tests in a continuous integration environment, you will need to configure your test runner, Karma, to run with a headless Chrome instance:

1. Update `karma.conf.js` to include a new headless browser option:

   src/karma.conf.js

   ```
   ...
   browsers: ['Chrome', 'ChromiumHeadless', 'ChromiumNoSandbox'],
   customLaunchers: {
     ChromiumHeadless: {
           base: 'Chrome',
           flags: [
             '--headless',
             '--disable-gpu',
             // Without a remote debugging port, Google Chrome exits
   immediately.
             '--remote-debugging-port=9222',
           ],
           debug: true,
       },
       ChromiumNoSandbox: {
         base: 'ChromiumHeadless',
         flags: ['--no-sandbox', '--disable-translate', '--disable-
   extensions']
         }
       },
   ```

The `ChromiumNoSandbox` custom launcher encapsulates all the configuration elements needed for a good default setup.

2. Update `protractor` configuration to run in headless mode:

e2e/protractor.conf.js
```
...
  capabilities: {
    browserName: 'chrome',
    chromeOptions: {
      args: [
        '--headless',
        '--disable-gpu',
        '--no-sandbox',
        '--disable-translate',
        '--disable-extensions',
        '--window-size=800,600',
      ],
    },
  },
...
```

 In order to test your application for responsive scenarios, you can use the `--window-size` option, as shown earlier, to change the browser settings.

3. Update the `package.json` scripts to select the new browser option in production build scenarios:

package.json
```
"scripts": {
  ...
  "test:prod": "npm test -- --watch=false"
  ...
}
```

 Note that `test:prod` doesn't include `npm run e2e`. e2e tests are integration tests that take longer to execute, so think twice about including them as part of your critical build pipeline. e2e tests will not run on the lightweight testing environment mentioned in the next section, so they will require more resources and time to execute.

Configuring testing environment

For a lightweight testing environment, we will be leveraging an Alpine-based installation of the Chromium browser:

1. Inherit from `slapers/alpine-node-chromium`
2. Append the following configuration to `Docker.integration`:

    Docker.integration
    ```
    ...
    FROM slapers/alpine-node-chromium as tester
    ENV BUILDER_SRC_DIR /usr/src
    ENV SRC_DIR /usr/src
    ENV TEST_SCRIPT test:prod

    RUN mkdir -p $SRC_DIR
    WORKDIR $SRC_DIR

    COPY --from=builder $BUILDER_SRC_DIR $SRC_DIR

    CMD 'npm run $TEST_SCRIPT'
    ```

The preceding script will copy the production build from the `builder` stage and execute your test scripts in a predictable manner.

Web server

The third and final stage generates the container that will be your web server. Once this stage is complete, the prior stages will be discarded and the end result will be an optimized sub-10 MB container:

1. Containerize your application with Docker
2. Append the `FROM` statement at the end of the file
3. `COPY` the production ready code from `builder` as shown here:

    Docker.integration
    ```
    ...
    FROM duluca/minimal-nginx-web-server:1.13.8-alpine
    ENV BUILDER_SRC_DIR /usr/src
    COPY --from=builder $BUILDER_SRC_DIR/dist /var/www
    CMD 'nginx'
    ```

4. Build and test your multi-stage `Dockerfile`:

```
$ docker build -f Dockerfile.integration .
```

 If you are pulling code from GitHub, ensure that your code is committed and pushed before building the container, since it will pull your source code directly from the repository. Use the `--no-cache` option to ensure that new source code is pulled. If you are copying code from your local or CI environment, then do *not* use `--no-cache` as you won't the speed gains from being able to reuse previously built container layers.

5. Save your script as a new npm script named `build:ci` as shown:

package.json
```
"scripts": {
    . . .
    "build:ci": "docker build -f Dockerfile.integration . -t
$npm_package_config_imageRepo:latest",
    . . .
}
```

CircleCI

CircleCI makes it easy to get started with a free tier and great documentation for beginners and pros alike. If you have unique enterprise needs, CircleCI can be brought on premise, behind corporate firewalls, or as a private deployment in the cloud.

CircleCI has pre-baked build environments for virtual configuration of free setups, but it can also run builds using Docker containers, making it a solution that scales to user skills and needs, as mentioned in the *Containerizing Build Environment* section:

1. Create a CircleCI account at `https://circleci.com/`

2. Sign up with GitHub:

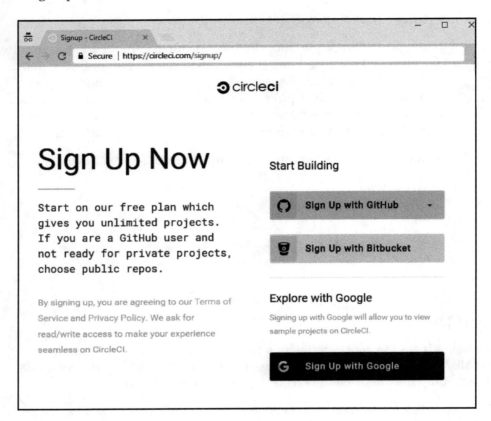

CircleCI Sign up page

3. Add a new project:

CircleCI Projects Page

On the next screen, you have an option to select **Linux** or **macOS** build environments. The macOS build environments are very useful for building iOS or macOS apps. However, there is no free-tier for those environments; only Linux instances with 1x parallelism are free.

4. Search for **lemon-mart** and click on **Setup project**
5. Select **Linux**
6. Select **Platform 2.0**
7. Select **Language** as **Other**, since we'll use a custom containerized build environment

8. In your source code, create a folder named `.circleci` and add a file named `config.yml`:

```
.circleci/config.yml
version: 2
jobs:
  build:
    docker:
      - image: docker:17.12.0-ce-git
    working_directory: /usr/src
    steps:
      - checkout
      - setup_remote_docker:
          docker_layer_caching: false
      - run:
          name: Build Docker Image
          command: |
            npm run build:ci
```

In the preceding file, a `build` job is defined, which is based on CircleCI's pre-built `docker:17.12.0-ce-git` image, containing the Docker and git CLI tools within itself. We then define build `steps`, which checks out the source code from GitHub with `checkout`, informs CircleCI to set up a Docker-within-Docker environment with the `setup_remote_docker` command and then executes the `docker build -f Dockerfile.integration .` command to initiate our custom build process.

> In order to optimize builds, you should experiment with layer caching and copying source code from the already checked out source code in CircleCI.

9. Sync your changes to Github
10. On CircleCI, click to **Create** your project

If everything goes well, you will have passing, *green*, build. As shown in the following screenshot, build #4 was successful:

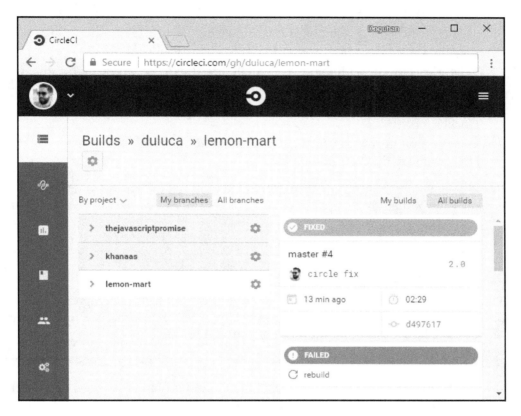

Green build on CircleCI

At the moment, the CI server is running, building the app in stage 1, then running the tests in stage 2, and then building the web server in stage 3. Note that we are not doing anything with this web server container image, such as deploying it to a server.

In order to deploy your image, you will need to implement a deploy step. In this step, you can deploy to a multitude of targets such as Docker Hub, Zeit Now, Heroku, or AWS ECS. The integration to these targets will involve multiple steps. At a highlevel, these steps are as follows:

1. Install target-specific CLI tool with a separate run step
2. Configure Docker with login credentials specific to the target environment, storing said credentials as CircleCI environment variables
3. Use `docker push` to submit the resulting web server image to the target's Docker registry
4. Execute a platform-specific `deploy` command to instruct the target to run the Docker image that was just pushed.

An example of how to configure such a deployment on AWS ECS from your local development environment is covered in `Chapter 16`, *Highly-Available Cloud Infrastructure on AWS*.

Code coverage report

A good way to understand the amount and the trends of unit tests coverage for your Angular project is through a code coverage report. In order to generate the report for your app, execute the following command from your project folder:

```
$ npx ng test --browsers ChromiumNoSandbox --watch=false --code-coverage
```

The resulting report will be created as HTML under a folder name coverage; execute the following command to view it in your browser:

```
$ npx http-server -c-1 -o -p 9875 ./coverage
```

Here's the folder-level sample coverage report generated by `istanbul.js` for LemonMart:

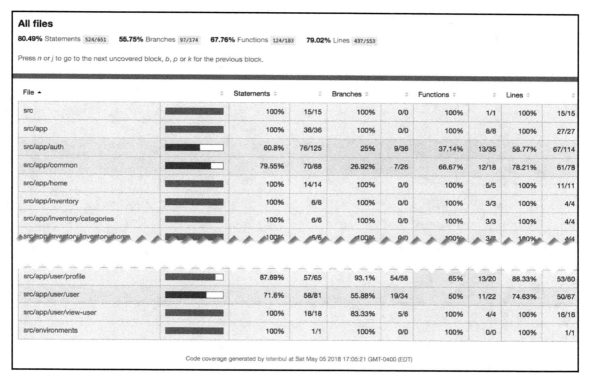

File ▲		Statements ⇕	⇕	Branches ⇕	⇕	Functions ⇕	⇕	Lines ⇕	⇕
src		100%	15/15	100%	0/0	100%	1/1	100%	15/15
src/app		100%	36/36	100%	0/0	100%	8/8	100%	27/27
src/app/auth		60.8%	76/125	25%	9/36	37.14%	13/35	58.77%	67/114
src/app/common		79.55%	70/88	26.92%	7/26	66.67%	12/18	78.21%	61/78
src/app/home		100%	14/14	100%	0/0	100%	5/5	100%	11/11
src/app/inventory		100%	6/6	100%	0/0	100%	3/3	100%	4/4
src/app/inventory/categories		100%	6/6	100%	0/0	100%	3/3	100%	4/4
src/app/inventory/inventory-home		100%	6/6	100%	0/0	100%	3/3	100%	4/4
src/app/user/profile		87.69%	57/65	93.1%	54/58	65%	13/20	88.33%	53/60
src/app/user/user		71.6%	58/81	55.88%	19/34	50%	11/22	74.63%	50/67
src/app/user/view-user		100%	18/18	83.33%	5/6	100%	4/4	100%	16/16
src/environments		100%	1/1	100%	0/0	100%	0/0	100%	1/1

All files

80.49% Statements 524/651   **55.75%** Branches 97/174   **67.76%** Functions 124/183   **79.02%** Lines 437/553

Press *n* or *j* to go to the next uncovered block, *b, p* or *k* for the previous block.

Code coverage generated by istanbul at Sat May 05 2018 17:05:21 GMT-0400 (EDT)

Istanbul code coverage report for LemonMart

You can drill down on a particular folder, like `src/app/auth`, and get a file-level report, as shown here:

All files src/app/auth

61.6% Statements 77/125   **25%** Branches 9/36   **38.24%** Functions 13/34   **59.65%** Lines 68/114

Press *n* or *j* to go to the next uncovered block, *b*, *p* or *k* for the previous block.

File		Statements		Branches		Functions		Lines	
auth-guard.service.ts		48.72%	19/39	0%	0/14	33.33%	3/9	47.22%	17/36
auth.service.fake.ts		84.62%	11/13	100%	0/0	60%	3/5	81.82%	9/11
auth.service.ts		57.69%	30/52	28.57%	4/14	21.43%	3/14	55.32%	26/47
cache.service.ts		75%	12/16	50%	3/6	60%	3/5	73.33%	11/15
role.enum.ts		100%	5/5	100%	2/2	100%	1/1	100%	5/5

Code coverage generated by istanbul at Thu May 10 2018 02:50:40 GMT-0400 (Eastern Daylight Time)

Istanbul code coverage report for src/app/auth

You can further drill down to get line-level coverage for a given file, like
`cache.service.ts`, as shown here:

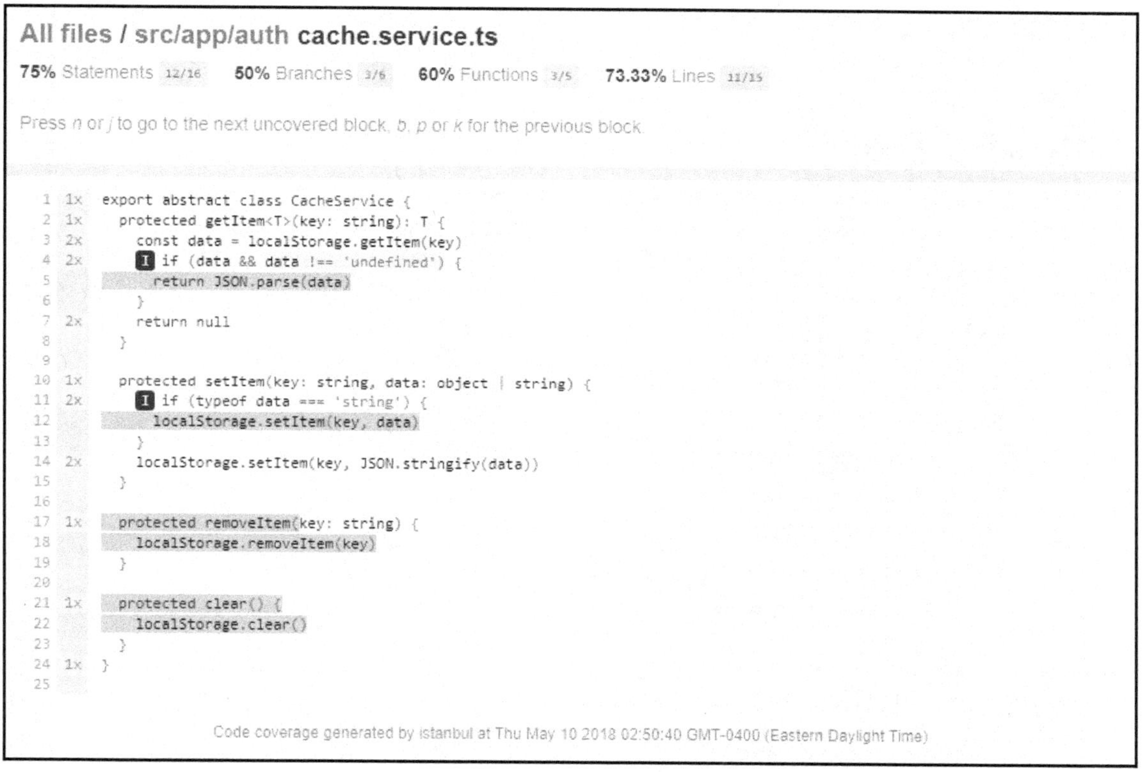

Istanbul Code Coverage Report for cache.service.ts

In the preceding image you can see that lines 5, 12, 17-18 and 21-22 are not covered by any
test. The **I** icon denotes that the if path was not taken. We can increase our code coverage
by implementing unit tests that exercise the functions that are contained within
`CacheService`. As an exercise, the reader should attempt to atleast cover one of these
functions with a new unit test and observe the code coverage report change.

Ideally, your CI server configuration should generate and host the code coverage report
with every test run in a readily accessible manner. Implement these commands as script in
`package.json` and execute them in your CI pipeline. This configuration is left as an
exercise for the reader.

Install `http-server` as a development dependency to your project.

API design

In full-stack development, nailing down the API design early on is important. The API design itself is closely correlated with how your data contract will look. You may create RESTful endpoints or use the next-gen GraphQL technology. In designing your API, frontend and backend developers should closely collaborate to achieve shared design goals. Some high-level goals are listed as follows:

- Minimize data transmitted between client and server
- Stick to well-established design patterns (that is, pagination)
- Design to reduce business logic present in the client
- Flatten data structures
- Do not expose database keys or relationships
- Version endpoints from the get go
- Design around major data components

It is important not to reinvent the wheel and take a disciplined, if not strict, approach to designing your API. The downstream effect of missteps in API design can be profound and impossible to correct once your application goes live.

I will go into details of designing around major data components and implement a sample Swagger endpoint.

Designing around major data components

It helps to organize your APIs around major data components. This will roughly match how you consume data in various components in your Angular application. We will start off by defining our major data components by creating a rough data entity diagram and then implementing a sample API for the user data entity with swagger.

Defining entities

Let's start by taking a stab at what kind of entities you would like to store and how these entities might relate to one another.

Here's a sample design for LemonMart, created using `draw.io`:

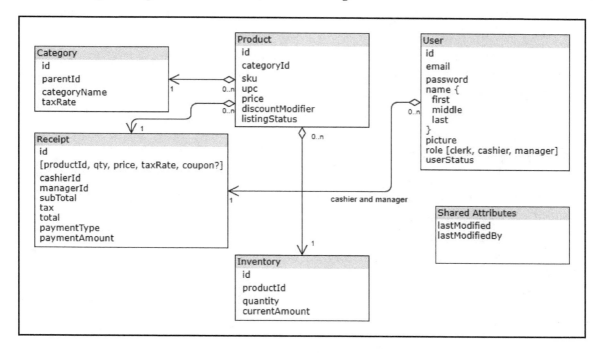

Data entity diagram for LemonMart

 At this moment, whether your entities are stored in a SQL or NoSQL database is inconsequential. My suggestion is to stick to what you know, but if you're starting from scratch, a NoSQL database like MongoDB will offer the most amount of flexibility as your implementation and requirements evolve.

Roughly speaking, you will need CRUD APIs for each entity. You can use Swagger to design your APIs.

Swagger

Swagger will allow you to design your web API. For teams, it can act as an interface between frontend and backend teams. Additionally, with API mocking, you can develop and complete API features before the implementation of the APIs even begins.

We will implement a sample Users API as we move on, to demonstrate how Swagger works.

The sample project comes with recommended extensions for VS Code. Swagger Viewer allows us to preview the YAML file without running any additional tools.

Defining a Swagger YAML file

The most widely used and supported version of the Swagger spec is `swagger: '2.0'`. The following example is given using the newer, standards-based, `openapi: 3.0.0`. The sample code repository contains both examples. However, at the time of publishing, most tooling in the Swagger ecosystem relies on version 2.0.

The sample code repository can be found at `github.com/duluca/lemon-mart-swagger-server`.

For your mock API server, you should create a separate git repository, so that this contract between your frontend and backend can be maintained separately.

1. Create a new GitHub repository, called `lemon-mart-swagger-server`
2. Start defining a YAML file with general information and target servers:

```
swagger.oas3.yaml
openapi: 3.0.0
info:
  title: LemonMart
  description: LemonMart API
  version: "1.0.0"

servers:
  - url: http://localhost:3000
    description: Local environment
  - url: https://mystagingserver.com/v1
    description: Staging environment
```

```
    – url: https://myprodserver.com/v1
      description: Production environment
```

3. Under `components`, define shared data `schemas`:

swagger.oas3.yaml

```
...
components:
  schemas:
    Role:
      type: string
      enum: [clerk, cashier, manager]
    Name:
      type: object
      properties:
        first:
          type: string
        middle:
          type: string
        last:
          type: string
    User:
      type: object
      properties:
        id:
          type: string
        email:
          type: string
        name:
          $ref: '#/components/schemas/Name'
        picture:
          type: string
        role:
          $ref: '#/components/schemas/Role'
        userStatus:
          type: boolean
        lastModified:
          type: string
          format: date
        lastModifiedBy:
          type: string
    Users:
      type: object
      properties:
        total:
          type: number
          format: int32
        items:
```

```
            $ref: '#/components/schemas/ArrayOfUser'
      ArrayOfUser:
        type: array
        items:
            $ref: '#/components/schemas/User'
```

4. Under `components`, add shared `parameters`, making it easy to reuse common patterns like paginated endpoints:

   swagger.oas3.yaml

```
  ...
    parameters:
      offsetParam: # <-- Arbitrary name for the definition that will
  be used to refer to it.
                      # Not necessarily the same as the parameter name.
        in: query
        name: offset
        required: false
        schema:
          type: integer
          minimum: 0
        description: The number of items to skip before starting to
  collect the result set.
      limitParam:
        in: query
        name: limit
        required: false
        schema:
          type: integer
          minimum: 1
          maximum: 50
          default: 20
        description: The numbers of items to return.
```

5. Under `paths`, define a `get` endpoint for the `/users` path:

```
  ...
  paths:
    /users:
      get:
        description: |
          Searches and returns `User` objects.
          Optional query params determines values of returned array
        parameters:
          - in: query
            name: search
            required: false
            schema:
```

```
        type: string
        description: Search text
    - $ref: '#/components/parameters/offsetParam'
    - $ref: '#/components/parameters/limitParam'
  responses:
    '200': # Response
      description: OK
      content: # Response body
        application/json: # Media type
          schema:
            $ref: '#/components/schemas/Users'
```

6. Under `paths`, add `get` user by ID and `update` user by ID endpoints:

swagger.oas3.yaml

```
...
  /user/{id}:
    get:
      description: Gets a `User` object by id
      parameters:
        - in: path
          name: id
          required: true
          schema:
            type: string
          description: User's unique id
      responses:
        '200': # Response
          description: OK
          content: # Response body
            application/json: # Media type
              schema:
                $ref: '#/components/schemas/User'
    put:
      description: Updates a `User` object given id
      parameters:
        - in: query
          name: id
          required: true
          schema:
            type: string
          description: User's unique id
        - in: body
          name: userData
          schema:
            $ref: '#/components/schemas/User'
          style: form
          explode: false
```

```
            description: Updated user object
        responses:
          '200':
            description: OK
            content: # Response body
                application/json: # Media type
                  schema:
                    $ref: '#/components/schemas/User'
```

To validate your Swagger file, you can use the online editor at `editor.swagger.io`.

Note the use of `style: form` and `explode: false`, which are the simplest way to configure an endpoint that expects basic form data. For more parameter serialization options or to simulate authentication endpoints and a slew of other possible configurations, refer to the documentation at `swagger.io/docs/specification/`.

Creating a Swagger server

Using your YAML file, you can generate a mock Node.js server using the Swagger Code Gen tool.

OpenAPI 3.0 with unofficial tooling

As mentioned in the earlier section, this section will use version 2 of the YAML file, which can generate a server using the official tooling. There are, however, other tools out there that can generate some code, but not complete enough to be easy to use:

1. If using OpenAPI 3.0 on the project folder, execute the following command:

```
$ npx swagger-node-codegen swagger.oas3.yaml -o ./server
...
Done!
Check out your shiny new API at C:\dev\lemon-mart-swagger-
server\server.
```

Under a new folder, called `server`, you should now have a Node Express server generated.

2. Install dependencies for the server:

```
$ cd server
$ npm install
```

You must then manually implement the missing stubs to complete the implementation of the server.

Swagger 2.0 with official tooling

Using official tooling and version 2.0, you can automate API creation and response generation. Once official tooling fully supports them, OpenAPI 3.0, the same instructions should apply:

1. Publish your YAML file on a URI that will be accessible by your machine:

```
https://raw.githubusercontent.com/duluca/lemon-mart-swagger-server/
master/swagger.2.yaml
```

2. In your project folder, execute the following command, replacing `<uri>` with the one pointing at your YAML file:

```
$ docker run --rm -v ${PWD}:/local swaggerapi/swagger-codegen-cli
$ generate -i <uri> -l nodejs-server -o /local/server
```

Similar to the preceding section, this will create a Node Express server under the server directory. In order to execute this server, carry on with the following steps.

3. Install the server's dependencies with `npm install`

4. Run `npm start`. Your mock server should now be up and running.

5. Navigate to `http://localhost:3000/docs`

6. Try out the API for `get /users`; you'll note that the **items** property is empty:

```
Request URL

 http://localhost:3000/v1/users?limit=20

Response Body

 {
   "total": 0.8008281904610115,
   "items": ""
 }

Response Code

 200
```

Swagger UI - Users endpoint

However, you should be receiving dummy data. We will correct this behavior.

7. Try out `get /user/{id}`; you'll see that you're receiving some dummy data back:

```
Request URL

 http://localhost:3000/v1/user/1

Response Body

 {
   "role": {},
   "userStatus": true,
   "lastModifiedBy": "lastModifiedBy",
   "name": {
     "middle": "middle",
     "last": "last",
     "first": "first"
   },
   "id": "id",
   "lastModified": "2000-01-23",
   "email": "email",
   "picture": "picture"
 }

Response Code

 200
```

Swagger UI - User by ID endpoint

The difference in behavior is because, by default, the Node Express server uses controllers generated under `server/controllers/Default.js` to read random data generated during server creation from `server/service/DefaultService.js`. However, you can disable the default controllers and force Swagger into a better default stubbing mode.

8. Update `index.js` to force the use of stubs and comment out controllers:

```
index.js
var options = {
    swaggerUi: path.join(__dirname, '/swagger.json'),
    // controllers: path.join(__dirname, './controllers'),
    useStubs: true,
}
```

9. Try out the `/users` endpoint again

As you can see here, the response is higher quality by default:

```
Request URL

  http://localhost:3000/v1/users?limit=20

Response Body

  {
    "total": 1,
    "items": [
      {
        "id": "Sample text",
        "email": "Sample text",
        "name": {
          "first": "Sample text",
          "middle": "Sample text",
          "last": "Sample text"
        },
        "picture": "Sample text",
        "role": "clerk",
        "userStatus": true,
        "lastModified": "2018-02-12",
        "lastModifiedBy": "Sample text"
      }
    ]
  }

Response Code

  200
```

Swagger UI - Users endpoint with dummy data

In the preceding, `total` is a whole number, `role` is defined correctly, and `items` is a valid array structure.

> To enable better and more customized data mocking, you can edit `DefaultService.js`. In this case, you would want to update the `usersGET` function to return an array of customized users.

Enable Cross-Origin Resource Sharing (CORS)

Before you're able to use your server from your application, you will need to configure it to allow for **Cross-Origin Resource Sharing** (**CORS**) so that your Angular application hosted on `http://localhost:5000` can communicate with your mock server hosted on `http://localhost:3000`:

1. Install the `cors` package:

   ```
   $ npm i cors
   ```

2. Update `index.js` to use `cors`:

   ```
   server/index.js
   ...
   var cors = require('cors')
   ...
   app.use(cors())

   // Initialize the Swagger middleware
   swaggerTools.initializeMiddleware(swaggerDoc, function(middleware)
   {
   ...
   ```

> Ensure that `app.use(cors())` is called right before `initializeMiddleware`; otherwise, other Express middleware may interfere with the functionality of `cors()`.

Verifying and publishing Swagger server

You can verify your Swagger server setup through the SwaggerUI, which will be located at `http://localhost:3000/docs`, or you can achieve a more integrated environment with the Preview Swagger extension in VS Code.

I will demonstrate how you can use this extension to test your API from within VS Code:

1. Select the YAML file in **Explorer**
2. Press *Shift + Alt + P* and execute the **Preview Swagger** command
3. You will see an interactive window to test your configuration, as illustrated:

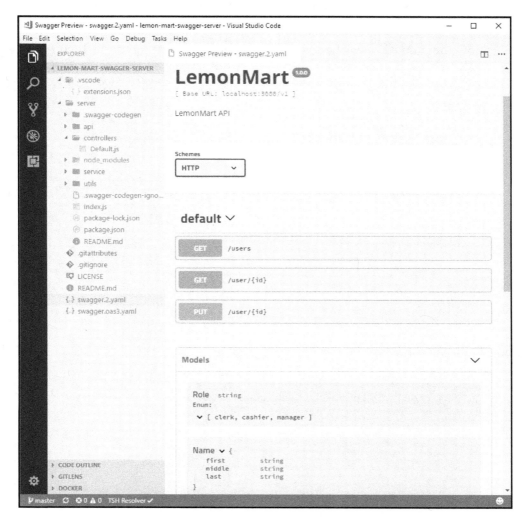

Preview Swagger Extension in Visual Studio Code

4. Click on the **Get** button for **/users**
5. Click on **Try it out** to see the results

In OpenAPI 3.0.0, instead of schemes, you will see a list of servers, including local and remote resources. This is a very convenient tool to explore various data sources as you code your frontend application.

Now that you have verified your Swagger server, you can publish your server to make it accessible to team members or **Automated Acceptance Test (AAT)** environments that require a predictable dataset to execute successfully.

Perform the following steps:

6. Add **npm Scripts for Docker** to the root level `package.json` file
7. Add a `Dockerfile`:

```
Dockerfile
FROM duluca/minimal-node-build-env:8.11.2

RUN mkdir -p /usr/src
WORKDIR /usr/src

COPY server .

RUN npm ci

CMD ["node", "index"]
```

Once you build the container, you are ready to deploy it.

I have published a sample server on Docker Hub at `https://hub.docker.com/r/duluca/lemon-mart-swagger-server`.

Summary

In this chapter, you learned how to create a container-based Continuous Integration environment. We leveraged CircleCI as a cloud-based CI service and highlighted the fact that you can deploy the outcome of your builds to all major cloud hosting providers. If you enable such automated deployment, you will achieve **Continuous Deployment (CD)**. With a CI/CD pipeline, you can share every iteration of your app with clients and team members and quickly deliver bug fixes or new features to your end users.

We also discussed the importance of good API design and established Swagger as a tool that is beneficial to frontend and backend developers alike to define and develop against a live data-contract. If you create a Swagger mock server, you can enable team members to pull the mock server image and use it to develop their frontend applications before backend implementation is completed.

Both CircleCI and Swagger are highly sophisticated tools in their own ways. The techniques mentioned in this chapter are straightforward on purpose, but they are meant to enable sophisticated workflows, giving you a taste of the true power of such tools. You can improve upon the efficiency and the capability of this technique vastly, but the techniques will depend on your specific needs.

Armed with CI and mocked APIs that we can send real HTTP requests to, we are ready to iterate rapidly while ensuring a high-quality deliverable. In the next chapter, we will dive deep into designing an authorization and authentication experience for your line-of-business app using token-based authentication and conditional navigation techniques to enable a smooth user experience, continuing the Router-first approach.

14
Design Authentication and Authorization

Designing a high-quality authentication and authorization system without frustrating the end user is a difficult problem to solve. Authentication is the act of verifying the identity of a user, and authorization specifies the privileges a user has to access a resource. Both processes, auth for short, must seamlessly work in tandem to address the needs of users with varying roles, needs, and job functions. In today's web, users have a high baseline level of expectations from any auth system they encounter through the browser, so this is a really important part of your application to get absolutely right the first time.

The user should always be aware of what they can and can't do in your app. If there are errors, failures, or mistakes, the user should be clearly informed as to why such an error occured. As your application grows, it is easy to miss all the ways an error condition could be triggered. Your implementation should be easy to extend or maintain, otherwise this basic backbone of your application will require a lot of maintenance. In this chapter, we will walk-through the various challenges of creating a great auth UX and implement a solid baseline experience.

We will be continuing the router-first approach to designing SPAs by implementing the authentication and authorization experience of LemonMart. In Chapter 12, *Create a Router-First Line-of-Business App*, we defined user roles, finished our build-out of all major routing and completed a rough walking-skeleton navigation experience of LemonMart, so we are well prepared to implement role-based routing and the nuances of pulling such an implementation.

In Chapter 13, *Continuous Integration and API Design*, we discussed the idea of designing around major data components, so you are already familiar with how a user entity looks like, which will come in handy in implementing a token-based login experience, including caching role information within the entity.

Before diving into auth, we will discuss the importance of completing high-level mock -ups for your application before starting to implement various conditional navigation elements, which may change significantly during the design phase.

In this chapter, you will learn about the following topics:

- Importance of high-level UX design
- Token-based authentication
- Conditional navigation
- Side Navigation bar
- Reusable UI Service for alerts
- Caching data
- JSON Web Tokens
- Angular HTTP interceptors
- Router guards

Wrapping up mock-ups

Mock-ups are important in determining what kind of components and user controls we will need throughout the app. Any user control or component that will be used across components will need to defined at the root level and others scoped with their own modules.

We have already identified the submodules and designed landing pages for them to complete the walking skeleton. Now that we have defined the major data components, we can complete mock-ups for the rest of the app. When designing screens at a high-level, keep several things in mind:

- Can a user complete common tasks required for their role with as little navigation as possible?
- Can users readily access all information and functionality of the app through visible elements on the screen?
- Can a user search for the data they need easily?
- Once a user finds a record of interest, can they drill-down into detail records or view related records with ease?
- Is that pop-up alert really necessary? You know users won't read it, right?

Keep in mind that there's no one right way to design any user experience, which is why when designing screens, always keep modularity and reusability in mind.

As you generate various design artifacts, such as mock-ups or design decisions, take care to post them on a wiki reachable by all team members:

1. On GitHub, switch over to the **Wiki** tab
2. You may check out my sample wiki at `Github.com/duluca/lemon-mart/wiki`, as shown:

GitHub.com LemonMart Wiki

3. When creating a wiki page, ensure that you cross-link between any other documentation available, such as **Readme**

4. Note that GitHub shows subpages on the wiki under **Pages**
5. However, an additional summary is helpful, such as the **Design Artifacts** section, since some people may miss the navigational element on the right
6. As you complete mock-ups, post them on wiki

   You can see a summary view of the wiki here:

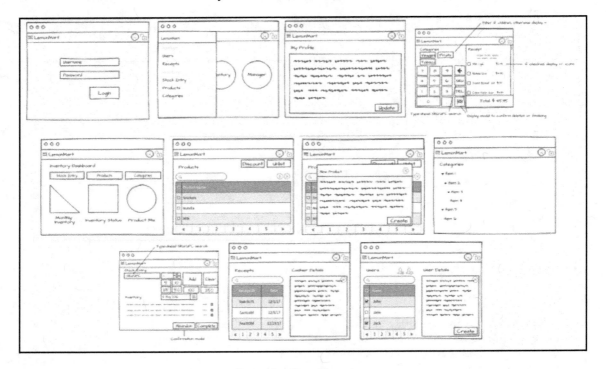

Summary view of Lemon Mart mock-ups

7. Optionally, place the mock-ups in the walking skeleton app so that testers can better envision the functionality that is yet to be developed

With the mock-ups completed, we can now continue the implementation of LemonMart with the Authentication and Authorization workflow.

Design authentication and authorization workflow

A well-designed authentication workflow is stateless so that there's no concept of an expiring session. Users are free to interact with your stateless REST APIs from as many devices and tabs as they wish, simultaneously or overtime. **JSON Web Token (JWT)** implements distributed claims-based authentication that can be digitally signed or integration protected and/or encrypted using a **Message Authentication Code (MAC)**. This means once a user's identity is authenticated through, let's say a password-challenge, they receive an encoded claim ticket or a token, which can then be used to make future requests to the system without having to reauthenticate the identity of a user. The server can independently verify the validity of this claim and process the requests without requiring any prior knowledge of having interacted with this user. Thus, we don't have to store session information regarding a user, making our solution stateless and easy to scale. Each token will expire after a predefined period and due to their distributed nature, they can't be remotely or individually revoked; however, we can bolster real-time security by interjecting custom account and user role status checks to ensure that the authenticated user is authorized to access server-side resources.

 JSON Web Tokens implement IETF industry standard RFC7519, found at `https://tools.ietf.org/html/rfc7519`.

A good authorization workflow enables conditional navigation based on a user's role so that users are automatically taken to the optimal landing screen; they are not shown routes or elements that are not suitable for their roles and if by mistake they try to access an authorized path, they're prevented from doing so. You must remember that any client-side role-based navigation is merely a convenience and is not meant for security. This means that every call made to the server should contain the necessary header information, with the secure token, so that the user can be reauthenticated by the server, their role independently verified and only then they are allowed to retrieve secured data. Client-side authentication can't be trusted, which is why password reset screens must be built with a server-side rendering technology so that both the user and the server can verify that the intended user is interacting with the system.

In the following sections, we will design a fully featured auth workflow around the **User** data entity, as follows:

```
User
id
email
password
name {
  first
  middle
  last
}
picture
role [clerk, cashier, manager]
userStatus
```

User entity

Add auth service

We will start by creating an auth service with a real and a fake login provider:

1. Add an authentication and authorization service:

   ```
   $ npx ng g s auth -m app --flat false
   ```

2. Ensure that the service is provided in `app.module`:

   src/app/app.module.ts
   ```
   import { AuthService } from './auth/auth.service'
   ...
   providers: [AuthService],
   ```

   Creating a separate folder for the service will organize various related components to authentication and authorization, such as the `enum` definition for Role. Additionally, we will be able to add an `authService` fake to the same folder, essential for writing unit tests.

3. Define user roles as an `enum`:

   src/app/auth/role.enum.ts
   ```
   export enum Role {
     None = 'none',
     Clerk = 'clerk',
     Cashier = 'cashier',
     Manager = 'manager',
   }
   ```

Implement a basic authentication service

Now, let's build a local authentication service that will enable us to demonstrate a robust login form, caching, and conditional navigation concepts based on authentication status and a user's role:

1. Start by installing a JWT decoding library, and for faking authentication, a JWT encoding library:

   ```
   $ npm install jwt-decode fake-jwt-sign
   $ npm install -D @types/jwt-decode
   ```

2. Define your imports for `auth.service.ts`:

   src/app/auth/auth.service.ts
   ```
   import { HttpClient } from '@angular/common/http'
   import { Injectable } from '@angular/core'

   import { sign } from 'fake-jwt-sign' // For fakeAuthProvider only
   import * as decode from 'jwt-decode'

   import { BehaviorSubject, Observable, of, throwError as
   observableThrowError } from 'rxjs'
   import { catchError, map } from 'rxjs/operators'

   import { environment } from '../../environments/environment'
   import { Role } from './role.enum'
   ...
   ```

3. Implement an `IAuthStatus` interface to store decoded user information, a helper interface, and the secure by-default `defaultAuthStatus`:

   src/app/auth/auth.service.ts
   ```
   ...
   export interface IAuthStatus {
     isAuthenticated: boolean
     userRole: Role
     userId: string
   }

   interface IServerAuthResponse {
     accessToken: string
   }

   const defaultAuthStatus = { isAuthenticated: false, userRole:
   Role.None, userId: null }
   ...
   ```

`IAuthUser` is an interface that represents the shape of a typical JWT that you may receive from your authentication service. It contains minimal information about the user and its role, so it can be attached to the `header` of server calls and optionally cached in `localStorage` to remember the user's login state. In the preceding implementation, we're assuming the default role of a `Manager`.

4. Define the `AuthService` class with a `BehaviorSubject` to anchor the current `authStatus` of the user and configure an `authProvider` that can process an `email` and a `password` and return an `IServerAuthResponse` in the constructor:

src/app/auth/auth.service.ts

```
...
@Injectable({
  providedIn: 'root'
})
export class AuthService {
   private readonly authProvider: (
     email: string,
     password: string
   ) => Observable<IServerAuthResponse>

  authStatus = new BehaviorSubject<IAuthStatus>(defaultAuthStatus)

  constructor(private httpClient: HttpClient) {
      // Fake login function to simulate roles
     this.authProvider = this.fakeAuthProvider
     // Example of a real login call to server-side
     // this.authProvider = this.exampleAuthProvider
  }
  ...
```

Note that `fakeAuthProvider` is configured to be the `authProvider` for this service. A real auth provider may look like the following code, where users' email and password are sent to a POST endpoint, which verifies their information, creating and returning a JWT for our app to consume:

example
```
private exampleAuthProvider(
  email: string,
  password: string
): Observable<IServerAuthResponse> {
  return
this.httpClient.post<IServerAuthResponse>(`${environment.baseUrl}/v
1/login`, {
    email: email,
```

```
    password: password,
  })
}
```

It is pretty straightforward, since the hard work is done on the server side. This call can also be made to a third party.

Note that the API version, `v1`, in the URL path is defined at the service and not as part of the `baseUrl`. This is because each API can change versions independently from each other. Login may remain `v1` for a long time, while other APIs may be upgraded to `v2`, `v3`, and such.

5. Implement a `fakeAuthProvider` that simulates the authentication process, including creating a fake JWT on the fly:

src/app/auth/auth.service.ts

```
...
private fakeAuthProvider(
  email: string,
  password: string
): Observable<IServerAuthResponse> {
  if (!email.toLowerCase().endsWith('@test.com')) {
    return observableThrowError('Failed to login! Email needs to
end with @test.com.')
  }

  const authStatus = {
    isAuthenticated: true,
    userId: 'e4d1bc2ab25c',
    userRole: email.toLowerCase().includes('cashier')
      ? Role.Cashier
      : email.toLowerCase().includes('clerk')
        ? Role.Clerk
        : email.toLowerCase().includes('manager') ? Role.Manager
: Role.None,
  } as IAuthStatus

  const authResponse = {
    accessToken: sign(authStatus, 'secret', {
      expiresIn: '1h',
      algorithm: 'none',
    }),
  } as IServerAuthResponse

  return of(authResponse)
}
...
```

The `fakeAuthProvider` implements what would otherwise be a server-side method right in the service, so you can conveniently experiment the code while fine-tuning your auth workflow. It creates and signs a JWT, with the temporary `fake-jwt-sign` library so that we can also demonstrate how to handle a properly-formed JWT.

> Do not ship your Angular app with the `fake-jwt-sign` dependency, since it is meant to be server-side code.

6. Before we move on, implement a `transformError` function to handle mixed `HttpErrorResponse` and string errors in an observable stream under `common/common.ts`:

   src/app/common/common.ts
   ```
   import { HttpErrorResponse } from '@angular/common/http'
   import { throwError } from 'rxjs'

   export function transformError(error: HttpErrorResponse | string) {
     let errorMessage = 'An unknown error has occurred'
     if (typeof error === 'string') {
       errorMessage = error
     } else if (error.error instanceof ErrorEvent) {
       errorMessage = `Error! ${error.error.message}`
     } else if (error.status) {
       errorMessage = `Request failed with ${error.status}
   ${error.statusText}`
     }
     return throwError(errorMessage)
   }
   ```

7. Implement the `login` function that will be called from `LoginComponent`, shown in the next section

8. Add `import { transformError } from '../common/common'`

9. Also implement a corresponding `logout` function, which may be called by the **Logout** button in the top toolbar, a failed login attempt, or if an unauthorized access attempt is detected by a router auth guard as the user is navigating the app, which is a topic covered later in the chapter:

   src/app/auth/auth.service.ts

```
...
login(email: string, password: string): Observable<IAuthStatus> {
  this.logout()

  const loginResponse = this.authProvider(email, password).pipe(
    map(value => {
      return decode(value.accessToken) as IAuthStatus
    }),
    catchError(transformError)
  )

  loginResponse.subscribe(
    res => {
      this.authStatus.next(res)
    },
    err => {
      this.logout()
      return observableThrowError(err)
    }
  )

  return loginResponse
}

logout() {
  this.authStatus.next(defaultAuthStatus)
}
}
```

The `login` method encapsulates the correct order of operations by calling the `logout` method, the `authProvider` with the `email` and `password` information, and throwing errors when necessary.

The `login` method adheres to the Open/Closed principle, from SOLID design, by being open to extension by our ability to externally supply different auth providers to it, but it remains closed to modification, since the variance in functionality is encapsulated with the auth provider.

In the next section, we will implement the `LoginComponent` so that users can enter their username and password information and attempt a login.

Implementing the login component

The `login` component leverages the `authService` that we just created and implements validation errors using reactive forms. The login component should be designed in a way to be rendered independently of any other component, because during a routing event, if we discover that the user is not properly authenticated or authorized, we will navigate them to this component. We can capture this origination URL as a `redirectUrl` so that once a user logs in successfully, we can navigate them back to it.

1. Let's start with implementing the routes to the `login` component:

   src/app/app-routing.modules.ts
   ```
   ...
     { path: 'login', component: LoginComponent },
     { path: 'login/:redirectUrl', component: LoginComponent },
   ...
   ```

2. Now implement the component itself:

   src/app/login/login.component.ts
   ```
   import { Component, OnInit } from '@angular/core'
   import { FormBuilder, FormGroup, Validators, NgForm } from
   '@angular/forms'
   import { AuthService } from '../auth/auth.service'
   import { Role } from '../auth/role.enum'

   @Component({
     selector: 'app-login',
     templateUrl: 'login.component.html',
     styles: [
       `
       .error {
          color: red
       }
       `,
       `
       div[fxLayout] {margin-top: 32px; }
       `,
     ],
   })
   export class LoginComponent implements OnInit {
     loginForm: FormGroup
     loginError = ''
   ```

```
    redirectUrl
    constructor(
      private formBuilder: FormBuilder,
      private authService: AuthService,
      private router: Router,
      private route: ActivatedRoute
    ) {
      route.paramMap.subscribe(params => (this.redirectUrl =
params.get('redirectUrl')))
    }

    ngOnInit() {
      this.buildLoginForm()
    }

    buildLoginForm() {
      this.loginForm = this.formBuilder.group({
        email: ['', [Validators.required, Validators.email]],
        password: ['', [
          Validators.required,
          Validators.minLength(8),
          Validators.maxLength(50),
        ]],
      })
    }

    async login(submittedForm: FormGroup) {
      this.authService
        .login(submittedForm.value.email,
submittedForm.value.password)
        .subscribe(authStatus => {
          if (authStatus.isAuthenticated) {
            this.router.navigate([this.redirectUrl || '/manager'])
          }
        }, error => (this.loginError = error))
    }
}
```

As the result of a successful login attempt, we leverage the router to navigate an authenticated user to their profile. In the case of an error sent from the server via the service, we assign that error to `loginError`.

3. Here's an implementation for a login form to capture and validate a user's `email` and `password`, and if there are any server errors, display them:

   src/app/login/login.component.html
   ```
   <div fxLayout="row" fxLayoutAlign="center">
   ```

```
<mat-card fxFlex="400px">
  <mat-card-header>
    <mat-card-title>
      <div class="mat-headline">Hello, Lemonite!</div>
    </mat-card-title>
  </mat-card-header>
  <mat-card-content>
    <form [formGroup]="loginForm" (ngSubmit)="login(loginForm)"
fxLayout="column">
      <div fxLayout="row" fxLayoutAlign="start center"
fxLayoutGap="10px">
        <mat-icon>email</mat-icon>
        <mat-form-field fxFlex>
          <input matInput placeholder="E-mail" aria-label="E-
mail" formControlName="email">
          <mat-error
*ngIf="loginForm.get('email').hasError('required')">
            E-mail is required
          </mat-error>
          <mat-error
*ngIf="loginForm.get('email').hasError('email')">
            E-mail is not valid
          </mat-error>
        </mat-form-field>
      </div>
      <div fxLayout="row" fxLayoutAlign="start center"
fxLayoutGap="10px">
        <mat-icon matPrefix>vpn_key</mat-icon>
        <mat-form-field fxFlex>
          <input matInput placeholder="Password" aria-
label="Password" type="password" formControlName="password">
          <mat-hint>Minimum 8 characters</mat-hint>
          <mat-error
*ngIf="loginForm.get('password').hasError('required')">
            Password is required
          </mat-error>
          <mat-error
*ngIf="loginForm.get('password').hasError('minlength')">
            Password is at least 8 characters long
          </mat-error>
          <mat-error
*ngIf="loginForm.get('password').hasError('maxlength')">
            Password cannot be longer than 50 characters
          </mat-error>
        </mat-form-field>
      </div>
      <div fxLayout="row" class="margin-top">
        <div *ngIf="loginError" class="mat-caption
```

```
error">{{loginError}}</div>
        <div class="flex-spacer"></div>
        <button mat-raised-button type="submit" color="primary"
[disabled]="loginForm.invalid">Login</button>
      </div>
    </form>
  </mat-card-content>
 </mat-card>
</div>
```

The **Login** button is disabled until email and password meets client site validation rules. Additionally, `<mat-form-field>` will only display one `mat-error` at a time, unless you create more space for more errors, so be sure place your error conditions in the correct order.

Once you're done implementing the `login` component, you can now update the home screen to conditionally display or hide the new component we created.

4. Update `home.component` to display login when a user opens up the app:

src/app/home/home.component.ts

```
template: `
  <div *ngIf="displayLogin">
    <app-login></app-login>
  </div>
  <div *ngIf="!displayLogin">
    <span class="mat-display-3">You get a lemon, you get a lemon,
you get a lemon...</span>
  </div>
  `,

export class HomeComponent implements OnInit {
  displayLogin = true
  ...
```

Don't forget to import the requisite dependent modules for the code above in to your Angular application. It is intentionally left as an exercise for the reader to locate and import the missing modules.

Your app should look similar to this screenshot:

LemonMart with login

There's still some work to be done, in terms of implementing and showing/hiding the sidenav menu, profile and logout icons, given the user's authentication status.

Conditional navigation

Conditional navigation is necessary in creating a frustration-free user experience. By selectively showing the elements that the user has access to and hiding the ones they don't, we allow the user to confidently navigate through the app.

Let's start by hiding the login component after a user logs in to the app:

1. On the `home` component, import the `authService` in `home.component`
2. Set the `authStatus` to a local variable named `displayLogin`:

src/app/home/home.component

```
...
import { AuthService } from '../auth/auth.service'
...
export class HomeComponent implements OnInit {
  private _displayLogin = true
  constructor(private authService: AuthService) {}

  ngOnInit() {
    this.authService.authStatus.subscribe(
      authStatus => (this._displayLogin =
!authStatus.isAuthenticated)
    )
  }

  get displayLogin() {
    return this._displayLogin
  }
}
```

 A property getter for displayLogin here is necessary, otherwise you may receive a **Error: ExpressionChangedAfterItHasBeenCheckedError: Expression has changed after it was checked message**. This error is a side effect of how the Angular component life-cycle and change detection works. This behavior may very well change in future Angular versions.

3. On the app component, subscribe to the authentication status and store the current value in a local variable named displayAccountIcons:

src/app/app.component.ts

```
import { Component, OnInit } from '@angular/core'
import { AuthService } from './auth/auth.service'
...
export class AppComponent implements OnInit {
  displayAccountIcons = false
  constructor(..., private authService: AuthService) {
    ...
  ngOnInit() {
    this.authService.authStatus.subscribe(
      authStatus => (this.displayAccountIcons =
authStatus.isAuthenticated)
    )
  }
  ...
}
```

4. Use `*ngIf` to hide all buttons meant for logged in users:

src/app/app.component.ts
```
<button *ngIf="displayAccountIcons" ... >
```

Now, when a user is logged out, your toolbar should look all clean with no buttons, as shown:

LemonMart toolbar after log in

Common validations

Before we move on, we need to implement validations for `loginForm`. As we implement more forms in Chapter 15, *Angular App Design and Recipes*, you will realize that it gets tedious, fast, to repeatedly type out form validations in either template or reactive forms. Part of the allure of reactive forms is that it is driven by code, so we can easily extract out the validations to a shared class, unit test, and reuse them:

1. Create a `validations.ts` file under the `common` folder
2. Implement email and password validations:

src/app/common/validations.ts
```
import { Validators } from '@angular/forms'

export const EmailValidation = [Validators.required,
Validators.email]
export const PasswordValidation = [
  Validators.required,
  Validators.minLength(8),
  Validators.maxLength(50),
]
```

 Depending on your password validation needs, you can use a `RegEx` pattern with the `Validations.pattern()` function to enforce password complexity rules or leverage the OWASP npm package, `owasp-password-strength-test`, to enable pass-phrases as well as set more flexible password requirements.

3. Update the `login` component with the new validations:

src/app/login/login.component.ts
```
import { EmailValidation, PasswordValidation } from
'../common/validations'
  ...
    this.loginForm = this.formBuilder.group({
      email: ['', EmailValidation],
      password: ['', PasswordValidation],
    })
```

UI service

As we start dealing with complicated workflows, such as the auth workflow, it is important to be able to programmatically display a toast notification for the user. In other cases, we may want to ask for a confirmation before executing a destructive action with a more intrusive pop-up notification.

No matter what component library you use, it gets tedious to recode the same boiler plate, just to display a quick notification. A UI service can neatly encapsulate a default implementation that can also be customized on a need basis:

1. Create a new `uiService` under `common`
2. Implement a `showToast` function:

src/app/common/ui.service.ts
```
import { Injectable, Component, Inject } from '@angular/core'
import {
  MatSnackBar,
  MatSnackBarConfig,
  MatDialog,
  MatDialogConfig,
} from '@angular/material'
import { Observable } from 'rxjs'

@Injectable()
export class UiService {
  constructor(private snackBar: MatSnackBar, private dialog:
MatDialog) {}

  showToast(message: string, action = 'Close', config?:
MatSnackBarConfig) {
    this.snackBar.open(
      message,
      action,
```

```
            config || {
              duration: 7000,
            }
          )
      }
    ...
    }
```

For a showDialog function, we must implement a basic dialog component:

1. Add a new `simpleDialog` under the `common` folder provided in `app.module` with inline template and styling

app/common/simple-dialog/simple-dialog.component.ts
```
@Component({
  template: `
    <h2 mat-dialog-title>data.title</h2>
    <mat-dialog-content>
      <p>data.content</p>
    </mat-dialog-content>
    <mat-dialog-actions>
      <span class="flex-spacer"></span>
      <button mat-button mat-dialog-close
*ngIf="data.cancelText">data.cancelText</button>
      <button mat-button mat-button-raised color="primary" [mat-
dialog-close]="true"
        cdkFocusInitial>
        data.okText
      </button>
    </mat-dialog-actions>
  `,
})
export class SimpleDialogComponent {
  constructor(
    public dialogRef: MatDialogRef<SimpleDialogComponent, Boolean>,
    @Inject(MAT_DIALOG_DATA) public data: any
  ) {}
}
```

 Note that `SimpleDialogComponent` should not have app selector like `selector: 'app-simple-dialog'` since we only plan to use it with `UiService`. Remove this property from your component.

2. Then, implement a `showDialog` function to
   display the `SimpleDialogComponent`:

app/common/ui.service.ts
```
...
showDialog(
    title: string,
    content: string,
    okText = 'OK',
    cancelText?: string,
    customConfig?: MatDialogConfig
  ): Observable<Boolean> {
    const dialogRef = this.dialog.open(
      SimpleDialogComponent,
      customConfig || {
        width: '300px',
        data: { title: title, content: content, okText: okText,
cancelText: cancelText },
      }
    )

    return dialogRef.afterClosed()
  }
}
```

ShowDialog returns an `Observable<boolean>`, so you can implement a follow-
on action, depending on what selection the user makes. Clicking on **OK** will
return `true`, and **Cancel** will return `false`.

In `SimpleDialogComponent`, using `@Inject`, we're able to use all variables sent
by `showDialog` to customize the content of the dialog.

 Don't forget to update `app.module.ts` and `material.module.ts` with
the various dependencies that are being introduced.

3. Update the `login` component to display a toast message after login:

src/app/login/login.component.ts
```
import { UiService } from '../common/ui.service'
...
constructor(... ,
    private uiService: UiService)
...
  .subscribe(authStatus => {
```

```
if (authStatus.isAuthenticated) {
    this.uiService.showToast(`Welcome! Role:
${authStatus.userRole}`)
    ...
```

A toast message will appear after a user logs in, as shown:

Material Snack bar

The `snackBar` will either take the full width of the screen or a portion depending on the size of the browser.

Caching with cookie and localStorage

We must be able to cache the authentication status of the logged in user. Otherwise, with every page refresh, the user will have go through the login routine. We need to update `AuthService` so that it persists the auth status.

There are three main ways to store data:

- `cookie`
- `localStorage`
- `sessionStorage`

Cookies should not be used to store secure data, because they can be sniffed or stolen by bad actors. In addition, cookies can store 4 KB of data and can be set to expire.

`localStorage` and `sessionStorage` are similar to each other. They are protected and isolated browser-side stores that allow for storing larger amounts of data for your application. You can't set an expiration date-time on either stores. `sessionStorage` values are removed, when the browser window is closed. The values survive page reloads and restores.

JSON Web Tokens are encrypted, and they include a timestamp for expiration, in essence, countering the weaknesses of `cookie` and `localStorage`. Either option should be secure to use with JWTs.

Let's start by implementing a caching service that can abstract away our method of caching authentication information that the `AuthService` can consume:

1. Start by creating an abstract `cacheService` that encapsulates the method of caching:

src/app/auth/cache.service.ts
```
export abstract class CacheService {
  protected getItem<T>(key: string): T {
    const data = localStorage.getItem(key)
    if (data && data !== 'undefined') {
      return JSON.parse(data)
    }
    return null
  }

  protected setItem(key: string, data: object | string) {
    if (typeof data === 'string') {
      localStorage.setItem(key, data)
    }
    localStorage.setItem(key, JSON.stringify(data))
  }

  protected removeItem(key: string) {
    localStorage.removeItem(key)
  }

  protected clear() {
    localStorage.clear()
  }
}
```

This cache service base class can be used to give caching capabilities to any service. It is not the same as creating a centralized cache service that you inject into another service. By avoiding a centralized value store, we avoid inter-dependencies between various services.

2. Update `AuthService` to extend the `CacheService` and implement caching of the `authStatus`:

auth/auth.service

```
...
export class AuthService extends CacheService {
  authStatus = new BehaviorSubject<IAuthStatus>(
    this.getItem('authStatus') || defaultAuthStatus
  )

  constructor(private httpClient: HttpClient) {
    super()
    this.authStatus.subscribe(authStatus =>
this.setItem('authStatus', authStatus))
    ...
  }
  ...
}
```

The technique demonstrated here can be used to persist any kind of data and intentionally leverages RxJS events to update the cache. As you may note, we don't need to update the login function to call `setItem`, because it already calls `this.authStatus.next`, and we just tap in to the data stream. This helps with staying stateless and avoiding side effects, by decoupling functions from each other.

 When initializing the `BehaviorSubject`, take care to handle the `undefined/null` case, when loading data from the cache and still provide a default implementation.

 You can implement your own custom cache expiration scheme in `setItem` and `getItem` functions or leverage a service created by a third party.

If you are going after a high-security application, you may choose to only cache the JWT to ensure an additional layer security. In either case, the JWT should be cached separately, because the token must be sent to the server in the header with every request. It is important to understand how token-based authentication works well, to avoid revealing compromising secrets. In the next section, we will go over the JWT life cycle to improve your understanding.

JSON Web Token life cycle

JSON Web Tokens compliment a stateless REST API architecture with an encrypted token mechanism that allow for convenient, distributed, and high-performance authentication and authorization of requests sent by clients. There are three main components of a token-based authentication scheme:

- Client-side, captures login information and hides disallowed actions for a good UX
- Server-side, validates that every request is both authenticated and has the proper authorization
- Auth service, generates and validates encrypted tokens, independently verifies authentication and authorization status of user requests from a data store

A secure system presumes that data sent/received between the major components mentioned is encrypted in-transit. This means your REST API must be hosted with a properly configured SSL certificate, serving all API calls over HTTPS, so that user credentials are never exposed between the client and the server. Similarly, any database or third-party service call should happen over HTTPS. Furthermore, any data store storing passwords should utilize a secure one-way hashing algorithm with good salting practices. Any other sensitive user information should be encrypted at-rest with a secure two-way encryption algorithm. Following this layered approach to security is critical, because attackers will need to accomplish the unlikely feat of compromising all layers of security implemented at the same time to cause meaningful harm to your business.

The next sequence diagram highlights the life-cycle of JWT-based authentication:

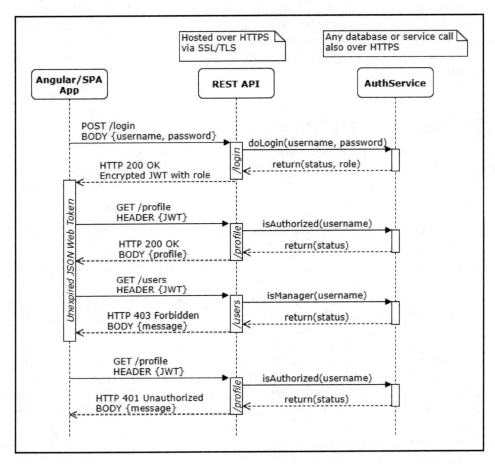

Life-Cycle of JWT-based authentication

Initially, a user logs in by providing their username and password. Once validated, the user's authentication status and role is encrypted to a JWT with an expiration date and time and is sent back to the browser.

Your Angular (or any other SPA) app can cache this token in local or session storage securely so that the user isn't forced to login with every request or worse yet, we don't store user credentials in the browser. Let's update the authentication service so that it can cache the token.

1. Update the service to be able to set, get, decode, and clear the token, as shown:

src/app/auth/auth.service.ts

```
. . .
  private setToken(jwt: string) {
    this.setItem('jwt', jwt)
  }

  private getDecodedToken(): IAuthStatus {
    return decode(this.getItem('jwt'))
  }

  getToken(): string {
    return this.getItem('jwt') || ''
  }

  private clearToken() {
    this.removeItem('jwt')
  }
```

2. Call `setToken` during login and `clearToken` during logout as highlight as follows:

src/app/auth/auth.service.ts

```
. . .
  login(email: string, password: string): Observable<IAuthStatus> {
    this.logout()

    const loginResponse = this.authProvider(email, password).pipe(
      map(value => {
        this.setToken(value.accessToken)
        return decode(value.accessToken) as IAuthStatus
      }),
      catchError(transformError)
    )
  . . .
  logout() {
    this.clearToken()
    this.authStatus.next(defaultAuthStatus)
  }
```

Every subsequent request will contain the JWT in the request header. You should secure every API to check for and validate the token received. For example, if a user wanted to access their profile, the `AuthService` would validate the token to check whether the user authenticated, but a further database call is required to check whether the user is also authorized to view the data. This ensures an independent confirmation of the users' access to the system and prevents any abuse of an unexpired token.

If an authenticated user makes a call to an API, where they don't have the proper authorization, say if a clerk wants to get access to a list of all the users, then the `AuthService` will return a falsy status and the client will receive a **403 Forbidden** response, which will be displayed as an error message to the user.

A user can make a request with an expired token; when this happens, a **401 Unauthorized** response is sent to the client. As a good UX practice, we should automatically prompt the user to login again and let them resume their workflow without any data loss.

In summary, real security is achieved by a robust server-side implementation and any client-side implementation is largely there to enable a good UX around good security practices.

HTTP interceptor

Implement an HTTP interceptor to inject the JWT into the header of every request sent to the user and also gracefully handle authentication failures by asking the user to log in:

1. Create `authHttpInterceptor` under `auth`:

   src/app/auth/auth-http-interceptor.ts
   ```
   import {
     HttpEvent,
     HttpHandler,
     HttpInterceptor,
     HttpRequest,
   } from '@angular/common/http'
   import { Injectable } from '@angular/core'
   import { Router } from '@angular/router'
   import { Observable, throwError as observableThrowError } from
   'rxjs'
   import { catchError } from 'rxjs/operators'
   import { AuthService } from './auth.service'

   @Injectable()
   export class AuthHttpInterceptor implements HttpInterceptor {
     constructor(private authService: AuthService, private router:
   ```

```
Router) {}
  intercept(req: HttpRequest<any>, next: HttpHandler):
Observable<HttpEvent<any>> {
    const jwt = this.authService.getToken()
    const authRequest = req.clone({ setHeaders: { authorization:
`Bearer ${jwt}` } })
    return next.handle(authRequest).pipe(
      catchError((err, caught) => {
        if (err.status === 401) {
          this.router.navigate(['/user/login'], {
            queryParams: { redirectUrl:
this.router.routerState.snapshot.url },
          })
        }

        return observableThrowError(err)
      })
    )
  }
}
```

Note that `AuthService` is leveraged to retrieve the token, and the `redirectUrl` is being set for the login component after a **401** error.

2. Update the `app` module to provide the interceptor:

src/app/app.module.ts
```
providers: [
  ...
  {
    provide: HTTP_INTERCEPTORS,
    useClass: AuthHttpInterceptor,
    multi: true,
  },
],
```

You can observe the interceptor in action, while the app is fetching the `lemon.svg` file, in the **Chrome Dev Tools** | **Network** tab, here:

Request header for lemon.svg

Side navigation

Enable mobile-first workflows and provide an easy navigation mechanism to quickly jump to desired functionality. Using the authentication service, given a user's current role, only display the links for features they can access. We will be implementing the side navigation mock-up, as follows:

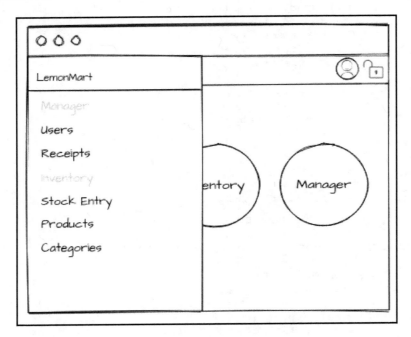

Side navigation mock-up

Let's implement the code for the side nav as a separate component, so that it is easier to maintain:

1. Create and declare a `NavigationMenuComponent` in `app.module`

   src/app/app.module.ts
   ```
   @NgModule({
     declarations: [
       ...
       NavigationMenuComponent,
     ],
   ```

The side navigation isn't technically required until after a user is logged in. However, in order to be able to launch the side navigation menu from the toolbar, we need to be able to trigger it from app.component. Since this component will be simple, we will eagerly load it. To do this lazily, Angular does have a Dynamic Component Loader pattern, which has a high implementation overhead that will only make sense if multi-hundred kilobyte savings will be made.

SideNav will be triggered from the toolbar, and it comes with a <mat-sidenav-container> parent container that hosts the SideNav itself and the content of the app. So we will need to render all app content by placing the <router-outlet> inside <mat-sidenav-content>.

2. Import MatSidenavModule and MatListModule to material.module

src/app/material.module.ts
```
@NgModule({
  imports: [
    ...
    MatSidenavModule,
    MatListModule,
  ],
  exports: [
    ...
    MatSidenavModule,
    MatListModule,
  ]
```

3. Define some styles that will ensure that the web app will expand to fill the entire page and remain properly scrollable on desktop and mobile scenarios:

src/app/app.component.ts
```
styles: [
  `.app-container {
    display: flex;
    flex-direction: column;
    position: absolute;
    top: 0;
    bottom: 0;
    left: 0;
    right: 0;
  }
  .app-is-mobile .app-toolbar {
    position: fixed;
    z-index: 2;
  }
```

```
.app-sidenav-container {
  flex: 1;
}
.app-is-mobile .app-sidenav-container {
  flex: 1 0 auto;
},
mat-sidenav {
  width: 200px;
}
`
],
```

4. Import an `ObservableMedia` service in `AppComponent`:

   src/app/app.component.ts
   ```
   constructor(
     ...
     public media: ObservableMedia
   ) {
   ...
   }
   ```

5. Update the template with a responsive `SideNav` that will slide over the content in mobile or push the content aside in desktop scenarios:

   src/app/app.component.ts
   ```
   ...
   template: `
     <div class="app-container">
       <mat-toolbar color="primary" fxLayoutGap="8px" class="app-
   toolbar"
         [class.app-is-mobile]="media.isActive('xs')">
         <button *ngIf="displayAccountIcons" mat-icon-button
   (click)="sidenav.toggle()">
           <mat-icon>menu</mat-icon>
         </button>
         <a mat-icon-button routerLink="/home">
           <mat-icon svgIcon="lemon"></mat-icon><span class="mat-
   h2">LemonMart</span>
         </a>
         <span class="flex-spacer"></span>
         <button *ngIf="displayAccountIcons" mat-mini-fab
   routerLink="/user/profile"
           matTooltip="Profile" aria-label="User Profile"><mat-
   icon>account_circle</mat-icon>
         </button>
         <button *ngIf="displayAccountIcons" mat-mini-fab
   routerLink="/user/logout"
   ```

```
      matTooltip="Logout" aria-label="Logout"><mat-
icon>lock_open</mat-icon>
      </button>
    </mat-toolbar>
    <mat-sidenav-container class="app-sidenav-container"
[style.marginTop.px]="media.isActive('xs') ? 56 : 0">
      <mat-sidenav #sidenav [mode]="media.isActive('xs') ? 'over' :
'side'"
                  [fixedInViewport]="media.isActive('xs')"
fixedTopGap="56">
        <app-navigation-menu></app-navigation-menu>
      </mat-sidenav>
      <mat-sidenav-content>
        <router-outlet class="app-container"></router-outlet>
      </mat-sidenav-content>
    </mat-sidenav-container>
  </div>
  `,
```

The preceding template leverages Angular Flex Layout media observable for a responsive implementation that was injected earlier.

Since the links that will be shown inside the `SiveNav` will be of variable length and subject various role-based business rules, it is a good practice to implement it in a separate component.

6. Implement a property getter for `displayAccountIcons` and a `setTimeout` so that you can avoid errors like `ExpressionChangedAfterItHasBeenCheckedError`

src/app/app.component.ts
```
export class AppComponent implements OnInit {
  _displayAccountIcons = false
  ...
  ngOnInit() {
    this.authService.authStatus.subscribe(authStatus => {
      setTimeout(() => {
        this._displayAccountIcons = authStatus.isAuthenticated
      }, 0)
    })
  }
```

```
      get displayAccountIcons() {
        return this._displayAccountIcons
      }
  }
```

7. Implement navigational links in `NavigationMenuComponent`:

src/app/navigation-menu/navigation-menu.component.ts

```
...
  styles: [
    `
    .active-link {
      font-weight: bold;
      border-left: 3px solid green;
    }
    `,
  ],
  template: `
    <mat-nav-list>
      <h3 matSubheader>Manager</h3>
      <a mat-list-item routerLinkActive="active-link"
routerLink="/manager/users">Users</a>
      <a mat-list-item routerLinkActive="active-link"
routerLink="/manager/receipts">Receipts</a>
      <h3 matSubheader>Inventory</h3>
      <a mat-list-item routerLinkActive="active-link"
routerLink="/inventory/stockEntry">Stock Entry</a>
      <a mat-list-item routerLinkActive="active-link"
routerLink="/inventory/products">Products</a>
      <a mat-list-item routerLinkActive="active-link"
routerLink="/inventory/categories">Categories</a>
      <h3 matSubheader>Clerk</h3>
      <a mat-list-item routerLinkActive="active-link"
routerLink="/pos">POS</a>
    </mat-nav-list>
    `,
...
```

`<mat-nav-list>` is functionally equivalent to `<mat-list>`, so you can use the documentation for that component for layout purposes. Observe the subheaders for **Manager**, **Inventory**, and **Clerk** here:

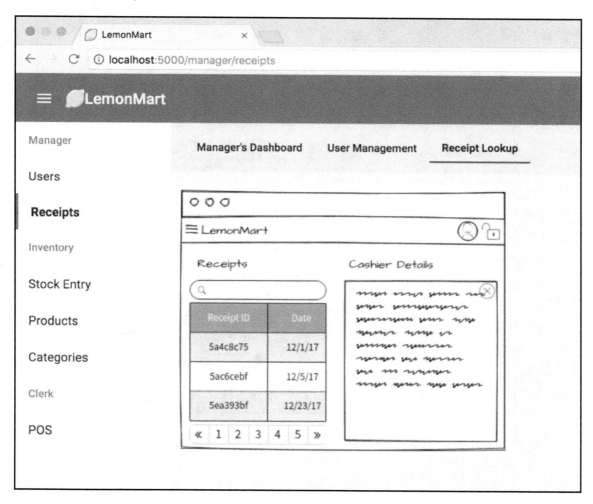

Manager dashboard showing receipt lookup on desktop

`routerLinkActive="active-link"` highlights the selected **Receipts** route, as shown in the preceding screenshot.

Additionally, you can see the difference in appearance and behavior on mobile devices as follows:

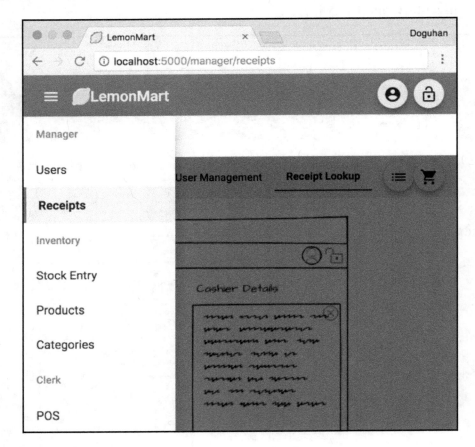

Manager dashboard showing receipt lookup on mobile

Log out

Now that we're caching the login status, we need to implement a log out experience:

1. In `AuthService`, implement a `logout` function:

   src/app/auth/auth.service.ts
   ```
   ...
     logout() {
       this.clearToken()
   ```

```
        this.authStatus.next(defaultAuthStatus)
    }
```

2. Implement the `logout` component:

   src/app/user/logout/logout.component.ts

```
import { Component, OnInit } from '@angular/core'
import { Router } from '@angular/router'
import { AuthService } from '../../auth/auth.service'

@Component({
  selector: 'app-logout',
  template: `
    <p>
      Logging out...
    </p>
  `,
  styles: [],
})
export class LogoutComponent implements OnInit {
  constructor(private router: Router, private authService:
AuthService) {}

  ngOnInit() {
    this.authService.logout()
    this.router.navigate(['/'])
  }
}
```

As you note, after a log out, user is navigated back to the home page.

Role-based routing after login

This is the most elemental and important part of your application. With lazy loading, we have ensured only the bare minimum amount of assets will be loaded to enable a user to login.

Once a user logs in, they should be routed to the appropriate landing screen as per their user role, so they're not guessing how they need to use the app. For example, a cashier needs to only access the POS to check out customers, so they can automatically be routed to that screen.

You find the mock up of the POS screen as illustrated:

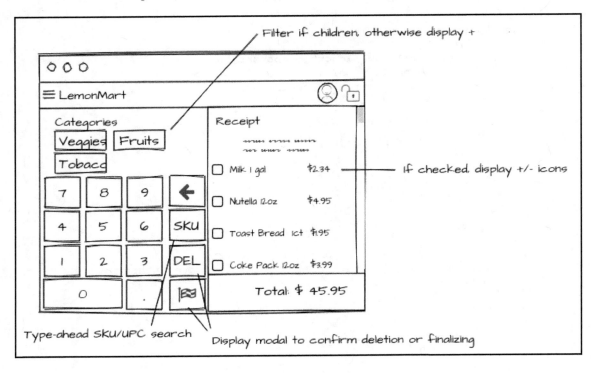

Point-of-Sale screen mock-up

Let's ensure that users get routed to the appropriate page after logging in by updating the
LoginComponent:

1. Update the login logic to route per role:

   app/src/login/login.component.ts

   ```
   async login(submittedForm: FormGroup) {
       ...
       this.router.navigate([
         this.redirectUrl ||
   this.homeRoutePerRole(authStatus.userRole)
       ])
       ...
   }

     homeRoutePerRole(role: Role) {
       switch (role) {
   ```

```
        case Role.Cashier:
          return '/pos'
        case Role.Clerk:
          return '/inventory'
        case Role.Manager:
          return '/manager'
        default:
          return '/user/profile'
    }
  }
```

Similarly, clerks and manager are routed to their landing screens to access the features they need to accomplish their tasks, as shown earlier. Since we implemented a default manager role, the corresponding landing experience will be launched automatically. The other side of the coin is intentional and unintentional attempts to access routes that a user isn't meant to have access to. In the next section, we will learn about router guards that can help check authentication and even load requisite data before the form is rendered.

Router Guards

Router Guards enable further decoupling and reuse of logic and greater control over the component lifecycle.

Here are the four major guards you will most likely use:

1. `CanActivate` and `CanActivateChild`, used for checking auth access to a route
2. `CanDeactivate`, used to ask permission before navigating away from a route
3. `Resolve`, allows for pre-fetching of data from route parameters
4. `CanLoad`, allows for custom logic to execute before loading feature module assets

Refer to the following sections for how to leverage `CanActivate` and `CanLoad`. `Resolve` guard will be covered in `Chapter 15`, *Angular App Design and Recipes*.

Auth Guard

Auth Guards enable good UX by allowing or disallowing accidental navigation to a feature module or component before it is loaded and any data requests are made to the server.

For example, when a Manager logs in, they're automatically routed to the `/manager/home` path. The browser will cache this URL, and it will be completely plausible for a clerk to accidentally navigate to the same URL. Angular doesn't know whether a particular route is accessible to a user or not and, without an `AuthGuard`, it will happily render the Manager's home page and trigger server requests that will end up failing.

 Regardless of the robustness of your frontend implementation, every REST API you implement should be properly secured server-side.

Let's update the router so that `ProfileComponent` can't be activated without an authenticated user and the `ManagerModule` won't load unless a manager is logging in using an `AuthGuard`:

1. Implement an `AuthGuard` service:

    src/app/auth/auth-guard.service.ts
    ```typescript
    import { Injectable } from '@angular/core'
    import {
      CanActivate,
      Router,
      ActivatedRouteSnapshot,
      RouterStateSnapshot,
      CanLoad,
      CanActivateChild,
    } from '@angular/router'
    import { AuthService, IAuthStatus } from './auth.service'
    import { Observable } from 'rxjs'
    import { Route } from '@angular/compiler/src/core'
    import { Role } from './role.enum'
    import { UiService } from '../common/ui.service'

    @Injectable({
      providedIn: 'root'
    })
    export class AuthGuard implements CanActivate, CanActivateChild,
    CanLoad {
      protected currentAuthStatus: IAuthStatus
      constructor(
        protected authService: AuthService,
        protected router: Router,
        private uiService: UiService
      ) {
        this.authService.authStatus.subscribe(
          authStatus => (this.currentAuthStatus = authStatus)
        )
      }
    ```

```
canLoad(route: Route): boolean | Observable<boolean> |
Promise<boolean> {
    return this.checkLogin()
}

canActivate(
    route: ActivatedRouteSnapshot,
    state: RouterStateSnapshot
): boolean | Observable<boolean> | Promise<boolean> {
    return this.checkLogin(route)
}

canActivateChild(
    childRoute: ActivatedRouteSnapshot,
    state: RouterStateSnapshot
): boolean | Observable<boolean> | Promise<boolean> {
    return this.checkLogin(childRoute)
}

protected checkLogin(route?: ActivatedRouteSnapshot) {
    let roleMatch = true
    let params: any
    if (route) {
        const expectedRole = route.data.expectedRole

        if (expectedRole) {
            roleMatch = this.currentAuthStatus.userRole ===
expectedRole
        }

        if (roleMatch) {
            params = { redirectUrl: route.pathFromRoot.map(r =>
r.url).join('/') }
        }
    }

    if (!this.currentAuthStatus.isAuthenticated || !roleMatch) {
        this.showAlert(this.currentAuthStatus.isAuthenticated,
roleMatch)

        this.router.navigate(['login', params  || {}])
        return false
    }

    return true
}

private showAlert(isAuth: boolean, roleMatch: boolean) {
```

```
        if (!isAuth) {
            this.uiService.showToast('You must login to continue')
        }

        if (!roleMatch) {
            this.uiService.showToast('You do not have the permissions to
view this resource')
        }
    }
}
```

2. Use the `CanLoad` guard to prevent loading of lazily loaded module, such as Manager's module:

    src/app/app-routing.module.ts
    ```
    ...
    {
        path: 'manager',
        loadChildren: './manager/manager.module#ManagerModule',
        canLoad: [AuthGuard],
    },
    ...
    ```

    In this instance, when the `ManagerModule` is being loaded, `AuthGuard` will be activated during the `canLoad` event, and the `checkLogin` function will verify the authentication status of the user. If the guard returns `false`, the module will not be loaded. At this point, we don't have the metadata to check the role of the user.

3. Use the `CanActivate` guard to prevent activation of individual components, such as user's `profile`:

    user/user-routing.module.ts
    ```
    ...
    { path: 'profile', component: ProfileComponent, canActivate:
    [AuthGuard] },
    ...
    ```

    In the case of `user-routing.module`, `AuthGuard` is activated during the `canActivate` event, and the `checkLogin` function controls where this route can be navigated to. Since the user is viewing their own profile, there's no need to check the user's role here.

4. Use `CanActivate` or `CanActivateChild` with an `expectedRole` property to prevent activation of components by other users, such as `ManagerHomeComponent`:

mananger/manager-routing.module.ts
```
. . .
  {
    path: 'home',
    component: ManagerHomeComponent,
    canActivate: [AuthGuard],
    data: {
      expectedRole: Role.Manager,
    },
  },
  {
    path: 'users',
    component: UserManagementComponent,
    canActivate: [AuthGuard],
    data: {
      expectedRole: Role.Manager,
    },
  },
  {
    path: 'receipts',
    component: ReceiptLookupComponent,
    canActivate: [AuthGuard],
    data: {
      expectedRole: Role.Manager,
    },
  },
. . .
```

Inside `ManagerModule`, we can verify whether the user is authorized to access a particular route. We can do this by defining some metadata in the route definition, like `expectedRole`, which will be passed into the `checkLogin` function by the `canActivate` event. If a user is authenticated but their role doesn't match `Role.Manager`, `AuthGuard` will return false and the navigation will be prevented.

5. Ensure that both `AuthService` and `AuthGuard` are provided in `app.module` and `manager.module` since they used in both contexts

As always, before moving on ensure that all your tests pass by executing `npm test` and `npm run e2e`.

Auth Service Fake and Common Testing Providers

We need to implement an `AuthServiceFake` so that our unit tests pass and use a pattern similar to `commonTestingModules` mentioned in `Chapter 12`, *Create a Router-First Line-of-Business App*, to conveniently provider this fake across our spec files.

To ensure that our fake will have the same public functions and properties as the actual `AuthService`, let's first start with creating an interface:

1. Add `IAuthService` to `auth.service.ts`

   src/app/auth/auth.service.ts

   ```
   export interface IAuthService {
     authStatus: BehaviorSubject<IAuthStatus>
     login(email: string, password: string): Observable<IAuthStatus>
     logout()
     getToken(): string
   }
   ```

2. Make sure `AuthService` implements the interface
3. Export `defaultAuthStatus` for reuse

   src/app/auth/auth.service.ts

   ```
   export const defaultAuthStatus = {
     isAuthenticated: false,
     userRole: Role.None,
     userId: null,
   }

   export class AuthService extends CacheService implements
   IAuthService
   ```

Now we can create a fake that implements the same interface, but provides functions that don't have any dependencies to any external authentication system.

1. Create a new file named `auth.service.fake.ts` under `auth`:

   src/app/auth/auth.service.fake.ts
   ```
   import { Injectable } from '@angular/core'
   import { BehaviorSubject, Observable, of } from 'rxjs'
   import { IAuthService, IAuthStatus, defaultAuthStatus } from
   './auth.service'
   ```

```
@Injectable()
export class AuthServiceFake implements IAuthService {
  authStatus = new BehaviorSubject<IAuthStatus>(defaultAuthStatus)
  constructor() {}

  login(email: string, password: string): Observable<IAuthStatus> {
    return of(defaultAuthStatus)
  }

  logout() {}

  getToken(): string {
    return ''
  }
}
```

2. Update `common.testing.ts` with `commonTestingProviders`:

src/app/common/common.testing.ts

```
export const commonTestingProviders: any[] = [
  { provide: AuthService, useClass: AuthServiceFake },
  UiService,
]
```

3. Observer the use of the fake in `app.component.spec.ts`:

src/app/app.component.spec.ts
```
...
  TestBed.configureTestingModule({
    imports: commonTestingModules,
    providers: commonTestingProviders.concat([
      { provide: ObservableMedia, useClass: ObservableMediaFake },
      ...
```

The empty `commonTestingProviders` array we created earlier is being concatenated with fakes that are specific to `app.component`, so our new `AuthServiceFake` should apply automatically.

4. Update the spec file for `AuthGuard` shown as follows:

src/app/auth/auth-guard.service.spec.ts

```
...
    TestBed.configureTestingModule({
        imports: commonTestingModules,
        providers: commonTestingProviders.concat(AuthGuard)
    })
```

5. Go ahead and apply this technique to all spec files that have a dependency on `AuthService` and `UiService`

6. The notable exception is in `auth.service.spec.ts` where you do *not* want to use the fake, since `AuthService` is the class under test, make sure it is configure shown as follows:

src/app/auth/auth.service.spec.ts

```
...
    TestBed.configureTestingModule({
        imports: [HttpClientTestingModule],
        providers: [AuthService, UiService],
    })
```

7. In addition `SimpleDialogComponent` tests require stubbing out some external dependencies like:

src/app/common/simple-dialog/simple-dialog.component.spec.ts

```
    ...
        providers: [{
            provide: MatDialogRef,
            useValue: {}
        }, {
            provide: MAT_DIALOG_DATA,
            useValue: {} // Add any data you wish to test if it is
    passed/used correctly
        }],
    ...
```

Remember, don't move on until all your tests are passing!

Summary

You should now be familiar with how to create high-quality authentication and authorization experiences. We started by going over the importance of completing and documenting high-level UX design of our entire app so that we can properly design a great conditional navigation experience. We created a reusable UI service so that we can conveniently inject alerts into the flow-control logic of our app.

We covered the fundamentals of token-based authentication and JWTs so that you don't leak any critical user information. We learned that caching and HTTP interceptors are necessary so that users don't have to input their login information with every request. Finally, we covered router guards to prevent users from stumbling onto screens they are not authorized to use, and we reaffirmed the point that the real security of your application should be implemented on the server side.

In the next chapter, we will go over a comprehensive list of Angular recipes to complete the implementation of our line-of-business app—LemonMart.

15
Angular App Design and Recipes

In this chapter, we will complete the implementation of LemonMart. As part of the router-first approach, I will demonstrate the creation of reusable routable components that also support data binding - the ability to lay out components using auxiliary routes of the router, using resolve guards to reduce boilerplate code and leveraging class, interfaces, enums, validators, and pipes to maximize code reuse. In addition, we will create multi-step forms and implement data tables with pagination, and explore responsive design. Along the way, in this book, we will have touched upon most of the major functionality that Angular and Angular Material has to offer.

In this chapter, the training wheels are off. I will provide general guidance to get you started on an implementation; however, it will be up to you to try and complete the implementation on your own. If you need assistance, you may refer to the complete source code that is provided with the book or refer to up-to-date sample on GitHub at `Github.com/duluca/lemon-mart`.

In this chapter, you will learn about the following topics:

- Object-oriented class design
- Routable reusable components
- Caching service responses
- HTTP POST requests
- Multi-step responsive forms
- Resolve guards
- Master/detail views using auxiliary routes
- Data tables with pagination

User class and object-oriented programming

So far, we have only worked with interfaces to represent data, and we still want to continue using interfaces when passing data around various components and services. However, there's a need to create a default object to initialize a `BehaviorSubject`. In **Object-oriented Programming (OOP)**, it makes a lot of sense for the `User` object to own this functionality instead of a service. So, let's implement a `User` class to achieve this goal.

Inside the `user/user` folder, define an `IUser` interface and a `User` class provided in `UserModule`:

src/app/user/user/user.ts
```
import { Role } from '../../auth/role.enum'

export interface IUser {
  id: string
  email: string
  name: {
    first: string
    middle: string
    last: string
  }
  picture: string
  role: Role
  userStatus: boolean
  dateOfBirth: Date
  address: {
    line1: string
    line2: string
    city: string
    state: string
    zip: string
  }
  phones: IPhone[]
}

export interface IPhone {
  type: string
  number: string
  id: number
}
```

```
export class User implements IUser {
  constructor(
    public id = '',
    public email = '',
    public name = { first: '', middle: '', last: '' },
    public picture = '',
    public role = Role.None,
    public dateOfBirth = null,
    public userStatus = false,
    public address = {
      line1: '',
      line2: '',
      city: '',
      state: '',
      zip: '',
    },
    public phones = []
  ) {}

  static BuildUser(user: IUser) {
    return new User(
      user.id,
      user.email,
      user.name,
      user.picture,
      user.role,
      user.dateOfBirth,
      user.userStatus,
      user.address,
      user.phones
    )
  }
}
```

Note that by defining all properties with default values in the constructors as `public`
properties, we hit two birds with one stone; otherwise, we will need to define properties
and initialize them separately. This way, we achieve a concise implementation.

You can also implement calculated properties for use in templates, such as being able to conveniently display the `fullName` of a user:

src/app/user/user/user.ts
```
get fullName() {
  return `${this.name.first} ${this.name.middle} ${this.name.last}`
}
```

 Using a `static BuildUser` function, you can quickly hydrate the object with data received from the server. You can also implement the `toJSON()` function to customize the serialization behavior of your object before sending the data up to the server.

Reusing components

We need a component that can display a given user's information. A natural place for this information to be presented is when the user navigates to `/user/profile`. You can see the mock-up `User` profile file:

User profile mock-up

User information is also displayed mocked up elsewhere in the app, at /manager/users:

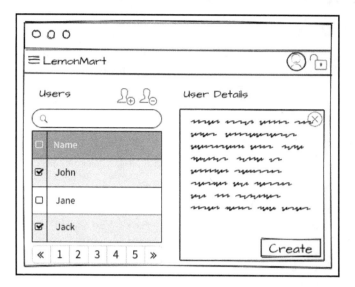

Manager user management mock-up

To maximize code reuse, we need to ensure that you design a User component that can be used in both contexts.

As an example, let's complete the implementation of two user profile-related screens.

User profile with multi-step auth-enabled responsive forms

Now, let's implement a multi-step input form to capture user profile information. We will also make this multi-step form responsive for mobile devices using media queries.

1. Let's start with adding some helper data that will help us display an input form with options:

   src/app/user/profile/data.ts
   ```
   export interface IUSState {
     code: string
     name: string
   }

   export function USStateFilter(value: string): IUSState[] {
     return USStates.filter(state => {
       return (
         (state.code.length === 2 && state.code.toLowerCase() ===
   value.toLowerCase()) ||
         state.name.toLowerCase().indexOf(value.toLowerCase()) === 0
       )
     })
   }

   export enum PhoneType {
     Mobile,
     Home,
     Work,
   }

   const USStates = [
     { code: 'AK', name: 'Alaska' },
     { code: 'AL', name: 'Alabama' },
     { code: 'AR', name: 'Arkansas' },
     { code: 'AS', name: 'American Samoa' },
     { code: 'AZ', name: 'Arizona' },
     { code: 'CA', name: 'California' },
     { code: 'CO', name: 'Colorado' },
     { code: 'CT', name: 'Connecticut' },
     { code: 'DC', name: 'District of Columbia' },
     { code: 'DE', name: 'Delaware' },
     { code: 'FL', name: 'Florida' },
     { code: 'GA', name: 'Georgia' },
     { code: 'GU', name: 'Guam' },
     { code: 'HI', name: 'Hawaii' },
   ```

```
        { code: 'IA', name: 'Iowa' },
        { code: 'ID', name: 'Idaho' },
        { code: 'IL', name: 'Illinois' },
        { code: 'IN', name: 'Indiana' },
        { code: 'KS', name: 'Kansas' },
        { code: 'KY', name: 'Kentucky' },
        { code: 'LA', name: 'Louisiana' },
        { code: 'MA', name: 'Massachusetts' },
        { code: 'MD', name: 'Maryland' },
        { code: 'ME', name: 'Maine' },
        { code: 'MI', name: 'Michigan' },
        { code: 'MN', name: 'Minnesota' },
        { code: 'MO', name: 'Missouri' },
        { code: 'MS', name: 'Mississippi' },
        { code: 'MT', name: 'Montana' },
        { code: 'NC', name: 'North Carolina' },
        { code: 'ND', name: 'North Dakota' },
        { code: 'NE', name: 'Nebraska' },
        { code: 'NH', name: 'New Hampshire' },
        { code: 'NJ', name: 'New Jersey' },
        { code: 'NM', name: 'New Mexico' },
        { code: 'NV', name: 'Nevada' },
        { code: 'NY', name: 'New York' },
        { code: 'OH', name: 'Ohio' },
        { code: 'OK', name: 'Oklahoma' },
        { code: 'OR', name: 'Oregon' },
        { code: 'PA', name: 'Pennsylvania' },
        { code: 'PR', name: 'Puerto Rico' },
        { code: 'RI', name: 'Rhode Island' },
        { code: 'SC', name: 'South Carolina' },
        { code: 'SD', name: 'South Dakota' },
        { code: 'TN', name: 'Tennessee' },
        { code: 'TX', name: 'Texas' },
        { code: 'UT', name: 'Utah' },
        { code: 'VA', name: 'Virginia' },
        { code: 'VI', name: 'Virgin Islands' },
        { code: 'VT', name: 'Vermont' },
        { code: 'WA', name: 'Washington' },
        { code: 'WI', name: 'Wisconsin' },
        { code: 'WV', name: 'West Virginia' },
        { code: 'WY', name: 'Wyoming' },
    ]
```

2. Install a helper library to programmatically access TypeScript enum values

```
$ npm i ts-enum-util
```

3. Add new validation rules to common/validations.ts

```
src/app/common/validations.ts
...

export const OptionalTextValidation = [Validators.minLength(2),
Validators.maxLength(50)]
export const RequiredTextValidation =
OptionalTextValidation.concat([Validators.required])
export const OneCharValidation = [Validators.minLength(1),
Validators.maxLength(1)]
export const BirthDateValidation = [
  Validators.required,
  Validators.min(new Date().getFullYear() - 100),
  Validators.max(new Date().getFullYear()),
]
export const USAZipCodeValidation = [
  Validators.required,
  Validators.pattern(/^\d{5}(?:[-\s]\d{4})?$/),
]
export const USAPhoneNumberValidation = [
  Validators.required,
  Validators.pattern(/^\D?(\d{3})\D?\D?(\d{3})\D?(\d{4})$/),
]
```

4. Now implement `profile.component.ts` as follows:

src/app/user/profile/profile.component.ts
```
import { Role as UserRole } from '../../auth/role.enum'
import { $enum } from 'ts-enum-util'
...
@Component({
  selector: 'app-profile',
  templateUrl: './profile.component.html',
  styleUrls: ['./profile.component.css'],
})
export class ProfileComponent implements OnInit {
  Role = UserRole
  PhoneTypes = $enum(PhoneType).getKeys()
  userForm: FormGroup
  states: Observable<IUSState[]>
  userError = ''
  currentUserRole = this.Role.None

  constructor(
    private formBuilder: FormBuilder,
    private router: Router,
    private userService: UserService,
    private authService: AuthService
  ) {}
```

```
ngOnInit() {
  this.authService.authStatus.subscribe(
    authStatus => (this.currentUserRole = authStatus.userRole)
  )

  this.userService.getCurrentUser().subscribe(user => {
    this.buildUserForm(user)
  })
  this.buildUserForm()
}
...
}
```

Upon load, we request the current user from `userService`, but this will take a while, so we must first build an empty form with `this.buildUserForm()`. On this function, you can also implement a resolve guard, as discussed in a later section, to load a user based on their `userId` provided on a route, and pass that data into `buildUserForm(routeUser)` and skip loading `currentUser` to increase reusability of this component.

Form groups

Our form has many input fields, so we will use a `FormGroup`, created by `this.formBuilder.group` to house our various `FormControl` objects. Additionally, children `FormGroup` objects will allow us to maintain the correct shape of the data structure.

Start building the `buildUserForm` function, as follows:

src/app/user/profile/profile.component.ts
```
...
  buildUserForm(user?: IUser) {
    this.userForm = this.formBuilder.group({
      email: [
        {
          value: (user && user.email) || '',
          disabled: this.currentUserRole !== this.Role.Manager,
        },
        EmailValidation,
      ],
      name: this.formBuilder.group({
        first: [(user && user.name.first) || '', RequiredTextValidation],
        middle: [(user && user.name.middle) || '', OneCharValidation],
        last: [(user && user.name.last) || '', RequiredTextValidation],
      }),
      role: [
```

```
      {
        value: (user && user.role) || '',
        disabled: this.currentUserRole !== this.Role.Manager,
      },
      [Validators.required],
    ],
    dateOfBirth: [(user && user.dateOfBirth) || '', BirthDateValidation],
    address: this.formBuilder.group({
      line1: [
        (user && user.address && user.address.line1) || '',
        RequiredTextValidation,
      ],
      line2: [
        (user && user.address && user.address.line2) || '',
        OptionalTextValidation,
      ],
      city: [(user && user.address && user.address.city) || '',
RequiredTextValidation],
      state: [
        (user && user.address && user.address.state) || '',
        RequiredTextValidation,
      ],
      zip: [(user && user.address && user.address.zip) || '',
USAZipCodeValidation],
    }),
    ...
  })
  ...
}
...
```

buildUserForm optionally accepts an IUser to prefill the form, otherwise all fields are set to their default values. The userForm itself is the top-level FormGroup. Various FormControls are added to it, such as email, with validators attached to them as needed. Note how name and address are their own FormGroup objects. This parent-child relationship ensures proper structure of the form data, when serialized to JSON, which fits the structure of IUser, in a manner that the rest of our application and server-side code can utilize.

You will completing the implementation of the `userForm` independently following the sample code provided for the chapter and I will be going over sections of the code piece by piece over the next few sections to explain certain key capabilities.

Stepper and responsive layout

Angular Material Stepper ships with the MatStepperModule. The stepper allows for form inputs to be broken up into multiple steps so that the user is not overwhelmed with processing dozens of input fields all at once. The user can still track their place in the process and as a side effect, as the developer we breakup our `<form>` implementation and enforce validation rules on a step-by-step basis or create optional workflows where certain steps can be skipped or required. As with all Material user controls, the stepper has been designed with a responsive UX in mind. In the next few sections, we will implement three steps covering different form-input techniques in the process:

1. Account Information
    - Input validation
    - Responsive layout with media queries
    - Calculated properties
    - DatePicker
2. Contact Information
    - Type ahead support
    - Dynamic form arrays
3. Review
    - Read-only views
    - Saving and clearing data

Let's prep the User module for some new Material modules:

1. Create a `user-material.module` containing the following Material modules:

```
MatAutocompleteModule,
MatDatepickerModule,
MatDividerModule,
MatLineModule,
MatNativeDateModule,
MatRadioModule,
MatSelectModule,
MatStepperModule,
```

2. Ensure `user.module` correctly imports:
    1. The new `user-material.module`
    2. The baseline `app-material.module`
    3. Required `FormsModule`, `ReactiveFormsModule` and `FlexLayoutModule`

As we start adding sub material modules, it makes sense to rename our root `material.module.ts` file to `app-material.modules.ts` inline with how `app-routing.module.ts` is named. Going forward, I will be using the latter convention.

3. Now, start implementing the first row of the Account Information step:

src/app/user/profile/profile.component.html

```html
<mat-toolbar color="accent">
  <h5>User Profile</h5>
</mat-toolbar>


<mat-horizontal-stepper #stepper="matHorizontalStepper">
  <mat-step [stepControl]="userForm">
    <form [formGroup]="userForm">
      <ng-template matStepLabel>Account Information</ng-template>
      <div class="stepContent">
        <div fxLayout="row" fxLayout.lt-sm="column"
[formGroup]="userForm.get('name')" fxLayoutGap="10px">
          <mat-form-field fxFlex="40%">
            <input matInput placeholder="First Name" aria-
label="First Name" formControlName="first">
            <mat-error
*ngIf="userForm.get('name').get('first').hasError('required')">
              First Name is required
            </mat-error>
            <mat-error
*ngIf="userForm.get('name').get('first').hasError('minLength')">
              Must be at least 2 characters
            </mat-error>
            <mat-error
*ngIf="userForm.get('name').get('first').hasError('maxLength')">
              Can't exceed 50 characters
            </mat-error>
          </mat-form-field>
          <mat-form-field fxFlex="20%">
            <input matInput placeholder="MI" aria-label="Middle
Initial" formControlName="middle">
            <mat-error
*ngIf="userForm.get('name').get('middle').invalid">
```

```
                Only inital
            </mat-error>
          </mat-form-field>
          <mat-form-field fxFlex="40%">
            <input matInput placeholder="Last Name" aria-
label="Last Name" formControlName="last">
            <mat-error
*ngIf="userForm.get('name').get('last').hasError('required')">
                Last Name is required
            </mat-error>
            <mat-error
*ngIf="userForm.get('name').get('last').hasError('minLength')">
                Must be at least 2 characters
            </mat-error>
            <mat-error
*ngIf="userForm.get('name').get('last').hasError('maxLength')">
                Can't exceed 50 characters
            </mat-error>
          </mat-form-field>
        </div>
        ...
      </div>
    </form>
  </mat-step>
...
</mat-horizontal-stepper>
```

4. Take care to understand how the stepper and the form configuration works so far, you should be seeing the first row render, pulling mock data:

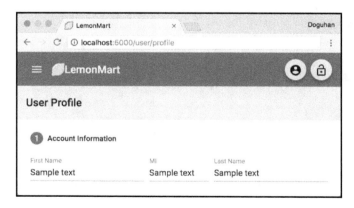

Multi-step form - Step 1

5. In order to complete the implementation of the form please refer to the sample code provided for this chapter or the reference implementation on `GitHub.com/duluca/lemon-mart`

 During your implementation, you will notice that the **Review** step uses a directive named `<app-view-user>`. A minimal version of this component is implemented in the ViewUser component section below. However, feel free to implement the capability inline for now and refactor your code during the Reusable component with binding and route data section.

In the following screenshot, you can see what a completed implementation of the multi-step form looks like on a desktop:

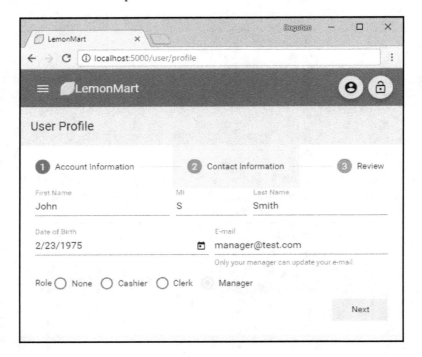

Multi-step form on desktop

Note that adding `fxLayout.lt-sm="column"` on a row with `fxLayout="row"` enables a responsive layout of the form, as shown:

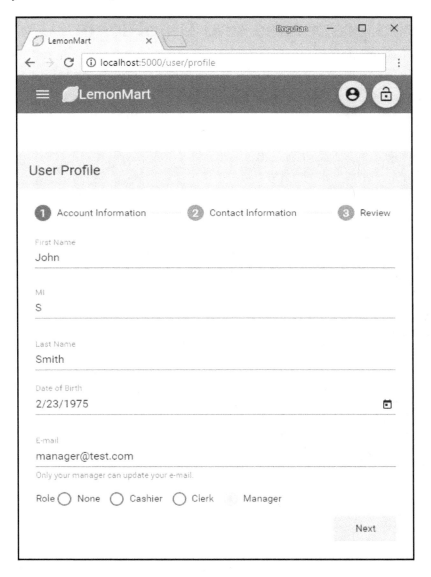

Multi-step form on mobile

Let's see how the **Date of Birth** field works in the next section.

Calculated properties and DatePicker

If you like to display calculated properties based on user input, you can follow the pattern shown here:

src/app/user/profile/profile.component.ts

```
...
get dateOfBirth() {
   return this.userForm.get('dateOfBirth').value || new Date()
}

get age() {
   return new Date().getFullYear() - this.dateOfBirth.getFullYear()
}
...
```

The usage of calculated properties in the template looks like this:

src/app/user/profile/profile.component

```
...
<mat-form-field fxFlex="50%">
  <input matInput placeholder="Date of Birth" aria-label="Date of Birth"
formControlName="dateOfBirth" [matDatepicker]="dateOfBirthPicker">
  <mat-hint *ngIf="userForm.get('dateOfBirth').touched">{{this.age}}
year(s) old</mat-hint>
  <mat-datepicker-toggle matSuffix [for]="dateOfBirthPicker"></mat-
datepicker-toggle>
  <mat-datepicker #dateOfBirthPicker></mat-datepicker>
  <mat-error *ngIf="userForm.get('dateOfBirth').invalid">
    Date must be with the last 100 years
  </mat-error>
</mat-form-field>
...
```

Here it is in action:

Selecting date with DatePicker

After the date is selected, the calculated age is displayed, as follows:

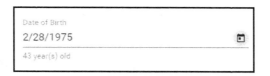

Calculated age property

Now, let's move on to the next step, **Contact Information** and see how we can enable a convenient way to display and input the state portion of the address field.

Type ahead support

In `buildUserForm`, we set a listener on `address.state` to support a type ahead filtering drop-down experience:

```
src/app/user/profile/profile.component.ts
...
this.states = this.userForm
  .get('address')
  .get('state')
  .valueChanges.pipe(startWith(''), map(value => USStateFilter(value)))
```

. . .

On the template, implement `mat-autocomplete` bound to the filtered states array with an `async` pipe:

src/app/user/profile/profile.component.html
```html
. . .
<mat-form-field fxFlex="30%">
  <input type="text" placeholder="State" aria-label="State" matInput
formControlName="state" [matAutocomplete]="stateAuto">
  <mat-autocomplete #stateAuto="matAutocomplete">
    <mat-option *ngFor="let state of states | async" [value]="state.name">
      {{ state.name }}
    </mat-option>
  </mat-autocomplete>
  <mat-error
*ngIf="userForm.get('address').get('state').hasError('required')">
    State is required
  </mat-error>
</mat-form-field>
. . .
```

Here's how it looks when a user enters the V character:

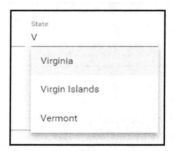

Dropdown with Typeahead Support

In the next section, let's enable the input of multiple phone numbers.

Dynamic form arrays

Note that `phones` is an array, potentially allowing for many inputs. We can implement this by building a `FormArray` with `this.formBuilder.array` and with several helper functions:

src/app/user/profile/profile.component.ts
```
...
  phones: this.formBuilder.array(this.buildPhoneArray(user ? user.phones :
[])),
...
  private buildPhoneArray(phones: IPhone[]) {
    const groups = []

    if (!phones || (phones && phones.length === 0)) {
      groups.push(this.buildPhoneFormControl(1))
    } else {
      phones.forEach(p => {
        groups.push(this.buildPhoneFormControl(p.id, p.type, p.number))
      })
    }
    return groups
  }

  private buildPhoneFormControl(id, type?: string, number?: string) {
    return this.formBuilder.group({
      id: [id],
      type: [type || '', Validators.required],
      number: [number || '', USAPhoneNumberValidation],
    })
  }
...
```

BuildPhoneArray supports initializing a form with a single phone input or filling it with the existing data, working in tandem with BuildPhoneFormControl. The latter function comes in handy when a user clicks on an **Add** button to create a new row for entry:

src/app/user/profile/profile.component.ts
```
...
  addPhone() {
    this.phonesArray.push(
      this.buildPhoneFormControl(this.userForm.get('phones').value.length +
1)
    )
  }

  get phonesArray(): FormArray {
    return <FormArray>this.userForm.get('phones')
  }
...
```

The `phonesArray` property getter is a common pattern to make it easier to access certain form properties. However, in this case, it is also necessary, because `get('phones')` must be typecast to `FormArray` so that we can access the `length` property on it on the template:

src/app/user/profile/profile.component.html

```
...
<mat-list formArrayName="phones">
  <h2 mat-subheader>Phone Number(s)</h2>
  <button mat-button (click)="this.addPhone()">
    <mat-icon>add</mat-icon>
    Add Phone
  </button>
  <mat-list-item *ngFor="let position of this.phonesArray.controls let
i=index" [formGroupName]="i">
  <mat-form-field fxFlex="100px">
    <mat-select placeholder="Type" formControlName="type">
      <mat-option *ngFor="let type of this.PhoneTypes" [value]="type">
      {{ type }}
      </mat-option>
    </mat-select>
  </mat-form-field>
  <mat-form-field fxFlex fxFlexOffset="10px">
    <input matInput type="text" placeholder="Number"
formControlName="number">
    <mat-error *ngIf="this.phonesArray.controls[i].invalid">
      A valid phone number is required
    </mat-error>
  </mat-form-field>
  <button fxFlex="33px" mat-icon-button
(click)="this.phonesArray.removeAt(i)">
    <mat-icon>close</mat-icon>
  </button>
  </mat-list-item>
</mat-list>
...
```

 The `remove` function is implemented inline.

Let's see how it should be working:

Multiple inputs using FormArray

Now that we're done with inputing data, we can move on to the last step of the stepper, **Review**. However, as it was mentioned earlier, the **Review** step uses the `app-view-user` directive to display its data. Let's build that view first.

ViewUser component

Here's a minimal implementation of the `<app-view-user>` directive that is a prerequisite for the **Review** step.

Create a new `viewUser` component under `user` as shown below:

src/app/user/view-user/view-user.component.ts
```
import { Component, OnInit, Input } from '@angular/core'
import { IUser, User } from '..//user/user'

@Component({
  selector: 'app-view-user',
  template: `
    <mat-card>
      <mat-card-header>
        <div mat-card-avatar><mat-icon>account_circle</mat-
icon></div>
        <mat-card-title>{{currentUser.fullName}}</mat-card-title>
```

```
          <mat-card-subtitle>{{currentUser.role}}</mat-card-subtitle>
        </mat-card-header>
        <mat-card-content>
          <p><span class="mat-input bold">E-mail</span></p>
          <p>{{currentUser.email}}</p>
          <p><span class="mat-input bold">Date of Birth</span></p>
          <p>{{currentUser.dateOfBirth | date:'mediumDate'}}</p>
        </mat-card-content>
        <mat-card-actions *ngIf="!this.user">
          <button mat-button mat-raised-button>Edit</button>
        </mat-card-actions>
      </mat-card>
    `,
    styles: [
      `
      .bold {
        font-weight: bold
      }
      `,
    ],
})
export class ViewUserComponent implements OnChanges {
  @Input() user: IUser
  currentUser = new User()

  constructor() {}

  ngOnChanges() {
    if (this.user) {
      this.currentUser = User.BuildUser(this.user)
    }
  }
}
```

The component above uses input binding with `@Input` to get user data, compliant with the `IUser` interface, from an outside component. We implement the `ngOnChanges` event, which fires whenever the bound data changes. In this event, we hydrate the simple JSON object stored in `this.user` as an instance of the class `User` with `User.BuildUser` and assign it to `this.currentUser`. The template uses this variable, because calculated properties like `currentUser.fullName` will only work if the data resides in an instance of the class `User`.

Now, we are ready to complete the multi-step form.

Review component and Save form

On the last step of the multistep form, users should be able to review and then save the form data. As a good practice, a successful POST request will return the data that was saved back to the browser. We can then reload the form with the information received back from the server:

src/app/user/profile/profile.component

```
...
async save(form: FormGroup) {
  this.userService
    .updateUser(form.value)
    .subscribe(res => this.buildUserForm(res), err => (this.userError =
err))
  }
...
```

If there are errors, they'll be set to userError to be displayed. Before saving, we will present the data in a compact form in a reusable component that we can bind the form data to:

src/app/user/profile/profile.component.html

```
...
<mat-step [stepControl]="userForm">
  <form [formGroup]="userForm" (ngSubmit)="save(userForm)">
  <ng-template matStepLabel>Review</ng-template>
  <div class="stepContent">
    Review and update your user profile.
    <app-view-user [user]="this.userForm.value"></app-view-user>
  </div>
  <div fxLayout="row" class="margin-top">
    <button mat-button matStepperPrevious color="accent">Back</button>
    <div class="flex-spacer"></div>
    <div *ngIf="userError" class="mat-caption error">{{userError}}</div>
    <button mat-button color="warn"
(click)="stepper.reset()">Reset</button>
    <button mat-raised-button matStepperNext color="primary" type="submit"
[disabled]="this.userForm.invalid">Update</button>
  </div>
  </form>
</mat-step>
...
```

This is how the final product should look:

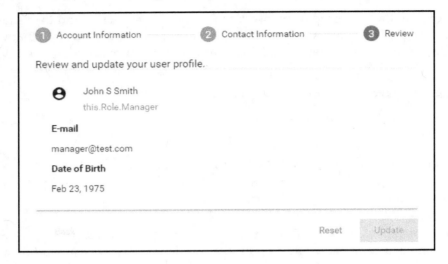

Review step

 Note the option to reset the form. Adding an alert dialog to confirm resetting of user input data would be good UX.

Now that the user profile input is done, we are about midway into our eventual goal of creating a master/detail view where a **Manager** can click on a user and view their profile details. We still have a lot more code to add, and along the way, we have fallen into a pattern of adding lots of boilerplate code to load the requisite data for a component. In the next section, we will learn about resolve guards so that we can simplify our code and reduce boilerplate.

Resolve guard

A resolve guard is a type of a router guard, as mentioned in `Chapter 14`, *Design Authentication and Authorization*. A resolve guard can load necessary data for a component by reading record IDs from route parameters, asynchronously load the data and have it ready by the time the component activates and initializes.

The major advantages for a resolve guard includes reusability of loading logic, reduction of boilerplate code, and also shedding dependencies, because the component can receive the data it needs without having to import any service:

1. Create a new `user.resolve.ts` class under `user/user`:

   src/app/user/user/user.resolve.ts
   ```
   import { Injectable } from '@angular/core'
   import { Resolve, ActivatedRouteSnapshot } from '@angular/router'
   import { UserService } from './user.service'
   import { IUser } from './user'

   @Injectable()
   export class UserResolve implements Resolve<IUser> {
     constructor(private userService: UserService) {}

     resolve(route: ActivatedRouteSnapshot) {
       return this.userService.getUser(route.paramMap.get('userId'))
     }
   }
   ```

2. You can use a resolve guard as shown:

   example
   ```
   {
     path: 'user',
     component: ViewUserComponent,
     resolve: {
       user: UserResolve,
     },
   },
   ```

3. The `routerLink` will look like this:

   example
   ```
   ['user', {userId: row.id}]
   ```

4. On the `ngOnInit` hook of the target component, you can read the resolved user like this:

   example
   ```
   this.route.snapshot.data['user']
   ```

You can observe this behavior in action in the next two sections, after we update `ViewUserComponent` and the router to leverage the resolve guard.

Reusable component with binding and route data

Now, let's refactor the `viewUser` component, so that we can reuse it in multiple contexts. One where it can load its own data using a resolve guard, suitable for a master/detail view and another, where we can bind the current user to it, as we have done in the Review step of the multi-step input form we built in the prior section:

1. Update `viewUser` component with the following changes:

   src/app/user/view-user/view-user.component.ts
   ```
   ...
   import { ActivatedRoute } from '@angular/router'

   export class ViewUserComponent implements OnChanges, OnInit {
     ...
     constructor(private route: ActivatedRoute) {}

     ngOnInit() {
       if (this.route.snapshot && this.route.snapshot.data['user']) {
         this.currentUser =
   User.BuildUser(this.route.snapshot.data['user'])
         this.currentUser.dateOfBirth = Date.now() // for data mocking
   purposes only
       }
     }
     ...
   ```

   We now have two independent events. One for `ngOnChanges`, which handles what value gets assigned to `this.currentUser`, if `this.user` has been bound to. `ngOnInit` will only fire once, when the component is first initialized or has been routed to. In this case, if any data for the route has been resolved then it'll be assigned to `this.currentUser`.

   To be able to use this component across multiple lazy loaded modules, we must wrap it in its own module.

2. Create a new `shared-components.module.ts` under `app`:

   src/app/shared-components.module.ts
   ```
   import { NgModule } from '@angular/core'
   import { ViewUserComponent } from './user/view-user/view-
   user.component'
   import { FormsModule, ReactiveFormsModule } from '@angular/forms'
   import { FlexLayoutModule } from '@angular/flex-layout'
   ```

```
import { CommonModule } from '@angular/common'
import { MaterialModule } from './app-material.module'

@NgModule({
  imports: [
    CommonModule,
    FormsModule,
    ReactiveFormsModule,
    FlexLayoutModule,
    MaterialModule,
  ],
  declarations: [ViewUserComponent],
  exports: [ViewUserComponent],
})
export class SharedComponentsModule {}
```

3. Ensure that you import `SharedComponentsModule` module into each feature module you intended to use `ViewUserComponent` in. In our case, these will be `User` and `Manager` modules.

4. Remove `ViewUserComponent` from the `User` module declarations

We now have the key pieces in place to begin the implementation of master/detail view.

Master/detail view auxiliary routes

The true power of router-first architecture comes to fruition with the use of auxiliary routes, where we can influence the layout of components solely through router configuration, allowing for rich scenarios where we can remix the existing components into different layouts. Auxiliary routes are routes that are independent of each other where they can render content in named outlets that have been defined in the markup, such as `<router-outlet name="master">` or `<router-outlet name="detail">`. Furthermore, auxiliary routes can have their own parameters, browser history, children, and nested auxiliaries.

In the following example, we will implement a basic master/detail view using auxiliary routes:

1. Implement a simple component with two named outlets defined:

   src/app/manager/user-management/user-manager.component.ts
   ```
   template: `
       <div class="horizontal-padding">
         <router-outlet name="master"></router-outlet>
         <div style="min-height: 10px"></div>
         <router-outlet name="detail"></router-outlet>
   ```

```
    </div>
```

2. Create a `userTable` component under `manager`

3. Update `manager-routing.module` to define the auxiliary routes:

   src/app/manager/manager-routing.module.ts

```
    ...
        {
          path: 'users',
          component: UserManagementComponent,
          children: [
            { path: '', component: UserTableComponent, outlet:
            'master' },
            {
              path: 'user',
              component: ViewUserComponent,
              outlet: 'detail',
              resolve: {
                user: UserResolve,
              },
            },
          ],
          canActivate: [AuthGuard],
          canActivateChild: [AuthGuard],
          data: {
            expectedRole: Role.Manager,
          },
        },
    ...
```

This means that when a user navigates to `/manager/users`, they'll see the `UserTableComponent`, because it is implemented with the `default` path.

4. Provide `UserResolve` in `manager.module` since `viewUser` depends on it

5. Implement a temporary button in `userTable`

   src/app/manager/user-table/user-table.component.html
```
<a mat-button mat-icon-button [routerLink]="['/manager/users', {
outlets: { detail: ['user', {userId: 'fakeid'}] } }]"
skipLocationChange>
  <mat-icon>visibility</mat-icon>
</a>
```

Consider that a user clicks on a **View detail** button like the one defined above, then `ViewUserComponent` will be rendered for the user with the given `userId`. In the next screenshot, you can see what the **View Details** button will look like after we implement the data table in the next section:

View Details button

You can have as many combinations and alternative components defined for master and detail, allowing for an infinite possibilities of dynamic layouts. However, setting up the `routerLink` can be a frustrating experience. Depending on the exact condition, you have to either supply or not supply all or some outlets in the link. For example, for the preceding scenario, if the link was `['/manager/users', { outlets: { master: [''], detail: ['user', {userId: row.id}] } }]`, the route will silently fail to load. Expect these quirks to be ironed out in future Angular releases.

Now that, we've completed the implementation of the resolve guard for `ViewUserComponent`, you can use Chrome Dev Tools to see the data being loaded correctly. Before debugging, ensure that the mock server we created in `Chapter 13`, *Continuous Integration and API Design*, is running.

6. Ensure that mock server is running by executing either `docker run -p 3000:3000 -t duluca/lemon-mart-swagger-server` or `npm run mock:standalone`.

7. In Chrome Dev Tools, set a break point right after `this.currentUser` is assigned to, as shown:

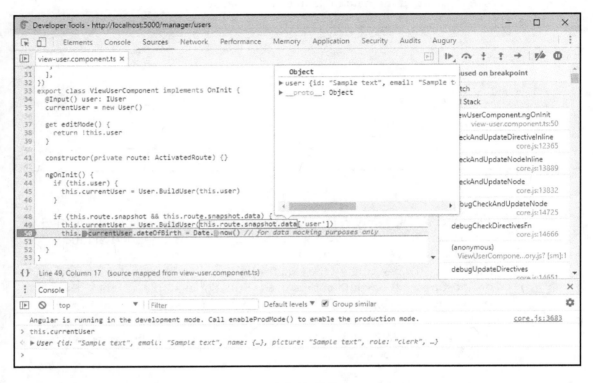

Dev Tools Debugging ViewUserComponent

You will observe that `this.currentUser` is correctly set without any boilerplate code for loading data inside the `ngOnInit` function, showing the true benefit of a resolve guard. `ViewUserComponent` is the detail view; now let's implement the master view as a data table with pagination.

Data table with pagination

We have created the scaffolding to lay out our master/detail view. In the master outlet, we will have a paginated data table of users, so let's implement `UserTableComponent`, which will contain a `MatTableDataSource` property named `dataSource`. We will need to be able to fetch user data in bulk using standard pagination controls like `pageSize` and `pagesToSkip` and be able to further narrow down the selection with user provided `searchText`.

Let's start by adding the necessary functionality to the `UserService`.

1. Implement a new interface `IUsers` to describe the data structure of paginated data

    src/app/user/user/user.service.ts
    ```
    ...
    export interface IUsers {
      items: IUser[]
      total: number
    }
    ```

2. Add `getUsers` to `UserService`

    src/app/user/user/user.service.ts
    ```
    ...
    getUsers(pageSize: number, searchText = '', pagesToSkip = 0):
    Observable<IUsers> {
      return
    this.httpClient.get<IUsers>(`${environment.baseUrl}/v1/users`, {
        params: {
          search: searchText,
          offset: pagesToSkip.toString(),
          limit: pageSize.toString(),
        },
      })
    }
    ...
    ```

3. Set up `UserTable` with pagination, sorting, and filtering:

    src/app/manager/user-table/user-table.component
    ```
    import { AfterViewInit, Component, OnInit, ViewChild } from
    '@angular/core'
    import { FormControl } from '@angular/forms'
    import { MatPaginator, MatSort, MatTableDataSource } from
    '@angular/material'
    ```

```
import { merge, of } from 'rxjs'
import { catchError, debounceTime, map, startWith, switchMap } from
'rxjs/operators'
import { OptionalTextValidation } from '../../common/validations'
import { IUser } from '../../user/user/user'
import { UserService } from '../../user/user/user.service'

@Component({
  selector: 'app-user-table',
  templateUrl: './user-table.component.html',
  styleUrls: ['./user-table.component.css'],
})
export class UserTableComponent implements OnInit, AfterViewInit {
  displayedColumns = ['name', 'email', 'role', 'status', 'id']
  dataSource = new MatTableDataSource()
  resultsLength = 0
  _isLoadingResults = true
  _hasError = false
  errorText = ''
  _skipLoading = false

  search = new FormControl('', OptionalTextValidation)

  @ViewChild(MatPaginator) paginator: MatPaginator
  @ViewChild(MatSort) sort: MatSort

  constructor(private userService: UserService) {}

  ngOnInit() {}

  ngAfterViewInit() {
    this.dataSource.paginator = this.paginator
    this.dataSource.sort = this.sort

    this.sort.sortChange.subscribe(() => (this.paginator.pageIndex
= 0))

    if (this._skipLoading) {
      return
    }

    merge(
      this.sort.sortChange,
      this.paginator.page,
      this.search.valueChanges.pipe(debounceTime(1000))
    )
      .pipe(
        startWith({}),
```

```
      switchMap(() => {
        this._isLoadingResults = true
        return this.userService.getUsers(
          this.paginator.pageSize,
          this.search.value,
          this.paginator.pageIndex
        )
      }),
      map((data: { total: number; items: IUser[] }) => {
        this._isLoadingResults = false
        this._hasError = false
        this.resultsLength = data.total

        return data.items
      }),
      catchError(err => {
        this._isLoadingResults = false
        this._hasError = true
        this.errorText = err
        return of([])
      })
    )
    .subscribe(data => (this.dataSource.data = data))
  }

  get isLoadingResults() {
    return this._isLoadingResults
  }

  get hasError() {
    return this._hasError
  }
}
```

After initializing the pagination, sorting, and the filter properties, we use the merge method to listen for changes in all three data streams. If one changes, the whole pipe is triggered, which contains a call to this.userService.getUsers. Results are then mapped to the table's datasource property, otherwise errors are caught and handled.

4. Create a `manager-material.module` containing the following Material modules:

```
MatTableModule,
MatSortModule,
MatPaginatorModule,
MatProgressSpinnerModule
```

5. Ensure `manager.module` correctly imports:
    1. The new `manager-material.module`
    2. The baseline `app-material.module`
    3. Required `FormsModule`, `ReactiveFormsModule` and `FlexLayoutModule`

6. Finally, implement the `userTable` template:

src/app/manager/user-table/user-table.component.html
```html
<div class="filter-row">
  <form style="margin-bottom: 32px">
    <div fxLayout="row">
      <mat-form-field class="full-width">
        <mat-icon matPrefix>search</mat-icon>
        <input matInput placeholder="Search" aria-label="Search"
[formControl]="search">
        <mat-hint>Search by e-mail or name</mat-hint>
        <mat-error *ngIf="search.invalid">
          Type more than one character to search
        </mat-error>
      </mat-form-field>
    </div>
  </form>
</div>
<div class="mat-elevation-z8">
  <div class="loading-shade" *ngIf="isLoadingResults">
    <mat-spinner *ngIf="isLoadingResults"></mat-spinner>
    <div class="error" *ngIf="hasError">
      {{errorText}}
    </div>
  </div>
  <mat-table [dataSource]="dataSource" matSort>
    <ng-container matColumnDef="name">
      <mat-header-cell *matHeaderCellDef mat-sort-header> Name
</mat-header-cell>
      <mat-cell *matCellDef="let row"> {{row.name.first}}
{{row.name.last}} </mat-cell>
    </ng-container>
    <ng-container matColumnDef="email">
```

```
        <mat-header-cell *matHeaderCellDef mat-sort-header> E-mail
</mat-header-cell>
        <mat-cell *matCellDef="let row"> {{row.email}} </mat-cell>
      </ng-container>
      <ng-container matColumnDef="role">
        <mat-header-cell *matHeaderCellDef mat-sort-header> Role
</mat-header-cell>
        <mat-cell *matCellDef="let row"> {{row.role}} </mat-cell>
      </ng-container>
      <ng-container matColumnDef="status">
        <mat-header-cell *matHeaderCellDef mat-sort-header> Status
</mat-header-cell>
        <mat-cell *matCellDef="let row"> {{row.status}} </mat-cell>
      </ng-container>
      <ng-container matColumnDef="id">
        <mat-header-cell *matHeaderCellDef fxLayoutAlign="end
center">View Details</mat-header-cell>
        <mat-cell *matCellDef="let row" fxLayoutAlign="end center"
style="margin-right: 8px">
          <a mat-button mat-icon-button
[routerLink]="['/manager/users', { outlets: { detail: ['user',
{userId: row.id}] } }]" skipLocationChange>
            <mat-icon>visibility</mat-icon>
          </a>
        </mat-cell>
      </ng-container>
      <mat-header-row *matHeaderRowDef="displayedColumns"></mat-
header-row>
      <mat-row *matRowDef="let row; columns: displayedColumns;">
      </mat-row>
    </mat-table>

    <mat-paginator [pageSizeOptions]="[5, 10, 25, 100]"></mat-
paginator>
</div>
```

With just the master view, the table looks like this screenshot:

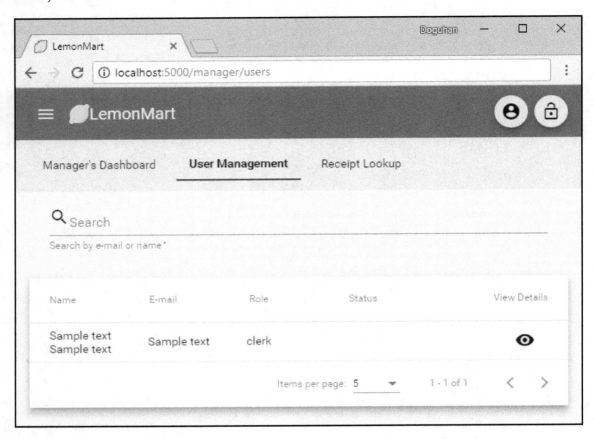

UserTable

If you click on the **View** icon, `ViewUserComponent` will get rendered in the detail outlet, as shown:

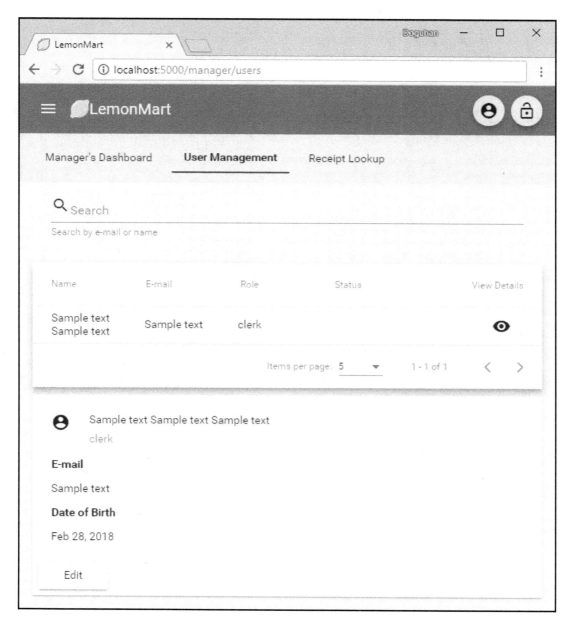

Master/Detail view

You can then wire up the **Edit** button and pass the `userId` to the `UserProfile` so that the data can be edited and updated. Alternatively, you can render the `UserProfile` in place in the detail outlet.

Data table with pagination completes the implementation of LemonMart for the purpose of this book. Now let's make sure all our tests our passing, before we move on.

Updating Unit Tests

Since we introduced a new `userService`, create a fake implementation for it, using the same pattern from `authService` and `commonTestingProviders` with it.

1. Implement `IUserService` interface for `UserService`

   src/app/user/user/user.service.ts
   ```
   export interface IUserService {
     currentUser: BehaviorSubject<IUser>
     getCurrentUser(): Observable<IUser>
     getUser(id): Observable<IUser>
     updateUser(user: IUser): Observable<IUser>
     getUsers(pageSize: number, searchText: string, pagesToSkip:
   number): Observable<IUsers>
   }
   ...
   export class UserService extends CacheService implements
   IUserService {
   ```

2. Implement the fake user service

   src/app/user/user/user.service.fake.ts
   ```
   import { Injectable } from '@angular/core'
   import { BehaviorSubject, Observable, of } from 'rxjs'

   import { IUser, User } from './user'
   import { IUsers, IUserService } from './user.service'

   @Injectable()
   export class UserServiceFake implements IUserService {
     currentUser = new BehaviorSubject<IUser>(new User())

     constructor() {}
   ```

```
getCurrentUser(): Observable<IUser> {
  return of(new User())
}

getUser(id): Observable<IUser> {
  return of(new User((id = id)))
}

updateUser(user: IUser): Observable<IUser> {
  return of(user)
}

getUsers(pageSize: number, searchText = '', pagesToSkip = 0):
Observable<IUsers> {
    return of({
      total: 1,
      items: [new User()],
    } as IUsers)
  }
}
```

3. Add the user service fake to `commonTestingProviders`

   src/app/common/common.testing.ts
   ```
   export const commonTestingProviders: any[] = [
     ...
     { provide: UserService, useClass: UserServiceFake },
   ]
   ```

4. Add `SharedComponentsModule` to `commonTestingModules`

   src/app/common/common.testing.ts
   ```
   export const commonTestingModules: any[] = [
     ...
     SharedComponentsModule
   ]
   ```

5. Instantiate default data for `UserTableComponent`

After fixing up its providers and imports, you will notice `UserTableComponent` is still failing to create. This is because, the component initialization logic requires `dataSource` to be defined. If undefined, the component can't be created. However, we can easily modify component properties in the second `beforeEach` method, which executes after the `TestBed` has injected real, mocked or fake dependencies to the component class. See the changes bolded below for test data setup:

src/app/manager/user-table/user-table.component.spec.ts
```
...
  beforeEach(() => {
    fixture = TestBed.createComponent(UserTableComponent)
    component = fixture.componentInstance
    component.dataSource = new MatTableDataSource()
    component.dataSource.data = [new User()]
    component._skipLoading = true
    fixture.detectChanges()
  })
...
```

By now, you may have noticed that just by updating some of our central configuration some tests are passing and the rest of tests can be resolved by applying the various patterns we have been using throughout the book. For example `user-management.component.spec.ts` uses the common testing modules and providers we have created:

src/app/manager/user-management/user-management.component.spec.ts
```
providers: commonTestingProviders,
imports: commonTestingModules.concat([ManagerMaterialModule]),
```

When you are working with providers and fakes, keep in mind what module, component, service or class is under test and take care to only provide fakes of dependencies.

`ViewUserComponent` is a special case, where we can't use our common testing modules and providers, otherwise we would end up creating a circular dependency. In this case, manually specify the modules that need to be imported.

6. Continue fixing unit test configurations until all of them are passing!

In this book, we didn't cover any functional unit testing, where we would test some business logic to test its correctness. Instead, we focused on keeping the auto-generated tests in working order. I highly recommend implementing unit tests to cover key business logic using the excellent framework provided by Angular out-of-the-box.

You always have the option to write even further elemental unit tests, testing classes and functions in isolation using Jasmine. Jasmine has rich test double functionality, able to mock and spy on dependencies. It is easier and cheaper to write and maintain these kinds of elemental unit tests. However, this topic is a deep one in its own right and is beyond the scope of this book.

Summary

In this chapter, we completed going over all major Angular app design considerations, along with recipes, to be able to implement a line-of-business app with ease. We talked about applying object-oriented class design to make hydrating or serializing data easier. We created reusable components that can be activated by the router or embedded within another component with data binding. We showed that you can POST data to the server and cache responses. We also created a rich multistep input forms that is responsive to changing screen sizes. We removed boilerplate code from components by leveraging a resolve guard to load user data. We then implemented a master/detail view using auxiliary routes and demonstrated how to build data tables with pagination.

Overall, by using the router-first design, architecture, and implementation approach, we approached our application's design with a good high-level understanding of what we wanted to achieve. Also, by identifying reuse opportunities early on, we were able to optimize our implementation strategy to implement reusable components ahead of time without running the risk of grossly over-engineering our solution.

In the next chapter, we will set up a highly-available infrastructure on AWS to host LemonMart. We will update the project with new scripts to enable no-downtime Blue-Green deployments.

16
Highly-Available Cloud Infrastructure on AWS

The web is a hostile environment. There are good and bad actors. Bad actors can try to poke holes in your security or try to bring down your website with a **Distributed Denial of Service (DDoS)** attack. Good actors, if you're lucky, will love your website and won't stop using it. They'll shower you with recommendations to improve your site, but also, they may run into bugs and they may be so enthusiastic that your site may slow down to a crawl due to high traffic. Real-world deployments on the web require a lot of expertise to get it right. As a full-stack developer, you can only know about so many nuances of hardware, software, and networking. Luckily, with the advent of cloud service providers, a lot of this expertise has been translated into software configurations, with the difficult hardware and networking concerns taken care of by the provider.

One of the best features of a cloud service provider is cloud scalability, which refers to your server automatically scaling out to respond to high volumes of unexpected traffic and scaling down to save costs when the traffic returns back to normal levels. **Amazon Web Services (AWS)** goes beyond basic cloud scalability and introduces high-availability and fault tolerant concepts, allowing for resilient local and global deployments. I have chosen to introduce you to AWS, because of its vast capabilities that go way beyond what I will touch in this book. With Route 53, you can get free DDoS protection; with API Gateway, you create API keys, with AWS Lambda you can handle millions of transactions for only a few dollars a month and with CloudFront you can cache your content at secret edge-locations that are scattered around major cities of the world. In addition, Blue-Green deployments will allow you to achieve no-downtime deployments of your software.

Overall, the tools and techniques you will be learning in this chapter are adaptable to any cloud provider and is fast becoming critical knowledge for any full-stack developer. We will be going over the following topics:

- Creating and protecting AWS accounts
- Right-sizing infrastructure

- Simple load testing to optimize instance
- Configuring and deploying to AWS ECS Fargate
- Scripted Blue-Green deployments
- Billing

Right-sizing infrastructure

The point of optimizing your infrastructure is to protect your companies revenue, while minimizing the cost of operating your infrastructure. Your goal should be to ensure that users don't encounter high-latency, otherwise known as bad performance or worse, unfulfilled or dropped requests, all the while making your venture remains a sustainable endeavor.

The three pillars of web application performance are as follows:

1. CPU utilization
2. Memory usage
3. Network bandwidth

I have intentionally left disk access out of the key consideration metrics, since only particular workloads executed on an application server or data store are affected by it. Disk access would rarely ever impact the performance of serving a web application as long as application assets are delivered by a **Content Delivery Network** (**CDN**). That said, still keep an eye on any unexpected runaway disk access, such as high frequency creation of temp and log files. Docker, for example, can spit out logs that can easily fill up a drive.

In an ideal scenario, CPU, memory, and network bandwidth use should be utilized evenly around 60-80% of available capacity. If you encounter performance issues due to various other factors such as disk I/O, a slow third-party service, or inefficient code, most likely one of your metrics will peek at or near maximum capacity, while the other two are idling or severely underutilized. This is an opportunity to use more CPU, memory, or bandwidth to compensate for the performance issue and also evenly utilize available resources.

The reason behind targeting 60-80% utilization is to allow for some time for a new instance (server or container) to be provisioned and ready to serve users. After your predefined threshold has been crossed, while a new instance is provisioned, you can continue serving the increasing number of users, thus minimizing unfulfilled requests.

Throughout this book, I have discouraged over-engineering or perfect solutions. In today's complicated IT landscape, it is nearly impossible to predict where you will encounter performance bottlenecks. Your engineering may, very easily, spend $100,000+ worth of engineering hours, where the solution to your problem may be a few hundred dollars of new hardware, whether it be a network switch, solid state drive, CPU, and more memory.

If your CPU is too busy, you may want to introduce more bookkeeping logic to your code, via index, hash tables, or dictionaries, that you can cache in memory to speed up subsequent or intermediary steps of your logic. For example, if you are constantly running array lookup operations to locate particular properties of a record, you can perform an operation on that record, saving the ID and/or the property of the record in a hash table that you keep in memory will reduce your runtime cost from $O(n)$ down to $O(1)$.

Following the preceding example, you may end up using too much memory with hash tables. In this case, you may want to more aggressively offload or transfer caches to slower, but more plentiful data stores using your spare network bandwidth, such as a Redis instance.

If your network utilization is too high, you may want to investigate usage of CDNs with expiring links, client-side caching, throttling requests, API access limits for customers abusing their quotas, or optimize your instances to have disproportionately more network capacity compared to its CPU or Memory capacity.

Optimizing instance

In an earlier example, I demonstrated the use of my `duluca/minimal-node-web-server` Docker image to host our Angular apps. Even though Node.js is a very lightweight server, it is simply not optimized to just be a web server. In addition, Node.js has single-threaded execution environment, making it a poor choice for serving static content to many concurrent users at once.

You can observe the resource that a Docker image is utilizing by executing `docker stats`:

```
$ docker stats
CONTAINER ID  CPU %  MEM USAGE / LIMIT   MEM %  NET I/O         BLOCK I/O
PIDS
27d431e289c9  0.00%  1.797MiB / 1.952GiB  0.09%  13.7kB / 285kB  0B / 0B
2
```

Here are comparative results of the system resources that a Node and NGINX-based servers utilize at rest:

Server	Image Size	Memory Usage
duluca/minimal-nginx-web-server	16.8 MB	1.8 MB
duluca/minimal-node-web-server	71.8 MB	37.0 MB

However, at rest values only tell a portion of the story. To get a better understanding, we must perform a simple load test to see memory and CPU utilization under load.

Simple load testing

To get a better understanding of the performance characteristics of our server, let's put them under some load and stress them:

1. Start your container using `docker run`:

    ```
    $ docker run --name <imageName> -d -p 8080:<internal_port>
    <imageRepo>
    ```

    If you're using `npm Scripts for Docker`, execute the following command to start your container:

    ```
    $ npm run docker:debug
    ```

2. Execute the following bash script to start the load test:

    ```
    $ curl -L http://bit.ly/load-test-bash | bash -s 100
    "http://localhost:8080"
    ```

    This script will send 100 requests/second to the server until you terminate it.

3. Execute `docker stats` to observe the performance characteristics.

Here are high-level observations of CPU and memory utilization:

CPU Utilization Statistics	Low	Mid	High	Max Memory
duluca/minimal-nginx-web-server	2%	15%	60%	2.4 MB
duluca/minimal-node-web-server	20%	45%	130%	75 MB

As you can see, there's a significant performance difference between the two servers serving the exact same content. Note that this kind of testing based on requests/second is good for a comparative analysis and does not necessarily reflect real-world usage.

It is clear that our NGINX server will give us the best bang for our buck. Armed with an optimal solution, let's deploy the application on AWS.

Deploy to AWS ECS Fargate

AWS **Elastic Container Service (ECS)** Fargate is a cost effective and an easy-to-configure way to deploy your container in the cloud.

ECS consists of four major parts:

1. Container Repository, **Elastic Container Registry (ECR)**, where you publish your Docker images
2. Services, Tasks and Task Definitions, where you define runtime parameters and port mappings for your container as a task definition that a service runs as tasks
3. Cluster, a collection of EC2 instances, where tasks can be provisioned and scaled out or in
4. Fargate, a managed cluster service, that abstracts away EC2 instances, load balancer, and security group concerns

 At the time of publishing, Fargate is only available in the AWS us-east-1 region.

Our goal is to create a highly-available blue-green deployment, meaning that at least one instance of our application will be up and running in the event of a server failure or even during a deployment.

Configuring ECS Fargate

You can access ECS functions under the AWS **Services** menu, selecting the **Elastic Container Service** link.

 If this is your first time logging in, you must go through a tutorial, where you will be forced to create a sample app. I would recommend going through the tutorial and deleting your sample app afterward. In order to delete a service, you'll need to update your service's number of tasks to 0. In addition, delete the default cluster to avoid any unforeseen charges.

Creating a Fargate Cluster

Let's start by configuring the Fargate Cluster, which act as a point of anchor when configuring other AWS services. Our cluster will eventually run a cluster service, which we will gradually build up in the following sections.

 At the time of publishing, AWS Fargate is only available in AWS US East region, with support for more regions and Amazon Elastic Container Service for Kubernetes (Amazon EKS) coming soon. Kubernetes is a widely preferred open source alternative to AWS ECS with richer capabilities for container orchestration with on-premises, cloud, and cloud-hybrid deployments.

Let's create the cluster:

1. Navigate to **Elastic Container Service**
2. Click on **Clusters** | **Create Cluster**
3. Select the **Networking only... powered by AWS Fargate** template

4. Click on the **Next** step and you see the **Create Cluster** step, as shown:

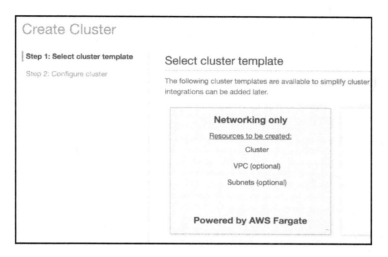

AWS ECS Create Cluster

5. Enter **Cluster name** as `fargate-cluster`
6. Create a **VPC** to isolate your resources from other AWS resources
7. Click on **Create Cluster** to finish the setup

You will see the summary of your actions, as follows:

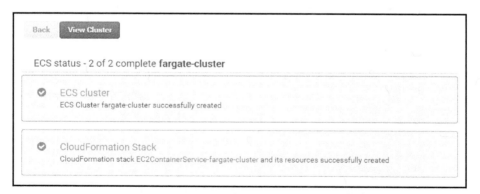

AWS ECS Fargate Cluster

Now that you have created a cluster within it's own **Virtual Private Cloud** (**VPC**), you can view it under **Elastic Container Service | Clusters**.

Creating container repository

Next, we need to set up a repository where we can publish the container images we build in our local or CI environment:

1. Navigate to **Elastic Container Service**
2. Click on **Repositories | Create Repository**
3. Enter repository name as `lemon-mart`
4. Copy the **Repository URI** generated on the screen
5. Paste the URI in `package.json` of your application as the new `imageRepo` variable:

   package.json
   ```
   ...
   "config": {
     "imageRepo": "000000000000.dkr.ecr.us-east-1.amazonaws.com/lemon-mart",
     ...
   }
   ```

6. Click on **Create Repository**
7. Click on **Next step** and then on **Done** to finish setup

In the summary screen, you will get further instructions on how to use your repository with Docker. Later in the chapter, we will go over scripts that will take care of this for us.

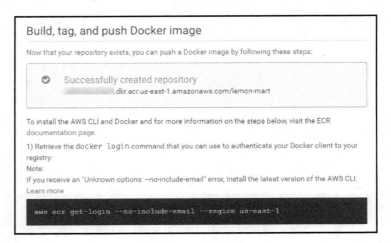

AWS ECS Repository

You can view your new repository under **Elastic Container Service | Repositories**. We will go over how to publish your image in the upcoming `npm Scripts for AWS` section.

Creating task definition

With a container target defined in our repository, we can define a task definition, which contains the necessary metadata to run our container, such as port mappings, reserved CPU, and memory allocations:

1. Navigate to **Elastic Container Service**
2. Click on **Task Definitions | Create new Task Definition**
3. Select **Fargate** launch type compatibility
4. Enter **Task Definition Name** as `lemon-mart-task`
5. Select **Task role** `none` (you can add one later to enable access other AWS services)
6. Enter **Task Size** `0.5 GB`
7. Enter **Task CPU** `0.25 CPU`
8. Click on **Add Container**:
    1. Enter **Container name** as `lemon-mart`
    2. For **Image**, paste the image repo URI from earlier, but append the `:latest` tag to it so that it always pulls the latest image in the repository, such as `000000000000.dkr.ecr.us-east-1.amazonaws.com/lemon-mart:latest`
    3. Set a **Soft limit** of `128 MB` for NGINX and `256 MB` for Node.js
    4. Under **Port mappings**, specify **Container port** as `80` for NGINX and `3000` for Node.js
9. Accept the remaining defaults

10. Click on **Add**; this is how your task definition will look before creating it:

Configure task and container definitions

A task definition specifies which containers are included in your task and how they interact with each other. You can also specify data volumes for your containers to use. Learn more

Task Definition Name* `lemon-mart-task`

Requires Compatibilities* FARGATE

Task size

The task size allows you to specify a fixed size for your task. Task size is required for tasks using the Fargate launch type and is optional for the EC2 launch type. Container level memory settings are optional when task size is set. Task size is not supported for Windows containers.

Task memory (GB) `0.5GB`

The valid memory range for 0.25 vCPU is: 0.5GB - 2GB.

Task CPU (vCPU) `0.25 vCPU`

The valid CPU for 0.5 GB memory is: 0.25 vCPU

Task memory maximum allocation for container memory reservation

0   384 shared of 512 MiB

Task CPU maximum allocation for containers

0   256 shared of 256 CPU units

Container Definitions

Add container

Container Name	Image	Hard/Soft m...	CPU Units	Essential	
lemon-mart		~/128		true	✖

*Required   Cancel   Previous   Create

AWS ECS Task Definition

11. Click on **Create** to finish setup

View your new **Task Definition** under **Elastic Container Service** | **Task Definitions**.

Note that the default settings will enable AWS CloudWatch logging, which is a way you can retroactively access console logs of your container instance. In this example, a CloudWatch Log Group named `/ecs/lemon-mart-task` will be created.

View your new Log Group under **Cloud Watch** | **Logs**.

 If you're adding a container that needs to persist data, the task definition allows you to define a volume and mount a folder to your Docker container. I've published a guide a for configuring AWS **Elastic File System** (**EFS**) with your ECS Container at `bit.ly/mount-aws-efs-ecs-container`.

Creating elastic load balancer

In a highly-available deployment, we will want to be running two instances of your container, as defined by the task definition we just created, across two different **Availability Zones** (**AZs**). For this kind of dynamically scaling out and scaling in, we need to configure an **Application Load Balancer** (**ALB**) to handle request routing and draining:

1. On a seperate tab, navigate to **EC2** | **Load Balancers** | **Create Load Balancer**
2. Create an **Application Load Balancer**
3. Enter **Name** `lemon-mart-alb`:

   In order to support SSL traffic under listeners, you can add a new listener for HTTPS on port `443`. An SSL setup can be achieved conveniently via AWS services and wizards. During the ALB configuration process, AWS offers links to these wizards to create your certificates. However, it is an involved process and one that can vary depending on your existing domain hosting and SSL certification setup. I will be skipping over SSL-related configuration in this book. You can find SSL related steps, published on the guide I've published at `bit.ly/setupAWSECSCluster`.

4. Under **Availability Zones**, select the **VPC** that was created for your **fargate-cluster**
5. Select all AZs listed
6. Expand **Tags** and add a key/value pair to be able to identify the ALB, like `"App": " LemonMart"`

7. Click on **Next**

8. Select **Default ELB security policy**

9. Click on **Next**

10. Create a new cluster specific security group, `lemon-mart-sg`, only allowing port `80` inbound or `443` if using HTTPS

> When creating your Cluster Service in the next section, ensure that the security group created here is the one selected during service creation. Otherwise, your ALB won't be able to connect to your instances.

11. Click on **Next**

12. Name a new **Target group** as `lemon-mart-target-group`

13. Change protocol type from `instance` to `ip`

14. Under **Health check**, keep the default route /, if serving a website on HTTP

Health checks are critical for scaling and deployment operations to work. This is the mechanism that AWS can use to check whether an instance has been created successfully or not.

> If deploying an API and/or redirecting all HTTP calls to HTTPS, ensure that your app defines a custom route that is not redirected to HTTPS. On HTTP server GET `/healthCheck` return simple 200 message saying `I'm healthy` and verify that this does not redirect to HTTPS. Otherwise, you will go through a lot of pain and suffering trying to figure out what's wrong, as all health checks fail and deployments inexplicably fail. `duluca/minimal-node-web-server` provides HTTPS redirection, along with an HTTP-only `/healthCheck` endpoint out of the box. With `duluca/minimal-nginx-web-server`, you will need to provide your own configuration.

15. Click on **Next**

16. Do *not* register any **Targets** or **IP Ranges**. ECS Fargate will magically manage this for you, if you do so yourself, you will provision a semi broken infrastructure

17. Click on **Next:Review**; your ALB settings should look similar to the one shown:

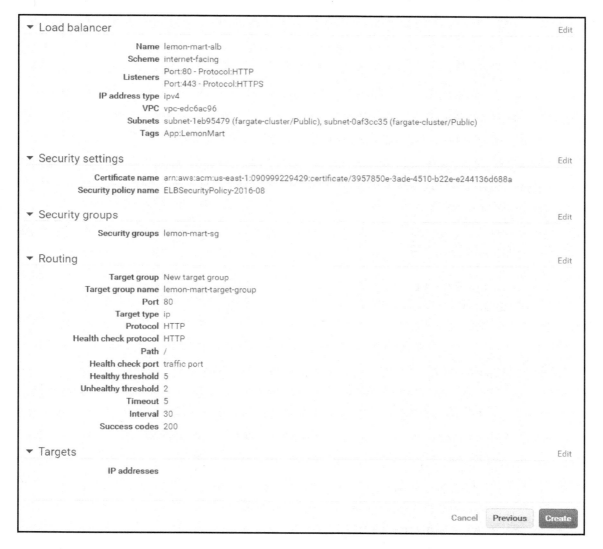

▼ Load balancer   Edit

Name	lemon-mart-alb
Scheme	internet-facing
Listeners	Port:80 - Protocol:HTTP
	Port:443 - Protocol:HTTPS
IP address type	ipv4
VPC	vpc-edc6ac96
Subnets	subnet-1eb95479 (fargate-cluster/Public), subnet-0af3cc35 (fargate-cluster/Public)
Tags	App:LemonMart

▼ Security settings   Edit

Certificate name	arn:aws:acm:us-east-1:090999229429:certificate/3957850e-3ade-4510-b22e-e244136d688a
Security policy name	ELBSecurityPolicy-2016-08

▼ Security groups   Edit

Security groups	lemon-mart-sg

▼ Routing   Edit

Target group	New target group
Target group name	lemon-mart-target-group
Port	80
Target type	ip
Protocol	HTTP
Health check protocol	HTTP
Path	/
Health check port	traffic port
Healthy threshold	5
Unhealthy threshold	2
Timeout	5
Interval	30
Success codes	200

▼ Targets   Edit

IP addresses	

Cancel   Previous   Create

AWS Application Load Balancer Settings

18. Click on **Create** to finish setup

You will be using the **lemon-mart-alb** when creating your Cluster Service in the next section.

Creating cluster service

Now, we will bring it all together by creating a service in our cluster using the task definition and the ALB we created:

1. Navigate to **Elastic Container Service**
2. Click on **Clusters | fargate-cluster**
3. Under **Services** tab, click on **Create**
4. Select **Launch type** Fargate
5. Select the task definition you created earlier

   Note that task definitions are versioned, such as lemon-mart-task:1. If you were to make a change to the task definition, AWS will create lemon-mart-task:2. You will need to update the service with this new version for your changes to take effect.

6. Enter **Service name** lemon-mart-service
7. **Number of tasks** 2
8. **Minimum healthy percent** 50
9. **Maximum percen**t 200
10. Click on **Next**

 Set minimum health percent to 100 for high-availability even during deployment. Fargate pricing is based on usage per second, so while deploying your application, you will be charged extra for the additional instances, while the old ones are being deprovisioned.

11. Under **Configure network**, select the same **VPC** as your cluster from earlier
12. Select all subnets that are available; there should be at least two for high-availability
13. Select the security group you created in the previous section—lemon-mart-sg
14. Select **Load Balancer** type as **Application Load Balancer**
15. Select the **lemon-mart-alb** option
16. Add **Container port** to the ALB, such as 80 or 3000, by clicking on the **Add to Load Balancer** button
17. Select the **Listener port** that you had already defined
18. Select the **Target group** you had already defined
19. Uncheck **Enable service discovery integration**
20. Click on **Next**

21. If you'd like your instances to scale out and in automatically, when their capacities are reach a certain limit, then set **Auto Scaling**

I would recommend skipping the set up of auto scaling during the initial setup of your service to make it easier to troubleshoot any potential configuration issues. You can come back and set it up later. Automatic task scaling policies rely on alarms, such as CPU Utilization.

22. Click on **Next** and review your changes, as illustrated:

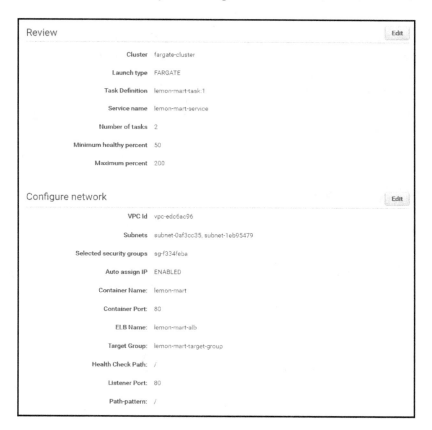

AWS Fargate cluster service settings

23. Finally, click on **Save** to finish setup

Observe your new service under **Elastic Container Service** | **Clusters** | **fargate-cluster** | **lemon-mart-service**. Until you publish an image to your container repository, your AWS service won't be able to provision an instance, since the health check will continually fail. After you publish an image, you will want to ensure that there are no errors present in the **Events** tab for your service.

AWS is a complicated beast and with Fargate, you can avoid a lot of complexity. However, if you're interested in setting up your own ECS cluster using your own Ec2 instances, you can get significant discounts with 1-3 year reserved instances. I have a 75+ setup guide available at `bit.ly/setupAWSECSCluster`.

We have executed a lot of steps manually to create our Cluster. AWS CloudFormation resolves this issue by offering configuration templates that you can customize to your needs or script your own templates from scratch. If you would like to get serious about AWS, this kind of code-as-infrastructure setup is definitely the way to go.

For production deployments, ensure that your configuration is defined by a CloudFormation template, so it can be easily reprovisioned, not if, but when a deployment related faux pas occurs.

Configuring the DNS

If you use AWS Route 53 to manage your domain, it is easy to assign a domain or a subdomain to an ALB:

1. Navigate to **Route 53** | **Hosted Zones**
2. Select your domain, like `thejavascriptpromise.com`
3. Click on **Create record set**
4. Enter **Name** as `lemonmart`
5. Set **Alias** to `yes`
6. Select the **lemon-mart-alb** from the load balancer list

7. Click on **Create** to finish setup

Route 53 - Create record set

Now, your site will be reachable on the subdomain you just defined, for
example `http://lemonmart.thejavascriptpromise.com`.

If don't use Route 53, don't panic. On your domain provider's website, edit the `Zone` file to
create an `A` record to the ELB's DNS address and you're done.

Getting the DNS Name

In order to get your load balancers' DNS address, perform these steps:

1. Navigate to **EC2 | Load Balancers**
2. Select the **lemon-mart-alb**

3. In the **Description** tab note the DNS name; consider this example:

   DNS name:
   ```
   lemon-mart-alb-1871778644.us-east-1.elb.amazonaws.com (A Record)
   ```

Prep Angular app

This section presumes that you have set up Docker and `npm Scripts for Docker` as detailed in `Chapter 10`, *Prepare Angular App for Production Release*. You can get the latest version of these scripts at `bit.ly/npmScriptsForDocker`.

Implement an optimized `Dockerfile`:

```
Dockerfile
FROM duluca/minimal-nginx-web-server:1.13.8-alpine
COPY dist /var/www
CMD 'nginx'
```

Note that if you're using `npm Scripts for Docker`, update the internal image port from `3000` to `80`, as shown:

```
"docker:runHelper": "cross-conf-env docker run -e NODE_ENV=local --name
$npm_package_config_imageName -d -p $npm_package_config_imagePort:80
$npm_package_config_imageRepo",
```

Adding npm Scripts for AWS

Just like `npm Scripts for Docker`, I have developed a set of scripts, called `npm Scripts for AWS`, that work on Windows 10 and macOS. These scripts will allow you to upload and release your Docker images in spectacular, no-downtime, blue-green fashion. You can get the latest version of these scripts at `bit.ly/npmScriptsForAWS`:

1. Ensure that `bit.ly/npmScriptsForDocker` are set up on your project
2. Create a `.env` file and set `AWS_ACCESS_KEY_ID` and `AWS_SECRET_ACCESS_KEY`:

   ```
   .env
   AWS_ACCESS_KEY_ID=your_own_key_id
   AWS_SECRET_ACCESS_KEY=your_own_secret_key
   ```

3. Ensure that your `.env` file is in your `.gitignore` file to protect your secrets

4. Install or upgrade to latest AWS CLI:
    - On macOS `brew install awscli`
    - On Windows `choco install awscli`

5. Log in to AWS CLI with your credentials:
    1. Run `aws configure`
    2. You'll need your **Access Key ID** and **Secret Access Key** from when you configured your IAM account
    3. Set **Default region name** like `us-east-1`

6. Update `package.json` to add a new `config` property with the following configuration properties:

package.json
```
...
"config": {
  ...
  "awsRegion": "us-east-1",
  "awsEcsCluster": "fargate-cluster",
  "awsService": "lemon-mart-service"
},
...
```

Ensure that you update `package.json` from when you configured `npm Scripts for Docker` so that the `imageRepo` property has the address of your new ECS repository.

7. Add AWS `scripts` to `package.json`, as illustrated:

package.json
```
...
"scripts": {
  ...
  "aws:login": "run-p -cs aws:login:win aws:login:mac",
  "aws:login:win": "cross-conf-env aws ecr get-login --no-include-email --region $npm_package_config_awsRegion > dockerLogin.cmd && call dockerLogin.cmd && del dockerLogin.cmd",
  "aws:login:mac": "eval $(aws ecr get-login --no-include-email --region $npm_package_config_awsRegion)"
}
```

`npm run aws:login` calls platform-specific commands that automate an otherwise multi-step action to get a Docker login command from the AWS CLI tool, as shown:

```
example
$ aws ecr get-login --no-include-email --region us-east-1
docker login -u AWS -p eyJwYX1...3ODk1fQ==
https://073020584345.dkr.ecr.us-east-1.amazonaws.com
```

You would first execute `aws ecr get-login` and then copy-paste the resulting `docker login` command and execute it so that your local Docker instance is pointed to AWS ECR:

```
package.json
...
"scripts": {
  ...
  "aws:deploy": "cross-conf-env docker run --env-file ./.env duluca/ecs-
  deploy-fargate -c $npm_package_config_awsEcsCluster -n
  $npm_package_config_awsService -i $npm_package_config_imageRepo:latest -r
  $npm_package_config_awsRegion --timeout 1000"
  }
...
```

`npm run aws:deploy` pulls a Docker container that itself executes blue-green deployment, using the parameters you have provided using the `aws ecr` commands. The details of how this works are beyond the scope of this book. To see more examples using native `aws ecr` commands, refer to the `aws-samples` repository at `github.com/aws-samples/ecs-blue-green-deployment`.

Note that the `duluca/ecs-deploy-fargate` blue-green deployment script is a fork of the original `silintl/ecs-deploy` image modified to support AWS ECS Fargate using PR `https://github.com/silinternational/ecs-deploy/pull/129`. Once `silintl/ecs-deploy` merges this change, I recommend using `silintl/ecs-deploy` for your blue-green deployments:

```
package.json
...
"scripts": {
  ...
  "aws:release": "run-s -cs aws:login docker:publish aws:deploy"
}
...
```

Finally, `npm run aws:release` simply runs `aws:login`, `docker:publish` from `npm Scripts for Docker` and `aws:deploy` commands in the right order.

Publish

Your project is configured to be deployed on AWS. You mostly need to use two of the commands we created to build and publish an image:

1. Execute `docker:debug` to test, build, tag, run, tail, and launch your app in a browser to test the image:

   ```
   $ npm run docker:debug
   ```

2. Execute `aws:release` to configure Docker login with AWS, publish your latest image build, and release it on ECS:

   ```
   $ npm run aws:release
   ```

3. Verify that your tasks are up and running at the **Service** level:

Clusters > fargate-cluster > Service: lemon-mart-service

Service : lemon-mart-service

Cluster	fargate-cluster	**Desired count**	2
Status	ACTIVE	**Pending count**	0
Task definition	lemon-mart-task:1	**Running count**	2
Launch type	FARGATE		
Platform version	LATEST		
Service role	aws-service-role/ecs.amazonaws.com/AWSServiceRoleForECS		

AWS ECS Service

Ensure that running count and desired count are the same.

4. Verify that your instances are running at the **Task** level:

AWS ECS task instance

Note the **Public IP** address and navigate to it; for example, `http://54.164.92.137` and you should see your application or LemonMart running.

5. Verify that the **Load Balancer** setup is correct at the DNS level.

6. Navigate to the **ALB DNS address**, for
   example `http://lemon-mart-alb-1871778644.us-east-1.elb.amazonaws`
   `.com`, and confirm that the app renders, as follows:

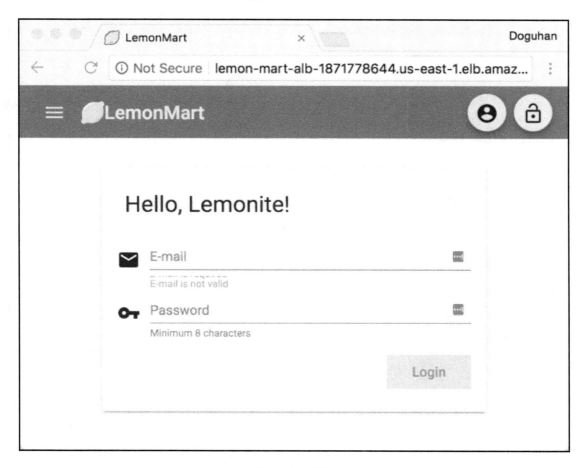

LemonMart running on AWS Fargate

Et voilà! Your site should be up and running.

In subsequent releases, following your first, you will be able to observe blue-green deployment in action, as shown:

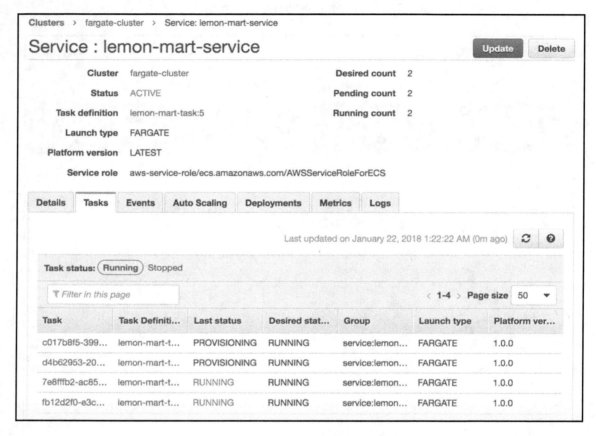

AWS Service during Blue-Green Deployment

There are two tasks running, with two new ones being provisioned. While the new tasks are being verified, running count will rise up to four tasks. After the new tasks are verified and the connections from old ones drained, the running count will return to two.

You can automate your deployments by configuring CircleCI with your AWS credentials, using a container that has the `awscli` tool installed and running `npm Scripts for AWS`. With this technique, you can achieve Continuous Deployment to a staging environment or Continuous Delivery to a production environment.

Summary

In this chapter, you learned about the nuances and various security considerations in properly protecting your AWS account. We went over the concepts of right-sizing your infrastructure. You conducted simple load testing in an isolated manner to find out relative differences in performance between two web servers. Armed with an optimized web server, you configured an AWS ECS Fargate cluster to achieve a highly-available cloud infrastructure. Using npm Scripts for AWS, you learned how to script repeatable and reliable no-downtime Blue-Green deployments. Finally, you became aware of the basic costs of running your infrastructure on AWS and other cloud providers such as Heroku, Zeit Now, and Digital Ocean.

Other Books You May Enjoy

If you enjoyed this book, you may be interested in these other books by Packt:

Hands-on Full Stack Development with Angular 5
Uttam Agarwal

ISBN: 978-1-78829-873-5

- Understand the core concepts of Angular framework
- Create web pages with Angular as front end and Firebase as back end
- Develop a real-time social networking application
- Make your application live with Firebase hosting
- Engage your user using Firebase cloud messaging
- Grow your application with Google analytics
- Learn about Progressive Web App

Learning Angular - Second Edition
Christoffer Noring, Pablo Deeleman

ISBN: 978-1-78712-492-9

- Set up the workspace and the project using webpack and Angular-Cli
- Explore the features of TypeScript and organize the code in ES6 modules
- Work with HTTP and Data Services and understand how data can flow in the app
- Create multiple views and learn how to navigate between them
- Make the app beautiful by adding Material Design
- Implement two different types of form handling and its validation
- Add animation to some standard events such as route change, initialization, data load, and so on
- Discover how to bulletproof your applications by introducing smart unit testing techniques and debugging tools

ASP.NET Core 2 and Angular 5
Valerio De Sanctis

ISBN: 978-1-78829-360-0

- Use ASP.NET Core to its full extent to create a versatile backend layer based on RESTful APIs
- Consume backend APIs with the brand new Angular 5 HttpClient and use RxJS Observers to feed the frontend UI asynchronously
- Implement an authentication and authorization layer using ASP.NET Identity to support user login with integrated and third-party OAuth 2 providers
- Configure a web application in order to accept user-defined data and persist it into the database using server-side APIs
- Secure your application against threats and vulnerabilities in a time efficient way
- Connect different aspects of the ASP. NET Core framework ecosystem and make them interact with each other for a Full-Stack web development experience

Leave a review - let other readers know what you think

Please share your thoughts on this book with others by leaving a review on the site that you bought it from. If you purchased the book from Amazon, please leave us an honest review on this book's Amazon page. This is vital so that other potential readers can see and use your unbiased opinion to make purchasing decisions, we can understand what our customers think about our products, and our authors can see your feedback on the title that they have worked with Packt to create. It will only take a few minutes of your time, but is valuable to other potential customers, our authors, and Packt. Thank you!

Index

www.ingramcontent.com/pod-product-compliance
Lightning Source LLC
LaVergne TN
LVHW081505050326
832903LV00025B/1392